Creativity in Context

Creativity in Context

Update to
The Social Psychology of Creativity

Teresa M. Amabile

HARVARD UNIVERSITY

with updates by

Teresa M. Amabile
Mary Ann Collins
Regina Conti
Elise Phillips
Martha Picariello
John Ruscio
Dean Whitney

Westview Press
A Member of the Perseus Books Group

Copyright © 1996 by Westview Press, Inc., A **Member of the Perseus Books Group**

Published in 1996 in the United States of America by Westview Press, Inc., 5500 Central Avenue, Boulder, Colorado 80301-2877, and in the United Kingdom by Westview Press, 12 Hid's Copse Road, Cumnor Hill, Oxford OX2 9JJ

Library of Congress Cataloging-in-Publication Data
Amabile, Teresa M.
    Creativity in context / Teresa M. Amabile.
        p. cm.
Includes bibliographical references and indexes.
    ISBN 0-8133-2827-6 (hc).—ISBN 0-8133-3034-3 (pbk.)
1. Creative ability.   2. Creative ability—Social aspects.
3. Motivation (Psychology)   I. Title.
BF411.A43   1996
153.3'5—dc20   96-11298
                                                                              CIP

The paper used in this publication meets the requirements of the American National Standard for Permanence of Paper for Printed Library Materials Z39.48-1984.

10   9   8   7   6   5   4   3   2

To my parents,
Charles and Carmela Amabile

Contents

Preface to the Updated Edition

When Westview Press expressed an interest in republishing *The Social Psychology of Creativity*, I was very pleased. The book, originally published in 1983, had been out of print for three years, and I felt frustrated whenever researchers or students called to ask where they might find a copy. However, although I was pleased to know that the book would once again be available, I was well aware of the many recent advances that are not represented in the original. It is my hope that this updated edition, retitled *Creativity in Context*, will both preserve the original and provide some insight into recent developments in the field. As indicated by the change in title, the updates will build upon and expand beyond the boundaries of the original work.

It has been 13 years since I began writing *The Social Psychology of Creativity*. Although those years have passed quickly, there have been significant changes in my research and in my thinking about creativity. I have worked with a great many new students and colleagues, and although we have continued to explore a number of the research questions outlined in the 1983 edition of this book, we have also moved in new directions. We have begun to study the ways in which social factors can serve to maintain creativity, going well beyond our earlier focus on the ways in which social factors can kill creativity. We have considered personality factors—stable individual differences—in motivational orientation and how they affect creativity in a number of domains. We have begun to think in detail about the cognitive mechanisms by which motivation might have an impact on creativity. And we have stretched the scope of our research by expanding to new populations (for example, professional artists and research scientists), new settings (specifically, business organizations), and new methods (such as surveys, interviews, and the examination of existing creative works).

As I began my study of creativity, over 20 years ago, I envisioned myself as carefully and methodically adding planks to the grand framework of psychological science. In retrospect, my work over these past two decades seems rather more like a surprising journey in search of the pieces to an important puzzle; although much of it was unpredictable, it does nonetheless fit together. This journey has taken me far beyond the domain of traditional social psychology, where I began, to many disparate domains that all hold pieces of this puzzle—cognitive, personality, developmental, and industrial psychology; organizational behavior; and organizational development. It has been a journey marked by both stability and change, by planning and chaos, by systematic research and opportunistic investigations. Although the puzzle now has a definite shape, there are still wide gaps. I am excited about sharing the discoveries we have made in our journey over the past few years; that is the purpose of this new, updated edition.

Let me provide a brief guide to the updated edition. The original Preface, the body of the book (Chapters 1–10), and the References section for the original 10 chapters are unchanged. We felt that it was important to preserve these original statements on the social psychology of creativity, because they largely served as the foundation for the field as it has developed in the past several years. The Updates directly follow each chapter; they were written by me and Mary Ann Collins, Regina Conti, Elise Phillips, Martha Picariello, John Ruscio, and Dean Whitney. Other colleagues provided detailed and valuable suggestions on drafts of the Update: Steve Kramer, Beth Hennessey, Karl Hill, Heather Coon, Mark Runco, Scott Isaksen, and Dean Simonton. Neither these colleagues nor those who coauthored the Updates with me can be held responsible for any errors that might be found there. Often they argued with me about the final presentation of a particular point; sometimes I listened, but sometimes I didn't! (I should also note that although I use the first person plural throughout the Updates, the "we" that I use in describing material from the 1983 edition really refers to me alone; I am responsible for most of the insightfulness *and* all of the wrongheadedness you might find there.)

In the original ten chapters we have placed a special symbol in the margin beside each section or paragraph for which the Update contains substantial new theory or data. That symbol appears in the margin beside this paragraph.

In the Updates, we review the major changes in theory and research that have occurred in the social psychology of creativity—and the field of creativity in general—since 1983. Although much of the theory and research reviewed in the Updates comes from our own work, we have tried to provide an overview of the work done by others in the field as well.

Much of my research over the past 12 years has been supported by external agencies and foundations, and I gratefully acknowledge their assistance: the National Institute for Child Health and Human Development, the National Institute of Mental Health, the Exxon Education Foundation, and the Center for Innovation Management Studies at Lehigh University.

A great many collaborators have contributed to my research—graduate students, undergraduate students, research assistants, research associates, and faculty colleagues. I wish to single out two individuals who have been particularly influential in developing this program of research over the past decade, and whose productive contributions have proved to be invaluable. Beth Hennessey began working with me as a graduate student in 1981, and after playing a seminal role in much of the research reported in this Update began a career as a faculty member at Wellesley College. In that capacity, she has continued to serve as a valued research associate, colleague, and friend. Karl Hill too began as a graduate student at Brandeis (in 1983) and during his years in my laboratory began to move the research program toward more complex, ecologically valid models. Karl continued *xiii*

to make valuable contributions to this work during his years as a faculty member at Wellesley College and then as a researcher at the University of Washington. I am most appreciative for all that Karl has given us, professionally and personally, over the years. Other collaborators include Kim Appelmans, Bob Burnside, Michele Castle, Mary Ann Collins, Regina Conti, Heather Coon, Barbara Grossman, Nur Gryskiewicz, Stan Gryskiewicz, Jessica Guite, Jenifer Harlem, Kathleen Holt, Nancy Koester, Marcie Korman, Tom Leahy, Ayelet Meron, Jill Nemiro, Elise Phillips, Martha Picariello, Sara Pollak, Shari Rist, John Ruscio, Amy Silverman, Debby Stephens, Monica Sultan, Sylvester Taylor, Sandra Teare, Elizabeth Tighe, and Dean Whitney. I am grateful for the camaraderie, the intellectual stimulation, and the productive work that these collaborators have given me. In particular, the members of "Amabile's Research Group" (ARG) during my 18 years at Brandeis University proved that it is possible to have high-level meetings that are consistently challenging, productive, and fun.

My new home, the Harvard Business School, has presented me with an exciting new set of colleagues whose diverse perspectives and challenging questions have already had a positive impact on the ideas expressed in the Updates.

My thinking has also been shaped these past several years by a number of colleagues in the field through their written work, their conversations with me, and their conference presentations: Frank Barron, Mike Csikszentmihalyi, Howard Gardner, Scott Isaksen, Michael Kirton, Sid Parnes, David Perkins, Mark Runco, Dorie Shallcross, Dean Simonton, Moe Stein, and Bob Sternberg. I found certain research conferences to be particularly stimulating: the 1988 Pitzer College creativity conference, the 1990 Harvard Graduate School of Education research conference, the 1992 International Creativity and Innovation Networking Conference, the 1994 KAI researchers' workshop, and many research presentations in the Creative Education Foundation's annual Creative Problem-Solving Institutes. I am grateful to my colleagues who organized and contributed to these conferences, and to the organizations that supported them.

I also wish to acknowledge the encouragement I received from the Creative Education Foundation in undertaking this update, and the excellent support that Michelle Baxter and the folks at Westview Press have given to me.

Finally, I wish to acknowledge my debt of gratitude to my parents, Charles and Carmela Amabile, who aroused in me a passionate intellectual curiosity, and to my husband, Steven Kramer, and my daughter, Christene DeJong, who continually inspire me to think and live creatively.

I invite the reader to enter into this puzzle of creativity and to consider the rewards of patiently trying to fill in the gaps.

Teresa M. Amabile

Preface to the 1983 Edition

The ideas presented in this book have been incubating for over 25 years. I was in the first grade, I believe, when the ideas that eventually developed into this social psychology of creativity first began to germinate. The occasion was art class, a weekly Friday afternoon event during which we were given small reproductions of the great masterworks and asked to copy them on notepaper using the standard set of eight Crayola® crayons. I had left kindergarten the year before with encouragement from the teacher about developing my potential for artistic creativity. During these Friday afternoon exercises, however, I developed nothing but frustration. Somehow, DaVinci's "Adoration of the Magi" looked wrong after I'd finished with it. I wondered where that promised creativity had gone.

I began to believe then that the restrictions placed on my artistic endeavors contributed to my loss of interest and spontaneity in art. When, as a social psychologist, I began to study intrinsic motivation, it seemed to me that this motivation to do something for its own sake was the ingredient that had been missing in those strictly regimented art classes. It seemed that intrinsic motivation, as defined by social psychologists, might be essential to creativity. My research program since then has given considerable support to that notion. As a result, the social psychology of creativity presented in this book gives prominence to social variables that affect motivational orientation.

The social psychology of creativity is such a new field of investigation that the phrase itself is almost impossible to find in the creativity literature. I first came across it shortly after I began my program of research. In a 1975 article, D. K. Simonton called for the development of a social psychology of creativity (Simonton, 1975a). His own work since then has been invaluable in providing information on the relationship between social environments and creative productivity over long periods of time. Simonton's archival research, which differs in many respects from mine, is reviewed at length in Chapter 8.

Aside from Simonton's work and my own, there is almost no empirical research on the impact of specific social factors on creativity. Creativity researchers have instead concentrated primarily on individual differences in creative abilities or constellations of personality traits that characterize outstandingly creative persons. While those areas of inquiry are important, there are a number of reasons to develop a social psychology of creativity. On a practical level, social variables represent one of the most promising avenues for influencing creative behavior. There is not much that can be done about innate abilities and personality characteristics. Furthermore, although cognitive skills necessary for creative performance can be developed, this process normally occurs over relatively long periods of time. By contrast, social environments influencing creativity can be changed easily and can have immediately observable effects on performance.

On a theoretical level, it is important to consider motivational variables in analyses of the creative process. This approach can contribute to theoretical social psychology by describing the impact of "traditional" social-psychological variables on cognitive performance, specifically creative performance. It can also contribute to theories of creativity by introducing a consideration of social factors and the motivational mechanisms by which they influence creativity.

The case for a social psychology of creativity is argued more fully in Chapter 1. There, I review the writings of several notably creative persons who have described the impact of social factors on their creativity. These arguments are then considered in the context of previous empirical research. In Chapter 2, I review existing definitions of creativity and methods for assessing creativity and, in Chapter 3, I present the definitions and assessment techniques I have applied in my own research. Chapter 4 outlines the theoretical framework that guides the discussion of creativity throughout the book. (A shorter discussion of the material in Chapters 2, 3, and 4 can be found in Amabile [1982b, 1983]).

Empirical research on social factors influencing creativity is presented in Chapters 5, 6, 7, and 8. Although much of the research in Chapters 5, 6, and 7 is mine, I also include a fairly exhaustive review of the work other researchers have done on evaluation, reward, choice, social facilitation, modeling, motivational orientation, and other social variables that might affect creativity. In Chapter 9, I draw practical implications from the research reviewed. In Chapter 10, I outline future research directions for a social psychology of creativity.

This book does not exhaustively review all previous creativity research. Rather, it reviews work on personality, testing, cognition, and creativity training that is most relevant to a social-psychological perspective on creativity. Information from this previous work is integrated with current social-psychological research in my attempt to lay the foundation for a comprehensive social psychology of creativity. This book is clearly not a complete statement. It is, instead, a description of the current state of the art and an outline of what a comprehensive model might be.

The research reported in this book was supported by a Young Scholars grant from the Foundation for Child Development, a series of Biomedical Research Support Grants from the National Institutes of Health, and a predoctoral fellowship from the National Institute of Mental Health. A grant from the Mazer Family Fund at Brandeis University was invaluable in the preparation of this manuscript. All of this support is gratefully acknowledged.

Several institutions generously allowed me and my students to conduct one or more of these studies within their walls: St. Jude's School in Waltham, Massachusetts, St. Clements's School in Somerville, Massachusetts, the Charles E. Cashman School in Amesbury, Massachusetts, the Lemberg Day Care Center at

Brandeis University, and the Veteran's Administration Hospital at Brockton, Massachusetts.

Dozens of people helped me develop the ideas presented here, conduct the research I report, and work this manuscript into its final form. First, after the debt of gratitude I owe my first teachers for making me wonder where my "creative potential" had gone, I owe thanks to my graduate mentors at Stanford, Mark Lepper and Lee Ross, for their part in the early development of my hypotheses on creativity. It was Mark's research and theorizing on intrinsic motivation that led me to consider the impact of motivational state on creative performance. Both Mark and Lee encouraged me in the risky business of creativity research and spent long hours discussing with me my earliest ideas on creativity. The other members of my doctoral dissertation committee, Daryl Bem and Philip Zimbardo, also gave me helpful insights at the earliest stages of this work.

Many colleagues, students, and friends contributed to this research. Steven Berglas and Ellen Langer collaborated with me on studies reported in this book, as did my graduate students, Margaret Stubbs, Beth Hennessey, and Maureen Whalen, and my undergraduate students, Phyllis Goldfarb, Shereen Brackfield, Lisa Berman, Donna Capotosto, and Nancy Goldberg. Anne Sandoval did a marvelous job with the data analyses for many of these studies. Several research assistants helped to conduct the studies, analyze the data, or locate resource material for this book: Barry Auskern, Linda Blazer, Tony Cadena, Scott Carlin, Ronit Goldlust, Barbara Grossman, Marie Handel, Leah Kaufman, Chihiro Mukai, Christopher Patsos, Gail Rubin, and Julia Steinmetz. In addition, my sisters, Carolyn Amabile and Phyllis Amabile, gave me important assistance in planning and conducting one of the studies described here.

Others contributed to the preparation of this book in various ways. Students in my "Psychology of Creativity" course at Brandeis have challenged and expanded my ideas on creativity. Teri Buchanan of Chevron U.S.A. most graciously provided me with complete transcripts from Chevron's 1981 national creativity exhibit. Verna Regan, Judy Woodman, and Karen Diehl of the psychology office at Brandeis helped to prepare pieces of the manuscript at various points. And Bill Harrington of Computer City helped to keep my Apple II-Plus smoothly processing the words that are served up here.

Although they cannot be held responsible for flaws in this book, several colleagues can be credited with helping to clarify my ideas and my prose. Robert Kidd, my advising editor, not only suggested this project initially, but he also provided generous encouragement throughout and helpful comments on a first draft of the book. Kenneth Gergen, Robert Hogan, Dean Keith Simonton, and David Campbell offered valuable suggestions for Chapters 2, 4, 8, and 9, respectively. Many other colleagues have given me comments over the past three years on drafts of proposals or manuscripts that found their way in some form into this book: Reid Hastie, Maurice Hershenson, Ray Knight, Ellen Langer, Leslie

McArthur, Ricardo Morant, Harvey Pines, David Schneider, Mark Snyder, Margaret Stubbs, Mick Watson, and Art Wingfield.

The staff of Springer-Verlag provided just the right blend of freedom, encouragement, guidance, and friendship to keep my motivation and creativity near their highest levels.

Finally, I owe my biggest debt of gratitude to my husband, William DeJong. In countless ways, he has been a true colleague and friend throughout the seven years of this research program. He discussed my ideas on creativity with me at every stage and was instrumental in their refinement. He helped as I developed and improved the research paradigm. Most importantly, he read and edited the entire first draft of this manuscript—a task which he did not take lightly. Bill's comments on conceptualization, consistency, and organization, together with his line-by-line editing, rendered this book considerably more readable than it would otherwise have been.

But Bill's contributions go far beyond those he made as a psychologist. He provided me with the time, space, and encouragement I needed to complete this project, and he did so by performing a number of acts that were clearly above and beyond the call of duty—from serving cups of tea and administering shoulder rubs as I hunched over the word processor at 2 A.M., to assuming the lion's share (and the lioness's, too) of child care for our two-year-old, Christene, to sending me off for a week at Cape Cod to complete the finishing touches on the book. Quite simply, this is his book, too.

T. M. A.

Part One
Understanding and Assessing Creativity

1

The Case for a Social Psychology of Creativity

It is nothing short of a miracle that the modern methods of instruction have not yet entirely strangled the holy curiosity of inquiry; for this delicate little plant, aside from stimulation, stands mainly in need of freedom; without this it goes to wreck and ruin without fail. It is a very grave mistake to think that the enjoyment of seeing and searching can be promoted by means of coercion and a sense of duty.

Einstein, 1949, p. 19

In this surprisingly lyrical passage from his autobiography, Einstein sounds a theme that will be repeated throughout this book: largely because they affect motivation, social factors can have a powerful impact on creativity.

To understand creativity, two basic questions must be answered. How is creative performance different from ordinary performance? What conditions are most favorable to creative performance—what personal abilities and characteristics, what social environments? With this book, I hope to lay the foundation for a social psychology of creativity. In this endeavor, I will concentrate on the second question by considering the social conditions that are most conducive to creativity. In examining the impact of social factors on creative performance, however, it is also necessary to consider the ways in which creative performance is different from ordinary performance. Thus, throughout the book, both questions will be addressed.

A Gap in Creativity Research

There are two reasons for developing a social psychology of creativity. The first, obvious reason is simply that there has previously been no such discipline. There is little relevant theory, there is only a small research literature on the effects of specific social and environmental influences on creativity and, more importantly, there are virtually no experimental studies of the effects of such influences. Clearly, this is not because there are few creativity studies overall. In 1950, *Psychological Abstracts* had 11 listings under "Creativity," less than .2% of the total number of articles abstracted. In 1960, this category represented .4% of the total; in 1966, it accounted for .8%, and by 1970 creativity articles made up fully 1% of all publications listed. Few of these studies were experimental, though, and even fewer concerned social-psychological factors. Between 1976 and 1978, no articles on creativity were published in the *Journal of Experimental Psychology, Psychological Review* or the *Journal of Experimental Social Psychology.* One article that could be considered related to creativity appeared in *Cognitive Psychology,* one in *Psychological Bulletin,* and four in the *Journal of Personality and Social Psychology.* During that same period, however, over 600 creativity articles were published in less experimentally oriented journals.

If creativity researchers have not been doing experimental studies of social-psychological effects on creative performance (and clearly they have not), what have they been doing? The major emphasis in creativity research over the past three decades has been on personality studies of creative individuals. This emphasis was directly predicted—or, perhaps, initiated—by Guilford in 1950: "the psychologist's problem is that of creative personality" (p. 444).

This research has taken several different forms. One long-standing approach involves the study of biographies and autobiographies of well-known creative individuals, attempting to define their peculiar qualities of intellect and personality (Galton, 1870; Cox, 1926). A second approach to the examination of individual differences in creative ability is the intensive laboratory study of one or a few creative individuals. Research carried out by MacKinnon and Barron (MacKinnon, 1962) at the Institute of Personality Assessment and Research at Berkeley is typical of this approach. These researchers carried out "living-in" assessments of artists and scientists who had been reliably nominated as creative by their peers. Over a weekend, each subject would be formally interviewed by different individuals, and would complete a large battery of personality and intelligence tests. Finally, the most common variety of individual-difference research on creativity examines ordinary individuals. Typically, an average population is chosen and the members are given personality, intelligence, and creativity tests. Those who achieve high creativity scores are compared along the other assessment dimensions with those who score low (e.g., Wallach & Kogan, 1965).

Some creativity research has focused on issues other than individual differences. For example, Newell, Shaw, and Simon (1962) have considered the cognitive skills necessary for creativity. They describe an information-processing approach to the problem, one in which creative activity is seen as the application of particular set-breaking heuristics. Their relatively sophisticated description of the creative process is linked to computer-based notions of human intellectual abilities. In contrast to the approach of Newell et al. (1962), most other work on the cognitive skills involved in creativity is less theoretical, relying on common-sense notions of the creative process and, occasionally, empirical findings from industry and education. The most familiar work in this category, Osborn's (1963) "brain-storming" program, is prototypical: sets of rules or heuristics are taught as guidelines for the generation of creative solutions to problems. Subsequently, ideas generated by people who have been trained in the program are compared with those of people who have not.

Finally, there have been a modest number of studies examining the effects of particular social or physical environments on creativity. Some studies have compared two populations from different environments on creativity test performance. For example, open classrooms have been compared to traditional classrooms (e.g., Klein, 1975), and large-city classrooms have been compared to those from smaller cities (Torrance et al., 1960). Other studies have used biographical data to investigate the effects of home and religious influences on the creativity of eminent people (e.g., Roe, 1952), or historical data to uncover the social, political, and cultural environments that foster or inhibit creativity (e.g., Simonton, 1975a).

The most active area of creativity research, then, has been the description of the peculiar characteristics of famous or widely recognized creative people, living and dead, or the description of differences in personality and intellect between people who do well on creativity tests and people who do not. Implicit in much of this work is the assumption that the important characteristics of creative people are largely innate (or at least largely immalleable), and that these characteristics clearly and reliably separate creative people from noncreative people.

As a result of the focus on individual differences, some potentially important areas of inquiry into creativity have been virtually ignored. There has been a concentration on the creative person, to the exclusion of "creative situations"—i.e., circumstances conducive to creativity. There has been a narrow focus on internal determinants of creativity to the exclusion of external determinants. And, within studies of internal determinants, there has been an implicit concern with "genetic" factors to the exclusion of contributions from learning and the social environment. 1

Previous research on creativity has had fundamentally different aims, in most respects, from those of a social psychology of creativity. Studies on the personality characteristics of outstandingly creative individuals have been concerned with identifying particular clusters of traits that can accurately describe such individuals. To an extent, these studies have been successful in fulfilling that goal. Studies on the characteristics that distinguish people who do well on creativity tests from those who do not do well are also concerned with individual-level description and, perhaps, with prediction. Again, this research has met with some success. Cognitive psychologists studying the creative process have identified some operating procedures of the human cognitive system that seem to lead with a high probability to novel and useful solutions. In contrast to these research endeavors, a social psychology of creativity aims to identify particular social and environmental conditions that can positively or negatively influence the creativity of most individuals.

Some Social Psychological Stories

The second reason for developing a social psychology of creativity is more important than the simple dearth of studies in this area: Social and environmental

---

1. When this symbol appears beside a paragraph, it means that the Update to this chapter contains substantially new theory or data on this point.

factors seem to play a crucial role in creative performance. There is considerable informal evidence that social-psychological factors have a significant impact on the productivity and creativity of outstanding individuals. Most of this evidence comes from autobiographies, letters, journals, and other first-person accounts by scientists, artists, writers, and others generally acknowledged for their creative achievements. Certainly, caution must be exercised in the use of such sources as evidence of actual psychological phenomena. One poet herself expressed doubt in the ability of creative persons to provide insight into their creativity:

> In answering the question, How are poems made? my instinctive answer is a flat, "I don't know." It makes not the slightest difference that the question as asked me refers solely to my own poems, for I know as little about how they are made as I do of anyone else's. What I do know about them is only a millionth part of what there must be to know. I meet them where they touch consciousness, and that is already a considerable distance along the road of evolution. (Lowell, 1930, p. 24)

There are three reasons, however, for considering first-person reports as legitimate sources of background material for developing a social psychology of creativity. First, the main focus of interest is not on introspections about thinking processes (which, as Lowell noted, are bound to be inaccurate or at least incomplete). Rather, the main focus is on creative persons' reports of social factors that impinged on them and the apparent stimulation or inhibition of their work that followed. Second, these reports are used only as sources of hypotheses about social factors, and not as tests of those hypotheses. Finally, although particular creative persons might certainly have experienced idiosyncratic reactions to social and environmental influences, if certain factors are repeatedly cited as important by creative people, it is likely that a real phenomenon is being identified.

Several creative people have provided excellent accounts of their daily working lives, often affording insight into influential social forces. (Not surprisingly, the majority of such accounts—particularly the more richly descriptive ones—come from writers.) In many of these reports, social forces are cited as harmful to creativity. This creates a peculiar paradox: May we accept the notion that such forces are indeed detrimental to creativity, if we draw the evidence from persons who distinguished themselves for their highly creative work? It seems more appropriate to find such evidence in the working lives of individuals who were never able to achieve wide acclaim for their work. But these individuals, of course, are not to be found among the names catalogued in collections of autobiographies, journals, and personal letters. We are forced, then, to use as a preliminary data source the writings of creative individuals who experienced normal peaks and depressions in their creative productivity, and then to examine experimentally the social forces that appear to have covaried with those fluctuations.

First-person accounts of creative activity contain ample evidence on the major issue considered in this book: the creativity-enhancing effect of working on something for its own sake, and the creativity-undermining effect of working on something for the sake of meeting an external goal. This contrast between internal (or intrinsic) and external (or extrinsic) motivation appears repeatedly in these accounts and, because of this obvious importance, it appears repeatedly in the social psychology of creativity developed in later chapters.

Albert Einstein: From External to Internal Control

Although Einstein wrote little of his life and work, what he did record contains a recurrent theme: His interest in science and, presumably, his creativity, were undermined by forces that exerted external control over his work. As a youth, he attended a regimented, militaristic school in Germany where the pressures of exam period so overwhelmed him that he temporarily lost his interest in science which was, even at that time, quite substantial. "This coercion had such a detering effect upon me that, after I had passed the final examination, I found the consideration of any scientific problems distasteful to me for an entire year" (1949, p. 18).

Partly in an attempt to escape from such a strictly regimented learning environment, Einstein left Munich for Zurich when he was 15, hoping to enroll in the Polytechnic Institute there. To his dismay, however, he failed the entrance examination and was required to enroll in a Swiss school for remedial coursework. According to one Einstein analyst (Holton, 1972), this episode represented a turning point in Einstein's schooling and, perhaps, in his scientific thinking as well. In sharp contrast to what he had known, this school was humanistic in orientation, stressing the individual's unencumbered search for knowledge. This social atmosphere was ideally suited to Einstein's independent style of thinking and working. There was little emphasis on memorization, much emphasis on individual laboratory work and student-initiated investigation, and a concentration on the development of relaxed, democratic exchanges between students and teachers. To the end of his life, Einstein remembered this school fondly: "It made an unforgettable impression on me, thanks to its liberal spirit and the simple earnestness of the teachers who based themselves on no external authority" (Holton, 1972, p. 106). It was here that Einstein devised the first *Gedankenexperiment* that would lead him to the theory of relativity.

Other creators have resisted external attempts to control their behavior. For example, Woody Allen reports enjoying his work as a stand-up comedian and a writer far more than his work as a filmmaker precisely because other people have so much more control over various aspects of filmmaking; in his other pursuits, he alone is in complete control of the outcome (Lax, 1975). Like many highly creative individuals, Allen shuns tasks that he feels pressured to do but earnestly attacks work that meets his own interests. He regularly played hooky from school as a child, and flunked out of NYU after his first semester. (The courses he failed in college included film production.) Starting at an early age, with great consistency, he rejected the expectations that others had for his performance. Rather than attending school, he would wander around Manhattan observing people or visiting magic stores or watching movies. Rather than conforming to someone else's notion of his proper education, he taught himself filmmaking, music, literature, philosophy, history, and magic. On the night he was awarded an Oscar for *Annie Hall,* he was doing what he always did on Monday night, and what he clearly preferred to society's recognition—playing clarinet with his jazz group in Manhattan.

The rejection of external constraints is evident in the writing of D.H. Lawrence, who wrote to a friend, "I always say, my motto is 'Art for my sake.' If I *want* to write, I write—and if I don't want to, I won't" (Allen, 1948, p. 225). Joyce Carol Oates suggests that her underlying reason for writing is the intrinsic pleasure that reading something good brings: "I write to discover what it is *I will have written.* A love of reading stimulates the wish to write—so that one can read, as a reader, the words one has written" (1982, p. 1). And Picasso said, "When we invented cubism, we had no intention of inventing cubism, but simply of expressing what was in us. Nobody drew up a program of action, and though our friends the poets followed our efforts attentively, they never dictated to us" (Zervos, 1952, p. 51).

Even the minor daily demands of relatives, friends, and colleagues can act as social constraints that undermine creativity. It appears that highly creative individuals must often resist those sources of external control, as well. Charles Dickens bluntly pointed this out in answer to a friend's invitation:

> "It is only half-an-hour"—"It is only an afternoon"—"It is only an evening," people say to me over and over again; but they don't know that it is impossible to command one's self sometimes to any stipulated and set disposal of five minutes—or that the mere consciousness of an engagement will sometimes worry a whole day. These are the penalties paid for writing books. Who ever is devoted to an art must be content to deliver himself wholly up to it, and to find his recompense in it. I am grieved if you suspect me of not wanting to see you, but I can't help it; I must go in my way whether or no. (Allen, 1948, p. 230)

Anne Sexton: Coping with External Constraint

In Anne Sexton's letters to friends, colleagues, and relatives (Sexton & Ames, 1977), one attitude toward her writing is prominent: a consistently high level of intrinsic motivation, a motivation to write poetry primarily because it was something she loved to do. Perhaps this should be expected of someone who, as a housewife at the age of 28, watched an Educational Television program called "How to Write a Sonnet" and decided to give it a try. She enjoyed it so much that, for the rest of her 46 years, she never stopped writing poetry. It became first her passionate avocation and then her vocation, carried out over obstacles that included a traveling-salesman husband, two young children, a household to run, and repeated bouts with serious depression. In an introduction to Sexton's letters, her daughter says, "Very quickly she established a working routine in a corner of the already crowded dining room. Piled high with worksheets and books, her desk constantly overflowed onto the dining room table; she wrote in every spare minute she could steal from childtending and housewifely duties" (p. 29).

Throughout her career as a writer, Sexton struggled (usually with success) against several types of external constraints, including evaluation, competition, and rewards. She once wrote to her psychiatrist, for example, that she had become a "cheap artist" since winning a Radcliffe grant, that success of this type was not good for her. At times, though, she was so obsessed with making as much money as possible that she would consider doing projects only for their commercial value:

> About the little whiz-bang piece (book, whatever) on psychiatrists. . . . a desperate attempt on my part to write something that will make me some money. . . . it is supposed to be funny and awful and a little nutty, i.e., not literature but rather a cheap but possibly commercial thing, supplemented with cartoons and all. I don't *want* my name on it. Not that my name isn't good enough but the book isn't good enough for my name. . . . (Sexton & Ames, 1977, p. 241)

Sexton seemed to be generally aware, however, of the detrimental effects that excessive concern with reward could have on creativity. When her friend W. D. Snodgrass won the Pulitzer Prize for poetry, she cautioned him against losing his original intrinsic motivation for writing:

> So okay. "Heart's Needle" is a great poem. But you have better than that inside you. To hell with their prize and their fame. You've got to sit down now and write some more "real" . . . write me some blood. That is why you were great in the first place. Don't let prizes stop you from your original courage, the courage of an alien. Be still, that alien, who wrote "real" when no one really wanted it. Because, that is the only thing that will save (and I do mean save) other people. Prizes won't. Only you will. (Sexton & Ames, 1977, pp. 109–110).

Sexton's cautious and ambiguous attitudes toward reward for creative work are captured well in this passage from a letter to her agent: "I am in love with money, so don't be mistaken, but first I want to write good poems. After that I am anxious as hell to make money and fame and bring the stars all down" (pp. 287–288).

In addition to overcoming her concerns about money, Sexton also struggled to avoid an excessive focus on external evaluation. One of her earliest poetry mentors, Robert Lowell, told her once to "write ten more really good poems," and she immediately found herself incapable of writing anything until she could decide that Lowell's dictum was of no importance. Like other creative writers, Sexton saw publication and critical acclaim as a kind of addictive drug; pleasing at first, it is never enough and quickly becomes the misplaced focus of one's work. She single-mindedly fought to remain her own critic, instead of allowing the outside world to dictate the worth and direction of her work. Indeed, she once facetiously suggested that poems be published anonymously to avoid this trap. Her advice to Erica Jong (after the publication of Jong's second novel) captures the essence of Sexton's ability to avoid the undermining effects of this social constraint:

Don't dwell on the book's reception. The point is to get on with it—you have a life's work ahead of you—no point in dallying around waiting for approval. . . . You have the gift—and with it comes responsibility—you mustn't neglect or be mean to that gift— you must let it do its work. It has more rights than the ego that wants approval. (Sexton & Ames, p. 414).

Despite her occasional focus on external praise and tangible reward, Sexton's primary concentration on the intrinsic satisfaction of writing was evident in a letter she wrote to her mother shortly after her work in poetry had begun:

Although there is nothing new in the manner in which I have written these, it seems new to most poet tasters. I do not write for them. Nor for you. Not even for the editors. I want to find something and I think at least "today" I think I will. Reaching people is mighty important, I know, but reaching the best of me is most important right now. (Sexton & Ames, pp. 32–33)

In keeping with this intrinsic orientation, Sexton often did succeed in functioning as her own worst critic. On more than one occasion, she sent poems to magazine editors virtually asking them *not* to print the poems because they did not meet her own high standards. "Now . . . the magazine acceptance ceased to work—now it's got to be a Good Poem (worst critic Anne Sexton)" (p. 78). From time to time, when she struggled with a loss of intrinsic motivation brought about by a fear of external reactions to her work, she attempted to explicitly reject external goals: "my ambition to write good poems is going to stop me from daring to write bad ones. But I feel a new confidence somewhere, a new daring . . . to write for its own sake and give up the goal. I am going (I hope) to love my poems again and bring them forth like children . . . even if they are ugly" (p. 153).

Sylvia Plath: A Losing Battle with External Constraint

If Anne Sexton appears to have been primarily driven by intrinsic motivation, Sylvia Plath appears to have struggled unsuccessfully for most of her working life against some powerful extrinsic motivations. Her earliest attempts at publication of poetry and fiction met with marked success; by the time she graduated from Smith College, she had won various writing awards, published in national magazines, served as guest editor at *Mademoiselle* magazine, and won a Fulbright scholarship to study at Cambridge. A desire to regain this early success that seemed so effortless, however, bedeviled her through persistent writer's blocks in later years: "Suddenly my life, which had always clearly defined immediate and long-range objectives—a Smith scholarship, a Smith degree, a won poetry or story contest, a Fulbright, a Europe trip, a lover, a husband—has or appears to have none" (Hughes & McCullough, 1982, p. 251).

Plath struggled with social constraints of many forms. Through her tortured adolescence and early adulthood, she repeatedly imagined the possible devastating effects that conventional marriage could have on her creativity: "I desire the things which will destroy me in the end. . . . I wonder if art divorced from normal and conventional living is as vital as art combined with living: in a word, would marriage sap my creative energy and annihilate my desire for written and pictorial expression" (Hughes & McCullough, 1982, p. 23).

Clearly, though, the greatest burden that impeded Plath's writing during her postcollege years is an extrinsic constraint that, perhaps more than any other specific social factor, appears to undermine the creativity of outstanding individuals: the expectation of external evaluation, and the attendant concern with external recognition. Plath's excessive concern with recognition often resulted in jealousy and competitive rage. For example, after writing one poem of pure description, she felt disgusted with her effort because, unlike Adrienne Rich, she seemed incapable of "getting philosophy" into her poems: "Until I do I shall lag behind A. C. R." (Hughes & McCullough, 1982, p. 296). Repeatedly, she was consumed by her desire to achieve more than others with whom she compared herself. "Yes, I want the world's praise, money & love, and am furious with anyone, especially with anyone I know or who has had a similar experience, getting ahead of me" (p. 305). On many occasions, these concerns clearly interfered with Plath's ability to work:

> All I need now is to hear that G. S. [George Starbuck] or M. K. [Maxine Kumin] has won the Yale and get a rejection of my children's book. A. S. [Anne Sexton] has her book accepted at Houghton Mifflin and this afternoon will be drinking champagne. Also an essay accepted by *PJHH*, the copycat. But who's to criticize a more successful copycat. Not to mention a poetry reading at McLean. . . . And now my essay, on Withens, will come back from *PJHH*, and my green-eyed fury prevents me from working. (p. 304)

Plath was fully aware that her early success had led her to become dependent on—almost addicted to—positive evaluation from others.

> I have been spoiled, so spoiled by my early success with *Seventeen,* with *Harper's,* and *Mademoiselle,* I figured if I ever worked over a story and it didn't sell, or wrote a piece for practice and couldn't market it, something was wrong. I was gifted, talented—oh, all the editors said so—so why couldn't I expect big returns for every minute of writing? (Hughes & McCullough, 1982, p. 250)

Repeatedly, Plath realized that she was obsessed with the idea of publication of her work, obsessed with a fear that she might not be admired and esteemed. Furthermore, she realized that this obsession was undermining her efforts to write creatively: "I dream too much of fame, posturings, a novel published, not people gesturing, speaking, growing and cracking into print" (p. 180)

Like Sexton, Plath tried consciously to adopt a more intrinsic orientation: "editors and publishers and critics and the World, . . . I want acceptance there, and to feel my work good and well-taken. Which ironically freezes me at my work, corrupts my nunnish labor of work-for-itself-as-its-own-reward" (Hughes & McCullough, 1982, p. 305). And, like Sexton, Plath attempted to distance herself from the constraint of external evaluation, to diminish its salience. She occasionally resolved, for example, to avoid showing her creative efforts to her poet-husband. At other times, she resolved to shut out all thought of critics except herself and her husband: "So I will try to wean myself into doing daily poetic exercises with a hell-who-cares-if-they're-published feeling. That's my trouble. . . . The main problem is breaking open rich, real subjects to myself and forgetting there is any audience but me & Ted" (p. 170). In one particularly interesting example of self-deception, she wrote in her journal, "I must feel the pain of work a little more & have five stories pile up here, five or ten poems there, before I start even hoping to publish and then, not counting on it: write every story, not to publish, but to be a better writer—and ipso facto, closer to publishing" (p. 173). At another point, she summed up the heart of the problem: She had become trapped by the desire for the external world to label her "a writer."

Apparently, this problem is a common one among writers and, perhaps, among individuals in other domains of creative activity, as well. In discussing what she saw as the major problem with American writers, Gertrude Stein remarked, "The trouble is a simple one. They become writers. They cease being creative men and soon they find that they are novelists or critics or poets or biographers" (Preston, 1952, p. 167). Stein pointed to Sherwood Anderson as a contrary example, someone who "is really and truly great because he truly does not care what he is and has not thought what he is except a man, a man who can go away and be small in the world's eyes and yet perhaps be one of the few Americans who have achieved that perfect freshness of creation and passion" (p. 167).

James Watson: A Race for Success

Almost from the day James Watson entered the Cambridge laboratory where he met and began to collaborate with Francis Crick, one motive was clear in their pursuit of the correct descriptive model for DNA: "Imitate Linus Pauling and beat him at his own game" (Watson, 1968, p. 37). They knew that they would have to use methods and theories that had been devised by Pauling in his work on alpha-helics. They knew that Pauling, like many chemists and biochemists, was also working on the DNA problem. And, finally, they were certain that there was a Nobel prize waiting for whomever first published a correct description of the DNA molecule.

This knowledge, along with their overriding desire to win this competition, was a salient force in Watson and Crick's work on the problem. Few pages go by in Watson's account of the research without mention of their obsession with this competition: "But if I went back to pure biology, the advantage of our small headstart over Linus might suddenly vanish" (Watson, 1968, p. 92). "Fortunately, Linus did not look like an immediate threat on the DNA front" (p. 93). When it appeared that Pauling would pull ahead in the race, as it appeared from a letter he had written his son (who was living in Cambridge and knew Watson and Crick), they despaired:

It was from his father. In addition to routine family gossip was the long-feared news that Linus now had a structure for DNA. No details were given of what he was up to, and so each time the letter passed between Francis and me the greater was our frustration. Francis then began pacing up and down the room thinking aloud, hoping that in a great intellectual fervor he could reconstruct what Linus might have done. As long as Linus had not told us the answer, we should get equal credit if we announced it at the same time. (p. 99)

And, when Pauling failed in his initial attempts, they were ecstatic:

Francis and I went over to the Eagle. The moment its doors opened for the evening we were there to drink a toast to the Pauling failure. Instead of sherry, I let Francis buy me a whiskey. Though the odds still appeared against us, Linus had not yet won his Nobel. (p. 104)

It is impossible to estimate the impact that this fierce competition had on Watson and Crick's creativity. Obviously, they did eventually succeed in their task. It is possible, of course, that they would have made their discovery sooner and with fewer false starts if they had not been so caught up in trying to beat another researcher "at his own game." Watson, however, gives no hint of this possibility: if anything, he seems to have viewed this competition as a spur to productivity at best and a simple fact of life in science at worst. In any case, it is clear from Watson's account that competition must be considered a salient social factor in creative endeavor.

What are the effects of winning the rewards that many creative people appear to so earnestly desire? Although, certainly, in many cases their work would be impossible without the support of grants, prizes, stipends, and ordinary salaries, at least some creative individuals appear to have suffered from the receipt of salient tangible rewards. Apparently, T. S. Eliot believed that the Nobel Prize would destroy his creativity. He was actually somewhat dejected after receiving it, and when a friend congratulated him and said, "High time!", Eliot replied, "Rather too soon. The Nobel is a ticket to one's own funeral. No one has ever done anything after he got it" (Simpson, 1982, p. 11). And Dostoevsky appears to have been virtually paralyzed by a large monetary advance for writing a novel which he had not yet even conceived:

And as for me, this is my story: *I worked and was tortured*. You know what it means to compose? No, thank God, you do not! I believe you have never written to order, by the yard, and have never experienced that hellish torture. Having received in advance from the *Russy Viestnik* so much money (Horror! 4,500 roubles). I fully hoped in the beginning of the year that poesy would not desert me, that the poetical idea would flash out and develop artistically towards the end of the year, and that I should succeed in satisfying everyone. . . . but on the 4th of December . . . I threw it all to the devil. I assure you that the novel might have been tolerable; but I got incredibly sick of it just because it was tolerable, and not *positively good*—I did not want that. (Allen, 1948, p. 231)

Thomas Wolfe: The Pressure of Success

In describing the horrendous doubt and confusion he experienced in attempting to write his second novel, Thomas Wolfe suggests that, ironically, the positive critical response to his first work was largely responsible:

> I would read about myself, for example, as one of the "younger American writers." I was a person who, some of the critics said, was to be watched. They were looking forward to my future book with interest and with a certain amount of apprehension. . . . Now, indeed, I could hear myself discussed, and somehow the fact was far more formidable than I had dreamed that it could be. . . . I was a young American writer, and they had hopes and fears about my future, and what would I do, or would it be anything, nothing, much, or little? Would the faults which they had found in my work grow worse or would I conquer them? Was I another flash in the pan? Would I come through? What would happen to me? (1936, p. 14)

Not only did the positive critical reception of his first book serve to paralyze Wolfe, but many citizens of his hometown, in which the first novel had ostensibly been set, were outraged at what he had portrayed. In some ways, this form of external evaluation was even more difficult for him to put out of mind:

> Month was passing into month; I had had a success. The way was opened to me. There was only one thing for me to do and that was work, and I was spending my time consuming myself with anger, grief, and useless passion about the reception the book had had in my native town, or wasting myself again in exuberant elation because of the critics and the readers' praise, or in anguish and bitterness because of their ridicule. (p. 25)

Time pressures became part of the burden success had laid on Wolfe; his "public"—especially his critics—were awaiting his second novel. Although no publisher had given him a deadline for completion of this second manuscript, he had a clear sense of the implicit expectations.

> At any rate, while my life and energy were absorbed in the emotional vortex which my first book had created, I was getting almost no work done on the second. . . . A young writer without a public does not feel the sense of necessity, the pressure of time, as does a writer who has been published and who must now begin to think of time schedules, publishing seasons, the completion of his next book. I realized suddenly with a sense of definite shock that I had let six months go by since the publication of my first book and that, save for a great many notes and fragments, I had done nothing. (1936, p. 26)

Once the time pressure became explicit, Wolfe's despair and distraction only intensified:

> Almost a year and a half had elapsed since the publication of my first book and already people had begun to ask that question which is so well meant, but which as year followed year was to become more intolerable to my ears than the most deliberate mockery: "Have you finished your next book yet?" "When is it going to be published?" . . . now, for

the first time, I was irrevocably committed so far as the publication of my book was concerned. I began to feel the sensation of pressure, and of naked desperation, which was to become almost maddeningly intolerable in the next three years. (pp. 49–50)

A Recurrent Theme: Intrinsic versus Extrinsic Motivation

The creative individuals whose first-person accounts of creative work I have reviewed here do not, of course, represent a random sample of writers, scientists, and artists. Nonetheless, their explicit and implicit statements about the influence of social factors on their work are in fact representative of the statements made by many others who have distinguished themselves for their creativity. Each of these factors appears regularly in first-person reports: a concern with evaluation expectation and actual evaluation; a desire for external recognition; a focus on competition and external reward; a reaction against time pressures; a deliberate rejection of society's demands; and a preference for internal control and intrinsic motivation over external control and extrinsic motivation.

These influences can be considered together as illustrations of one general principle: Intrinsic motivation is conductive to creativity, but extrinsic motivation is detrimental. It appears that when people are primarily motivated to do some creative activity by their own interest in and enjoyment of that activity, they may be more creative than they are when primarily motivated by some goal imposed on them by others. Although this principle appears in some form in nearly all of the first-person accounts presented earlier, it is clear that there are large differences in the degree to which external goals undermined creativity. Sylvia Plath, for example, appeared to be crippled for long periods of time by a concern with evaluation and competition and the demands that others made on her. For Anne Sexton, on the other hand, these seem not to have been major issues. Why the difference? It is possible that the two writers differed in their fundamental abilities and temperaments. There are ways, however, in which social factors could also have played a part. Through early socialization, Sexton might have learned strategies for ignoring or overcoming external constraint. Or, perhaps, there were important differences in the levels of constraint in the working environments of these two writers. It is not possible, by simple examination of the introspective accounts, to arrive at any reliable conclusions to this issue; experimental research is required. In any case, however, it can be said that social psychological factors *are* important in creativity and, among these, the most crucial may be those that either lead people to concentrate on the intrinsically interesting aspects of a task or lead them to concentrate on some extrinsic goal.

The intrinsic motivation principle will be the cornerstone of the social psychology of creativity developed in this book. Before that principle is examined in detail, however, it will be necessary to lay a methodological and conceptual foundation. Chapter 2 deals with the meaning and measurement of creativity, and Chapter 3 presents in detail a consensual assessment technique used in much of the research that appears in later chapters. Chapter 4 presents a working model of the creative process, highlighting the role of social-psychological factors. Chapters in the second section of the book include research evidence on several specific factors used in tests of the intrinsic motivation hypothesis: evaluation, reward, and task constraint of other types. In addition, these chapters present research on social factors that do not derive directly from the intrinsic motivation principle: social facilitation, modeling, and educational environments, among others. The final section of the book includes chapters on the application of social-psychological principles to creativity enhancement and on integrating a social psychology of creativity into a comprehensive theoretical framework.

Update

As of 1983, besides our own program of research there was only one other researcher who had produced a significant body of work on the social psychology of creativity: Dean Simonton. In the years since, many researchers and theorists have seriously turned their attention toward the impact of social factors on creativity. For example, Harrington and his colleagues conducted an empirical study of long-term parental influences on creativity (Harrington et al., 1987) and developed an "ecology of human creativity" theory that includes social influences (Harrington, 1990). Several other theorists have included social psychological factors in their recent conceptualizations—for example, Csikszentmihalyi (1988) in his "systems view of creativity," Gardner (1988) in his "interdisciplinary perspective," Gruber (1988) in his "evolving systems" approach to creativity, Sternberg and Lubart (1991) in their "investment theory" of creativity, and Woodman, Sawyer, and Griffin (1993) in their interactionist theory of organizational creativity.

Although creativity theorists had, several decades earlier, speculated on the importance of environmental "press" (Mooney, 1963), it is only in recent years that creativity conferences, edited books, and journals have explicitly focused attention on the issue (e.g., Gryskiewicz & Hills, 1992; Isaksen, Murdock, Firestien, & Treffinger, 1993). The field of creativity research has two major new journals, *Creativity Research Journal* and *Creativity and Innovation Management,* in addition to the long-standing *Journal of Creative Behavior.* Over the past few years, many of the conceptual and empirical articles in each of these journals have dealt explicitly or implicitly with social psychological variables. Moreover, though they are still rare, articles on creativity have appeared with increasing frequency in mainstream psychology journals.

Thus, it appears that the case for a social psychology of creativity has been made successfully. It also appears that the creativity field overall has enjoyed an increase of activity in both conceptual development and rigorous empirical research. But the social psychology of creativity is still in its early stages, and a focus on creative persons, creative personalities, and creativity skills still dominates the field. Even considering the sizable advances reported in this update, there are still many unanswered questions about social influences on creativity.

The first edition of this chapter asserted that "largely because they affect motivation, social factors can have a powerful impact on creativity." With twelve more years of research behind us, we reaffirm that basic theme. Whatever an individual's talents, domain expertise, and creative thinking skills, that individual's social environment—the conditions under which he or she works—can significantly increase or decrease the level of creativity produced. It still appears that the primary mechanism (or at least a primary mechanism) of this influence is the individual's motivational state. Intrinsic motivation, which is the drive to engage in some activity because it is interesting and involving, appears to be essential for high levels of creativity. And intrinsic motivation can be significantly affected by the social environment.

In examining this proposition, we initially focused on individuals (both children and adults) in experimental studies where we carefully manipulated social factors and studied the effects on artistic and verbal creativity. The first edition of this book reported the results of these early experiments. We have since expanded our program of research to include problem-solving creativity and to add nonexperimental methods (surveys, interviews, and archival sources) for studying influences on the creativity of individuals, groups, and organizations. In so doing, we have moved beyond a focus on intrinsic and extrinsic motivation. Although the intrinsic motivation principle (formerly termed the intrinsic motivation hypothesis) is still crucial in our theory of creativity, we have paid more detailed attention to other aspects of social influence on creativity. And, as we shall make clear in the Update to Chapter 4, the intrinsic motivation principle itself has been revised.

Indeed, we have even expanded beyond our original concern with social psychological factors, in large part because the social psychological perspective has finally begun to find its way into mainstream research and theory. The first edition of this book presented the outline of a comprehensive theory of creativity, a theory in which social and motivational factors were highlighted. As will become evident in the updates of Chapters 2 through 10, in the years since, we have attempted to become more inclusive in the factors we studied and the theoretical perspectives we incorporated. We have also attempted to move toward a comprehensive systems view that includes interacting networks of factors influencing—and being influenced by—creativity. The social psychology of creativity as it was originally conceived grew largely from a desire to explore uncharted territories of the creativity question that stretched well beyond the personality psychology of creativity that was then overwhelmingly dominant in the field. Now we regularly include personality measures in our studies of social influences, and we have begun to use cognitive measures as well. We have, we hope, begun to practice the integration of disciplines we preached twelve years ago.

2

The Meaning and Measurement of Creativity

Creativity researchers are often accused of not knowing what they are talking about. The definition and assessment of creativity have long been a subject of disagreement and dissatisfaction among psychologists, creating a criterion problem that researchers have tried to solve in a variety of ways. Some have proposed that creativity can be identified with particular, specifiable features of products or persons or thought processes. Others have suggested that creativity be defined by the quality of the response that a product elicits from an observer. And there are those who suggest that creativity cannot be defined—that it is unknown and unknowable. I will argue in this chapter that, in different ways, each of these approaches can be useful for solving the criterion problem in creativity research.

Kosslyn (1980) has suggested that "it is not necessary to begin with a crisp definition of an entity in order to study it. . . . It is hard to define something one knows little about" (p. 469). Certainly, this observation can apply to creativity research. Although it would be inaccurate to say that we know little about creativity, given the rather rich store of data we have on the personality characteristics of creative individuals, it is still true that we do not know enough to specify a precise, universally applicable definition of the term. We cannot draw up a list of special traits, for example, and say that the work done by persons exhibiting those traits must necessarily be creative. Similarly, we cannot enumerate a set of objectively identifiable features that distinguish all creative products. And we cannot at this time outline the crucial characteristics of creative thought processes. Clearly, though, there is scientific precedence for conducting research in the absence of a widely accepted objective definition of the entity under study.

This is not to say, however, that we can postpone indefinitely any concerns about defining creativity. There are at least three general questions that must be asked at the outset of any research program, and definitions play a role in answering each of them: (1) What are we talking about? This is the question that is most difficult to answer in a precise way, but, as I argued earlier, a precise answer is not crucial. As long as the entity under consideration can be recognized with reasonably good consensus, it makes sense to proceed with a scientific examination of that entity. I will demonstrate later in this chapter that, in fact, this widespread consensus does hold for the recognition of creativity. (2) How can we study it? To answer this question, a clearly specified operational definition is necessary, one suggesting a methodology that can be systematically replicated. (3) How does it work? A complete answer to this question, of course, requires a comprehensive process theory. In order to attempt the formulation of such a theory, it is important to have at least a working conceptual definition of the entity; in the present case, we must begin with some notions about the important features of creative products, persons, or processes.

In this chapter, I will review previous attempts to define and assess creativity, arguing that most researchers have been too quick in their efforts to objectify the criteria of creativity. Following this, I will present an operational definition of creativity based on subjective judgment and a companion conceptual definition that serves as the foundation for the theoretical notions to be developed more fully in Chapter 4.

Previous Approaches to Creativity Definition

Many of the earliest definitions of creativity focused on the creative *process.* Such definitions were based on the notion that anything resulting from this process could be called creative. Perhaps the most remarkable process definition is John Watson's:

> *How the new comes into being:* One natural question often raised is: How do we ever get new verbal creations such as a poem or a brilliant essay? *The answer is that we get them by manipulating words, shifting them about until a new pattern is hit upon.* (Watson, 1928, p. 198)

In commenting upon this behavioristic view of human creativity, Koestler (1964) suggested that "for the anthropomorphic view of the rat, American psychology substituted a rattomorphic view of man" (p. 560). Koestler proposed that, instead of random associations, creativity involves a "bisociative process"—the deliberate connecting of two previously unrelated "matrices of thought" to produce a new insight or invention. According to him, the process includes "the displacement of attention to something not previously noted, which was irrelevant in the old and is relevant in the new context; the discovery of hidden analogies as a result" (1964, p. 119).

Other theorists have similarly concentrated on thought processes in their definitions of creativity. Gestalt psychologists (e.g., Wertheimer, 1945) suggested that creativity and insight arise when the thinker grasps the essential features of a problem and their relation to a final solution. Newell et al. (1962) stated that "creative activity appears simply to be a special class of problem-solving activity characterized by novelty, unconventionality, persistence, and difficulty in problem formulation" (p. 66). And some developmental psychologists (e.g., Feldman, 1980; Gruber & Barrett, 1974) have proposed that creative thinking shares many features in common with Piagetian transformations.

J. P. Guilford's 1950 address to the American Psychological Association is widely considered to have been a major impetus to the psychological study of creativity. In that address, Guilford defined creativity in terms of the *person,* a focus that became dominant during the 1950s and is still popular in much creativity research today:

> In its narrow sense, creativity refers to the abilities that are most characteristic of creative people. . . . In other words, the psychologist's problem is that of creative personality. . . . I have often defined an individual's personality as his unique pattern of traits. A trait is any relatively enduring way in which persons differ from one another. The psychologist is particularly interested in those traits that are manifested in performance; in other words, in behavior traits. Behavior traits come under the broad categories of aptitudes, interests, attitudes, and temperamental qualities . . . Creative personality is then a matter of those patterns of traits that are characteristic of creative persons. (1950, p. 444)

The person approach to the definition of creativity, although seldom explicitly stated, has in fact guided most empirical research on creativity (Nicholls, 1972).

Despite the implicit emphasis on the person in creativity research, most explicit definitions have used the creative *product* as the distinguishing sign of creativity. For example, Jackson and Messick (1965) proposed that creative products elicit a distinct set of aesthetic responses from observers: surprise, satisfaction, stimulation, and savoring. Bruner (1962) similarly focused on the response that creative products elicit from observers. He saw the creative product as anything that produces "effective surprise" in the observer, in addition to a "shock of recognition" that the product or response, while novel, is entirely appropriate. Most product definitions of creativity include these characteristics of novelty and appropriateness. Barron (1955a) proposed that, to be judged as "original," (1) the response "should have a certain stated uncommonness in the particular group being studied" and (2) it must be "to some extent adaptive to reality" (pp. 478–479). In other words, the incidence of the response must be statistically uncommon, and the response must be in some way appropriate to the problem. MacKinnon (1975), with whom Barron collaborated on an intensive study of creative persons, adopted Barron's two criteria and added a third: "true creativeness involves a sustaining of the original insight, an evaluation and elaboration of it, a developing of it to the full" (p. 68). Stein (1974) similarly suggested a definition that builds on the basic notions of novelty and appropriateness: creativity results in the production of some novel result that is useful, tenable, or satisfying, and represents a real "leap" away from what has previously existed.

Although many previous creativity definitions implicitly assume or explicitly state that creativity in persons or in products is to be considered a continuous quantity, it appears to be common wisdom among many laypersons and psychologists that creativity is a dichotomous variable. For example, this proposition is implicit in Guilford's (1950) discussion of creative persons, and it is explicit in Ghiselin's (1963) articulation of criteria for creativity:

This quality of uniqueness, recognizable and definable, either is present in full force or is absent entirely. The products to be dealt with are not more or less suffused with creativity, as an object may be tinged with color in one or another degree of saturation. Either a product of the mind is creative in one respect or another or else it is not creative in any. (p. 37)

In addition, some theorists assume different kinds of creativity: scientific, musical, artistic, verbal. This assumption underlies such philosophically diverse theories as Koestler's (1964) bisociative theory of creativity and Guilford's (1967) structure-of-intellect theory. These questions of the underlying dimensionality of creativity and the similarity of different domains of creativity are important ones; they are discussed at greater length later in the chapter.

In sum, even though person approaches have guided most previous research on creativity, formal definitions of creativity based on personality traits are as rare as formal definitions based on characteristics of the creative process. In formal discourse, product definitions are generally considered as ultimately the most useful for creativity research, even among those who study the creative personality or the creative process. Few creativity studies, however, have used assessment techniques that closely follow any explicit definition of creative products.

Previous Approaches to Creativity Measurement

Most empirical work on creativity has employed one of three assessment techniques. A few researchers have attempted an objective analysis of products. Some have relied on subjective judgments of products or persons as creative. The vast majority, however, have used creativity tests; the most popular of these are similar in form and administration to conventional intelligence tests. Before considering whether alternative approaches are warranted, it is important to examine each of these three techniques, its heuristic value, range of application, and shortcomings.

Creativity Tests

Creativity tests, the most popular method of assessment in empirical studies, can be grouped into three broad categories: personality tests, biographical inventories, and behavioral assessments.

Personality inventories. The first category includes traditional personality inventories from which "creativity scales" have been derived—for example, Gough's (1957) California Psychological Inventory (Helson, 1965), Cattell and Eber's (1968) Sixteen Personality Factor Questionnaire (Cattell & Butcher, 1968), Gough and Heilbrun's (1965) Adjective Check List (Gough, 1979), and Heist and Yonge's (1968) Omnibus Personality Inventory (Heist, 1968). In addition, there are personality tests that were specifically designed only to assess traits characteristic of creative individuals—for example, the "How Do You Think?" test (Davis &

Subkoviak, 1975), the "Group Inventory for Finding Creative Talent" (GIFT) (Rimm, 1976; Rimm & Davis, 1976), and the "What Kind of Person Are You?" test (Torrance & Khatena, 1970).

Gough's (1979) Creative Personality Scale for the Adjective Check List is representative of the first group of personality tests. The research leading to the development of this scale studied 12 samples in a variety of fields, comprising 1,701 subjects whose creativity had been reliably assessed by experts in those fields. Working from the 300 adjectives that make up the full self-report ACL, Gough identified a subscale of 30 adjectives that reliably differentiated the more creative from the less creative individuals. Of these 30 items, 18 were found to be positively related to creativity: capable, clever, confident, egotistical, humorous, individualistic, informal, insightful, intelligent, interests wide, inventive, original, reflective, resourceful, self-confident, sexy, snobbish, and unconventional. The 12 negatively weighted items were: affected, cautious, commonplace, conservative, conventional, dissatisfied, honest, interests narrow, mannerly, sincere, submissive, and suspicious. Torrance and Khatena's (1970) "What Kind of Person Are You?" is typical of personality tests that were specifically designed to assess creativity. On this instrument, subjects select adjectives to describe themselves within a forced-choice format. Generally, for example, highly creative individuals describe themselves as altruistic rather than courteous, curious rather than self-confident, and self-starting rather than obedient.

Biographical inventories. A second approach to the assessment of creative personality has been the administration of biographical inventories (e.g., Cattell, 1959; Ellison, 1960; Holland & Astin, 1961; McDermid, 1965; Owens, Schumacher, & Clark, 1957). Most of these inventories were originally devised on an intuitive basis and refined through testing samples of individuals rated high in creativity and those rated low or average. For example, the Alpha Biographical Inventory (Institute for Behavioral Research in Creativity, 1968) was developed through extensive testing of NASA scientists and engineers (Taylor & Ellison, 1964). It includes several hundred items on childhood, interests and hobbies, notable experiences, and so on. The Biographical Inventory: Creativity (Schaefer, 1969a) includes 165 items grouped into five categories: family history, educational history, leisure activities, physical characteristics, and miscellaneous. Finally, Taylor (1963) administered a 50-item biographical inventory to 94 researchers at the Navy Electronics Laboratory in San Diego, comparing the results against supervisors' ratings of subjects' creativity and productivity. This research uncovered a number of intriguing differences between those rated as more creative and those rated as less creative. The more creative men preferred the fields of mathematics, physics, electronics, communications, and other physical sciences in college (as opposed to radio, electricity, electrical laboratory, and engineering). They dated significantly more frequently in college (or were married in college). As children they lived in homes that were well-equipped with work benches and tools (as opposed to homes with no tools). And, as children, they read significantly more books. Finally, they were more ambitious in their careers.

Behavioral tests. Most people familiar with the creativity literature would, when asked to describe a typical "creativity test," mention one of several behavioral assessments that are more test-like than the personality or biographical inventories. Most often, these behavioral assessments include a battery of tests similar in administration and form to traditional intelligence tests. Many of the tests that Guilford (1967) originally devised to tap the divergent thinking component in his structure-of-intellect theory (1956) have served as the model for many creativity tests. Guilford's "Unusual Uses" test, for example, requires the subject to name as many uses as possible for a common object (such as a brick). The most widely used test batteries, however, and the criteria against which many other creativity tests have been validated, are the Torrance Tests of Creative Thinking (TTCT, also called the Minnesota Tests of Creative Thinking, Torrance, 1962).

The TTCT call for oral, written, or drawn responses which can be scored separately by category, although results are sometimes combined into a single creativity score for each individual. Test administration follows a standard procedure. Children (for whom the tests were originally designed) are usually given the tests in a group by their teacher, with fairly stringent time limits. Instructions given to the children suggest that correct responses are those which are unusual and clever. The responses to the test items are scored in terms of four criterion components of creativity (derived mainly from Guilford's theory): (1) fluency, the production of large numbers of ideas; (2) flexibility, the production of a large variety of ideas; (3) elaboration, the development, embellishment, or filling out of ideas; and (4) originality, the use of ideas that are not obvious or banal, or are statistically infrequent.

The TTCT can be grouped into three categories: nonverbal tests, verbal tests using nonverbal stimuli, and verbal tests using verbal stimuli. An example of a nonverbal test is the "Circles Task," in which the child is asked to sketch as many different objects as possible using 36 identical blank circles, and to provide a title for each sketch. Fluency is scored as the total number of circles used. Flexibility is scored as the total number of "different categories" of objects represented. Originality is scored by assigning one point to each response represented in less than 5% of the normative population, and two points to each response represented in less than 2% of the population. Finally, elaboration is scored as the number of "pertinent details" used in the sketches. A verbal test using nonverbal stimuli is the "Product Improvement" test, where the child is shown a toy dog and told, "try to think of the cleverest, most interesting and most unusual ways of changing this toy dog so that boys and girls will have more fun playing with it." An example of a verbal test using verbal stimuli is the "Consequences" test, where the subject is given 5 minutes to write an answer to a question such as, "What would happen if man could become invisible at will?" Most of the tests are scored on all four criterion components of fluency, flexibility, originality, and elaboration.

Most other creativity tests are similar in form, content, administration, and scoring to the TTCT. For example, although the authors of the Wallach and Kogan tests (1965) strongly recommend a nonevaluative, game-like, untimed administration, the form, content, and scoring of these tests do not differ substantially from those for the TTCT. The Wallach and Kogan tests include five subtests, each of which requires children to make a verbal response to a series of questions. In the "Instances" test, children are asked, "Name all the round things you can think of," "Name all the things you can think of that will make a noise," and so on. The "Alternate Uses" test is essentially the same as the "Unusual Uses" tests devised by Guilford and by Torrance. In the "Similarities" test, children are asked to name as many similarities as they can between two objects, such as a potato and a carrot or a radio and a telephone. The "Pattern Meanings" and "Line Meanings" tests require children to name as many things as they can think of when viewing particular abstract patterns or line drawings. For each test, a "uniqueness" score is obtained by noting the total number of responses the child gave that were completely unique in the group being studied. A "number" score is obtained by counting all responses.

Although they are rare, there have been some attempts to devise tests of the creative process. For example, Ghiselin, Rompel, and Taylor (1964) created a "Creative Process Checklist," designed to assess states of attention and affect in scientists at the moment of invention. These researchers asked scientists to recall such moments and choose adjectives to describe their experience before, during, or after "the act of grasping (or shaping) a new insight" or "solving a problem." There were some differences between scientists they considered "creative" ("high in creativity and low in material success") and those they considered "materially successful" ("low in creativity and high in material success"). Within this rather peculiar dichotomy, Ghiselin and his colleagues found that the creative scientists most often described their attention in the early stages of thought on a problem as "diffused" and "scanning," while the successful scientists described their attention as "focused" and "sharp." Following the insight, creative scientists were more likely to feel "delighted," while successful scientists were more likely to feel "relieved," "satisfied," "exalted," "full," and "excited."

What does it mean when someone scores high (or low) on a creativity test? Is it appropriate to consider high scorers as "creative persons"? Although many authors and users of creativity tests might suggest that such a label is appropriate, greater caution in interpretation is warranted. Ward (1974), for example, argues that test scores should not be considered measures of creativity but, instead, should be given narrower labels that more accurately capture the particular abilities assessed. My own position is similar to this. In Chapter 4, I suggest that creative performance emerges from three necessary components, from combinations of innate skills, learned abilities, and task attitudes. Any given creativity test might tap one or more of those abilities or dispositions, but it is most unlikely that a single test will tap all the elements of the three components in a general way. Thus, in attempting to better predict creative achievement, it is important to specify which domains and elements of creativity are assessed with any particular test.

Environmental influences on test performance. Although there is evidence that creativity tests do assess relatively stable attributes and abilities, it is interesting to note that various social and environmental factors can influence test outcomes. For example, a number of studies have found that subjects' scores on creativity tests will improve if they are simply told that they are taking a creativity test. In one such study (Speller & Schumacher, 1975), boys and girls were given Guilford's (1963) Unusual Uses Test (for bricks, brooms, bottles, newspapers, clothes hangers, and tires) with instructions that introduced the test either as a "creativity exercise" or a "word exercise." Fluency scores were significantly affected, with the "creativity" subjects scoring higher than the "word exercise" subjects. In another study (Manske & Davis, 1968), subjects' originality scores increased when they were instructed to be "original," their practicality scores increased when they were instructed to be "practical," and their total number of responses increased when they were instructed to be "wild." If they were told to be both practical and original, their scores did not differ from those under nonspecific instructions, although fewer responses were given overall. Finally, in a study where subjects were told to respond to the Adjective Check List (Gough & Heilbrun, 1965) as a creative person would, they appeared to be significantly more "creative" than they did when asked to complete the ACL as they would without specific instructions (Ironson & Davis, 1979).

Testing environments may also influence test outcomes. Wallach and Kogan (1965) suggested that creativity tests be administered in "a context free from or minimally influenced by the stresses that arise from academic evaluation and a fear of the consequences of error" (p. 321). Additionally, they suggested that testing situations be "unfettered by such forms of pressure as the imposition of time limits" (p. 64). Wallach and Kogan based these prescriptions on both their analysis of subjects' performance over time on creativity tests, and on the introspective reports of outstandingly creative individuals. Although there is some contradictory evidence (see Hattie, 1977), a large number of studies have in fact shown differences in creativity test scores under different testing conditions and different time constraints (e.g., Adams, 1968; Boersma & O'Bryan, 1968; Christensen, Guilford, & Wilson, 1957; Dentler & Mackler, 1964; Dewing, 1970; Lieberman, 1965; Mednick, Mednick, & Jung, 1964; Murphy, 1972; Nicholls, 1972; Van Mondfrans, Feldhusen, Treffinger, & Ferris, 1971; Wilner, 1974).

Perhaps most interesting, however, are the studies demonstrating effects of contextual cues in the testing environment on test performance. In an ingenious experiment, Glucksberg (1964) presented subjects with the task of completing an electrical circuit for which the supplied wire was too short; the only way in which the circuit could be completed was by inserting a screwdriver to connect the wire. Subjects presented with a screwdriver whose blade looked similar to the wire (in color and brightness) and whose handle looked similar to the posts on the circuit board solved the problem in significantly less time than did subjects whose screwdrivers looked dissimilar to the other elements of the problem.

Higgins and Chaires (1980) gave subjects Duncker's (1945) functional fixedness problem, which asks them to mount a candle on a screen using only the candle and some thumbtacks. The problem can only be solved by emptying the thumbtacks out of their box and using the box as a platform. Subjects who had previously learned "undifferentiated constructions" for remembering pairs of objects (e.g., "tray of tomatoes") were significantly less likely to solve Duncker's problem than were subjects who had learned "differentiated constructions" for the same object pairs (e.g., "tray and tomatoes"). Finally, although the drawing of a picture cannot truly be considered a "creativity test," some intriguing effects of prior environmental stimulation were obtained in a study in which subjects were asked to draw a picture after viewing two slides presented either separately or superimposed on a screen (Sobel & Rothenberg, 1980). Those who had viewed the superimposed slides produced drawings rated as significantly more creative than those produced by subjects viewing the separate slides.

Certainly it is unlikely that all of these results showing social and environmental influences on creativity test performance can be explained by a single theoretical construct. The important point to be made here, however, is that the tests do not assess *only* stable individual differences in creative abilities and attitudes. Even on tests that are designed to measure such differences, social and contextual factors may at times play a crucial role in performance.

A critique of creativity tests. Despite the evidence that creativity tests can be influenced by situational or contextual factors, there are a number of reasons for considering creativity tests unsatisfactory for wide use in a social psychology of creativity. In fact, some of the problems with creativity tests could hamper *any* empirical application. First, although there have been some studies suggesting that certain creativity tests do assess qualities that correspond to real-world creative performance (e.g., Torrance, 1962, 1972a), the construct validity (concurrent and predictive) of many tests has been seriously questioned by recent empirical work (cf. Bastos, 1974; Goolsby & Helwig, 1975; Holland, 1968; Jordan, 1975; Kazelskis, 1972), as has the convergent validity of different test procedures considered together (cf. Hocevar, 1981). The validity problem is especially troublesome since many of the creativity tests are validated against one another.

Second, as mentioned earlier, it appears that many of the creativity tests assess such narrow ranges of abilities that it is inappropriate to label a particular test performance as generally indicative of "creativity." For example, there is evidence that "originality" scores on the Torrance Tests of Creative Thinking are heavily influenced by verbal fluency (Dixon, 1979; Hocevar, 1979a, 1979b, 1979c). Although verbal fluency might well be a skill that contributes importantly to creativity in certain domains of endeavor, labeling these scores as "originality" may be misleading.

Third, the purportedly objective scoring procedures in many of the creativity tests are, in fact, basically subjective. For some scoring procedures, results must depend on the test scorer's intuitive assessment of what is creative. Even when scoring guidelines have been specified in sufficient detail to allow little room for the scorer's own interpretation, performance on the tests is rated according to the test constructor's intuitive assessment of what is creative, and not according to objective criteria of novelty, appropriateness, satisfyingness, and so on. Motivated perhaps by the apparent success of objective tests of intelligence, creativity researchers might have been too quick in attempting to objectify the assessment of creativity. Many creativity tests do measure abilities and dispositions that are probably important for creative performance. But it is inappropriate to label their results as directly indicative of some global quality that can be called creativity. I suggest that such judgments can ultimately only be subjective.

Thus, there are a number of difficulties inherent in using creativity tests for empirical research. For the specific purpose of developing a social psychology of creativity, however, the most crucial feature of the creativity tests is that they were primarily developed as tools for individual difference research. They were expressly designed to be sensitive to individual differences in performance in a wide variety of domains or individual differences in particular personality traits; indeed, there is abundant evidence that many of the tests do assess relatively stable individual differences (e.g., Gakhar & Luthra, 1973; Holland, 1968; Torrance, 1972a, 1972b). Precisely to the extent that they are able to detect subtle individual differences, however, these tests are inappropriate for experimental studies of social and environmental influences on creativity (Feldman, 1980). Normally, social psychologists seek to control for and, as much as possible, eliminate individual-difference (within-group) variability in the crucial dependent measures, in order that those measures might more easily detect the "signal" of between-group differences produced by experimental manipulations (Carlsmith, Ellsworth, & Aronson, 1976). Thus, in developing a social psychology of creativity, it is unwise to rely upon assessment techniques that were expressly designed to reveal consistent individual differences.

At several points throughout this book, I will support my arguments, in part, with results obtained by researchers using creativity tests. This may seem odd, in light of my criticisms of those tests. Nonetheless, there are several reasons to include the results of such studies here. First, many of those studies were, in fact, investigations of individual differences—for which the tests are well-suited. Second, it clearly is possible that strong social-psychological factors might significantly influence performance on such tests. Third, when cited, these studies are accompanied by cautions concerning the validity problems of the tests used. Despite the problems involved, if there are a number of creativity-test studies pointing to a particular conclusion, and if those results agree with studies using other methods, then the test-dependent outcomes should be regarded as informative.

Objective Analysis of Products

A second approach to creativity assessment, used only infrequently, is the objective analysis of products. Ghiselin (1963), for example, suggested that it should be possible to analyze objectively the "intrinsic quality" of products to determine whether they are creative. Although he did not present any specific methodological guidelines for accomplishing this feat, Ghiselin's optimistic expectation still has a seductive appeal. If it were possible to somehow quantify our notions of what makes a creative product and to specify objective means for assessing those quantities, the criterion problem would be permanently solved. Few researchers have even attempted a clear-cut quantification of creativity, but one meticulous effort in this direction deserves some comment.

In a study of the relationship between a melody's fame and its originality (see Chapter 8), Simonton (1980b) developed a completely reliable and objective method for quantifying originality. He used two dictionaries of musical themes to select all of those themes for which the composition date and the composer's birthdate were known, yielding 15,618 themes by 479 classical composers. Simonton then used the first six notes of each theme to determine its originality. Each note was paired with each succeeding note, yielding five two-note transitions for each theme. By computer analysis, each such transition was assigned a score based on the rarity of both the notes and the intervals between them, within the entire population of two-note transitions. These rarity scores were then summed for each theme, producing an overall originality score.

Clearly, this methodology is exciting in its adoption of a clear operational definition, its elegant simplicity, and its rigorous objectivity. Nonetheless, despite the potential utility of this approach, it would be inappropriate to embrace it as an ultimate objective methodology for the assessment of creativity. For one thing, the technique would be considerably more difficult to apply to other domains of endeavor which, unlike music, do not lend themselves well to mathematical description. In addition, though, and more importantly, this technique cannot distinguish the creative from the merely bizarre. As noted earlier, virtually all conceptual definitions of creativity include notions such as value or appropriateness in addition to novelty. Indeed, Simonton (1980b) implies that his originality measure must be coupled with some measure of the theme's acceptability in arriving at an assessment of creativity: "Hence, as the originality of a melody increases relative to the entire classical repertoire, the frequency of its performance first increases to a peak and thereafter decreases, with the least favored themes being the most original. In general terms, creativity is a curvilinear function of originality" (p. 981).

I will return to the feasibility of specifying objective features of creative products when I describe some results of my own program of research. At this point, I will foreshadow a later argument by saying that, ultimately, the assessment of creativity simply cannot be achieved by objective analysis alone. Some type of subjective assessment is required.

Subjective Judgments

Though used much less frequently than creativity tests, the subjective assessment of persons or products as creative has a much longer history. For his *Hereditary Genius* (1870), Galton relied on biographical dictionaries to select outstanding literary men and scientists—a technique that depended, clearly, on the subjective judgments of both Galton and those who compiled the dictionaries. Castle (1913), in a study of eminent men and women, used biographical dictionaries to choose an initial sample and then refined the sample by keeping only those who appeared in three additional sources and had the greatest amount of space devoted to them. Cox (1926), in gathering data for a personality study of 300 geniuses, drew her sample from a list of the 1,000 most eminent individuals in history that had been compiled by J. Cattell (1903) on the basis of space allotment in biographical dictionaries. And Simonton, in a study of various sociocultural influences on creativity (1975a), relied on frequency of citation in histories, anthologies, and biographical dictionaries as a measure of creativity.

Other studies use the judgments of a select group of experts to assess the creativity of particular individuals. Roe (1952) asked a panel of experts in each of four scientific disciplines to select the most eminent people in their field. For example, she asked six biologists to rate fellow biologists who belonged to the National Academy of Sciences or the American Philosophical Society. In a study of various influences on musical creativity, Simonton (1977a) chose 10 eminent classical composers on the basis of their rank ordering by the members of the American Musicological Society (Farnsworth, 1969).

Probably the most thorough application of this expert-nomination procedure can be found in the research on creative architects conducted by MacKinnon (1962) and his colleagues at the Institute for Personality Assessment and Research at Berkeley. The dean and four of his colleagues in the College of Architecture at the University of California were asked to rate and nominate the 40 most creative architects in the United States. They were provided with a definition of creativity, which included: "constructive ingenuity, ability to set aside established conventions and procedures when appropriate, a flair for devising effective and original fulfillments of the major demands of architecture, and original thought" (p. 137). MacKinnon rank-ordered the resulting 86 names on the basis of the ratings and his subjective assessments of summaries of the architects' work.

Rather than relying on the subjective judgments of a *person's* creativity, some studies use subjective judgments of a particular *product's* creativity. For example, Sobel and Rothenberg (1980) had subjects draw sketches after viewing slide stimuli presented either separately or superimposed. The sketches were subsequently rated by two accomplished artists who were given three dimensions on which to make their ratings:

1. *Originality of sketches:* the sketch presents a fresh, new or novel design, structure, image, or conception.

2. *Value of sketches:* the artistic worth of the sketch, determined by factors such as effectiveness, visual interest or visual power, coherence or unity, intelligibility, emotional impact, "says" or "conveys" something.
3. *Overall creative potential of the art product:* degree to which the product is both original and of value. (p. 957)

The judges were asked to form judgments of the overall creative potential of each sketch and to then assign each sketch a rating on a 5-point scale ranging from 1 [equals] "sketch is very bad—lacks originality and value or is not an artistic product, either in content or in execution" to 5 [equals] "sketch is excellent—highly original and highly valuable" (pp. 957–958).

In another study where subjects actually produced art works in the laboratory (Getzels & Csikszentmihalyi, 1976), four different groups of judges (two expert and two nonexpert) rated drawings on each of three dimensions: "originality," "craftsmanship," and "overall aesthetic value." Rather than providing the judges with specific definitions of these dimensions, these researchers asked them to use their own subjective criteria.

An intriguing and still unanswered question about the use of subjective judgments is, what, exactly, do judges mean when they call something "creative"? What features of products predict their responses? What phenomenological response states lead them to apply that label? In one of the few studies that reports judges' definitions of creativity, Lewis and Mussen (1967) found that teachers, when asked to comment on their creativity ratings of children's art, said that "original art" is contemporary, abstract, and spontaneous, while art with "artistic merit" (presumably different from "original art") is old, representational, dull, and mainly pleasing.

In an intriguing theoretical paper, Jackson and Messick (1965) suggest that judgments of outstanding creativity are composed of four aesthetic responses occurring together: (1) *surprise* is the aesthetic response to *unusualness* in a product, judged against *norms* for such products; (2) *satisfaction* is the response to *appropriateness* in a product, judged within the *context* of the work; (3) *stimulation* is the response to *transformation* in the product, evidence that the product breaks away from the *constraints* of the situation as typically conceived; and (4) *savoring* is the response to *condensation* in a product, the judged *summary power* or ability of the product to condense a great deal of intellectual or emotional meaning in a concise and elegant way. Unfortunately, there has been little empirical work on Jackson and Messick's scheme or, in fact, on any other framework for understanding subjective judgments of creativity. Although it has been demonstrated that judges can rate products according to "transformational power" (Feldman, Marrinan, & Hartfeldt, 1972), it has not been demonstrated that judges do, in fact, use transformational power (or any of the other proposed criteria) when left to their own devices for assessing creativity.

Studies employing subjective judgment have clearly avoided one of the problems noted earlier with the creativity tests. In their use of judges' ratings, such studies employ an assessment technique in which the subjective nature of the measure is direct and unveiled, in contrast to the seeming objectivity of the creativity tests. In other respects, however, many of the previously used subjective assessment methodologies present difficulties. First, many subjective assessment procedures fail to differentiate between the creativity of the products and other constructs, such as technical correctness or aesthetic appeal (cf. Hocevar, 1981). Second, the meaning of interjudge reliability can be questioned in studies where the experimenter presents judges with his own definition of creativity for them to apply or trains judges beforehand to agree with one another (e.g., Eisner, 1965; Rivlin, 1959; Wallen & Stevenson, 1960). Of course, in those studies where only one judge is used, it is impossible to discuss the reliability of assessment, and the meaning of that assessment must be seriously questioned. In addition, it is clear that measures of creativity based on eminence as indicated in historical sources are contaminated by personal, political, and other factors not necessarily related to creativity (cf. Stein, 1974; Wallach, 1970).

Most important here, however, are the ways in which previous subjective assessment methodologies might be inappropriate for use in social psychological research. Techniques employing global assessment of an individual as creative on the basis of his life's work are likely to detect relatively stable characteristics and would, therefore, be better suited to personality than to social-psychological research. Although these techniques might have some utility in the study of global effects of stable social factors (such as family structure), they would be inappropriate for the study of relatively unstable influences (such as temporary working conditions).

Even those assessment procedures that have judges rate single products, however, may be too sensitive to large and stable individual differences in performance. The theoretical framework for creativity presented in Chapter 4 proposes that creative performance depends on three components: skills relevant to a particular domain, skills relevant to creative thinking, and motivation for the particular task in question. Within this conceptualization, social-psychological factors have their primary influence on the task motivation component. Clearly, the assessment of creativity will be most sensitive to task motivational effects if the influence of domain-relevant and creativity-relevant skills can be controlled or eliminated. Thus, to the extent that the task presented to subjects draws upon special talents or experience-related skills—as do the tasks in most previous subjective-assessment methodologies—the assessment will be insensitive to social-psychological effects. Finally, many researchers using subjective assessment fall prey to a difficulty also encountered by those using creativity tests: The research is conducted in the absence of clear operational definitions. This occurs either because the researchers fail to articulate explicitly the definition of creativity guiding their research, or because they present conceptual definitions that are not directly tied to assessment procedures. Nearly all current definitions of creativity are conceptual rather than operational and were not intended to be translated into actual assessment criteria. Thus, despite the existence of intuitively reasonable definitions of creativity, current assessment techniques are not closely linked to them.

There are, then, a number of problems with current creativity assessment techniques. Methods attempting to objectively identify features of products as creative are not widely applicable and, ultimately, cannot be used as sole indicators of creativity. Creativity tests, though seemingly objective, are in fact based in subjective creativity judgments. Moreover, most of these tests are ill-suited to social-psychological research because of their sensitivity to individual differences. Directly subjective assessment methods often suffer from unreliability or from sampling procedures that render them, too, sensitive to individual differences. And virtually all previous methods of creativity assessment have been devised in the absence of clear operational definitions. This last issue is so central that it must be the starting point for improvements on previous techniques.

I suggest that the first step toward solving the criterion problem in creativity research is the adoption of two complementary definitions of creativity: an operational definition that is readily applicable to empirical research, and an underlying conceptual definition that can be used in building a theoretical formulation of the creative process.

A Consensual Definition of Creativity

The creativity assessment technique used in my program of research is grounded in a consensual definition of creativity—an explicitly operational definition that implicitly underlies most subjective assessment methodologies (cf. Amabile, 1982b):

> A product or response is creative to the extent that appropriate observers independently agree it is creative. Appropriate observers are those familiar with the domain in which the product was created or the response articulated. Thus, creativity can be regarded as the quality of products or responses judged to be creative by appropriate observers, and it can also be regarded as the process by which something so judged is produced.

Like most current definitions of creativity, the consensual definition is based on the creative *product*, rather than the creative process or person. Given the current state of psychological theory and research methodology, a definition based on process is not feasible. Although some progress has been made in this regard (e.g., Newell et al., 1962), a clear and sufficiently detailed articulation of the creative process is not yet possible. In addition, and more importantly, the identification of a thought process or subprocess as creative must finally depend upon the fruit of that process—a product or response. Likewise, even if we can clearly specify a constellation of personality traits that characterizes outstandingly creative people, the identification of people on whom such personality research would be validated must depend in some way upon the quality of their work. Thus, the definition that is most likely to be useful for empirical research is one grounded in an examination of products.

As I mentioned earlier, some theorists (e.g., Ghiselin, 1963) suggest that it will be possible to articulate criteria of creativity that are clearly stated and can be readily translated into an assessment methodology. But this hope of delineating clear objective criteria for creativity is still to be met. Indeed, I suggest that, ultimately, it is not possible to articulate objective criteria for identifying products as creative. Just as the assessment of attitude statements as more or less favorable (Thurstone & Chave, 1929) or the identification of individuals as "physically attractive" (Walster, Aronson, Abrahams, & Rottman, 1966) is a subjective judgment, so too is the assessment of creativity. Surely there are particular characteristics of attitude statements or persons or products that observers look to in rating them on scales of favorability or physical attractiveness or creativity. But, in the final analysis, the choice of those particular characteristics is a subjective one.

For the purposes of empirical research, then, it seems appropriate to abandon the hope of finding objective criteria for creativity and, instead, to adopt a definition that relies upon clearly subjective criteria. This is the aim of the consensual definition just presented. The consensual definition conceptually identifies creativity with the assessment operations. It may indeed be possible to identify particular objective features of products that correlate with subjective judgments of creativity or to specify subjective correlates of those judgments, but this definition makes it unnecessary to identify those objective features or the characteristics of those subjective reactions beforehand.

In the application of this operational definition, several important assumptions are made about the nature of creativity and creativity judgment. First, of course, I assume that products or observable responses must ultimately be the hallmark of creativity, and that it is not possible a priori to specify which objective features of new products will be considered "creative." Rather, as with most concepts used in social-psychological research (cf. Gergen, 1982), criteria for creativity require an historically bound social context.

Furthermore, I assume that although creativity in a product may be difficult to characterize in terms of features, and although it is difficult to characterize the phenomenology of observers' responses to creative products clearly (Feldman, 1980), creativity is something that people can recognize and often agree upon, even when they are not given a guiding definition (Barron, 1965).

In addition, in accord with previous theorists (e.g., Simon, 1967a), I propose that there is one basic form of creativity, one basic quality of products that observers are responding to when they call something "creative," whether they are working in science or the arts.

Finally, I assume that there are degrees of creativity, that observers can say with an acceptable level of agreement that some products are more creative or less creative than others. This assumption of a continuous underlying dimension is common in psychological theorizing on creativity. Cattell and Butcher (1968), for example, stated that creativity "may be manifested . . . at widely differing levels, from discovering the structure of the atom to laying out a garden" (p. 279). Nicholls

(1972) has argued against the assumption of a normally distributed personality trait of creativity, but he does concede that the assumption of continuity in judgments of creative *products* is a reasonable one. It is important to note that, although this explicit assumption is common in the psychological study of creativity, the popular assumption that creativity is a dichotomous quality—that people and things are either creative or not creative—is still implicit in much of the creativity literature.

A Conceptual Definition of Creativity

Although it is necessary to specify an operational definition of creativity that relies solely on subjective criteria, such a definition is not, by itself, sufficient for use in a theory of creativity. Although empirical studies of human creativity cannot at this time apply specific criteria for identifying creative products, any theoretical formulation of creativity must make assumptions about these criteria and their characteristics. Thus, to lay the foundation for a theoretical model of creativity, it is necessary to make assumptions about the nature of observers' responses when they call something "creative."

The theoretical framework of creativity presented in the following chapter is based in a conceptual definition of creativity that comprises two essential elements:

> A product or response will be judged as creative to the extent that (a) it is both a novel and appropriate, useful, correct or valuable response to the task at hand, and (b) the task is heuristic rather than algorithmic.

This conceptual definition is closely aligned with most of the product definitions described earlier, in its inclusion of novelty and appropriateness as two hallmark characteristics of creativity. In addition, however, this definition specifies that the task must be heuristic rather than algorithmic (cf. McGraw, 1978; Taylor, 1960). As typically defined (e.g., Hilgard & Bower, 1975), algorithmic tasks are those for which the path to the solution is clear and straightforward—tasks for which an algorithm exists. By contrast, heuristic tasks are those not having a clear and readily identifiable path to solution—tasks for which algorithms must be developed.[1] As used here, "path to solution" should be taken in its most general sense, referring to that set of cognitive and motor operations that will lead to an acceptable response or product in the domain of endeavor. By definition, algorithmic tasks have a clearly identified goal, but heuristic tasks might or might not have a clearly identified goal; the important distinction is that, for heuristic tasks, the *path to the solution* is not completely straightforward. In fact, however, in many cases, heuris-

---

[1] One implication of this, of course, is that an experimenter who wishes to present subjects with a "creativity test" must use a task for which there is no widely familiar algorithm.

tic tasks do not have clearly defined solutions *or* goals, and it is part of the problem-solver's task to identify them. Thus, as many theorists have noted (e.g., Campbell, 1960; Getzels & Csikszentmihalyi, 1976; Souriau, 1881), problem discovery is an important part of much creative activity.

An example of algorithmic and heuristic tasks might help to illuminate the distinction. If a chemist applied, step by step, well-known synthesis chains for producing a new hydrocarbon complex, that synthesis would not be considered creative according to this conceptual definition, even if it led to a product that was novel (had not been synthesized before) and appropriate (had the properties required by the problem). Only if this chemist had to develop an algorithm for the synthesis could the result be called creative. Similarly, an artist who followed the algorithm "paint pictures of different sorts of children with large sad eyes, using dark-toned backgrounds" would not be producing creative paintings, even if each painting were unique and technically perfect.

Clearly, there is a large class of tasks that may be considered either algorithmic or heuristic, depending on the particular goal and the level of knowledge of the performer in question. For example, if the goal of a task is simply to bake a cake, a recipe can be followed exactly, and the task will be considered algorithmic. If the goal is to bake a new kind of cake, a recipe will have to be invented, and the task will be considered heuristic. Certainly, some tasks may *only* be algorithmic—for example, solving an addition problem. Other tasks can only be considered heuristic—for example, finding a cure for leukemia—since no one knows the path to the solution. Most tasks, however, can be considered one or the other.

Furthermore, the determination of the label "algorithmic" or "heuristic" depends on the individual performer's knowledge about the task. If an algorithm for task solution exists but the individual has no knowledge of it, the task can be considered heuristic for that individual. For example, a student who independently proves a well-known theorem in geometry would certainly be said to have solved a heuristic task. To the extent that the proof is also seen as novel and correct, the student's work can be considered creative.

The specification of tasks as algorithmic or heuristic raises an important question about the assessment of creativity: Is the assessment to be made on normative or ipsative criteria? By including the algorithmic-heuristic dimension, the conceptual definition seems to rely on ipsative criteria. That is, if the task is heuristic *for the individual in question*, then novel and appropriate solutions generated by that individual can be considered creative. In contrast, the consensual definition appears to rely on normative criteria; in that definition, no mention is made of the observers' awareness of the creator's knowledge.

I suggest that creativity assessment, though primarily based on normative criteria, must rely to some degree on ipsative criteria as well. Creativity judges must have information (or make their own assumptions) about the creator in order to determine whether the task is heuristic, and the extent to which the response is novel and appropriate within the relevant comparison population. Clearly, collages made by small children require a different judgmental set for artist-judges than do those made by accomplished artists. Ipsative information is used to assess the nature of the task and the appropriate comparison group. Once this is done, however, creativity judgments are made on normative bases.

In presenting the consensual definition, I argued that the assessment of creativity must, ultimately, be culturally and historically bound. What aspect of observers' judgments is so bound? Is it their judgments of novelty, or appropriateness, or the algorithmic/heuristic nature of the task? I suggest that each of these is importantly influenced by cultural context and historical time. Observers are obviously influenced by knowledge of what products and responses have, in the past, been made in the domain in question. In this way, assessments of novelty are determined.[2] Observers are also influenced by cultural constraints specifying appropriate and inappropriate responses. And, finally, observers must rely to some extent on their knowledge of the zeitgeist in the field, in order to make a determination of whether the solution path has been clearly specified (rendering the task algorithmic) or is still unknown (leaving the task heuristic).

Although they serve different functions, the operational and conceptual definitions are closely related. The conceptual definition underlies the theoretical framework to be presented in Chapter 4. A useful conceptualization of creativity must explain how the crucial characteristics of creative products evolve in the process of task engagement. In essence, the conceptual definition is a best guess as to what characteristics appropriate observers are looking for when they assign ratings of "creativity" to products. Clearly, though, the characteristics proposed in that definition cannot be directly translated into an empirically useful definition, because it is not yet possible to specify objectively "novelty" or "appropriateness" or "straightforwardness" with any generality. Thus, although it is necessary to articulate a conceptual definition, a satisfactory operational definition must return to the final criterion for creativity assessment—reliable subjective judgment.

In the next chapter, I will describe a program of research that developed and tested the adequacy of a subjective assessment technique based on the operational definition I have proposed.

Update

Conceptually, we—and most of the field—still endorse the spirit of Morris Stein's (1953) definition of creativity as "that process which results in a novel work that

---

[2] Retrospective judgments of novelty must also be made in the same way. In assessing the creativity of a product made in the past, observers take into account information about the social and historical context in which the work was done. For example, in asserting that the film *Citizen Kane* was highly creative, modern film critics are judging it against the state of cinematic art at the time it was made, and not against the current zeitgeist.

is accepted as tenable or useful or satisfying by a group at some point in time." This definition combines two of the key elements of our own conceptual definition of creativity—novelty, and acceptability or appropriateness. In addition, it implies the utility of our operational definition of creativity, which rests on the consensus judgments of some social group at some point in time.

In the original edition of this book, we noted that there was no direct tie between our conceptual and operational definitions of creativity. The operational definition is necessary for the development of useful assessment methods; it specifies that a product is creative to the extent that appropriate observers agree it is creative. The conceptual definition is necessary for building a theory of creativity; it states that creativity is a novel, appropriate response to a heuristic (or open-ended) task. Essentially, the conceptual definition rests on assumptions about what observers are responding to when they identify a product as highly creative.

In the past few years, we have begun to gather some evidence on observers' criteria for creativity. In one study, Elise Phillips asked expert artists who had just served as judges of the creativity of other artists' works to rank-order a large number of qualities of art products in terms of how influential each of those qualities was in their assessment of creativity: emotion conveyed in the work; the idea behind the work (subject matter); the imaginativeness of the work; expressiveness; movement in the work; excitement; use of color; symmetry/asymmetry; complexity/simplicity; abstract expression; realistic expression; and use of form (Phillips, 1993). There was a fair degree of agreement in the rank-ordering of these qualities, and there was particular agreement in the top criteria. Of the 10 experts, 7 chose "imaginativeness" (novelty) as the most important criterion in their creativity assessments. Clearly, however, these data are just a start. Considerably more work is required to forge strong links between the conceptual and operational definitions.

It is important to reiterate several other assumptions that served as foundations for our original definitions and to note that, in the years since, a number of other theorists have asserted the utility of the same assumptions. For example, we argued that creativity assessments must, ultimately, be socially, culturally, and historically bound. It is impossible to assess the novelty of a product without some knowledge of what else exists in a domain at a particular time. It is impossible to assess appropriateness without some knowledge of utility or meaning in a particular context. And it is impossible for these assessments to be made—or indeed for creative products themselves to be made—in a cultural, social, or historical vacuum. These points have been forcefully made in recent years by a number of theorists, including Simonton (1984) and Csikszentmihalyi (1988).

We also argued in the 1983 edition that it is reasonable to assume a continuum of creativity—from the lowest "garden variety" levels where ordinary individuals are doing everyday things in appropriate ways that are somewhat novel, to the highest levels of creativity where geniuses are producing notable work that transforms fields and even societies. There is still considerable controversy in the field about this assumption. Some fully embrace the utility of the continuum notion, as we do (e.g., Isaksen & Dorval, 1993; Kirton, 1976; Sternberg & Lubart, 1991). However, several recent theorists either implicitly or explicitly assume that creativity is a discontinuous quality wherein the genius levels are both qualitatively and quantitatively different from all other work done in their domains (e.g., Feldman et al., 1994; Gardner, 1988; Gruber, 1988). A corollary assumption is that the processes producing the highest levels of work are qualitatively different as well, and that only they deserve the label "creative process."

However, we have repeatedly found that our expert judges are able to reliably assign degrees of creativity to the works we show them, whether those works are produced by "ordinary people" or by high-level professionals in a particular field. Moreover, we believe that without compelling evidence to the contrary, it is most parsimonious to assume a continuum of creativity in both products and processes.

It is true that there often appears to be a discontinuity in the creativity of products. Surely the works of Picasso seem to be qualitatively different from the works produced by beginning art students. We argue that this apparent discontinuity could well arise from a continuous but highly skewed distribution of creativity where nearly all products in a domain exhibit no creativity or low levels of creativity, and as levels of creativity increase, dramatically fewer products appear. Even between high levels and the very highest levels, there would be large apparent gaps in the quality of the products.

Moreover, we argue that even products that differ enormously in their creativity levels could arise from the same basic underlying process. As of yet, there is no clear evidence to settle the argument. However, a metaphor drawn from research in dynamical systems theory may be helpful in describing how a single underlying process can lead to qualitatively different outcomes (Amabile & Tighe, 1993).

The system used in this metaphor is that of a horse on a treadmill where the treadmill increases its speed at a constant rate. When the treadmill begins moving slowly, the horse walks. At some point the speed of the treadmill becomes great enough that the horse's movements become qualitatively different; the horse is now trotting. At some later point the horse breaks into a canter and, finally, into a gallop. A quantitative change in the speed of the treadmill has produced a qualitative change in the gait pattern of the horse. An observer glancing at the horse at Time 1 (walking) would see movement that looked quite different from what she might see if she glanced at Time 3 (cantering). Each of these movement patterns looks qualitatively different, yet the underlying system in the treadmill (and in the horse) has remained the same.

We argue that it is possible, given quantitatively different levels of each of the components of creativity (such as skill or motivation), for a single underlying process to lead to products that appear qualitatively different. There can be a continuity of process whether or not there are true qualitative changes (or discontinuities) in the creativity of products. And, even if such discontinuities exist, we believe that studying creativity at its lower levels can still illuminate the creativity of genius.

In understanding the social psychological conditions that can foster or inhibit creativity, it may be particularly useful to study creativity at its more modest levels. For one thing, there is more of it out there to study. For another thing, in the absence of extraordinarily high levels of talent, individuals may be particularly likely to display wide levels of variability in their creative output as a function of the social situation. These fluctuations can be investigated either between persons (as we have done in most of our research) or within persons. Of course, examining variability within persons would represent a departure from the normative consensual assessment of creativity, where products from several individuals in a given domain are compared to one another. It would require a more *ipsative* (or individually based) consensual assessment of creativity, where a person's work at one point in time is compared to that person's work in the same domain at other points in time. Both approaches can and should be used in creativity research with both high-level and modest-level creativity, as appropriate. The individually based assessment of creativity may be particularly useful in understanding social influences over the life span (holding talent and expertise more or less constant) and in understanding the development of children's creativity.

We critiqued creativity tests in the original chapter, arguing that they were unsuitable for most social psychological research on creativity and that, indeed, they might be unsuitable for most purposes. In the years since, a number of new critiques of creativity tests have been published. For example, Hocevar and Bachelor (1989) soundly criticize personality-based creativity tests as well as divergent-thinking tests and recommend a focus on creative accomplishments and creative products. Despite the continuing popularity of creativity tests, due in part to their ease of administration and scoring, it appears that many researchers are beginning to favor reliable subjective assessments of the creativity of products. This, of course, is our own approach as described in Chapter 3. We now suggest that creativity tests and subjective assessments of products are both useful for creativity research, but in different ways. The tests likely measure particular cognitive styles and skills that are conducive to creativity (called "Creativity-Relevant Processes" in our theory), whereas the method of consensual subjective assessment is more useful for broad overall measures of a product's creativity.

3

A Consensual Technique for Creativity Assessment

The consensual definition of creativity, my assumptions about the nature of creativity assessment, and the requirements of an appropriate methodology for a social psychology of creativity led to the development of the consensual assessment technique used in my research. Before presenting studies that employed the technique and assessing the extent to which it meets the criteria for creativity measurement in social psychology, I will describe the major features of the technique in some detail.

In selecting an appropriate task, there are three requirements that must be met. First, of course, the task must be one that leads to some product or clearly observable response that can be made available to appropriate judges for assessment. Second, the task should be open-ended enough to permit considerable flexibility and novelty in responses. Third, since it is desirable for social-psychological research that there not be large individual differences in baseline performances on the task, it should be one that does not depend heavily on certain special skills— such as drawing ability or verbal fluency—that some individuals have undoubtedly developed more fully than others. Certainly, for tasks that do depend heavily on special skills, it is possible to reduce extreme interindividual variability by choosing only individuals with a uniform level of baseline performance. However, this solution is impractical for most social-psychological studies of creativity, since it is rather difficult in most domains to identify large numbers of persons with uniform levels of skill in the domain. For this reason, while it is probably advisable in any case to eliminate subjects with deviantly high or low levels of experience with the domain in question, preliminary studies in a laboratory-based social psychology of creativity should use tasks that virtually all members of the population can perform adequately, without evidence of large individual difference variability.

There are also a number of requirements for the assessment procedure. First, the judges should all have experience with the domain in question, although the level of experience for all judges need not be identical. The specification of "appropriate observers" in the consensual definition is similar to Stein's (1967) suggestion that a creative product is accepted as useful, tenable, or satisfying by a group of "significant others," defined as "a formally or informally organized group of persons that has the ability and expertise to evaluate developments in its own field" (Stein, 1974, p. 35). Basically, the consensual assessment technique requires that all judges be familiar enough with the domain to have developed, over a period of time, some implicit criteria for creativity, technical goodness, and so on.

Among researchers who use subjective assessments of creativity, there has been some concern over characteristics of the judges: Should the judges be chosen on the basis of homogeneous views of creativity, as some have suggested (e.g., Korb & Frankiewicz, 1976)? Should people judge their own products on creativity? Should the judges themselves be shown to have produced creative work? The first question reaches the heart of the criterion problem. It is extremely difficult, given our current state of knowledge, to describe the nature of creativity judgments in any general way. Thus, it seems most appropriate to simply rely on the assumption that experts in a domain do share creativity criteria to a reasonable degree. As for the second question, there is evidence that self-judgments may not agree well with observers' judgments (Berkowitz & Avril, 1969). And, concerning the third issue, some studies have shown no differences between the judgments of "creative" and "uncreative" individuals (e.g., Baker, 1978; Lynch & Edwards, 1974). For these reasons, assessments should be made by external observers who have not been preselected on any dimension other than their familiarity with the domain.

The second procedural requirement is that the judges make their assessments independently. The essence of the consensual definition is that experts in a domain can recognize creativity when they see it, and that they can agree with one another in this assessment. If experts say (reliably) that something is highly creative, we must accept it as such. The integrity of the assessment technique depends on agreement being achieved without attempts by the experimenter to assert particular criteria or attempts by the judges to influence each other. Thus, the judges should not be trained by the experimenter to agree with one another, they should not be given specific criteria for judging creativity, and they should not have the opportunity to confer while making their assessments.

Third, in preliminary work on developing the technique for a given task, judges should be asked to make assessments on other dimensions in addition to creativity. Minimally, they should make ratings of the technical aspects of the work and, if appropriate, its aesthetic appeal as well. This would then make it possible to determine whether creativity is related to or independent of those dimensions in subjective assessments of the product in question. Assessments of other aspects of the work would also make it possible to compare social-environmental effects on those aspects with social-environmental effects on creativity. This is important because, theoretically, there might be reasons to predict that a given social factor will have differential effects on creativity and on technical performance.

Fourth, judges should be instructed to rate the products relative to one another on the dimensions in question, rather than rating them against some absolute standards they might have for work in their domain. This is important because, for most studies, the levels of creativity produced by the "ordinary" subjects who participate will be low in comparison with the greatest works ever produced in that domain.

Finally, each judge should view the products in a different random order, and each judge should consider the various dimensions of judgment in a different random order. If all judgments were made in the same order by all judges, high levels of interjudge reliability might reflect method artifacts.

Once the judgments are obtained, ratings on each dimension should be analyzed for interjudge reliability. In addition, if several subjective dimensions of judgment have been obtained, these should be factor analyzed to determine the degree of independence between creativity and the other dimensions. Finally, if the products lend themselves to a straightforward identification of specific objective features, these features may be recorded and correlated with creativity judgments.

As implied by the consensual definition of creativity, the most important criterion for this assessment procedure is that the ratings be reliable. By definition, interjudge reliability in this method is equivalent to construct validity. If appropriate judges independently agree that a given product is highly creative, then it can and must be accepted as such. In addition, it should be possible to separate subjective judgments of creativity from judgments of technical goodness and from judgments of aesthetic appeal (cf. Hocevar, 1981). Obviously, for some domains of endeavor, it may be relatively difficult to obtain ratings of aesthetic appeal and technical quality that are not highly correlated with ratings of creativity. After all, the conceptual definition includes elements of appropriateness or correctness in the conceptualization of creativity. However, it is important to demonstrate that it is at least possible to separate these dimensions. Otherwise, the discriminant validity of the measure would be in doubt; judges might be rating something as "creative" *simply* because they like it or because they find it to be technically well done.

Judges' ratings can be used to determine if the original task presented to subjects was appropriate for the purposes of a social psychological methodology. Certainly, if virtually all of the subjects in a random sample of a population are able to complete the task and report no technical difficulty in doing so (e.g., in manipulating the materials, in finishing within a reasonable period of time), this would suggest that the task was well-chosen for these purposes. If later judging of the products reveals a low correlation between judged creativity and experience-related characteristics of the subjects (e.g., age, experience with the particular type of materials), then the task can be considered a satisfactory one.[1]

---

[1] Certainly, in the extremes, experience-related variables will be important regardless of the particular task chosen. For this reason, care should be taken in eliminating extremes in ability level on the task in question. Thus, for example, if a verbal task were being used, it would be inappropriate to include an age range of 5–15 years in the population for a given study, even if the task had been chosen to minimize the importance of particular verbal skills. Likewise, if an artistic task were being used with a population of college students, it would be inappropriate to include students who have been doing studio art for several years along with students who have no involvement in art, even if the task does not depend in any obvious way upon draftsmanship.

The Consensual Assessment of Artistic Creativity

In an effort to establish firmly the utility of the consensual assessment technique, I have carried out a program of research using the technique in the assessment of both artistic creativity and verbal creativity (cf. Amabile, 1982b). I will present here the results of that research that are most directly relevant to evaluating the assessment technique. A number of these studies will be described more fully in later chapters, since they were designed to test particular hypotheses on the social psychology of creativity.

Study 1: Children's Artistic Creativity

Subjects and judges. The subjects for the study in which this technique was initially developed (Amabile, 1982a) were 22 girls, ages 7–11, who lived in an apartment complex in Palo Alto, California. All girls of these ages in this complex were invited to attend one of two "Art Parties" to be held during a weekend afternoon in the recreation hall; invitations were randomly distributed. There were fifteen girls in one group and seven in the other. All were of relatively low socioeconomic status.

Since this was the first investigation of this assessment technique, three different groups of judges, varying in expertise with art, were used—(1) *psychologists:* 12 members of the Stanford University psychology department (faculty and graduate students); (2) *art teachers:* 21 members of an art education course in the Stanford University School of Education (many of whom were elementary and secondary school art teachers); and (3) *artists:* 7 undergraduate and graduate artists from the art department at Stanford University (each of whom had spent at least 5 years working in studio art).

Materials. All subjects were given identical sets of materials to work with: over 100 pieces of lightweight paper in several different sizes, shapes, and colors (all arranged identically for each subject), a container of glue, and a 159 × 209 piece of white cardboard.

Procedure. The girls were seated at long tables and given their materials.[2] One of the three female experimenters explained that she needed some art designs made by children, so she was first asking them to make a design for her to keep. They were told that, later, they could make some more designs to take home with them.

---

[2] With the exception of one study that specifically investigated social facilitation effects, this is the only creativity study I have conducted in which subjects worked in groups. They were, however, encouraged by the experimenters to avoid copying or interfering with the other girls. To facilitate individual effort, the children were seated at widely spaced places at the tables. It was the observation of the experimenters, who were present throughout the session, that there was very little imitation of ideas or techniques.

The art works were always referred to as "designs," never as "pictures" or "patterns." This was done to convey as little experimenter expectation as possible regarding the appropriate level of representation in the collages.

After the initial introduction, the experimenter went on to demonstrate how to glue the shapes onto paper, and the children practiced with some scrap materials. Following this, the children were told they could use the materials in any way they wished to make a design that was "silly." This silliness theme was used as a means of obtaining a relatively high baseline level of creativity, and of reducing one source of variability—the themes children might employ—that could serve to make the judges' task more difficult. After 18 minutes (at which time virtually everyone had finished), the children were asked to stop.

All judges were told that the designs had been made by children in 18 minutes. Each psychologist-judge, working individually, was asked to rank the designs from most to least creative, using his or her own subjective definition of creativity. The art teachers were shown professionally made slides of the 22 designs and were also asked to use their own subjective definitions of creativity in making their independent assessments. They were asked to assign each design to one of five categories immediately after viewing it: (1) very uncreative; (2) rather uncreative; (3) undecided; (4) rather creative; (5) very creative.

The artist-judges were recruited to spend 4 hours in an individual session judging the 22 designs on a variety of dimensions. As with the other two groups of judges, the artists were allowed to inspect all 22 designs before beginning their ratings, and were told that the designs had been made by children in 18 minutes. These judges evaluated each of the 22 designs on 23 different dimensions, including creativity, technical goodness, and aesthetic appeal. A nonrestrictive "definition" of each dimension was provided at the top of its rating sheet. Table 3-1 lists these dimensions, and their definitions. The judges were asked to keep the different dimensions of judgment as separate from one another as possible. They were also instructed to rate the collages relative to one another on each dimension, rather than rating them against some absolute standard for art.

The artist-judges were presented with continuous scales for making each judgment. These scales had five equally spaced reference points marked, three of which were labeled: high, medium, and low. The judges were told to make each judgment by placing an X anywhere on the scale. They were asked to make their judgments under the assumption that the scale had equal spacing between the five reference points, and they were encouraged to make use of the entire range of the scale. On 4 of the 23 dimensions (creativity, technical goodness, liking, and silliness), these judges were also asked to assign each design to one of three categories (high, medium, and low) and to rank all 22 designs from highest to lowest on the given dimension.

The designs were arranged in a different random order for each judge, and the dimensions were judged in different random orders (e.g., all designs judged on balance, then all judged on creativity, and so on). The rating, ranking, and cate-

Table 3-1. Dimensions of Judgment for Artist-Judges, Study 1

Dimension	Descriptive Definition Given Judges
Creativity	Using your own subjective definition of creativity, the degree to which the design is creative.
Novel use of materials	The degree to which the work shows novel use of materials.
Novel idea	The degree to which the design itself shows a novel idea.
Liking	Your own subjective reaction to the design; the degree to which you like it.
Overall aesthetic appeal	In general, the degree to which the design is aesthetically appealing.
Pleasing placement of shapes	The degree to which there is a pleasing placement of shapes in the design.
Pleasing use of color	The degree to which the design shows a pleasing use of color.
Display	If it were possible, the interest you would have in displaying this design in your home or office.
Technical goodness	The degree to which the work is good technically.
Overall organization	The degree to which the design shows good organization.
Neatness	The amount of neatness shown in the work.
Effort evident	The amount of effort that is evident in the product.
Balance	The degree to which the design shows good balance.
Variation of shapes	The degree to which the design shows good variation of shapes.
Degree of representationalism	The degree to which the design shows an effort to present recognizable real-world objects.
Degree of symmetry	The degree to which the overall pattern is symmetrical.
Expression	The degree to which the design conveys a literal, symbolic, or emotional meaning to you.
Silliness	The degree to which the design conveys a feeling of silliness, as when a child is feeling and acting "silly."
Detail	The amount of detail in the work.
Spontaneity	The degree of spontaneity conveyed by the design.
Movement	The amount of movement in the design.
Complexity	The level of complexity of the design.

Table 3-2.   Interjudge Reliabilities for Seven Artist Judges, Study 1

Dimension of Judgment	Reliability of Scale Ratings	Reliability of Rankings	Reliability of Category Groupings
Creativity	.77	.78	.69
Novel use of materials	.84	—	—
Novel idea	.70	—	—
Liking	.52	.51	.43
Aesthetic appeal	.54	—	—
Pleasing placement of shapes	.26	—	—
Pleasing use of color	.47	—	—
Display	.40	—	—
Technical goodness	.72	.82	.80
Organization	.87	—	—
Neatness	.77	—	—
Effort evident	.76	—	—
Planning evident	.91	—	—
Balance	.38	—	—
Variation in shapes	.88	—	—
Representationalism	.96	—	—
Symmetry	.95	—	—
Expression	.82	—	—
Silliness	.65	.72	.63
Detail	.87	—	—
Spontaneity	.75	—	—
Movement	.83	—	—
Complexity	.89	—	—

gory grouping tasks were described to judges beforehand, and the judges were given loose time limits to help them pace themselves through the judgment tasks. The experimenter stayed with the judges throughout the session, checking that judgments were made in the proper order, and that the time limits were met.

Results. Interjudge reliabilities (Winer, 1971) of the 23 dimensions of judgment rated by the artist-judges are presented in Table 3-2.[3] It can be seen that, for the ratings, 16 of the 23 dimensions have reliabilities of .70 or greater, and 10 of the

---

[3] The technique of calculating interjudge reliabilities presented by Winer (1971) involves an analysis of between-design and within-design variance in ratings, and the result depends on the number of judges used. The Spearman-Brown calculation of reliabilities (Nunnally, 1967), which depends on the number of judges and the average interjudge correlation, yields results for these analyses that are virtually identical to those obtained by the analysis of variance technique. Since the Spearman-Brown calculations are considerably simpler, they were used in subsequent studies.

Table 3-3.   Correlations Between Dimensions of Judgment for Artist-Judges, Study 1

Dimension	Correlation with Creativity	Correlation with Technical Goodness
Dimensions correlated significantly with creativity		
Creativity	—	.13
Novel use of materials	.81[a]	.04
Novel idea	.90[a]	.19
Liking	.72[a]	.31
Variation in shapes	.62[b]	.06
Symmetry	−.59[b]	.27
Detail	.54[b]	.19
Spontaneity	.57[b]	−.34
Movement	.57[b]	−.20
Complexity	.76[a]	−.02
Dimensions correlated significantly with technical goodness		
Technical goodness	.13	—
Planning	−.04	.80[a]
Organization	−.13	.82[a]
Neatness	−.26	.72[a]
Balance	−.24	.64[b]
Pleasing placement of shapes	.32	.60[b]
Pleasing use of color	.25	.47[c]
Representationalism	−.18	.54[b]
Expression	−.05	.52[c]
Dimensions correlated significantly with both		
Aesthetic appeal	.43[c]	.59[b]
Display	.56[b]	.56[b]
Effort evident	.64[b]	.55[b]

Note. Correlations with no superscripts are not statistically significant.
[a]$p < .001$.
[b]$p < .01$.
[c]$p < .05$.

23 have reliabilities greater than .80. Interjudge agreement in the other two groups of judges was also fairly high. The reliability of the creativity rankings made by the 12 psychologist-judges was .73; that of the creativity ratings made by the 21 teacher-judges was .88. There was good agreement between the different groups of judges on their creativity assessments, although the level of expertise of the judges did appear to make some difference. The correlation between the psychologist-judges' mean creativity ranking for each design and the artist-judges' mean creativity ranking was .44, $p < .05$. The correlation between the art teachers and the artist-judges, however, was considerably higher: .65, $p < 01$.

Table 3-4. Factor Analysis on 23 Dimensions of Judgment for Artist-Judges, Varimax Rotation, Study 1[a]

| | Factor Loading | |
| | | |
Dimension	Factor 1: Creativity	Factor 2: Technical Goodness
Creativity cluster		
Creativity	.68	−.23
Novel use of materials	.78	−.21
Novel idea	.55	−.18
Effort evident	.85	.23
Variation in shapes	.72	−.04
Detail	.95	.09
Complexity	.91	−.30
Technical cluster		
Technical goodness	.16	.54
Organization	−.08	.67
Neatness	−.34	.51
Planning	.10	.83
Representationalism	.00	.95
Symmetry	−.34	.48
Expression of meaning	−.01	.92
Aesthetic judgments		
Liking	.22	−.04
Aesthetic appeal	−.04	.14
Would you display it?	.22	.28

[a]From Amabile, T. M. Social psychology of creativity: A consensual assessment technique. *Journal of Personality and Social Psychology,* 1982, *43,* 1004. Copyright 1982 by the American Psychological Association. Reprinted by permission of the publisher.

Several of the dimensions assessed by the artist-judges did indeed correlate with their judgments of creativity (see Table 3-3). In addition, it appears that this group of judgments was psychologically separate for the judges from their assessments of technical competence and aesthetic appeal. A factor analysis done on the mean ratings of all 23 dimensions of judgment for each design (varimax rotation) revealed two major factors that were largely orthogonal. These appear to be a creativity factor and a technical goodness factor. Many of the 23 dimensions clustered neatly about these two factors; loadings on the factors are presented in Table 3-4. It is important to note that liking for and aesthetic appeal of the collages loaded low on both of these main factors, as did the rated "silliness" of the designs.

A number of objective measures were made on the collages by two independent raters who agreed at nearly 100%. They measured the number of pieces used, number of colors used, number of shape categories used (circles, squares, cres-

Table 3-5.   Correlations Between Objective Features of the Designs and Artist-Judges'
Ratings of Creativity, Study 1

Objective Feature	Correlation with Rated Creativity
Number of colors used	.48[b]
Number of pieces used	.64[a]
Number of shape categories used	.52[b]
Number of pieces altered	.37[b]
Number of pieces overlapping	.62[a]

Note. "Number of shape categories" signifies the number of shape types the subject chose (e.g., circles, squares, crescents, etc.); "number of pieces altered" signifies the number of pieces that were altered in some way (ripped, folded, etc.); "number of pieces overlapping" signifies the number of pieces that partially or completely overlapped another piece.
[a] $p < .01$.
[b] $p < .05$.

cents, etc.), the number of pieces altered in some way (ripped, folded, etc.), and the number of pieces that overlapped other pieces, in addition to half a dozen other objective features of the collages. Many of these features did indeed correlate significantly with the artist-judges' ratings of creativity (see Table 3-5).

Finally, age of the child did not correlate significantly with any of the three groups of judges' assessments of creativity, although it did correlate with the artist-judges' rated technical goodness of the collages, $r = .46$, $p < .05$.

Study 2: Adults' Artistic Creativity

The subjects in this second test of the consensual assessment technique (Amabile, 1979) were 95 women enrolled in an introductory psychology course at Stanford University. Using materials similar to those used in Study 1, each subject worked individually on a collage for 15 minutes. Again, subjects were asked to convey a feeling of silliness with their designs.

Fifteen artists, nine males and six females, served as judges of the designs made by subjects in this study. Each judge had at least 5 years of experience doing studio art (painting, drawing, or design). Most were graduate students enrolled in the Stanford art department, and one was a professional artist living in Palo Alto. The judging procedure was identical to that used in Study 1. However, instead of the 23 dimensions that artist-judges in Study 1 had assessed, these judges were given only 16 dimensions. These dimensions were chosen by discarding those that had low interjudge reliabilities in Study 1 or had not clustered with the creativity or technical goodness judgments. The 16 dimensions of judgment were (1) expression of meaning, (2) degree of representationalism, (3) silliness, (4) detail, (5) degree of symmetry, (6) planning evident, (7) novelty of the idea, (8) balance, (9) novelty in use of materials, (10) variation of shapes, (11) effort evident, (12) complexity, (13) neatness, (14) overall organization, (15) creativity, and (16) technical goodness.

Table 3-6. Interjudge Reliabilities for Fifteen Artist Judges, Study 2

Dimension of Judgment	Reliability
Creativity	.79
Novel use of materials	.90
Novel idea	.82
Technical goodness	.76
Organization	.70
Neatness	.86
Effort evident	.84
Planning evident	.87
Balance	.48
Variation in shapes	.84
Representationalism	.95
Symmetry	.90
Expression	.86
Silliness	.89
Detail	.82
Complexity	.81

The interjudge reliability of the creativity judgments was .79. In general, the reliabilities of all the subjective judgments were quite high: 15 of the 16 dimension reliabilities were .70 or higher, 12 of the 16 were above .80, and the median reliability was .84 (see Table 3-6). Only one dimension of judgment, balance, fell far below an acceptable reliability level. As in Study 1, a factor analysis (varimax rotation) was performed on the dimensions of judgment. With three exceptions, the 16 dimensions clustered almost exactly as they had in the analysis of Study 1. There were two nearly orthogonal factors: one composed of creativity, novel material use, novel idea, effort evident, variation of shapes, detail, and complexity, and one composed of neatness, organization, planning evident, balance, and expression of meaning. The asymmetry dimension (the negative of the symmetry judgments) loaded sufficiently low on the creativity factor (.28) that it did not cluster with the others. In addition, representationalism loaded nearly zero on both factors, and the single dimension of "technical goodness" not only loaded high on the technical factor, it also loaded fairly high on the creativity factor. Study 2 is described in more detail in Chapter 5.

Because Studies 1 and 2 were the preliminary investigations of the consensual assessment technique, they included many more dimensions of judgment than did later studies. My description of these later studies will be somewhat less detailed.

Studies 3–6: Further Investigations of Children's Art

In Study 3 (Berglas, Amabile, & Handel, 1981), 55 boys and 56 girls made collages using materials similar to those provided in the two earlier studies. The children were drawn from grades 2–6 at a parochial school in eastern Massachusetts. Each child worked individually on the collage for 15 minutes. The judges were six undergraduate artists at Brandeis University, all majoring in studio art; each had at least 4 years of studio art experience. Working under the standard judging procedure, these artists rated each collage on creativity and technical goodness. The interjudge reliabilities were .77 for creativity and .72 for technical goodness. Judgments of creativity correlated .26 with judgments of technical goodness. Again, the correlation between subject age and rated creativity of the collage was nonsignificant, $r = .12$, while the correlation between subject age and rated technical goodness *was* significant, $r = .28$, $p < .01$. There were no significant differences between boys and girls in rated creativity. This study is described in more detail in Chapter 5.

In Study 4 (Stubbs & Amabile, 1979), subjects were 47 girls and boys enrolled in grades 1 and 2 at a nontraditional "open" school in eastern Massachusetts. Using the standard materials, each child worked individually on making a collage for 15 minutes. In addition, the children completed a version of Guilford's Unusual Uses test (along with other measures to be described in more detail in Chapter 7). The judges were seven artists and seven nonartists. Each of the seven artists was a studio art major at Brandeis University, with at least 4 years of experience in studio art.[4] The nonartists were graduate students in psychology, undergraduates, and elementary school teachers (teaching in schools other than the one where the study had been conducted). Following the standard procedures, each judge rated each collage on creativity and on technical goodness.

The interjudge reliability for creativity judgments was .81 for the artists, .83 for the nonartists, and .89 when all 14 judges were considered together. The reliability for technical goodness judgments was .72 for the artists, .80 for the nonartists, and .83 for all 14 judges. For creativity judgments, the correlation between artists and nonartists was .69, $p < .001$. Over all judges, the correlation between creativity and technical goodness judgments was .77. Interestingly, rated creativity of the collages in this study correlated significantly with scores on the Unusual Uses test ($r = .48$), a finding that supports results of other research comparing creativity test scores with subjective assessments of products (e.g., Rimm & Davis, 1980). Study 4 is described in more detail in Chapter 8.

Study 5 (Stubbs, 1981) included 79 boys and girls, ages 5–8, from grades K–2 at three elementary schools in the Boston area. Each child made a collage according to the standard procedure. Subsequently, seven student-artists, each with at least 3 years of studio art experience, rated the collages on creativity and technical goodness. Both reliabilities were comparable to those obtained in the other studies: .78 for creativity, and .76 for technical goodness. The correlation between the two dimensions of judgment was .28.

---

[4] Some of these judges also served in Study 3.

In Study 6 (Amabile & Gitomer, 1984), 14 boys and 14 girls from a day-care center (ages 2–6) made collages individually according to the standard procedure. The collages were judged on creativity, technical goodness, and liking by eight student-artists, each of whom had at least 3 years of studio art experience. The reliabilities were .79 for creativity, .92 for technical goodness, and .76 for liking. Creativity judgments correlated .71 with technical goodness judgments, and .72 with liking judgments. There were no significant differences between boys and girls on any dimensions of judgment. Study 6 is described in more detail in Chapter 6.

Studies 7–13: Further Investigations of Adults' Art

Subjects in Study 7 were 10 male and 10 female undergraduates enrolled in an introductory psychology course at Stanford University. They were given 20 minutes to work alone, making a collage that "conveyed a feeling of silliness," using materials similar to those used in the studies with children. Half of the males and half of the females were asked, in addition, to "be as creative as possible."

Each design was rated on creativity by seven male and seven female nonartist judges, using the standard procedure. These judges were graduate students in psychology and undergraduates in a variety of fields at Stanford University. Each judge worked independently, rating the collages only on creativity. The interjudge reliability for these ratings was .93. Instructions to "be creative" had no impact on the creativity of the collages, but there was a nearly significant sex difference. Females made collages that were rated higher in creativity than those made by males ($p < .052$). There were no significant differences between the ratings assigned by female judges and those assigned by male judges. Because of the superiority of females over males in their collage creativity (a finding that was also obtained by Roweton, 1975), most of the subsequent studies with adults in this program of research used only female subjects.

Forty undergraduate women at Brandeis University participated in Study 8 (Amabile, Goldfarb, & Brackfield, 1990, Study 2). Using the standard technique, each subject was given 15 minutes to make a collage that "conveyed a feeling of silliness." The 10 judges, who were undergraduate students working on their honors projects in studio art, each rated the collages on creativity and technical goodness. The reliabilities were .93 and .91, respectively, and the correlation between the two dimensions was .70. This study is described in more detail in Chapters 5 and 7.

In Study 9 (Brackfield, 1980), 50 undergraduate women made collages that were subsequently judged by 10 undergraduate artists on creativity. The reliability of these ratings was .92.

Sixty undergraduate women made collages in Study 10 (Amabile, Goldberg, & Capotosto, 1982, Study 1), and fourteen undergraduate artists rated the collages on creativity with a reliability of .75. This study is considered in more detail in Chapter 6.

Table 3-7.   Summary of Major Findings on Artistic Creativity Judgments

Study No.	Subjects	Judges	Reliability
1	22 girls	12 psychologists	73
		21 art teachers	.88
		7 artists	.77
2	95 women	15 artists	.79
3	111 boys and girls	6 artists	.77
4	47 boys and girls	7 artists	.72
		7 nonartists	.80
5	79 boys and girls	7 artists	.78
6	28 boys and girls	8 artists	.79
7	20 women and men	14 nonartists	.93
8	40 women	10 artists	.93
9	50 women	10 artists	.92
10	60 women	14 artists	.75
11	120 women	12 artists	.80
12	52 men	15 artists	.79
13	48 women and men	10 artists	.77

In Study 11 (Amabile, Goldberg, & Capotosto, 1982, Study 2), 120 undergraduate women made collages that were subsequently judged on creativity by 12 undergraduate artists. The reliability of these judgments was .80.

Subjects in Study 12 (Berman, 1981) were 52 males at the Veteran's Association Hospital in Brockton, Massachusetts. Forty-two were patients with psychiatric disorders and ten were ward attendants. These subjects made collages according to the standard procedure. Fifteen college art students and high school art teachers served as judges of the creativity of the collages. The interjudge reliability was .79.

In Study 13 (conducted in collaboration with Barry Auskern), 24 male and 24 female undergraduates made collages that were subsequently judged on creativity by 10 student artists. The reliability of these ratings was .77. In contrast to the results of Study 7, the sex difference in this study was not significant.

The 13 studies on the consensual assessment of artistic creativity are summarized in Table 3-7.

The Consensual Assessment of Verbal Creativity

The results of studies using the consensual assessment technique for artistic creativity are encouraging, but it is important to demonstrate that this methodology is applicable to other domains as well. In the studies reported below, a technique for the consensual assessment of verbal creativity was developed and tested. Although most of these studies used the same creativity task (the writing of a brief poem), three experimented with other verbal activities. Like the studies of artistic creativity, many of these are discussed at greater length in subsequent chapters because they tested particular hypotheses about creativity.

Study 14: An Initial Investigation Using Poetry

Subjects and judges. Forty-eight female students enrolled in an introductory psychology course at Brandeis University served as subjects in this study (Amabile, Goldfarb, & Brackfield, 1990, Study 1). Two groups of expert judges assessed the finished products—Haiku poems. Group 1 was composed of 10 graduate students and senior honors students recruited from the English department of Brandeis University. All had at least 3 years' experience studying poetry at an advanced level and writing poetry themselves. Several were published poets. Group 2 was composed of 10 poets who lived in Cambridge, Massachusetts. Most were graduate students in the English department of Harvard University, but some were not associated with any university. All of these judges had published in academic or nonacademic literary magazines.

Procedure. Each subject was given 20 minutes to work individually on writing an "American Haiku" poem.[5] The American Haiku is a simplified form of unrhymed poetry consisting of five lines: line 1 is a single noun; line 2 consists of two adjectives describing the noun; line 3 consists of three verb forms relating to the noun; line 4 contains any number of words (a phrase or sentence about the noun); line 5 repeats the noun of line 1. After the initial instructions, subjects were presented with two examples of American Haiku poems. All subjects were provided with the first line of the poem they were to write—the word "Joy"—in an effort to reduce variability and to make the judging task somewhat easier.

The judges in Group 1 participated together in a single session. Of course, since the judging task involved reading, each judge could work independently. Indeed, the judges were not allowed to discuss the poems or the judging task until the session was completed. The judges first read the instructions that subjects had received, and were then told that the female undergraduate subjects had had 20 minutes in which to write their poems. Each judge was allowed to read through a copy of all 48 poems prior to making any judgments. The judges rated each poem on creativity, using their "own subjective definition of creativity." They were instructed to rate the poems relative to one another, rather than rating them against some absolute standard for poetry. Rating scales similar to those used in the collage judging were employed here—continuous scales with five equally spaced reference points marked, three of which were labeled: high, medium, and low. The judges were told to make each judgment by placing an X anywhere on the scale. They were asked to view the scale as having equal spacing between the five reference points and they were encouraged to make use of the

---

[5] The term "Haiku" is used here in a generally descriptive sense. The only clear similarities between "American Haiku" and traditional Japanese Haiku are the brevity of the poems and the clearly defined structure. In a strict sense, the poems written in these studies are best considered "cinquains." (See Amabile, 1982c.)

Table 3-8.   Dimensions of Judgment for Poet-Judges in Group 2, Study 14

Dimension	Descriptive Definition Given Judges
Creativity	The degree to which the poem is creative, using your own subjective definition of creativity.
Liking	How well you like the poem, using your own subjective criteria for liking.
Consistency of theme	The degree to which a consistent theme is expressed throughout the poem.
Novelty of word choice	The degree to which the word choice is novel.
Appropriateness of word choice	The degree to which the word choice is appropriate to the theme.
Richness of imagery	The degree to which vivid imagery is used.
Originality of idea	The degree to which the thematic idea is original.
Pleasing flow of words	The degree to which the flow of words in the poem is pleasant.
Sophistication of expression	The degree to which the expression in the poem is sophisticated.
Use of the poetic form	The degree to which the use of the "American Haiku" form is correct, according to the directions given.
Emotionality	The amount and depth of emotion the poem conveys.
Grammar	The degree to which the poem is grammatically correct.
Rhythm	The degree to which rhythm is used effectively in the poem.
Clarity	The degree to which the poem is expressed clearly.

entire range of the scale. The poems were judged in a different random order by each judge.

The judges in Group 2 also participated in a group session. The procedure was identical to that followed for judges in Group 1, except that these judges rated each of 24 poems on 14 different dimensions.[6] Table 3-8 lists these dimensions, as well as the nonrestrictive "definitions" that judges were provided for each. The

---

[6] Half of the original 48 poems were randomly chosen for assessment by Group 2. This was done because the task of rereading each poem for rating on each of the 14 dimensions was quite time-consuming. It was decided that this procedure, however, would be preferable to one in which each poem was rated on all 14 dimensions before the next poem was rated on any; the procedure of rating all poems at once on a given dimension was adopted to increase the likelihood that judges would apply their subjective criteria for each dimension more consistently.

Table 3-9.   Interjudge Reliabilities for Ten Judges in Group 2, Study 14

Dimension of Judgment	Reliability
Creativity	.90
Liking	.80
Consistency of theme	.87
Novelty of word choice	.89
Appropriateness of word choice	.78
Richness of imagery	.92
Originality of idea	.90
Pleasing flow of words	.83
Sophistication of expression	.91
Use of form	.82
Emotionality	.74
Grammar	.63
Rhythm	.71
Clarity	.75

judges were asked to keep the different dimensions of judgment as separate from one another as possible. The dimensions were judged in a different random order by each judge (e.g., all poems judged on creativity, then all judged on richness of imagery, and so on). The judges were given loose time limits to help them pace themselves through the judgment tasks.

Results. The interjudge reliabilities of virtually all subjective judgments were quite high. The reliability of creativity judgments for Group 1 was .87 and, for Group 2, .90. As can be seen in Table 3-9, 13 of the 14 reliabilities were above .70, and 9 were at or above .80. A factor analysis (varimax rotation) of the 14 dimensions did not produce as clear a separation between factors as was obtained with judgments on the collages. All of the dimensions loaded positively on the two main factors, and some loaded rather high on both. However, it is possible to identify meaningful clusters of dimensions. There was a "creativity" factor, consisting of creativity, novelty of word choice, originality of idea, sophistication of expression, and rhythm; a "style" factor, consisting of clarity, appropriateness of word choice, and consistency of theme; and a "technical" factor, consisting of grammar and use of the poetic form. The loadings of these dimensions on each of the three factors are presented in Table 3-10. Study 14 is described in more detail in Chapters 5 and 7.

Studies 15–18: Additional Tests of the Poetry Method

Subjects in Study 15 (done in collaboration with Lisa Berman and Ronit Goldlust) were 40 undergraduate females recruited from the introductory psychology class at Brandeis University. They wrote American Haiku poems under the same procedure used for Study 14. The judges were six poets living in the Cambridge,

Table 3-10. Factor Analysis on 14 Dimensions of Judgment for Group 2, Varimax Rotation, Study 14[a]

	Factor Loading		
Dimension	Factor 1: Creativity	Factor 2: Style	Factor 3: Technical
Creativity cluster			
Creativity	.91	.30	.21
Novelty of word choice	.91	.25	.24
Originality of idea	.88	.36	.06
Sophistication	.90	.31	.13
Rhythm	.78	.36	.10
Style cluster			
Clarity	.23	.89	.27
Appropriateness	.47	.82	.20
Consistency	.44	.81	.16
Technical cluster			
Grammar	.19	.17	.90
Use of form	.14	.22	.91

[a]From Amabile, T. M. Social psychology of creativity: A consensual assessment technique. *Journal of Personality and Social Psychology,* 1982, *43,* 1008. Copyright 1982 by the American Psychological Association. Reprinted by permission of the publisher.

Massachusetts area.[7] These judges worked individually on the assessment tasks in their homes. They were sent written instructions and copies of the 40 poems, and were asked to follow the same judging procedures they had followed in the group session for Study 14. Each judge rated each of the 40 poems on creativity, clarity of expression, and use of poetic form.

Although somewhat lower than the interjudge reliabilities obtained in Study 14, two of the three reliabilities here did meet acceptable levels. The reliability of creativity judgments was .77; poetic form judgments, .91; and clarity judgments, .62. Creativity judgments correlated -.16 with poetic form judgments, and .38 with clarity judgments; both correlations are nonsignificant.

Study 16 (Amabile & Zingmond, 1982) included 30 male and 29 female undergraduates who wrote Haiku poems according to the standard instructions. The reliability of creativity judgments for 12 poet-judges was .82. There were no significant sex differences.

In Study 17 (done in collaboration with Barry Auskern; see Study 13 above), 24 male and 24 female undergraduates wrote Haiku poems that were rated on creativity by eight poet-judges. The reliability of these ratings was .77. Again, there were no significant sex differences.

Subjects in Study 18 (Amabile, 1985) were 72 creative writers at Boston University who each wrote two Haiku poems according to the standard instruc-

---

[7] All of these judges had served in Study 14.

tions. The reliability for 12 poet-judges' creativity ratings on the first group of poems was .82, and their reliability for the second group of poems was .78. This study is described in greater detail in Chapter 7.

Studies 19–21: Other Measures of Verbal Creativity

These three studies tested different tasks for assessing verbal creativity within the consensual assessment technique. In both, subjects made verbal responses that were then rated by judges according to the standard procedure. In Study 19 (Stubbs & Amabile, 1979), subjects were 47 girls and boys enrolled in grades 1 and 2 at a nontraditional "open" school in eastern Massachusetts (the same subjects described under Study 4 above). Each child was shown a standard set of six pictures (always in the same sequence) depicting a child playing with a dog. The children were asked to tell a short story to the pictures, saying one thing about each. These stories were tape-recorded, transcribed, and presented in their transcribed version to two former elementary school teachers for rating on the standard creativity scales used in other studies.[8] A simple correlation coefficient between the ratings made by the two judges revealed an extremely high level of agreement: $r = .87$. These children also completed Guilford's Unusual Uses test and, like the collage creativity (see Study 4), the storytelling creativity correlated significantly with scores on this test ($r = .40$). Study 19 is described more fully in Chapter 8.

Study 20 (Hennessey, 1982) also investigated storytelling creativity in children. One hundred fifteen boys and girls in grades 1–5 at a parochial school were asked to first look through a book without words and then tell a story by saying one thing about each page. The book (Mayer, 1967) tells a story through 30 pages of pictures. Although the basic story line is clear, the pictures are sufficiently ambiguous that there is a great deal of room for flexibility in the children's storytelling. These stories were tape-recorded, transcribed, and presented to three elementary school teachers for ratings on creativity. As in Study 19, the level of agreement between these independent creativity judgments was quite good; interjudge reliability was .91.

In Study 21 (done in collaboration with Ellen Langer), subjects were 48 male and female adults recruited from a variety of settings. Individually, they were each shown the same set of five cartoons and asked to write "amusing" captions for them.[9] Since it was assumed that any well-read individual would qualify as an appropriate judge for cartoon captions, the captions (with the cartoons) were shown to 10 faculty members and graduate students at Brandeis University. These judges used the standard procedure to rate the captions on creativity and humor. The re-

---

[8] Only two judges were used in this exploratory study because of the time involved in reading all of the stories, and because it was expected that a relatively high level of agreement would be obtained. These two judges were acquaintances, but had not trained together and had never taught together. Neither had worked in the school from which subjects were drawn.

[9] These cartoons were chosen from *The New Yorker* and other magazines. They were selected to be ambiguous enough that a variety of humorous responses were possible. The original captions were removed before the cartoons were presented to subjects.

Table 3-11.   Summary of Major Findings on Verbal Creativity Judgments

Study No.	Task	Subjects	Judges	Reliability
14	Haiku poems	48 women	10 poets	87
		24 women	10 poets	90
15	Haiku poems	40 women	6 poets	.77
16	Haiku poems	59 women and men	12 poets	.82
17	Haiku poems	48 women and men	8 poets	77
18	Haiku poems	72 women and men (creative writers)	12 poets	82 (Poem 1) .78 (Poem 2)
19	Storytelling	47 boys and girls	2 teachers	.87 (simple r)
20	Storytelling	115 boys and girls	3 teachers	.91
21	Cartoon captions	48 women and men	10 people	.85

liability of the creativity ratings was .85, and that of the humor ratings was .82. The two dimensions of judgment were correlated at .69.

The studies of verbal creativity are summarized in Table 3-11.

A Summary of Major Findings

These studies were designed, in part, to develop and test a reliable subjective method for assessing creativity in different domains. They were successful on a number of counts, revealing several strengths of the methodology. Of primary importance, these studies have shown that it is possible to obtain high levels of agreement in subjective judgments of creativity, even when the judges are working independently and have not been trained to agree in any way. The reliability of the storytelling creativity ratings in two preliminary studies of that method—.87 with only two judges, and .91 with three—is particularly encouraging. Thus, according to the consensual definition of creativity presented earlier, the subjective ratings can be considered a valid measure of creativity for these collages, poems, stories, and cartoon captions. The validity of these measures will be strengthened in Part Two of the book, where I present several studies using the consensual assessment technique to test hypotheses about the social psychology of creativity. In those studies, this technique provided measures of a construct that behaved as creativity was predicted to behave on the basis of particular theoretical derivations.

The level of interjudge agreement on creativity ratings may depend to some degree upon the magnitude of effort required of judges. In Study 2, where each artist-judge spent approximately 4 hours rating 95 collages on each of 16 different dimensions, the mean interjudge correlation was only .21. By contrast, in Study 8, where each artist-judge spent only about one-half hour rating 40 collages on two dimensions, the mean interjudge correlation was .57. Thus, when the judging task is particularly demanding, judge fatigue and difficulty in maintaining consistent criteria throughout the judging task should be anticipated. Under such circumstances, it is wise to increase the number of judges used.

Interestingly, the level of expertise of the judges appears not to matter as much as might have been expected for these tasks. In the studies on artistic creativity, there is no clear superiority of artists over nonartists in average interjudge correlations. Moreover, it does not appear that nonartists and artists were subjectively defining creativity in very different ways. In those studies where both types of judges were used (Studies 1 and 4), the degree of agreement between artists and nonartists is quite high (.44 and .65, respectively, for the two groups of nonartists in Study 1, .69 in Study 4). Similarly, the level of agreement between poets and nonpoets in the ratings for Study 14 was quite high—.80. And good reliabilities were obtained from "ordinary" individuals in their ratings of the creativity of cartoon captions.

These data, of course, raise the question of who is to be considered an "expert" for the purposes of the present methodology and, thus, who is to be considered an "appropriate" judge. It appears that the only requirement is a familiarity with the domain of endeavor in which the product was made. Thus, the high level of agreement in Study 14 might have arisen because the Haiku form is so simple, and because most educated individuals in our culture are familiar with it. Similarly, it is likely that all the groups of judges in the collage studies shared some requisite minimal familiarity with collages, and that the people judging the cartoon captions shared some requisite minimal familiarity with magazine cartoons.

It seems, then, that for some domains any individuals with a moderate level of exposure to the domain are appropriate. On the other hand, there are types of products which probably require judges who have received special training in the field, because the domains are so complex or are not generally familiar (such as medical research or atonal music). Without special selection of experts, the judges' familiarity with the domain would be in doubt, and their level of agreement would almost certainly suffer. Thus, in applying the consensual assessment technique, it is most prudent to select judges who do have a special familiarity with the domain.

The studies of artistic creativity also demonstrated that subjective judgments of the creativity of art works can be separated from judgments of their aesthetic appeal and technical goodness. In Study 1, aesthetic judgments loaded very low on both the creativity and the technical goodness factors in the factor analysis. And in both Study 1 and Study 2 (where enough dimensions were judged to warrant a factor analysis), there was a clear separation between the technical goodness and creativity factors. It is important to note, however, that the single dimension labeled "technical goodness" does not seem to capture the technical component of subjective judgments consistently. Although the correlation between the single creativity and technical goodness dimensions was only .13, .26, and .28 in Studies 1, 3, and 5, respectively, it was .68, .77, .71, and .70 in Studies 2, 4, 6, and 8, respectively. Since the factor analysis did consistently yield a good separation between the creativity and technical goodness *factors,* it may be that a scale labeled something other than "technical goodness" would better capture that distinct set of features that includes neatness, organization, planning, and so on, and that ratings on such a scale would be more consistently distinct from ratings on the creativity scale.

There was a separation between the creativity factor and the others in a factor analysis of Haiku poem ratings in Study 14, although this separation was not quite as clear as that between the artistic judgments in Studies 1 and 2. As noted earlier, although ratings of liking for the poems did not cluster closely with the creativity dimensions on that factor analysis, the single liking dimension was highly correlated with the single creativity dimension. Thus, it appears that although it may be possible for some types of products to obtain creativity judgments that are clearly uncontaminated by assessments of liking, for other types of products, creativity judgments may be more tightly bound up with assessments of aesthetic appeal. The same may obtain for ratings of creativity and ratings of humor in humorous materials.

A preliminary attempt was made in Studies 1 and 2 to investigate the nature of judges' reactions when they labeled something as "creative," to determine if they were aware of feeling, for example, that creative work was both novel and appropriate. An open-ended question at the end of each judging task asked each artist to describe how he or she had arrived at the creativity ratings by listing the crucial features of the collages and by describing their subjective reactions. Although responses for many of the dimensions (e.g., neatness, organization, and even aesthetic appeal) were straightforward and easily classified, responses for the creativity dimensions were unclear and difficult to interpret. There was a great deal of variability in these answers, and most of them were heavily spiced with jargon. These answers suggest that, as proposed earlier, creativity may be something that is difficult for people to describe, but is still relatively easy for them to identify with a good degree of reliability.

Because of the difficulty in obtaining clear phenomenological descriptions of judges' creativity ratings, it is especially important that the creativity ratings were found to correlate with a number of other dimensions of subjective judgment (novelty of idea, complexity, and so on). With these data, we can begin to describe judges' responses to these particular products. In addition, it is important that creativity ratings in Study 1 correlated significantly with some objectively measureable features of the collages. The analysis of objective features might ultimately be useful, for at least some products, in identifying objective features that consistently correlate with the subjective judgments of creativity. If it is possible to do so with a high degree of consistency across products made by different groups of subjects and across ratings made by different groups of judges, then these features might be used as indicators of the way in which judges decide to apply the label "creative" to such products.

These studies demonstrated that the consensual assessment technique can be adapted for very different kinds of tasks. The collage-making is completely nonverbal, involving the manipulation of paper and glue. By contrast, the task of writing an American Haiku poem requires the composition of five original lines.

The storytelling and caption-writing tasks also represent diverse domains. It seems probable, therefore, that this methodology could be successfully employed for a variety of tasks in a wide range of domains.

It is of particular significance for a social psychology of creativity that it is possible, as demonstrated in these studies, to find a creativity assessment task that does not depend heavily on the special skills that some individuals may have developed more highly than others. Certainly, some individual-difference variability is tapped by these tasks. Although most studies including both males and females showed no sex difference on creativity, one study (#7) did; and, in Study 4, collage and storytelling creativity correlated significantly with a traditional measure of "trait" creativity—the Unusual Uses test. Nonetheless, the consistent lack of significant correlation between children's ages and their collage creativity or storytelling creativity provides powerful evidence that performance on these tasks does not depend heavily on special skills. Furthermore, the artistic and verbal creativity tasks were quite manageable and enjoyable for virtually all children and adults who did them. Thus, the types of tasks used in these studies promise to be generally useful in experimental studies of social and environmental influences on creativity.

Comparison with Previous Techniques

The consensual assessment technique can be seen as the conceptual reverse of the technique used in traditional "objective" creativity tests. In those tests, component tasks and subtasks are scored to yield a global assessment of an individual's creativity, an assessment that is ultimately based on the subjective judgment of the psychometricians who devised the subtasks or the raters who score them. Instead, the present technique begins with a global, explicitly subjective assessment of creativity. This global judgment is then clearly demonstrated to be a reliable one. Once this is done, the judgment of creativity can be broken down into component parts; that is, it can be examined to determine which other subjective judgments and, perhaps, which objective features of the product predict this judgment of creativity. As the studies presented here demonstrate, some progress toward this goal has already been made.

Moreover, this subjective assessment technique appears to have more ecological validity as a measure of creativity than many of the creativity tests. Using materials that allow for considerable flexibility in response, subjects actually create something—a collage, a poem, a story—that real-world creators might make. Then, using an approach that has clear precedents in social-psychological research (e.g., Thurstone & Chave, 1929; Walster et al., 1966), reliable subjective judgments of the products are obtained from appropriate observers. Thus, not only does the task itself mimic real-world performance, but the assessment technique mimic real-world evaluations of creative work.

A few previous studies have used subjective assessment methods that are similar to the consensual assessment technique (e.g., Domino, 1974; Helson & Crutchfield, 1970; Kruglanski, Friedman, & Zeevi, 1971; MacKinnon, 1962; Sobel & Rothenberg,

1980). Indeed, some of these studies have obtained results similar to mine. For example, Ryan and Winston (1978) found that adult raters' judgments of the creativity of children's drawings were correlated with the "form diversity" of the drawings; this finding recalls that of Study 1, where creativity ratings correlated with ratings of the variability in shapes used. In another study (Trowbridge & Charles, 1966), subjective ratings of the creativity of children's paintings were separable from ratings of technical competence. Moreover, for children in the age range represented in my studies, that study found no substantial correlation between age and rated creativity, although there was a correlation between age and rated technical competence. These results exactly match those obtained in Study 1.

Of all previous techniques, that which comes the closest to the present methodology was employed by Getzels and Csikszentmihalyi (1976) in an intriguing study they conducted on the work of aspiring artists. These researchers come very close to my own statements on creativity measurement when they assert that "aesthetic judgments are based on vague and subjective criteria, yet they are consistent and predictable" (p. 120). Getzels and Csikszentmihalyi obtained drawings from 31 graduate students in art and had judges use scales to independently rate these drawings on each of three dimensions: "originality," "craftsmanship," and "overall aesthetic value." Their method is also similar to the present method in that judges were asked to use their own subjective criteria for each of these dimensions. And they obtained rather good interjudge correlations on originality ratings with small groups of judges: .31 by five artists, .47 by five art teachers, .45 by mathematics students, and .35 by business students. Finally, they obtained reasonably good consistencies between the ratings of experts and nonexperts. Originality judgments of the artists correlated .77 with those of the art teachers, .56 with those of the mathematics students, and .64 with those of the business students.

Nonetheless, there are some clear differences. First, the task chosen by Getzels and Csikszentmihalyi obviously depends heavily on domain-relevant skills, so it would probably be unsuitable as a general technique for studying social psychological influences on creativity. (Getzels and Csikszentmihalyi were not focusing on social psychological influences but on problem definition in art.) Second, these researchers did not tie their assessment method to a definition of creativity, and did not address themselves to the validity of their measurements. Indeed, they asserted that, "what is at issue here is the *consistency* of aesthetic preferences, not their validity" (p. 110). My own view, of course, is that consistent judgments of creativity by appropriate observers *must* be taken as valid. Third, to "systematize" evaluations, Getzels and Csikszentmihalyi forced the judges' evaluations of the 31 drawings to conform to a "pre-normalized" 9-point scale, such that one drawing was to be rated 1 on the scale, one was to be rated 9, two were to be rated 2 and 8 each, four were rated 3 and 7 each, five were rated 4 and 6, and seven were given the "average" rating of 5. This procedure was followed for each of the three dimensions judged. It may be that the ratings obtained under this system were different from those that judges would have made if their use of the scales was not constrained. Finally, there was no clear separation between the dimensions of judgment; "originality" was highly correlated with both "craftsmanship" and "overall aesthetic value." Thus, there is no evidence that creativity was really being assessed as a separate construct.

In comparison with previous subjective assessment techniques, the methodology I have presented can be more generally useful for social psychological studies for a number of reasons. First, it calls for tasks that are structured so as to be relatively independent of skills such as writing or drawing ability. Second, in contrast to many subjective-assessment studies in which judges make global ratings of a *person's* creativity, with this technique judges make ratings of specific *products*. In addition, the reliability of creativity judgments across several groups of appropriate observers has been firmly established in the present method, in the absence of any attempt to train judges to agree (an approach used in many previous studies). Finally, the existence of a unique subjective construct called "creativity" has been demonstrated. Although my studies did not always obtain a clear separation between creativity and other dimensions, some of the studies do provide convincing evidence that it is at least possible to consider creativity a separate subjective construct.

Limitations and Future Possibilities

Despite its advantages, the consensual assessment technique cannot be considered a universally useful methodology. Indeed, it has some distinct limitations. First, if practical considerations are primary, this method is decidedly impractical in the short run. The choosing of an appropriate task and an appropriate judge population, the judging of the products by several individuals (sometimes on several dimensions), and the statistical analyses are all extremely time-consuming.

In addition, to the extent that the task chosen is one that does not depend heavily on particular abilities and experience-related skills, the approach is probably not a useful one for identifying enduring individual differences in creativity. However, since tasks can be chosen with this end in mind (i.e., the inclusion of an appropriate range of skills to be tapped), with modification this method might prove to be a reasonable one even for such individual-difference studies.

Also, it may be difficult to apply this assessment technique to products that are at the frontiers of a particular domain of endeavor. Consider, for example, revolutionary theories in science or revolutionary works of art. It would be difficult to apply this method to assess the creativity of these products because it is precisely their revolutionary nature that makes it difficult for people, even supposed experts in their fields, to agree on the level of creativity evident. In fact, this problem could be considered within the context of the "familiarity" criterion I proposed earlier. These products are so different that no one is sufficiently familiar with the domain to serve as an "appropriate" judge—perhaps because the products create their own new domain.

Finally, a related caveat is that the reliability—and hence the validity—of the judgments obtained by this method are necessarily limited by historical time and place. It is doubtful, for example, that a group of Italian Renaissance painters would agree well with a group of contemporary American artists in their creativity judgments of a set of Impressionist art works. Clearly, the shared subjective criteria of creativity in any domain of endeavor do change over time and do differ across cultures. This fact, however, should not be considered a limitation of the consensual assessment technique. Many previous theorists have suggested that the judgment of creativity is always historically and culturally bound.[10] It seems unreasonable to expect that universal and enduring criteria—even subjective criteria—could ever be agreed upon.

Although my preliminary studies lay the groundwork for the consensual assessment methodology, further refinement and extension of the technique are required in a number of areas. First, attempts should be made to extend the subjective assessment methodology to other domains of endeavor and other types of tasks within the artistic and verbal domains already explored. In particular, storytelling and the writing of cartoon captions should be explored in more detail, with judges rating the products on a number of dimensions that may be factor-analyzed, as were the dimensions for collage and poetry judgments.

Second, a finer identification of objective and subjective correlates of creativity judgments may be possible. As I noted earlier, a comprehensive description of these correlates could point the way to a clearer understanding of what people mean when they call something "creative." Such an understanding might also be obtained through a more extensive probing of judges' explanations for their ratings on creativity.

Third, the limits of interjudge reliability should be explored, especially where the products being judged are in relatively new domains or represent truly pioneering work.

Fourth, since the results presented earlier suggested that certain characteristics of the judging task—such as the number of products or dimensions to be judged—can influence interjudge agreement, it is important to determine what other features of the judging task might also influence reliability.

Fifth, more work is needed on the identification of "appropriate" judges for particular types of products, and on the influence of judge characteristics on interjudge reliability.

Sixth, the preliminary studies showed a reasonable but not a perfect separation between creativity and other dimensions of subjective judgment. Thus, it is important to determine under what circumstances and for what types of products and domains of endeavor creativity judgments will and will not be clearly separable from assessments of technical and aesthetic qualities.

---

[10] For example, Stein (1975, p. 253) defines creativity as "a process that results in a novel product or idea which is accepted as useful, tenable, or satisfying by a significant group of others *at some point in time*" (emphasis added).

Finally, attempts should be made to determine whether alterations could be made in this subjective assessment technique to render it useful not only for the social psychology of creativity, but for the identification of individual differences in creativity as well.

A Wider Context

My arguments on the utility of the consensual assessment technique for a social psychology of creativity raise a more general point about the aims and the methods of personality and social psychology. Most simply stated, it is the purpose of personality psychology to identify stable characteristics and abilities and to study the ways in which they are related to other characteristics and abilities. Thus, personality researchers generally look for consistency of behavior over time and across situations, and they look for evidence of a given trait in a variety of behavioral domains. For these purposes, measures that are particularly sensitive to stable baseline individual differences are most useful. On the other hand, most simply stated, it is the purpose of social psychology to investigate the impact of social and environmental factors on most people, or on the "average" person. Thus, social psychologists are less interested in within-group variability (and in fact usually seek to reduce it in their studies) than they are in situationally induced between-group differences in behavior. Such differences, although they may be large and important ones, are usually less enduring than the individual differences that personality researchers seek to identify. For their purposes, then, social psychologists require measures that are not particularly sensitive to baseline individual differences, but do allow room for variability in response. This difference between appropriate methods applies not only to creativity assessment, but also to measurement in a wide range of other behavioral domains that are of interest to both social and personality psychology.

In summary, then, rather than proposing a new and easily applicable creativity test, the consensual assessment technique instead presents a general methodology that can produce clear and reliable subjective judgments of creativity. This approach, unwieldy as it may seem in the short run, does promise to be applicable to a broad range of domains and tasks within domains. As such, it can be useful for studies in a wide range of areas—in particular, for the social psychology of creativity. In the long run, then, more than any single creativity test, this approach may contribute to the rigorous empirical investigation of many creativity questions that have previously remained unexamined.

Update

We have continued to use the consensual assessment technique (CAT) for creativity assessment described in the 1983 edition, and we have continued to find it a valuable methodology. The primary value is the same as that cited in the earlier edition: It relies on real products that the subjects have made, in domains that frequently appear in the real world.

In this update, we will present our current thinking about and current uses of the technique, which include several modifications to the original. In addition, we present data from new creativity tasks we have devised.

Reliability Calculation

The 1983 edition presents two methods that we originally used for calculating the interjudge reliability of subjective creativity assessments. The first is a technique recommended by Winer (1971) that involves an analysis of between- and within-variance in judge ratings. The second utilizes the Spearman-Brown prediction formula (Nunnally, 1967, p. 223), which is based on the number of judges (n) and the mean interjudge correlation (r):

$$\text{reliability} = \frac{n\,r}{1 + (n - 1)\,r}$$

These two techniques yield highly similar results, as does the Cronbach's coefficient alpha as calculated by the "reliability" procedure in SPSS (Statistical Package for the Social Sciences). Because it is extremely simple and straightforward to use, in recent years we have relied upon the SPSS-calculated alpha as our measure of interjudge reliability.

Very recently, we have once again revisited the issue of interjudge reliability calculation. Our current standard method for calculating reliability, the coefficient alpha, is based on the underlying assumption that "judge" is a fixed effect. That is, the reliability can conceptually be understood as estimating the degree of agreement if the same set of judges were to again assess the products rated. However, although this assumption is not, strictly speaking, in opposition to our aims in the CAT, it would probably be better to consider judge as a random effect. In so doing, the reliability would be generalized to a larger population of judges from which the current set of judges was drawn. This assumption is met if interjudge reliability is calculated according to the intraclass correlation ICC (2,k) method (Bartko, 1976; Shrout & Fleiss, 1979). In practice, this method often yields results that are similar to our standard method (coefficient alpha).

New Reliability Data on Collages and Haiku Poems

The 1983 edition described the methodology for and reported reliability data on two major creativity tasks that we had devised: paper collage and "American Haiku" (or cinquain) poetry. In the intervening years we have often used these tasks in our studies, and good reliabilities almost always result. Table A presents these recent data.

Table A.   New Creativity Reliability Data on Collages and Haiku Poems

Data From	Subjects	Judges	Reliability
Collages			
Amabile, Hennessey, & Grossman, 1986 (Study 2)	80 children	11 artists	.80
Amabile, Hennessey, & Grossman, 1986 (Study 3)	60 undergraduate women	14 artists	.75
Hennessey, Amabile, & Martinage, 1989 (Study 2)	58 children	12 elementary school teachers	.70
Hennessey & Zbikowski, 1993	41 children	15 artists	.79
1991	40 undergraduates	12 artists	.77
Collins & Amabile, 1992	87 undergraduates	8 artists and art students	.78
Ruscio, Whitney, & Amabile, 1995	151 undergraduates	10 artists	.80
Conti, Collins, & Picariello, 1995 (1)	50 children	5 adults familiar with children's art	.82
Conti, Collins, & Picariello, 1995 (2)	118 children	5 art teachers	.72
Haiku Poems (Cinquains)			
Ruscio, Whitney, & Amabile, 1995	151 undergraduates	4 English graduate students	.89
Hennessey, 1989 (1)	37 children	4 teachers	.82
Hennessey, 1989 (2)	29 children	4 teachers	.82
Picariello, 1992	46 children (2 poems)	7 teachers or former teachers	.82 .86

Note. All studies were conducted by members of Amabile's Research Group at Brandeis University. Studies that were not reported in manuscripts are referred to only by year. Reliabilities are coefficient alpha.

New Creativity Tasks

In the 1983 edition we proposed that the CAT could be extended to a wide variety of tasks in a wide variety of domains. In our own program of research we have created a large number of new creativity tasks to which we have applied the CAT with considerable success (e.g., Hennessey & Amabile, 1988). These tasks can be grouped into three broad domains: verbal creativity (stories and other prose passages), artistic creativity (line drawings, paintings, still-life sketches, and a variety of artistic media), and problem-solving creativity (computer programming, desert island survival problems, ideas for new high-tech services, and construction of a structure out of ordinary household materials).

Importantly, not only have we expanded the tasks and products used in our research, but we have also expanded the subject populations studied. We have now applied the CAT to products generated by professional artists, professional art students, computer programming students, student poets, and employees of a high-tech company, as well as our traditional subject populations of undergraduates and elementary school children. Table B presents reliability data on each of these new tasks.

Notice that in both Table A and Table B there are some interesting differences between task domains in the degree of interjudge reliability that is generally obtained. Overall, we obtain acceptably reliable assessments with fewer judges for verbal tasks and problem-solving tasks than for artistic tasks.

Table B   Creativity Reliability Data on New Creativity Tasks.

Data From	Task/Product	Subjects	Judges	Reliability
		Artistic Tasks		
Pollak, 1992	Art students' works (within subjects)	29 art students	9 art teachers	.73
Pollak, 1992	Art students' portfolios (between subjects)	29 art students	9 art teachers	.72
Amabile, Phillips, & Collins, 1994	Art in various media (within subjects)	23 professional artists	10 professional artists	.74
Amabile, Phillips, & Collins, 1994	Artists' portfolios (between subjects)	23 professional artists	10 professional artists	.92
Collins & Amabile, 1992	Line drawings	87 undergraduates	8 artists and art students	.76
Collins & Amabile, 1992	Sponge paintings	87 undergraduates	8 artists and art students	.77
Hennessey, 1989 (1)	Computer line drawings	37 children	7 psychology grad. students	.83
Hennessey, 1989 (2)	Computer line drawings	39 children	7 psychology grad. students	.87
Hennessey, 1989 (3)	Computer line drawings	73 children	7 psychology grad. students	.90
Phillips, 1992 (1)	Paintings (within subjects)	4 artists	8 familiar with art	.53
Phillips, 1992 (1)	Painting portfolios (between subjects)	4 artists	8 familiar with art	.91
Phillips, 1992 (2)	Paintings (within subjects)	4 artists	8 (4 familiar with art)	.55
Phillips, 1992 (2)	Painting portfolios (between subjects)	4 artists	8 (4 familiar with art)	.86
Phillips, 1992 (3)	Artworks in various media (within subjects)	4 artists	6 art students	.54
Phillips, 1992 (3)	Portfolios in various media (between subjects)	4 artists	6 art students	.91

Table B   Creativity Reliability Data on New Creativity Tasks (*Continued*)

Data From	Task/Product	Subjects	Judges	Reliability
		Verbal Tasks		
Amabile, Hennessey, & Grossman, 1986 (Study 1)	Stories told to a picture book without words	115 children	3 elementary school teachers	.91
Amabile, Hennessey, & Grossman, 1986 (Study 2)	Stories told to a picture book without words	80 children	3 elementary school teachers	.83
Hennessey, Amabile, & Martinage, 1989	Stories told to a picture book without words	113 children	3 elementary school teachers	.80
Hennessey & Zbikowski, 1993	Stories told to a picture book without words	41 children	3 elementary school teachers	.67
Hill, 1991	Prose passages	214 undergraduates	8 creative writing students	.88
Tighe, 1992	3 different prose passages	82 undergraduates	5 English teachers	.84, .84, and .72
1992	Prose passages	60 undergraduates	4 writing students	.75
1993	2 different prose passages	184 undergraduates	4 writing students	.79 and .79
1992	Poems of various styles	38 student poets	9 professional poets	.81
Hill, Amabile, Coon, & Whitney, 1994	Prose passages	202 undergraduates	4 writers	.80
Conti, Amabile, & Pollak, 1995	Psychology essays	75 undergraduates	5 psychology teachers	.75
Picariello, 1994	2 different essays	131 children	3 teachers	.72 and .78
		Problem Solving Tasks		
Conti & Amabile, 1995	Computer programs	32 computer students	9 computer grad. students	.75
Ruscio, Whitney, & Amabile, 1995	Structures from ordinary materials	143 undergraduates	4 psychology students	.87
Collins, 1992	Survival ideas	56 undergraduates	3 psychology grad. students	.80
1993	Ideas for high-tech products	20 high-tech employees	3 high-tech employees	.61
Conti, 1992	Business solutions	60 undergraduates	5 MBA students	.80

Note. All studies were conducted by members of Amabile's Research Group at Brandeis University. Studies that were not reported in manuscripts are referred to only by year. Reliabilities are coefficient alpha.

Issues and Changes in the Consensual Assessment Technique

We have made several modifications in our practice of the CAT over the past twelve years. Most of these have been minor, but some have been fairly significant. Most of the changes were motivated by a desire to simplify or to experiment with the technique to determine its flexibility and robustness. Other changes, however, were motivated by shifts in our conceptualization of what creativity assessment requires and how our goals can best be achieved. Here we review the primary changes and the issues motivating them.

Who Are "Appropriate" Judges?

In the 1983 edition we asserted that appropriate judges are those familiar with the domain in which the product was produced or the response articulated. We occasionally used the term "expert" to describe appropriate judges, but we are now convinced that for most products in most domains, judges need not be true experts in order to be considered appropriate. Even in the 1983 edition we reported data demonstrating that there were strong correlations between true experts in a domain (for example, artists judging children's art) and nonexperts who were merely familiar with the domain (for example, psychologists judging children's art). We have since confirmed this view. For example, we have found that the graduate students in our laboratory produce creativity ratings of children's poems that correlate well with elementary school teachers' ratings of the same poems (e.g., Picariello, 1992). And in other cases where we lack the validation of a set of experts, we have at least found that nonexperts can yield reliable ratings—for example, psychology graduate students assessing structures constructed by undergraduates in the laboratory (Ruscio, 1994).

Nonetheless, it would be a mistake to assume that everyone (or even every psychology graduate student) can be considered an appropriate judge for products in every domain. In many domains, some formal training in the field may be necessary for judges to even understand the products they are assessing. For example, for our computer-programming task, where the subjects were computer science undergraduate students, we found it necessary to use computer science graduate students as our judges (Conti & Amabile, 1995). And in a study where the products were artworks in the portfolios of professional artists, we found some differences between expert and nonexpert groups of judges (Phillips, 1992). Moreover, we even found differences among judges within the art field; the professional artists agreed better with one another than an art historian agreed with any of them. It may be that for certain high-level products, being steeped in the specific domain really does lead to more valid assessments of creativity.

We suggest that the best guideline is to use judges who have at least some formal training or experience in the target domain, if at all possible. This guideline becomes more important if the domain is one with which most people are not conversant, and the level of judge expertise becomes more important as the level of subjects' expertise in the domain increases. In other words, the judges should be closely familiar with works in the domain at least at the level of those being produced by the subjects. The degree of familiarity required in the judges will depend not only on the domain and the level at which the subjects are operating, but also on the ultimate purpose of the assessments (Runco & Smith, 1992).

In the 1983 edition, we briefly considered the question of whether people can serve as judges of the creativity of their own work. There was at the time a small body of evidence suggesting that self-assessments were not useful, but the question was far from closed. Of course, if only self-assessments were used as the measure of creativity, it would be impossible to assess interjudge reliability. This would effectively render such a measure invalid. However, it is still of interest to consider the accuracy of self-assessment if we view reliable judge ratings as the external criterion of accuracy.

In some of our studies, we have found that self-assessments correlate moderately positively (in the range of .30 to .40) with mean judge assessments. One example comes from our study of computer science students' computer programs (Conti & Amabile, 1995). Another comes from our study of professional artists' artworks (Amabile, Phillips, & Collins, 1994)—although we found that the artists tended to rate their own works considerably higher than did the judges. This level of agreement is particularly impressive when we consider that the judges and the subjects were using somewhat different comparisons for their assessments. In the computer-programming study, the judges were making their ratings relative to other programs written by other subjects in the study, but the subjects were simply providing a general rating of their own programs' creativity. In the professional artist study, the judges were making their ratings of each particular artwork relative to 19 other artworks by the same artist, but the artists were making their ratings of each artwork relative to all other artworks they had made in the previous six years. We should note, however, that in other of our studies, self-assessments of creativity are essentially uncorrelated with judge assessments—for example, in the structure-building study (Ruscio, 1994). We suspect that the crucial variable may be the degree to which the subjects are familiar with the creativity task before they engage in it. The computer programmers and the artists all had considerable experience, but the structure-building task was designed to be one that the subjects (introductory psychology students) would find quite unfamiliar.

What Are the Essential Characteristics of the Task?

We still believe that several features of experimental creativity tasks are crucial for application of the CAT. Such tasks must: (a) be feasible in the sense that virtually all subjects in the study can produce something that can be assessed by judges, (b) present all subjects with the same set of materials, instructions, and working conditions (except, of course, for materials, instructions, or working conditions that may constitute any independent variable under study), (c) allow for considerable flexibility in responses, (d) result in some form of product that can readily be observed by judges, and (e) result in products that can be reliably rated by appropriate judges. Within these parameters, researchers can and should practice their own creativity in devising interesting and useful tasks. And, of course, "naturally occurring" tasks that meet the last three criteria (such as the artworks made by professional artists) are appropriate for application of the CAT in nonexperimental studies.

There is one feature of creativity tasks we originally recommended that we now believe requires clarification and modification. We recommended that the tasks not depend heavily on any special skills. This recommendation was made specifically for studies primarily focusing on social psychological factors as independent variables. To the extent that there were large individual differences in performance resulting from differential skill levels, it would become more difficult to detect the "signal" of social psychological effects over the "background noise" of those individual differences. There are three circumstances, however, under which it is acceptable and perhaps even advisable to use tasks that do depend on special skills. The first such circumstance is a social psychological study in which all of the subjects have an equivalent degree of expertise in the domain. An example is our study of the effects of working for commission (versus doing self-initiated work) on the creativity of professional artists (Amabile, Phillips, & Collins, 1994). In such a study, although skill differences will certainly exist, they should not dominate social influences (as long as those influences are at least moderate). The second circumstance is a study that is specifically oriented toward studying the contribution of skills to product creativity (e.g., Amabile, Hill, Hennessey, & Tighe, 1994; Hill, 1991; Hill, Amabile, Coon, & Whitney, 1994). The third circumstance is one in which the independent variable is a social psychological factor but a repeated-measures design is used (Pollak, 1992).

What Are the Essential Elements of the Procedure?

In the 1983 edition, we argued that if judges are trained in their creativity ratings, their subsequent interjudge reliability will be suspect. That is, rather than truly agreeing with one another, they may simply be reflecting the standard that they were taught. For this reason, we suggested as the most conservative approach that judges not even be given specific definitions of creativity. The "nondefinitional definition" we typically provide to judges is, "Using your own subjective definition of creativity, rate the degree to which each [collage, poem, structure, and so on] is creative relative to the other [collages, poems, structures, and so on]."

In our recent research, however, we have encountered one situation in which judges seemed unable to work without some guiding definition. This particular study was conducted in a large corporation (Amabile, Conti, Coon, Lazenby, & Herron, in press). The dependent variable was the creativity of each of a large number of technical development projects as assessed by experts within the corporation who were familiar with a great many such projects. In our initial discussions with high-level technical personnel within the corporation, it became clear that they (and presumably their colleagues) were uncomfortable with the idea of rating the creativity of these projects in the absence of some guiding definition. In particular, they were concerned that assessments of the likely commercial success of the product or process would account for much of the variance in creativity ratings. Because commercial success is largely determined by factors that have nothing to do with the creativity of the initial product or process idea, we agreed to supply the judges with a general creativity definition that explicitly excluded commercial success. (The definition did include novelty and appropriateness.) Thus, although we believe that in most situations it is advisable to allow judges to use their own subjective definitions, we also recognize that there may be some special circumstances under which definitions should be provided.

There are other procedural modifications that we have made when the circumstances of the study seemed to call for them. As a general rule, all judges should rate all products. This ensures that all products are being rated relative to one another, and it greatly simplifies the reliability calculations. However, at times this is impossible. Such a situation arose in the study just described. No expert within the corporation was familiar with all of the projects to be rated, and different experts were familiar with somewhat different sets of projects. For example, Project 1 might be rated by 12 judges, Project 2 might be rated by 4 judges (3 of whom had also rated Project 1), and Project 3 might be rated by 4 judges (2 of whom had also judged Project 2, and 1 of whom had also judged Project 1). In this case we had no choice but to use the data we received; we calculated interjudge reliability by using intraclass correlation.

Finally, as the CAT was originally described, judges should rate all products on one dimension (such as creativity) before rating all products on any other dimension (such as technical quality). This was recommended as a means of maintaining consistency in judges' subjective criteria for a particular dimension and allowing the separability of the different dimensions. However, we have found that this methodology is simply not practical in certain situations. For example, in a study where 100 long prose passages must be rated on each of 3 dimensions, the judges' task would be insufferably long and tedious if each of those prose passages had to be read 3 times (once for each dimension rated). In such situations, as always, we allow the judges to familiarize themselves with the products to be rated before they actually begin the rating task. However, rather than insisting that they read all 100 passages, we give them a random sample for this initial familiarization (say, 20%). Next, we stress to judges the importance of maintaining clarity in their subjective definitions of the different dimensions and the importance of separating the dimensions as much as possible. We then allow them to read each passage once, after which they rate the passage on each of the dimensions under consideration before moving on to the next passage.

Within-Subject Product Assessments

As of the publication of the 1983 edition, we had not conducted a study that involved more than one product per subject. However, for social psychological studies as well as for other studies, it is often advantageous to use repeated-measures designs. Perhaps the most important reason is that it allows for a broader view of the creativity of an individual's work rather than a single snapshot. A repeated-measures design was used in the study where we investigated possible differences in creativity between professional artists' commissioned works and their non-commissioned (self-initiated) works (Amabile, Phillips, & Collins, 1994). We presented expert-artist judges with 10 commissioned and 10 noncommissioned works from each artist, asking them to rate each work relative to the other 19 works from that particular artist. Not surprisingly, this rating task was considerably more difficult for judges than was the task of rating individual works from different subjects relative to one another; the works of any one artist are unlikely to differ dramatically among themselves on creativity or technical quality. Nonetheless, although interjudge reliabilities were somewhat lower than those obtained in between-subjects rating tasks, the creativity reliability was acceptable (greater than .70). Thus, the CAT can be useful for within-subjects as well as between-subjects creativity assessment.

Is Creativity a Separate Quality?

In the 1983 edition, we showed that it is possible to obtain judge ratings of creativity that are essentially uncorrelated (or only weakly correlated) with judge ratings of technical quality or aesthetic appeal. However, we also presented data demonstrating that, in many cases, creativity will be positively correlated with other dimensions, such as technical quality. We argued that although it is important to demonstrate that it is at least possible to separate creativity from other product qualities, in practice, creativity will often be related to other qualities.

The studies we have conducted in the past twelve years have shown that, in many cases creativity is indeed correlated with dimensions such as technical quality. Those correlations generally range from .20 to .50 (or even higher occasionally). Our pattern of results seems to suggest that these dimensions may be most highly correlated in expert-level works, such as the works of professional artists. It may be that high-level creativity is not possible without an extraordinary command of technique. Even in garden-variety products from ordinary subjects (such as collages produced by psychology students in our laboratory), we should perhaps not be surprised when creativity is related to quality or appeal. After all, our conceptual definition of creativity includes not only a novelty component but also an appropriateness component. However, it still is appropriate to obtain creativity ratings that are as "pure" as possible. In practice, we have found that judges' ratings of creativity and technical quality of artworks will be less highly correlated if they rate another dimension (such as aesthetic appeal) in between (Phillips, 1992). Perhaps focusing judges' attention on their aesthetic reaction to the work "cleans the slate" for judgments on other, more evaluative, dimensions such as technical quality and creativity.

Can the CAT Be Used for Individual-Difference Assessment?

We originally presented the CAT as most useful for social psychological studies of creativity in contrast to the popular creativity tests designed to be sensitive to individual differences in creativity. We argued that if the tasks chosen for use in the CAT were as free as possible from reliance on special domain skills, then individual-difference variability would be minimized and the possibility of detecting social-environmental effects would be maximized. We have since broadened our view.

In a number of our recent studies we have found that the CAT can indeed be useful in individual-difference research. In two studies, for example, professional artists (or student artists) were rated on creativity relative to one another (Amabile, Phillips, & Collins, 1994; Pollak, 1992). The basis for these expert-judge assessments was a portfolio of works from each artist. Thus, the portfolios were rated as a whole, relative to one another. Not only were independent judges able to assign relative creativity ratings to these artists with a high degree of reliability, but the mean creativity ratings correlated significantly with other individual-difference measures in each of these studies. We have also found that judges can reliably rate children's collections of works (in this case, short poems) relative to one another (Picariello, 1992). Even in studies where only one product is obtained from each subject, we have found significant correlations between judge-rated creativity and certain individual-difference measures (e.g., Amabile, Hill, Hennessey, & Tighe, 1994; Collins & Amabile, 1992). Moreover, when we correlated the CAT creativity measures from different products produced by the same subjects in different studies, there was a considerable degree of consistency (Conti, Coon, & Amabile, in press).

Does this mean that the CAT is less appropriate for social psychological studies, or that it is better than creativity tests for individual creativity assessment? No. It means that, as our theoretical model (Chapter 4) proposes, the creativity of a particular product results from the confluence of several different influences, including the individual's motivation (which can be strongly influenced by the social environment), the individual's expertise in the domain, and the individual's level of creative-thinking skill. Clearly, the technique is useful for its originally intended purpose in the social psychology of creativity. Several of our studies have demonstrated significant effects of social-environmental variables on creativity as assessed by the CAT; most of these were studies where "ordinary" subjects engaged in tasks that did not require special skills. Moreover, we have not done any empirical work pitting CAT measures against traditional tests of creative-thinking skills. We can say, however, that the CAT can be used effectively in both social psychological and individual-difference studies of creativity.

There is an important caution, however. The CAT may be useful in identifying differences between the creative performances of different individuals in *a certain type of task* in a *particular domain* at *particular points in time*. It would be inappropriate to use these product-creativity scores as a measure of a person's overall degree of creativity (a concept that, we would argue, is inappropriate in itself). For example, on the basis of the expert ratings of our professional artists' portfolios, we can say that for the six-year time period represented, certain of the artists produced more creative work overall in their primary medium than did other of the artists. But we cannot say that certain artists are more creative people, or even more creative artists, than the others.

Sex Differences in Creativity

Although it is not directly relevant to the use of the CAT, a consideration of subject populations is important for the general issue of creativity measurement. In one of the early CAT studies reported in the 1983 edition, we found a marginally significant sex difference: women produced collages that were rated as more creative than those produced by men. In order to avoid possible complicating effects, we relied primarily on female subjects in many of our later studies. We have long since abandoned this practice, in large part because we did not wish to develop a social psychology of female creativity. In the many studies where we have included both men and women, or boys and girls, we have occasionally found sex differences—generally with children. From the small body of data we have collected, it appears that girls may be more creative on some verbal tasks (Picariello, 1994), and boys may be more creative on some artistic tasks (Phillips, 1993). However, such sex differences have been rare in our results.

Other Uses of the Consensual Assessment Technique

A number of other researchers have used the CAT in their creativity research over the past few years. For example, the technique has been used successfully in a study of the creativity of children's artworks (Koestner, Ryan, Bernieri, & Holt, 1984), in a study of children's creativity in various domains (Baer, 1994), and in a study of the creativity of adults on products in several different domains (Sternberg & Lubart, 1991, 1993). Besemer & O'Quin (1986) and O'Quin & Besemer (1989) have begun to develop a creativity assessment technique that, like the CAT, is based on subjective assessments of several judges. Their Creative Product Semantic Scale (CPSS), however, is considerably more formalized than the CAT. It presents judges with a questionnaire that includes seventy-one items and requires them to rate each product on each of those items.

A relatively unusual but quite promising use of the CAT is in the assessment of *creative process*. Beth Hennessey asked adults to create line drawings on computer screens using particular keys to select colors, start points, and end points for each line (Hennessey, 1994). The computer was programmed to record all lines that the subject drew, in real time. Thus, it was possible to later view the screen just as it would have looked as the subject was drawing—including erased lines—with the exact sequence of drawing moves captured. Hennessey found that undergraduate judges who viewed the entire sequence for each subject could reliably assess the creativity of the *process* the subjects undertook to produce these drawings (with reliabilities of .83 for a group of 30 judges, and .81 for a group of 15 judges). As with product assessments, the process assessments were made for one task-process relative to the others using the judges' own subjective definitions.

Summary

Research over the past several years has demonstrated that the consensual assessment technique is robust, yielding reliable subjective assessments of creativity even when the procedure is varied to some extent. To be sure, some difficulties are encountered when the procedure strays far from the standard originally established in the 1983 edition. We can summarize the most important features of the technique quite simply; these should not be drastically altered if at all possible. Any experimental task should be one that allows for variability in acceptable responses, and all subjects should be given the same materials and guidelines. Moreover, the task should be one in which most subjects can actually produce an observable product or response. For experimental studies, the judges should be shown the basic task materials and instructions given to subjects. For all studies, both experimental and naturalistic, the judges should have at least a moderate degree of familiarity with the domain in which the products were produced, and the level at which they were produced. The judges should view all products (or a substantial subset) before they begin to make their ratings, and they should be told to rate the products relative to one another. Finally, the judges should work independently.

The CAT has broader uses than we originally envisioned. It can be used to obtain reliable assessments of several of the same person's products on their relative creativity. Moreover, its results can be useful as individual-difference measures of creative performance on particular tasks in particular domains for a given time period, especially when several instances of each individual's work are available for judges to examine. Finally, it can be expanded to new domains and new tasks that are quite different from those we originally envisioned. Thus, although the CAT is considerably more time-consuming than standard creativity tests, we argue that it affords greater flexibility to creativity researchers. We also argue that because it relies on actual products made by subjects, it affords greater validity for many purposes as well.

4
A Theoretical Framework

The primary goal of this book is to develop the foundations of a social psychology of creativity. In order to accomplish this goal, however, it is necessary to meet a second goal of equal importance: to integrate the social-psychological approach within a more general theoretical framework for a comprehensive psychology of creativity. In the past, the psychological study of creativity has been hampered by the tendency of individual investigators to narrow their theoretical focus to a single concern—the distinctive personality characteristics of outstandingly creative persons, or the special cognitive abilities of creative artists and scientists, or (less frequently) the social environments that hinder or foster creativity. However sound the empirical research directed toward those single issues, this approach has led to a theoretical fragmentation within the psychology of creativity.

As a social psychology of creativity develops, then, it must not be proposed as an answer to all questions of creativity, any more than a personality approach or a cognitive approach can be proposed as a complete answer. It is true that social-psychological issues have been largely ignored in the study of creativity. I argue here that it is not enough to concentrate empirical research on those issues; they must be integrated into a general framework that includes personality and cognition. This chapter will present such a framework for the psychology of creativity, illustrating the place of social psychology in that framework and outlining the contributions that social-psychological research can make to a full understanding of the creative process.

The conceptualization of creativity presented here (cf. Amabile, 1983) can be considered a componential one, since it suggests a set of components as necessary and sufficient for creative production in any domain.[1] At the outset, it is essential to describe what this conceptualization is and what it is not. It is not a fully artic-

---

[1] Sternberg (1977a, 1977b, 1978, 1979) has used the term "componential" extensively in his theory of human reasoning. There is a basic commonality between his and the present use of the term. In both conceptualizations, all of the "components" are seen as necessary, and the set of components is seen as essentially complete. Sternberg's model is more highly developed, being subdivided into hierarchical levels which include performance components, acquisition components, transfer components, retention components, and metacomponents (processes controlling the lower components). Although, in Sternberg's model, the components are *processes*, in the present conceptualization of creativity, the components are sets of elements that control, determine, and enter into processes.

ulated theory, presented at a level of detail that allows the derivation of a limited set of testable propositions. It is not based on one particular program of empirical research. In some of its aspects, it is largely speculative.

The componential conceptualization is best considered a working model for a theory of creativity, a proposal of what a formal theory of creative performance might include. Grounded in the diverse data on creativity that have accumulated over the past 30 years, it includes the dispositional, cognitive, and social factors that appear to determine creativity. It is presented here for its potential heuristic value in generating research designed to account for various creativity phenomena. In this book, the componential conceptualization serves two major functions: It guides the formulation of specific hypotheses tested in my own research on social influences, and it serves as a framework for both reviewing past creativity research and generating the prescriptions that will be made for an applied social psychology of creativity.

Preliminary Assumptions and Observations

The componential conceptualization of creativity is grounded in a set of formal and informal observations about creative production, as well as a set of assumptions about the nature of creativity:

1. It is assumed that there is a continuum from the low levels of creativity observed in everyday life to historically significant advances in science, literature, and the arts. In contrast to popular views of creativity as a discrete entity, this assumption implies that it is possible for anyone with normal cognitive abilities to produce work that is creative to some degree in some domain of endeavor.
2. A closely related assumption is that there can be degrees of creativity within a particular individual's work.
3. At least for high levels of creativity, there often seems to be a special "match" between individuals and domains (Feldman, 1980). There appears to be a particularly good fit, for example, between one individual and chess-playing, or between another individual and musical composition.
4. The ages at which peak creativity is achieved in different domains varies widely (Dennis, 1966; Lehman, 1953; Simonton, 1975a).
5. Although different individuals may differ widely in their potential for creative performance in any given domain, it does appear to be possible to increase creativity to some extent (Stein, 1974; 1975). Specifically, although innate abilities ("talents") in a given domain do appear to be important for high levels of creativity, formal education seems essential in most outstanding creative achievements (Feldman, 1980).
6. Talents, education, and cognitive skills do not by themselves appear to be sufficient for high levels of creativity.

7. Particular clusters of personality traits are found fairly consistently among individuals exhibiting high levels of creativity (see Stein, 1974, for a review) but, again, they are not sufficient in and of themselves. Certainly, any given individual—even one exhibiting a particular "creative" personality-trait constellation—is not creative at all times or in all domains.

8. A great many outstanding creative individuals (e.g., Poincare, 1924) have described the phenomenon of "incubation": After ceasing to consciously work on a difficult problem, they sometimes experience an apparent flash of illumination, during which the solution appears to them unexpectedly.

9. Although an eagerness to work diligently appears to be an essential component of high levels of creativity (Golann, 1963) and although a number of introspective accounts describe creativity as marked by deep involvement in the activity at hand, these accounts also stress the importance of intellectual playfulness and freedom from external constraints (e.g., Einstein, 1949).

10. Although it appears that extrinsic constraints can be detrimental to creativity (a central theme to be developed more fully later), there are individuals who appear to produce consistently creative work under clear and salient extrinsic constraints.

These assumptions and observations guided the development of the componential framework. They will be considered at greater length after the framework is presented in detail.

The Components of Creative Performance

The componential framework of creativity includes three major components, as outlined in Figure 4-1. In keeping with the consensual definition of creativity offered in Chapter 2, "creativity" here refers to the production of responses or works that are reliably assessed as creative by appropriate judges. These three components, then, are presented as factors essential for the production of such responses and works.[2]

Within this framework, "Domain-Relevant Skills" can be considered as the basis for any performance in a given domain. This component includes factual knowledge, technical skills, and special talents in the domain in question. "Creativity-Relevant Skills" include cognitive style, application of heuristics for the exploration of new cognitive pathways, and working style. "Task Motivation" includes motivational variables that determine an individual's approach to a given task. As conceptualized here, the three components operate at different levels of specificity. Creativity-relevant skills operate at the most general level; they may in-

---

[2] The term "factor" is used here in the colloquial sense of elements, circumstances, or conditions contributing to a process or outcome. This use is to be distinguished from the more narrowly statistical use of the term in the psychology of intelligence (e.g., Spearman, 1927).

1

<u>DOMAIN-RELEVANT SKILLS</u>

<u>INCLUDES:</u>

- KNOWLEDGE ABOUT THE DOMAIN
- TECHNICAL SKILLS REQUIRED
- SPECIAL DOMAIN-RELEVANT "TALENT"

<u>DEPENDS ON:</u>

- INNATE COGNITIVE ABILITIES
- INNATE PERCEPTUAL AND MOTOR SKILLS
- FORMAL AND INFORMAL EDUCATION

2

<u>CREATIVITY-RELEVANT SKILLS</u>

<u>INCLUDES:</u>

- APPROPRIATE COGNITIVE STYLE
- IMPLICIT OR EXPLICIT KNOWLEDGE OF HEURISTICS FOR GENERATING NOVEL IDEAS
- CONDUCIVE WORK STYLE

<u>DEPENDS ON:</u>

- TRAINING
- EXPERIENCE IN IDEA GENERATION
- PERSONALITY CHARACTERISTICS

3

<u>TASK MOTIVATION</u>

<u>INCLUDES:</u>

- ATTITUDES TOWARD THE TASK
- PERCEPTIONS OF OWN MOTIVATION FOR UNDERTAKING THE TASK

<u>DEPENDS ON:</u>

- INITIAL LEVEL OF INTRINSIC MOTIVATION TOWARD THE TASK
- PRESENCE OR ABSENCE OF SALIENT EXTRINSIC CONSTRAINTS
- INDIVIDUAL ABILITY TO COGNITIVELY MINIMIZE EXTRINSIC CONSTRAINTS

Figure 4-1.   Components of Creative Performance

fluence responses in any content domain. Thus, some highly creative individuals may indeed appear to be creative "types," behaving atypically in many domains of behavior. Domain-relevant skills, on the other hand, operate at an intermediate level of specificity. This component includes all skills relevant to a general domain (e.g., verbal production), rather than skills relevant to only a specific task within a domain (e.g., writing a Haiku poem on autumn). It is assumed that, within a particular domain, skills used in any specific task will have a great deal of overlap with skills used in any other task. Finally, task motivation operates at the most specific level; motivation may be very specific to particular tasks within domains and may even vary over time for a particular task. Thus, for example, a student may have a high level of motivation for writing computer programs, but may have a low level of motivation for working problems in formal logic.

Figure 4-1 includes several elements within each of the three components. At our current level of knowledge, although it is reasonable to assume that all three components are necessary for creativity, it is not possible to specify which of the individual elements is necessary. It might, for example, be possible for a composer to produce a symphony that observers would agree was quite creative without that composer having any particular "talent" for hearing in imagination all the instruments playing together. On the other hand, it might be that such talent is essential. The point is that only future research can indicate which elements constitute a complete set within any one of the components, and which elements are indeed essential. Thus, the elements included in Figure 4-1 within each component are presented as examples of the kind of elements that the component contains.

Domain-Relevant Skills

Domain-relevant skills comprise the individual's complete set of response possibilities from which the new response is to be synthesized, and information against which the new response is to be judged. This component can be seen as the set of cognitive pathways for solving a given problem or doing a given task. Some of the pathways are more common, well-practiced, or obvious than others, and the set of pathways may be large or small. The larger the set, the more numerous the alternatives available for producing something new, for developing a new combination of ideas. As Newell and Simon (1972) have so poetically described it, this set can be considered the problem-solver's "network of possible wanderings" (p. 82).[3]

This component includes familiarity with and *factual knowledge* of the domain in question: facts, principles, opinions about various issues in the domain, knowledge of paradigms, performance "scripts" for solving problems in the domain (Schank & Abelson, 1977), and aesthetic criteria. Clearly, it is only possible to be

---

[3] There is a great deal of overlap between the present conceptualization of domain-relevant skills and Newell and Simon's (1972) conceptualization of "problem space." However, Newell and Simon do not explicitly include the technical motor skills or special talents that are here seen as part of domain-relevant skills.

creative in nuclear physics if one knows something (and probably a great deal) about nuclear physics. The component of domain-relevant skills also includes *technical skills* that may be required by a given domain, such as laboratory techniques or studio art techniques, and special *domain-relevant "talents"* that may contribute to creative productivity. As proposed, this set of skills depends upon innate cognitive, perceptual, and motor abilities, as well as formal and informal education in the domain of endeavor.

Although the research literature on domain-relevant skills is scant, notions similar to those presented here can be found in the work of several previous theorists. In what is perhaps the most well-known intuitive description of the creative process, Wallas (1926) suggested that the first step is the "preparation" stage, which depends upon "the whole process of intellectual education" (p. 92). Similarly, Koestler (1964) refers to the importance of "ripeness" in determining whether the "bisociation" of two different "matrices of thought" will take place: "the statistical probability for a relevant discovery to be made is the greater the more firmly established and well exercised each of the still separate skills, or thought-matrices, are" (p. 108). And Newell et al. (1962) propose that "there is a high correlation between creativity (at least in the sciences) and proficiency in the more routine intellective tasks that are commonly used to measure intelligence" (p. 145). To this, I add the qualification that there is a high correlation between creativity and proficiency in the more routine *domain-relevant* intellective tasks.

In discussions of creativity, there is often a lack of clarity about the meaning of "talent." Talent, in the present context, refers simply to a special skill for which an individual appears to have a natural aptitude. To be considered a talent, a skill need not be completely absent in the general population, but the high level of that skill in a talented individual clearly distinguishes him or her from the general population. Moreover, the skill need not (and probably can never) appear in its most mature state with no special training or experience; certainly, a talent can be developed.

Mental imagery presents a good example of what is here meant by "talent." Although most individuals assert that they experience some type of mental imagery (cf. Kosslyn, 1980), some outstandingly creative people appear to have had an extraordinary talent for calling upon visual, auditory, or even kinesthetic images. Consider Albert Einstein's *Gedankenexperiment* in which he saw himself traveling alongside a beam of light (Einstein, 1949; Holton, 1972). Mozart described his vivid auditory imagery: "Nor do I hear in my imagination the parts *successively,* but I hear them, as it were, all at once" (Mozart, 1878, p. 212). Nikola Tesla, the inventor of the AC generator, claimed to generate images of machines that were more detailed than any blueprint; he would test his imagined devices by having them run in his mind for weeks, periodically "checking" them for signs of wear (McKim, 1972). And the poet Stephen Spender (1952) regarded mental imagery as indispensible for his craft: "The poet, above all else, is a person who never forgets certain sense impressions which he has experienced and which he can relive again and again as though with all their original freshness" (p. 121).

It seems reasonable, then, to propose that different types of vivid mental imagery are important domain-relevant skills for creativity in several different fields, and to consider outstanding levels of this skill as "talent." Although present methodologies do not lend themselves well to an investigation of individual differences in mental imagery abilities, there is reason to believe that such methodologies could be developed and that they could lead to advances in the study of creativity (cf. Kosslyn, 1980).

The nature of domain-relevant information and the manner in which it is stored can make an important difference in creative production. Wickelgren (1979) has argued that "the more we concentrate on . . . heavily contextualized (specific) concepts and propositions, the less capacity we will have available to learn general principles and questions that crosscut different areas and perspectives" (p. 382). In other words, knowledge organized according to general principles will be of greater utility than specific, narrowly applicable collections of facts. Likewise, performance scripts organized according to general approaches to problems rather than strict response algorithms should be more likely to contribute to high levels of creativity. Thus, according to this perspective, the popular notion that a great deal of knowledge in a given domain can be detrimental to creativity is incorrect. In general, an increase in domain-relevant skills can only lead to an increase in creativity—provided that the domain-relevant information is organized appropriately. This proposition fits well with the assertion of previous theorists (e.g., Campbell, 1960) that larger stores of properly coded knowledge increase the probability of outstanding responses. In other words, while it is possible to have "too many algorithms," it is not possible to have too much knowledge.

There has been virtually no research directly examining the role of domain-relevant skills in the production of creative work. There is some evidence, however, supporting the notion that exposure to a wide array of information in a domain can enhance creativity. In a series of studies on physical scientists, those named as most creative by their peers were the most likely to seek information on their discipline actively and to have exposure to information within different scientific disciplines (Kasperson, 1978a, 1978b). Other research has shown that highly creative and productive scientists tend to be unusually familiar with the scientific zeitgeist (Simonton, 1979), and that bilingual children tend to score higher on verbal creativity than their monoglot peers (Okoh, 1980). In addition, some indirect evidence may be found in biographical and personality assessments of outstandingly creative individuals (e.g., Cox, 1926; MacKinnon, 1962; Roe, 1952). Summaries of this research generally stress the importance of intellectual abilities in creativity (e.g., Cattell & Butcher, 1968), and at least one archival study has found direct evidence of the crucial role of formal education (Simonton, 1978).

Creativity-Relevant Skills

Herein lies the "something extra" of creative performance. Most simply, an individual's use of creativity-relevant skills determines the extent to which his product or response will surpass previous products or responses in the domain. Assuming an appropriate level of motivation, performance will be "good" or "adequate" or "acceptable" if the requisite domain-relevant skills exist. However, even with these skills at an extraordinarily high level, an individual will be incapable of producing work that will be considered creative if creativity-relevant skills are lacking.

This component includes, first, a *cognitive style* characterized by a facility in understanding complexities and an ability to break set during problem-solving. Several features of cognitive style appear to be relevant to creativity:[4]

A. *Breaking perceptual set* (as suggested by Boring, 1950; Katona, 1940; and Wertheimer, 1959). Duncker's (1945) studies in "functional fixedness," for example, demonstrated that subjects who solved his problem "creatively" were those who could see a thumbtack box as a platform for a candle, rather than as just a container.

B. *Breaking cognitive set* (or exploring new cognitive pathways). Newell et al. (1962) suggest that problem-solving can result in creative solutions when an old set of unsuccessful problem-solving strategies is abandoned and the search, as a result, moves off in a new direction.

C. *Understanding complexities.* There is evidence that cognitive complexity, an appreciation of and facility in working with complexity, is related to creativity in at least some domains of endeavor (Quinn, 1980).

D. *Keeping response options open as long as possible.* In a study of student artists, Getzels and Csikszentmihalyi (1976) found that those who approached their canvas without a definite plan produced more creative paintings than those who knew in advance what they were going to do. Kuhn (1963) views this ability to avoid foreclosure of alternatives as essential for scientific creativity: "Ability to support a tension that can occasionally become almost unbearable is one of the prize requisites for the very best sort of scientific research."

E. Suspending judgment. Schiller once advised a friend who complained about being uncreative: "In the case of the creative mind, it seems to me, the intellect has withdrawn its watchers from the gates, and the ideas rush in pell-mell, and only then does it review and inspect the multitude" (Brill, 1938, p. 193). Suspension of judgment is the cardinal rule of Osborn's (1963) brainstorming program and, apparently, the facet of that program that is most responsible for positive results (Stein, 1975).

F. Using "wide" categories. Individuals who categorize information in "wide" as opposed to "narrow" categories, who see relationships between apparently

---

[4] Taken collectively, these features of cognitive style appear to fit within two major styles that Prentky (1980) has suggested as conducive to creativity: A-type, "characterized by extensive scanning that often incorporates much peripheral, extraneous information, erratic mental 'thrashing' of large amounts of information, and a hyper-alertness that facilitates the whole process" (p. 70) and C-type, "characterized by a constricted scan that screens out all but essential information, a narrow focus on bits of information, and a compulsiveness that permits slow mastication, digestion, and storage of large amounts of information" (p. 72).

diverse bits of information, may be more likely to produce creative works and responses (Cropley, 1967).

G. *Remembering accurately.* Campbell (1960) has proposed that those who can code, retain, and recall large amounts of detailed information will probably have an advantage in creative performance; there is, indeed, some empirical evidence to support this proposition (Pollert, Feldhusen, Van Mondfrans, & Treffinger, 1969).

H. *Breaking out of performance "scripts."* I proposed earlier that domain-relevant skills include performance "scripts" (Schank & Abelson, 1977) or "algorithms," set sequences of steps for performing tasks or solving problems in a given domain. It may be important for creativity to be able to break out of well-used scripts occasionally, or at least to be able to examine them, instead of proceeding through them uncritically (Langer, 1978; Langer & Imber, 1979).

I. *Perceiving creatively.* Koestler (1964) has suggested the critical role of seeing things differently from the way most people see them, of being able to take advantage of serendipity by recognizing the importance of new information.

The creativity-relevant skills component also includes *knowledge of heuristics* for generating novel ideas. A heuristic can be defined as "any principle or device that contributes to a reduction in the average search to solution" (Newell et al., 1962, p. 78). Thus, a heuristic may be considered as a general rule that can be of aid in approaching problems or tasks. Several theorists and philosophers of science have proposed creativity heuristics: (a) "When all else fails, try something counterintuitive" (Newell et al., 1962). (b) "Make the familiar strange" (Gordon, 1961). (c) Generate hypotheses by analyzing case studies, use analogies, account for exceptions, and investigate paradoxical incidents (McGuire, 1973). (d) Play with ideas; engage in "mental gymnastics" (Wickelgren, 1979).

Clearly, creativity heuristics are best considered as ways of approaching a problem that can lead to set-breaking and novel ideas, rather than as strict rules that should be applied by rote. Although these heuristics may be stated explicitly by the person using them, they may also be known at a more implicit level and used without direct awareness. Moreover, the utility of a given heuristic may be idiosyncratic to a particular individual. It is said that Salvador Dali liked to use in his paintings the hypnogogic images that came to him as he fell asleep. To this end, he would sit at a table when sleepy, prop his chin up with a spoon, and then wait to be awakened as his head dropped during the first moments of slumber.

A *work style* conducive to creative production is a third element of creativity-relevant skills. Evidence suggests that the ideal work style has several features: (a) an ability to concentrate effort and attention for long periods of time (Campbell, 1960; Hogarth, 1980; Prentky, 1980); (b) an ability to use "productive forgetting" when warranted—an ability to abandon unproductive search strategies and temporarily put aside stubborn problems (Simon, 1966); (c) a persistence in the face of difficulty (Roe, 1953; Walberg, 1971); and (d) a high energy level, a willingness to work hard, and an overall high level of productivity (Bergman, 1979; Bloom, 1956; Davis & Rimm, 1977; Simonton, 1980b; Wallach & Kogan, 1965).

Within the componential conceptualization, personality traits identified with creative behavior are considered an important contributor to creativity-relevant skills. Although individual-difference research on creativity has produced results that are, at times, contradictory, a limited set of traits appears repeatedly in summaries of empirical work on the characteristics of creative persons (e.g., Davis & Rimm, 1977; Feldman, 1980; Golann, 1963; Stein, 1974; Taylor & Barron, 1963): (a) a high degree of self-discipline in matters concerning work; (b) an ability to delay gratification; (c) perseverance in the face of frustration; (d) independence of judgment; (e) a tolerance for ambiguity; (f) a high degree of autonomy; (g) an absence of sex-role stereotyping (Biller, Singer, & Fullerton, 1969); (h) an internal locus of control (DuCette, Wolk, & Friedman, 1972); (i) a willingness to take risks (McClelland, 1956; Glover, 1977; Glover & Sautter, 1977); and (j) a high level of self-initiated, task-oriented striving for excellence (Barron, 1963; Chambers, 1964; MacKinnon, 1965; Roe, 1952).

One personality trait that appears consistently in such lists is particularly relevant to the main hypothesis presented in this book—the intrinsic motivation hypothesis of creativity. This trait is independence, an absence of conformity in thinking and dependence on social approval. In a series of pioneering studies, Crutchfield (1955, 1959, 1962) found that individuals who had been identified as highly creative were much less likely to conform in the Asch situation than were those identified as less creative. Other research, ranging from creativity-training programs (Parnes & Meadow, 1963) to studies of misbehaving students (Kaltsounis & Higdon, 1977; Stone, 1980), has confirmed the finding that conformity to social pressure is negatively related to creativity. Most interesting for a social psychology of creativity, however, is some evidence suggesting that social pressures to conform can have general detrimental effects on creativity (Cashdan & Welsh, 1966; Torrance, 1967). Later, I will argue that various forms of social constraint can influence creative performance in much the same way that the various "uncreative" personality traits do.

Some creativity-relevant skills, then, depend on personality characteristics. Others, however, may be directly taught through training. And, as individuals gain experience with idea-generation, they may devise their own strategies for creative thinking. A great deal of previous research has investigated these elements, including work on creativity training programs such as brainstorming (Osborn, 1963) and synectics (Gordon, 1961), and research on the "creative personality" (e.g., Barron, 1955a; Cattell & Butcher, 1968; MacKinnon, 1962; Wallach & Kogan, 1965).

Task Motivation

Few theorists have given extensive attention to the role of motivational variables in creativity. There are some, however, who have suggested that creativity is most likely to appear under intrinsic motivation—a motivational state generated by the individual's reaction to intrinsic properties of the task, and not generated by extrinsic factors. Koestler (1964), for example, speculated that the highest forms of creativity are generated under conditions of freedom from control, since it is under these conditions that a person may most easily reach back into the "intuitive regions" of the mind. Koestler saw this regression to unconscious, playful levels of thought as essential for creative production.

Carl Rogers (1954) also speculated on the importance of reliance upon self and freedom from external control in creativity. One of three "inner conditions" that he deemed necessary for creativity is an internal locus of evaluation. With an internal locus, an individual is primarily concerned with self-evaluation of his work; the evaluation of others is only a secondary concern. In addition, Rogers proposed the absence of external evaluation as an environmental condition essential to fostering creativity.

Other psychologists have suggested that self-perceptions of personal freedom are necessary for creative thought and expression. As noted earlier, Crutchfield (1962) postulated a basic antipathy between conformity and creative thinking, asserting that "conformity pressures tend to elicit kinds of motivation in the individual that are incompatible with the creative process" (p. 121). According to Crutchfield, such conformity pressures can lead to extrinsic, "ego-involved" motivation, in which the creative solution is a means to an ulterior end. This contrasts sharply with intrinsic, "task-involved" motivation, in which the creative act is an end in itself. In describing the mechanism by which conformity pressure might be injurious to creative thinking, Crutchfield said:

> The outer pressure and inner compulsion to conform arouse extrinsic, ego-involved motives in the problem solver. His main efforts tend to become directed toward the goals of being accepted and rewarded by the group, of avoiding rejection and punishment. The solution of the problem itself becomes of secondary relevance, and his task-involved motivation diminishes. In being concerned with goals extrinsic to the task itself, and particularly as rendered anxious about potential threats in the situation, his cognitive processes become less flexible, his insights less sensitive. (p. 125)

These three theorists, working within philosophy, humanistic psychology, and social psychology, have each suggested that a freedom from extrinsic constraint will enhance creative thinking. This is the basic notion behind the inclusion of task motivation in the componential framework. I propose that intrinsic motivation is conducive to creativity, whereas extrinsic motivation is detrimental. Here, intrinsic motivation can be viewed as both a state and a trait (although this "trait" should not be thought of as general and pervasive, but specific to particular classes of activities). Individuals may have relatively enduring levels of interest in particular activities, but levels of interest may also be importantly influenced by social and environmental variables, as well.

Thus, within the componential formulation, task motivation includes two elements: the individual's baseline attitude toward the task (the "trait"), and the individual's perceptions of his reasons for undertaking the task in a given instance (the "state"). A baseline attitude toward the task is formed, quite simply, when the individual performs a cognitive assessment of the task and the degree to which it matches his existing preferences and interests. Perceptions of one's motivation for undertaking the task in a given instance, on the other hand, depend largely upon external social and environmental factors—specifically, the presence or absence of salient extrinsic constraints in the social environment. Extrinsic constraints are defined as factors that are intended to control or could be perceived as controlling the individual's performance on the task in a particular instance. As such, these constraints are extrinsic to the task itself; they are not an essential feature of task performance, but are introduced by other people. A salient extrinsic constraint is one whose controlling implications are clear to the individual during task engagement. In sum, then, such constraints should lead to decreases in intrinsic task motivation and, as a result, decreases in creativity. According to this formulation, creative performance may be seen as analogous to "latent learning"; it occurs primarily when task-irrelevant motivation (extrinsic motivation) is low (Kimble, 1961).

In addition to external constraints, internal factors, such as an individual's ability to cognitively minimize the salience of such extrinsic constraints, might also influence task motivation. Thus, the final level (and type) of motivation in a particular instance will vary from the baseline level of intrinsic motivation as a function of extrinsic constraints that may be present in the situation and the individual's strategies for dealing with these constraints.

The propositions on task motivation presented in this framework derive primarily from social-psychological notions of intrinsic motivation (deCharms, 1968; Deci, 1975; Lepper & Greene, 1978a). In these conceptualizations, a person is said to be intrinsically motivated to engage in an activity if that person views such engagement as an end in itself, and not as a means to some extrinsic goal. Most recent intrinsic motivation research has been concerned with the "overjustification" hypothesis, derived from the attribution theories of Bem (1972), Kelley (1967, 1973), and deCharms (1968). These theorists propose that, under certain conditions, there will be an inverse relationship between the salient external constraints imposed upon an individual's engagement in an activity and that individual's intrinsic motivation to perform that activity. Several studies, employing a variety of extrinsic constraints—including tangible reward for performance, surveillance, and externally imposed deadlines—have supported this hypothesis (e.g., Amabile, DeJong, & Lepper, 1976; Condry, 1977; Deci, 1971, 1972a, 1972b; Kruglanski, 1975; Lepper & Greene, 1975; Lepper, Greene, & Nisbett, 1973; Ross, 1975).

This discussion of prevailing social-psychological notions of intrinsic and extrinsic motivation betrays a bias that might well be unwarranted. Virtually all social-psychological theorists dealing with this question have proposed a cognitive explanation of the overjustification phenomenon: Initially interested in an activity, an individual who is led to engage in that activity in the presence of some salient extrinsic constraint will judge himself to be motivated by the constraint and not by his own interest. Empirical research has, in fact, produced data suggesting that attributions do mediate changes in interest (e.g., Kruglanski, Alon, & Lewis, 1972; Pittman, Cooper, & Smith, 1977). It will be made clear in subsequent chapters, however, that the evidence for viewing this process as *solely* cognitive is rather weak. Thus, despite the cognitive terminology I use to discuss the role of task motivation in the componential framework, it is important to assert that positive affect may be a critical component of intrinsic motivation and that negative affect may be a critical component of extrinsic motivation.

The inclusion of task motivation as an important component in this framework, along with propositions on the detrimental effects of extrinsic constraint, should not be taken to suggest that creative production is effortless, that it will (as some humanists suggest) flow spontaneously when the mind and body are most relaxed and unbothered. On the contrary, I propose that, while freedom from external pressure is most conducive to creativity, freedom from internal discipline and effortfulness can be detrimental. The creativity-relevant skills of disciplined effort are no less essential than an intrinsic orientation to the task.

In sum, I propose that any of a wide variety of extrinsic constraints will, by impairing intrinsic motivation, have detrimental effects on creative performance. Task motivation can be seen in this context as the most important determinant of the difference between what a person *can* do and what he *will* do. The former is determined by the level of domain-relevant and creativity-relevant skill; the latter is determined by these two in conjunction with an intrinsically motivated state.

A Componential Framework

A theory of creativity must describe how the components just presented might contribute to the creative process. Figure 4-2 presents a schematic representation of a framework that can be used to develop a theory of the creative process. This framework describes the way in which an individual might assemble and use information in attempting to arrive at a solution, response, or product. In information-processing terms, task motivation is responsible for initiating and sustaining the process. It determines whether the search for a solution will begin and whether it will continue, and it also determines some aspects of response generation. Domain-relevant skills are the material drawn upon during operation; they determine what pathways will be available during the search for a response, and what criteria will be used to assess the response possibilities that are generated. Creativity-relevant skills act as an executive controller during response generation, influencing the way in which the search for responses will proceed. In the figure, broken lines indicate the influence of the components on different stages of the creative process. Only the influences presumed to be the most important, however, are depicted.

The process outlined here is proposed to be the same for both high and low levels of creativity. Moreover, it is proposed that the level of creativity of a product or response will vary as a function of the levels of each of the three components.

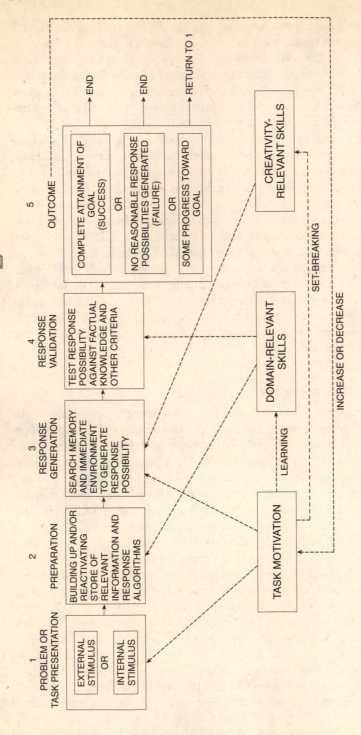

Figure 4.2. Componential framework of creativity. Broken lines indicate the influence of particular factors on others. Solid lines indicate the sequence of steps in the process. Only direct and primary influences are depicted here.

Each component is necessary, and none is sufficient for creativity in and of itself. Thus, although this framework cannot be considered a detailed mathematical model of the creative process, it is, in a general sense, a multiplicative model. No component may be absent if some recognizable level of creativity is to be produced. The levels of the three components for an individual's attempt at a given task determine that individual's overall level of creativity on that task.

A Sequence of Response Generation

The initial step in the proposed sequence is the presentation of the task to be engaged in or the problem to be solved. Task motivation has an important influence at this stage: If the individual has a high level of intrinsic interest in the task, this interest will be sufficient to engage the process. Under these circumstances, the individual, in essence, poses the problem to himself. In other situations, however, the problem is presented by another individual. It is possible, of course, for someone else to pose a problem to us that we find particularly interesting. It is likely, however, that in many cases an externally posed problem is not intrinsically interesting to the individual. Getzels and his colleagues (Getzels, 1975; Getzels & Csikszentmihalyi, 1976) have suggested that "discovered problems" are more likely to be solved creatively than are "presented problems," and many theorists have argued that problem-discovery is an important part of much creative activity (e.g., Campbell, 1960; Souriau, 1881).

The second stage may be considered preparatory to actual generation of responses or solutions. At this point, the individual builds up or reactivates a store of information relevant to the problem or task, including a knowledge of response algorithms for working problems in the domain in question. In the case where domain-relevant skills are impoverished at the outset, this stage may be quite a long one during which a great deal of learning takes place (Bain, 1874; Mach, 1896; Poincare, 1924; Souriau, 1881). On the other hand, if the domain-relevant skills are already sufficiently rich to afford an ample set of possible pathways to explore during task engagement, the reactivation of this already-stored set of information and algorithms may be almost instantaneous, occupying little real time. In this instance, preparation can be considered as a kind of "warming up" (Wickelgren, 1979), a calling up of relevant ideas.

It is in the third stage that the level of novelty of the product or response is determined. Here the individual generates response possibilities by searching through the available pathways and exploring features of the environment that are relevant to the task at hand. During each "run" through the sequence, the individual follows a particular cognitive pathway to a solution or response. Both creativity-relevant skills and task motivation play a role at this stage. The existing repertoire of creativity-relevant skills will determine the flexibility with which cognitive pathways are explored, the attention given to particular aspects of the task, and the extent to which a particular pathway is followed in pursuit of a solution. In addition, creativity-relevant skills can influence the subgoals of the response generation stage by determining whether a large number of response possibilities will be generated through a temporary suspension of critical judgment or a decision to keep response options open. This in itself may be important for creativity, since there is some evidence of a positive relationship between quality and quantity of creative ideas (Milgram, Milgram, Rosenbloom, & Rabkin, 1978). Task motivation, if it is intrinsic rather than extrinsic, can add to the existing repertoire of skills a willingness to "play" with this particular task—to take risks, and to attend to aspects of the environment that might not be obviously relevant to attainment of a solution.

When a task is heuristic, necessitating a search of response pathways, what determines which pathways are explored? Campbell (1960) has suggested that possibilities are produced by a blind or random process. Certainly, the search can be narrowed down by various methods. But, Campbell suggests, some amount of blind search is always required with tasks of this nature. The more possibilities there are to be explored and the better the strategies for exploring them rapidly, the greater the likelihood of producing a novel yet appropriate response. Some degree of chance, however, is always an element (Hogarth, 1980).

Domain-relevant skills again figure prominently in the fourth stage, the validation of the response possibility that has been chosen on a particular trial. Using domain-relevant techniques of analysis, the response possibility is tested for correctness or appropriateness against the knowledge and assessment criteria included within domain-relevant skills. Thus, it is this stage that determines the extent to which the product or response will be useful, correct, or valuable—the second response characteristic that, together with novelty, is essential in order for the product to be considered "creative" according to the conceptual definition proposed earlier.

The fifth stage represents the decision-making that must be carried out on the basis of the test performed in stage 4. If the test has been passed perfectly, if there is complete attainment of the original goal, the process terminates. If there is complete failure, if no reasonable response possibility has been generated, the process will also terminate. If there is some progress toward the goal—if at least a reasonable response possibility has been generated or if, in Simon's (1978) terms, there is some evidence of "getting warmer"—the process returns to the first stage, where the problem is once again posed. Whether there is failure or success or partial success, information gained from the trial will be added to the existing repertoire of domain-relevant skills. Thus, it might be expected that prior experience with a problem will allow greater creativity in solving it, and that more creative responses will occur relatively late in any given process of task engagement. There is some empirical evidence to support both of these propositions (Milgram & Rabkin, 1980; Schubert, 1977). If task motivation remains sufficiently high, another trial will be attempted, perhaps with information gained from the previous trial being used to pose the problem in a somewhat different form. If, however, task motivation has dropped below some critical minimum, the process will terminate.

As tasks become more complex, the application of this outline to the production of creative responses on those tasks also becomes increasingly more complex. Work on any given task or problem may involve a long series of loops through the process, until success in a final product is achieved. Indeed, work on what seems to be a single task may actually involve a series of rather different subtasks, each with its own separate "solution." These subtasks may be hierarchically arranged, and the completion of any single subtask may in itself involve several runs through the process until success is finally achieved. For example, the superordinate goal of "writing a poem" involves several subtasks, including finding a theme, deciding on a meter to use, choosing major and minor guiding images, inventing metaphors and similes, writing particular words, phrases, and lines. Each of these can be seen as a task or a subtask whose achievement is necessary for successful poetry-writing. Thus, success on a task depends in part upon the outcomes of subtasks and the difficulty of achieving success on those subtasks.

Range of applicability. Despite its description in information-processing terms, the componential framework should be applicable not only to problem-solving creativity (in mathematics and the sciences, for example) but also to artistic creativity (in literature or the graphic arts, for example). Thus, "problem" refers to any task that an individual sets for himself or has set before him. "Solution" can be taken to mean any idea for successfully completing that task, whether it takes the form of an idea for a research hypothesis or an idea for a sonnet. And a solution is "correct" to the extent that it is an appropriate response to the initial problem.

The componential framework is a general model of the process of task engagement. As such, it not only describes the way in which creative or uncreative responses to heuristic tasks may be generated, it also describes the way in which responses to algorithmic tasks may be generated. If a task is purely algorithmic, the solution may be arrived at in a straightforward manner by applying a particular algorithm. If the algorithm exists among the individual's domain-relevant skills (stage 2), stage 3 consists of following that one particular cognitive pathway to the solution.[5] Thus, with algorithmic tasks, the componential framework may still be applied; the difference is that, in this instance, there is no room for exploration of various pathways, no room for novelty, and, hence, no room for creativity.

Feedback and Interaction Between Components

Within the componential framework, the outcome of a particular trial—whether success or failure or partial success—can directly influence task motivation,

---

[5] Of course, if the algorithm is not part of the individual's repertoire, the task must be considered heuristic for that individual. In this case, there are three possibilities: (1) no response will be generated, (2) an inappropriate algorithm will be applied and an incorrect response generated, or (3) the individual will invent the correct algorithm; such an outcome would, clearly, be considered creative.

thereby setting up a feedback cycle through which future engagement in the same or similar tasks can be affected. If complete success has been achieved, there will be no motivation to undertake exactly the same task again, but in most instances, intrinsic motivation for similar tasks within the domain should increase. This proposition must be qualified, however, by reference to the nature of the original task. If that task was a simple one with little challenge, intrinsic interest in similar tasks will most probably not increase. The role of challenge in intrinsic motivation has been stressed by several previous theorists (e.g., Berlyne, 1965; Csikszentmihalyi, 1975; Hunt, 1965; Malone, 1981; White, 1959).

If complete failure was encountered on the trial—if no reasonable responses were generated—intrinsic motivation for the task should decrease. In other words, motivation will decrease when the outcome of the test reveals that the problem-solver is essentially no closer to the goal than when he began. If partial success has been met, intrinsic motivation will increase when the problem solver has the sense of "getting warmer" in approaching the goal.

This proposition that process outcome can influence task motivation is compatible with Harter's (1978) theory of effectance motivation. Harter built upon White's (1959) definition of the "urge toward competence," a motivation "which impels the organism toward competence and is satisfied by a feeling of efficacy" (Harter, 1978, p. 34). According to Harter's theory, failure at mastery attempts will lead eventually to decreases in intrinsic motivation and striving for competence. However, success at a challenging task will lead to intrinsic gratification, feelings of efficacy, and increases in intrinsic motivation—which, in turn, will lead to more mastery attempts. In essential agreement with Harter, a number of social-psychological theorists (e.g., deCharms, 1968; Deci, 1975; Deci & Ryan, 1980; Lepper & Greene, 1978b) have proposed that success—confirmation of competence—will lead to increased task motivation, while failure—a confirmation of incompetence—will have the opposite effect.

Through this influence on task motivation, outcomes can also indirectly affect domain-relevant and creativity-relevant skills. A higher level of motivation may lead to additional learning about the task and related subjects, thereby increasing domain-relevant skills. The proposition that task motivation can also influence creativity-relevant skills fits well with the intrinsic motivation hypotheses of several theorists (e.g., Csikszentmihalyi, 1975; Deci, 1975). The intrinsically motivated state, which I propose as the task motivation most conducive to creative performance, is typically characterized as one in which the individual adopts an attitude of intellectual playfulness and total absorption in the activity at hand. It is reasonable to suppose that this state would be most conducive to the set-breaking cognitive flexibility, the risk-taking that appear to be essential for high levels of creativity. Moreover, a sustained high level of intrinsic task motivation may make set-breaking and cognitive risk-taking more probable and more habitual, thereby increasing the permanent repertoire of creativity skills.

Relationship to Previous Theories

The componential conceptualization of creativity integrates several notions proposed by previous theorists. For example, as early as 1950, Guilford suggested that skills, personality characteristics, and motivational level are all important determinants of creative behavior:

> Creative abilities determine whether the individual has the power to exhibit creative behavior to a noteworthy degree. Whether or not the individual who has the requisite abilities will actually produce results of a creative nature will depend upon his motivational and temperamental traits. (Guilford, 1950, p. 444)

Although this statement is vague, in that it does not specify what the requisite abilities or traits might be, and although it does not consider social/environmental influences on motivation, Guilford does present the kernel of a componential model of creativity.

The sequence outlined in Figure 4-2 resembles models of the creative process proposed by previous theorists. For example, Helmholtz (Whiting, 1958) described the process as consisting of saturation (gathering facts), incubation (considering material in new combinations), and illumination (a glimpse of the solution). In perhaps the best-known description of the creative process, Wallas (1926) added a fourth element to arrive at this sequence: preparation, incubation, illumination, and verification (testing the validity of the final solution).[6] Stein (1967) described the creative process as consisting of three stages: hypothesis formation, hypothesis testing, and communication. And Hogarth (1980) proposed four stages: preparation, production, evaluation, and implementation; in addition, he described sets of aids and barriers to each of the stages. Taken together, these diverse theoretical descriptions of creativity present an outline of the creative process that is similar to the sequence depicted in Figure 4-2. It begins with a preparatory stage of thought on some problem, moves on to the generation of possible solutions, and ends with some evaluation of the solution(s) generated.

In addition to the general sequence, there are a number of specific elements in the componential framework that can be found in the writing of previous theorists. For example, Cropley (1967) discusses the importance of cognitive styles, which appear in the model as creativity-relevant skills; Getzels and Jackson (1962) point to the importance of some minimal level of intellectual skills; MacKinnon (1975) suggests the personality characteristics that may be most important to creativity; Torrance (1962) outlines the features of "creative environments"; Maddi (1975) points to the importance of self-discipline and concentration of effort;

---

[6] This final step, it seems was first suggested by the mathematician Poincaré (1924) in a lecture on mathematical creativity.

Parnes (1975) enumerates several techniques that can be used to increase the level of creativity-relevant skills; and Bruner (1962) maintains that creative activity requires a use of heuristics rather than well-worn algorithms.

Some Implications of the Model

The intelligence-creativity question. The componential framework suggests an answer for the intelligence-creativity controversy that has, in the past, been prominent in the creativity literature. A number of studies have shown a nonhomoscedasticity of variance in the bivariate distribution of IQ and creativity scores (Barron, 1961; Getzels & Jackson, 1962; Schubert, 1973; Wallach, 1971). At low levels of intelligence, there appears to be an almost uniformly low level of creativity. However, at higher levels of intelligence, all levels of creativity are found. Here, the IQ-creativity correlation is quite low. Most reviews of the literature support this finding (e.g., Stein, 1968; Wallach, 1971), although there is some question about the possibility of identifying a threshold of IQ below which high levels of creativity cannot be found (cf. Child & Croucher, 1977).

The perennial question has been, are creativity and intelligence basically the same thing, or are they not? The componential conceptualization suggests, simply, that intelligence (as typically conceived) is a component of creative ability. It is a necessary, but not a sufficient, contributing factor. Some minimum level of intelligence is required for creative performance because intelligence is, presumably, directly related to the acquisition of domain-relevant skills and the application of creativity heuristics. However, there are factors necessary for creativity that would not be assessed by traditional intelligence tests: intrinsic motivation toward the task, for example, and personality dispositions conducive to deep levels of concentration or uninhibited intellectual risk-taking.

Age and creativity. The componential framework can be useful in suggesting an explanation for the vastly different average ages at which peak creativity is achieved in different domains of endeavor. The key to this explanation is that certain domain-relevant skills may be relatively less crucial for creative work in some domains than in others. For example, in philosophy and the natural sciences, an enormous amount of formal and informal education is necessary for an individual to even begin to produce significantly creative work. By contrast, a relatively low level of exposure to formal training in music might be sufficient to allow an individual to compose creative work if his other skills and task motivation were high.

Thus, it is not surprising that the average age of outstanding creativity in the arts is reached in the 30s and 40s, while the average age of outstanding creativity in philosophy is reached in the 60s (Dennis, 1966; Lehman, 1953). Similarly, writers of creative poetry tend to be younger than writers of creative prose. Simonton (1975c) explains this finding by suggesting that literary "maturity," marked by lexical and syntactical sophistication, is required for writing outstanding prose.

Mozart was capable at the age of 6 of composing music that is still considered creative because his innate domain-relevant skills and creativity-relevant skills were so outstanding that, coupled with a high level of interest in music, they provided him with all he really required to do creative work in his domain. When his experience grew, his creativity increased, as would be predicted by the multiplicative nature of the componential model. Indeed, although creative achievement might be seen at a relatively young age among composers of music, Simonton (1980b) has found that musicians' *peak* creativity appears later in life.

Incubation and illumination. A number of creative individuals have described the phenomenon of incubation on a difficult problem, followed by an apparent flash of illumination. During incubation, they cease consciously working on the problem; during illumination, the solution appears to them unexpectedly, with surprising suddenness. (See, for example, Poincare, 1924.) Simon (1966) has proposed an information-processing account of these phenomena, suggesting that they are the result of a process of selective forgetting. According to this explanation, solution efforts are guided by a hierarchy or "tree" of goals and subgoals. If a subgoal is reached, it can be forgotten, but the tree of unattained goals is preserved. According to Simon, this goal-tree is retained in relatively short-term memory, but the information that is gained during attempts to solve the problem is retained in long-term memory. If the problem is set aside for a while, parts of the original goal-tree will fade. When the individual returns to the problem, he can retrieve from long-term memory the store of information gained on previous attempts and use it to construct a new and more directly useful goal-tree. Since this new set of goals is based on better information, the time to solution is expected to be faster.

There is nothing in Simon's account that is incompatible with the componential model. However, the componential model suggests an additional mechanism for incubation and illumination. This motivational mechanism may operate in tandem with the previously proposed informational mechanisms, or it may produce these phenomena in the absence of selective forgetting. In many cases, the passage of time during the "incubation" period may cause the social context in which the original problem was posed to become less salient. Specifically, if salient extrinsic constraints were imposed on the individual's initial attempts at solving the problem, those constraints might be expected to become less salient over time. Thus, when the individual returns to work on the problem, intrinsic motivation might be restored and creativity might be more likely as a result.

Playfulness and involvement. A number of introspective accounts describe the phenomenology of creativity as marked by deep involvement in the activity at hand, coupled with a kind of intellectual playfulness. For example, Einstein (1949) described creativity as "combinatorial play." Tchaikovsky described the consuming involvement in his work that accompanied a creative idea:

It would be vain to try to put into words that immeasurable sense of bliss which comes over me directly a new idea awakens in me and begins to assume a definite form. I forget everything and behave like a madman. Everything within me starts pulsing and quivering; hardly have I begun the sketch ere one thought follows another. In the midst of this magic process it frequently happens that some external interruption wakes me from my somnambulistic state . . . Dreadful, indeed, are such interruptions. (1906, pp. 57–58)

The propositions on task motivation within the componential model offer a reasonable account of these phenomena. As I will argue later, the intrinsically motivated state is essential for high levels of creativity because, under extrinsic motivation, some attention is directed toward the attainment of the extrinsic goal and away from the exploration of new pathways. Moreover, if intrinsic motivation is sufficiently undermined by extrinsic constraint, task engagement will be avoided altogether. In contrast, under high intrinsic motivation, most of the individual's attention will be directed toward the task itself, toward an exploration of its details and of possibly relevant aspects of the task environment. The higher the level of intrinsic motivation, the deeper this concentration on the task. Finally, if we can define task engagement for extrinsic reasons as "work," and task engagement for intrinsic reasons as "play," it will be expected that, phenomenologically, states of highly creative activity will seem like play.

Predictions of Creativity

Given particular levels of each of the three components, the componential framework of creativity can be used to make qualitative predictions of the outcomes of task engagement. Of primary importance, of course, it can predict the level of creativity of the product, response, or solution. In addition, however, it can predict certain other characteristics of responses (such as technical correctness) as well as some features of future task engagement.

The propositions of the componential model can be represented as six general principles guiding predictions. The first, overriding principle is that the components combine in a multiplicative fashion. The higher the levels of each of the components, the more creative the product.

Second, the level of domain-relevant skills primarily influences the appropriateness or correctness of the response; these skills determine the initial set of pathways to be searched for a solution as well as the final validation of the response possibilities that are generated.

Third, the level of creativity-relevant skills primarily determines the novelty of the response. Through the operation of creativity heuristics, attention can be directed to novel or nonobvious aspects of the task or the environment, aspects that can lead to the discovery of novel solutions. In addition, a cognitive style that can deal adequately with complexities will make higher levels of creativity possible, as will a working style characterized by perseverance when the initial pathways explored are not fruitful.

Fourth, the level and type of task motivation not only determine whether an individual will engage in the task, but they also influence the novelty of the response in much the same way as creativity-relevant skills. If intrinsic motivation is high, the individual will engage in the task. If it is low, he will only engage in the task if sufficient extrinsic motivation is present. If the individual is induced to engage in the activity under conditions of low intrinsic motivation, he may exhibit low creativity even if he has a store of previously learned creativity heuristics. In an attempt to attain the hierarchically superior extrinsic goal, the individual may rely upon well-worn response algorithms which do not require attention to nonobvious aspects of the task or the environment. Conversely, even if the individual does not have a permanent repertoire of creativity heuristics, an intrinsic task motivation may accommodate set-breaking and the exploration of new cognitive pathways. Thus, even if the individual has not previously learned the heuristic of looking for counterintuitive response possibilities, the "playful" approach to a task engendered by high levels of intrinsic motivation might eventually lead the individual to generate nonobvious responses anyway.

Fifth, the process of task engagement is cyclical. Assuming the absence of extrinsic constraints in the future, the primary determinants of future task engagement are the initial level of task motivation and success or failure at initial runs through the process.

Sixth, the level of intrinsic task motivation after initial runs through the process can influence subsequent levels of domain-relevant and creativity-relevant skills. High task motivation can lead to learning in both components. Higher levels of these components will, of course, make creativity more probable in the future.

Table 4-1 outlines the predictions that would be made for all possible combinations of two extreme levels of each of the components. In this presentation of predictions, the task is assumed to be a heuristic one. Obviously, the level designations of the components are only relative. Moreover, the outline does not include the case where one of the components is absent entirely. In this instance, the level of creativity of the product (if there were in fact any product) would be judged as essentially zero.

It is possible to construct familiar scenarios corresponding to each of the cases described in Table 4-1. Case A describes the "star" in any field of endeavor. This individual is extremely well-educated in the domain in question, both in terms of factual knowledge and technical skills ("tools of the trade"). In addition, he may have particular talents that are relevant to work in this area. This category includes, for example, the poet who has a masterful command of vocabulary, grammar, and syntax, along with an ability to vividly recapture visual, auditory, and kinesthetic images; it also includes the well-schooled research scientist who possesses an extraordinary memory for detail. Moreover, these individuals have a store of heuristics for generating novel ideas, a cognitive style that can deal well with complexities and ambiguities, and a set of work habits that are conducive to

Table 4-1. Predictions Derived from the Componential Framework

Case	Initial Level of Domain-Relevant Skills	Permanent Repertoire of Creativity-Relevant Skills	Level of Intrinsic Task Motivation	Product or Response Characteristics[a]	Future Engagement in Similar Tasks
A	High	High	High	Judged high in creativity.[b] Overall, a "significant" work.	High interest in future engagement. Similar performance expected.
B	High	High	Low	If person engages in task, product judged moderate in creativity.	Low interest in future engagement. Similar performance expected.[c]
C	High	Low	High	Product judged moderate in creativity. "Predictable," "correct" responses. Creativity not expected to be as low as in case D, because high task motivation should lead to a temporarily high (or at least moderate) level of the creativity-relevant skills of set-breaking and cognitive risk-taking.	Moderate interest in future engagement. Improved creativity would be expected, since the temporary creativity-relevant skills could be incorporated into a permanent repertoire.
D	Low	Low	Low	If person engages in task, product judged low in creativity. "Predictable," "correct" responses.	Low interest in future engagement. Similar performance expected.[c]

E	Low	High	High	Product judged moderate in creativity. Responses will tend to be "eccentric" or "bizarre," with little significance.	Moderate interest in future engagement. Improved creativity would be expected, since the high level of motivation could lead to learning of domain-relevant skills.
F	Low	High	Low	If person engages in task, product judged relatively low in creativity. Responses will tend to be "eccentric" or "bizarre," with little significance.	Low interest in future engagement. Similar performance expected.[c]
G	Low	Low	High	Product judged relatively low in creativity. Some novelty expected, since high task motivation should lead to a temporarily high (or at least moderate) level of the creativity-relevant skills of set-breaking and cognitive risk-taking. "Eccentric" or "bizarre" responses.	Moderate interest in future engagement. Improved creativity would be expected, since the temporary creativity-relevant skills could be incorporated into a permanent repertoire, and since a high level of motivation could lead to learning of domain-relevant skills.
H	Low	Low	Low	If person engages in task, product judged low in creativity. Generally poor performance.	Low interest in future engagement. Similar performance expected.[c]

[a] For this example, the task is presumed to be a heuristic one for which domain-relevant skills are moderately important.

[b] All statements about creativity judgment refer to independent assessments by appropriate observers, where the judgments are made relative to all products in the domain. Relative judgments within a subset of products can also be predicted from the componential model.

[c] This is the performance to be expected if the person is induced (by external constraints) to engage in the task.

a well-disciplined concentration of effort. In Case A, these individuals are working on tasks that hold a high level of intrinsic interest for them. They can be expected to produce work judged high in creativity and generally "significant." Their
level of interest in the task (or similar tasks, once the one at hand is completed in
a wholly satisfactory manner) will remain high, and creativity can be expected in
the future.

Case B describes a situation where such talented, well-schooled individuals are
induced to work on a task that does not hold intrinsic interest for them. This
might be the case, for example, where an outstanding artist is commissioned to
produce a painting on a theme of little interest to her. Here, creativity would not
be expected to be nearly as high as in Case A, and there would be little interest in
future engagement in similar tasks unless extrinsic incentives were once again
provided.

In Case C, the individual has learned all the necessary domain-relevant skills
and has a high level of interest in the task, but lacks creativity-relevant skills. This
might describe an intelligent student of music who, much to her delight, is allowed to undertake her first composition. However, she knows no rules of thumb
for generating themes that differ significantly from those she has learned so well.
As a result, her composition is relatively low in creativity, although her high level
of intrinsic interest might lead her to "play" with the elements of composition
long enough to discover some set-breaking techniques. On subsequent attempts,
these techniques, now part of her permanent repertoire, would be used more
readily and easily, resulting in higher levels of creativity.

In Case D, such an individual begins with a *low* level of intrinsic interest in the
task; for example, perhaps she was assigned the chore of composing for academic
evaluation. Here, creativity would be expected to be even lower (although the response would be formally "correct"), and subsequent interest would be quite low.

Case E describes the rare situation where an individual who knows very little
about a given domain is nonetheless interested in a task within that domain and
applies a set of creativity heuristics to performance of that task. The classic dilettante would fall into this category—the individual who enthusiastically attacks a
problem with little expertise and, because of an ability to produce unusual responses, achieves a result that is considered merely bizarre or eccentric. Thus, although novelty of response is high, appropriateness is low; the result is a product
judged only moderate in creativity. It is possible, though, that such an individual
might be sufficiently interested in the task to learn the requisite domain-relevant
skills for application to subsequent work in the domain.

In Case F, an individual with an impressive store of creativity-relevant skills is
induced to engage in an activity in which he has little interest or expertise. This
would, perhaps, describe a person who, having distinguished himself for creativity in his own field (for example, science) was induced to work in a quite unrelated area (for example, university administration). Attempts at creative responses
in such a situation would lead to results that were unusual or strange, with little

significance. Because of the low level of initial motivation and the lack of success, subsequent interest would be low and similar performances could be expected in the future.

In Case G, the dilettante (who is interested in an area of which he has little knowledge) does not even possess a store of creativity-relevant skills. Responses would be judged low on creativity but, because the high level of interest might in itself lead to playful exploration of ideas, responses would have some measure of novelty. Due to the lack of domain-relevant skills, however, they would tend to be bizarre, inappropriate responses. If motivation remained sufficiently high, improved creativity might be expected in the future as a result of the learning of creativity-relevant and domain-relevant skills.

Finally, Case H describes an individual who is essentially "out of his element." In this situation, a person lacking in creativity-relevant skills is induced to engage in an activity in which his expertise and his interest are both low. Responses will be judged low in creativity, and subsequent performance, if it could be induced by extrinsic constraints, would be similarly poor.

The research presented and reviewed in this book considers social-environmental influences on all three components of creative production, but particularly on task motivation. Thus, the qualitative predictions from Table 4-1 that are most relevant to the issues considered here are those contrasting Case A with Case B, C with D, E with F, and G with H. In other words, these are the pairs of cases where domain-relevant and creativity-relevant skills are essentially equivalent, but task motivation differs. Creativity of final products and responses should differ as a direct result.

The Intrinsic Motivation Hypothesis of Creativity

Perhaps the most important difference between the componential framework of creativity and previous formulations is the prominence given to task motivation. Most of the research presented in this book directly tests or is relevant to an evaluation of the intrinsic motivation hypothesis of creativity: *the intrinsically motivated state is conducive to creativity, whereas the extrinsically motivated state is detrimental.* Because this hypothesis is so central to the social psychology of creativity, it is important to consider its implications in some detail.

Intuitively, the intrinsic motivation hypothesis of creativity derives from suggestions that a nonconstrained social environment is most conducive to creativity (Wallach & Kogan, 1965). Consider, for example, Einstein's (1949) recollections about the effects of social constraints on his scientific creativity:

> In this field [Physics], however, I soon learned to scent out that which was able to lead to fundamentals and to turn aside from everything else, from the multitude of things which clutter up the mind and divert it from the essential. The hitch in this was, of course, the fact that one had to cram all this stuff into one's mind for the examinations, whether one liked it or not. This coercion had such a deterring effect upon me that, after I had passed

the final examination, I found the consideration of any scientific problems distasteful to me for an entire year. In justice I must add, moreover, that in Switzerland we had to suffer far less under such coercion, which smothers every truly scientific impulse, than is the case in many another locality. There were altogether only two examinations; aside from these, one could just about do as one pleased. This was especially the case if one had a friend, as did I, who attended the lectures regularly and who worked over their content conscientiously. This gave one freedom in the choice of pursuits until a few months before the examination, a freedom which I enjoyed to a great extent and have gladly taken into the bargain the bad conscience connected with it as by far the lesser evil. (pp. 18–19)

Intrinsic motivation has been variously defined by a number of theorists. Harlow (1950) used the term to refer to the interest his monkeys showed in puzzle manipulation. Taylor (1960), in presenting his "information processing theory of motivation," suggested an inherent interest in cognitively engaging tasks. A similar notion was developed by Hunt (1965), who defined intrinsic motivation as "motivation inherent in information processing and action." In a discussion specifically focused on creativity, Crutchfield (1962) aptly described the intrinsically and extrinsically motivated states:

> What motives impel the creative act? Is the creative act merely a means in the service of other ends, or is it sought as an end in itself? How does the nature of the motivation for a given creative act affect the likelihood of its achievement?
>
> The person may be driven to create by needs for material gain, such as money or promotion in his job. He may be driven by needs for status or for affiliation with others. He may be driven by needs for self-enhancement or self-defense. In all these cases, the particular need has merely extrinsic and arbitrary relation to the inherent nature of the specific creative task. The achievement of the creative solution is a *means* to an ulterior end, rather than the end in itself. We may refer to such cases as ones of *extrinsic, ego-involved* motivation for creative thinking.
>
> In clear contrast is that motive which has to do with the intrinsic value in the attaining of the creative solution itself. Here the problem is inherently challenging, the person is "caught" by it and compelled to be immersed in it, and with achievement of a solution the creator is "by joy possessed." Like Harlow's monkeys, who solve problems for the "fun" of it (1950), the creative man may invent a new device, paint a picture, or construct a scientific theory for the sheer intrinsic pleasures involved. . . . This, then, is the kind of motivation in which the creative act is an *end*, not a means. We may refer to this as *intrinsic, task-involved* motivation for creative thinking. (pp. 121–122)

Crutchfield goes on to propose that intrinsic motivation will lead to higher levels of creativity than extrinsic motivation. Indeed, some personality data he collected (1961) do suggest that high levels of intrinsic motivation characterize the work of notably creative persons.

Recently, social psychologists (e.g., Lepper, Greene, & Nisbett, 1973) have defined intrinsic motivation more cognitively: an individual is intrinsically motivated if he perceives himself as engaging in an activity primarily out of his own interest in it; he is extrinsically motivated if he perceives himself as engaging in the activity in order to obtain some extrinsic goal. All of these definitions, however, share the same elements: Persons who engage in an activity for its own sake are intrinsically motivated; persons who engage in an activity to achieve some goal external to task engagement are extrinsically motivated. I hypothesize that these differences in motivation can lead to significant differences in creative performance.

Theoretically, the intrinsic motivation hypothesis of creativity derives from the social-psychological theories of motivation discussed earlier. These theories have primarily been concerned with the way in which salient extrinsic constraints can undermine subsequent intrinsic interest to perform an activity. Some theorists, however, have recently begun to speculate about the effects of extrinsic constraint upon *immediate* performance. The conceptualization that most directly deals with creative performance is that of McGraw (1978), who suggests that performance on algorithmic tasks should be enhanced by increases in extrinsic motivation, but performance on heuristic tasks (creativity tasks) should be adversely affected. Lepper and Greene (1978a) propose a "means-end" analysis of task motivation, arguing that a person will pay attention to those aspects of the task that are necessary to attain the goal (such as simply finishing), but may neglect other aspects (such as novelty of response). Kruglanski and his colleagues (1977) present a "minimax" formulation of task behavior that is compatible with these notions. In this conceptualization, a person working under an "exogenous" (extrinsic) motivation may adopt a minimax strategy, in which he would "strive to do the least possible of the task for the most possible of the reward" (p. 142). Presumably, under these conditions, creativity would suffer unless it was required for achievement of the reward, and the individual knew what operations would constitute a "creative" performance.

It is important to consider the relationship between intrinsic and extrinsic motivation. Although many organizational theories of job satisfaction include the common assumption that the two forms of motivation are additive (e.g., Porter & Lawler, 1968; Vroom, 1964), social psychological theories propose that they interact, with high levels of extrinsic motivation precluding high levels of intrinsic motivation (e.g., Calder & Staw, 1975; Lepper et al., 1973). In this view, if a task is intrinsically interesting, the imposition of salient extrinsic constraints on task engagement will lead to the self-perception that one is performing that task primarily to attain the extrinsic goal. Intrinsic motivation will decrease accordingly. Although there is considerable empirical evidence to support this hydraulic view of motivation (cf. Calder & Staw, 1975), it is possible that, if we consider affective as well as cognitive consequences of task engagement and extrinsic constraint, we might find some conditions under which an additive model would apply. I will return to this notion in greater length in Chapter 6.

There has been little previous research directly examining the intrinsic motivation hypothesis of creativity. In the following chapters, I will review that research and present my own work on the problem. Before presenting evidence of a detrimental effect of social constraint on creativity, however, it is necessary to consider more closely the mechanism by which motivational orientation might influence creativity. In proposing a mechanism by which this social-psychological phenomenon occurs, I will rely on conceptualizations of algorithms, heuristics, and attention, from cognitive psychology, and conceptualizations of individual differences, from personality psychology.

The Operation of Motivational Effects on Creativity

Algorithms, heuristics, and attention. Cognitive psychology provides notions that can be useful in proposing a mechanism by which task motivation influences response generation. Simon (1967b) has postulated that the most important function of motivation is the control of attention. He proposes that motivation determines which goal hierarchy will be activated at any given time, and suggests that the more intense the motivation to achieve a goal, the less attention will be paid to aspects of the environment that are seemingly irrelevant to achieving that goal. This proposition can explain the consistent finding that incidental or latent learning is impaired by the offer of reward for task performance (e.g., Kimble, 1961; Spence, 1956). It can also explain the detrimental effects of extrinsic constraint on creativity.

Extrinsically motivated behavior is narrowly directed toward achieving the extrinsic goal that has been imposed, whether that goal be attaining a reward, meeting a deadline, achieving the approval of an observer, or obtaining a positive evaluation from an expert. In order for a creative response to be produced, however, it is often necessary to temporarily "step away" from the perceived goal (Newell et al., 1962), to direct attention toward seemingly incidental aspects of the task and the environment. The more single-mindedly a goal is pursued, the less likely it may be that alternative solution paths will be explored.

There is some indirect evidence to support this notion. In one study (Ward, 1969), children generated ideas in environmentally barren settings (empty rooms) or environmentally rich settings (rooms containing objects and pictures providing cues to possible answers). Highly creative children performed significantly better in the cue-rich environment than in the barren environment, suggesting that environmental scanning may be an important creativity-relevant skill. Other research with children supports this finding (Friedman, Raymond, & Feldhusen, 1978). In addition, there is some intriguing empirical evidence from the animal literature that high levels of food-directed motivation lead animals to ignore crucial aspects of the environment in problem-solving (Birch, 1945).

In a sense, then, the difference between extrinsic and intrinsic motivation—for the purposes of a conceptualization of creativity—can be seen as the difference between divided and undivided attention to the task itself and task-relevant information. The extreme state of undivided attention to the task itself under high levels of intrinsic motivation is aptly described by Csikszentmihalyi (1978): "a contraction of the perceptual field," a "heightened concentration on the task at hand." Attentional capacity in humans is quite limited (cf. Simon, 1967b); an extrinsically motivated individual will direct at least some of his limited attention to the contingency and his progress toward meeting it (Lepper & Greene, 1978a). As a result, extrinsically motivated people will be less able than intrinsically motivated people to devote complete attention to the task and task-relevant aspects of the environment. In short, an extrinsic motivation will decrease the probability that the creativity heuristics of exploration, set-breaking, and risk-taking will be applied. There will be a heavy reliance upon response algorithms that already exist within the store of domain-relevant skills.

Individual differences in response to constraints. There are clear and nontrivial differences between individuals in the extent to which the imposition of extrinsic constraints will undermine creativity. Particular individuals might be more or less "immune" to such constraints in a wide range of activities or in certain narrowly specified activities. Indeed, their observable creativity might actually seem to be enhanced by extrinsic constraints. For example, Watson and Crick (see Watson, 1968) were certainly cognizant of the tangible and social rewards that would accrue to anyone describing the structure of the DNA molecule. They did, nonetheless, produce clearly creative work.

One determinant of differences in response to constraints might be the individual's degree of familiarity with a given task—a domain-relevant skill. Over time, as successful experience with a particular class of tasks is accrued, algorithms may be developed from heuristics. That is, general approaches to searching possible solution pathways in the domain may be specified at a sufficient level of detail that they become algorithms. They can, in the future, be applied more or less by rote in the applicable domain. Thus, the production of novel and appropriate responses can become relatively routine for someone with a great deal of successful experience in the domain in question. Indeed, although these responses would be called "creative" by appropriate observers, such cases lie on a boundary where the definition of creativity becomes unclear. In these instances, the tasks are heuristic for nearly everyone, since the path to the solution is not at all straightforward. But for an individual with a great deal of successful experience in the domain, these tasks may actually have become algorithmic.

This, then, is one condition under which creativity might be seen even in the face of salient extrinsic constraints: The extrinsic goal involves finding a "creative" solution or response, *and* the individual already has algorithms for achieving a solution that will be so judged. In this case, the divided attention produced by the external contingency will not be detrimental, because the individual does not need to apply creativity heuristics.

There are two other conditions under which extrinsic constraints would not be expected to be detrimental. Both have to do with particular personality characteristics and related creativity heuristics or work habits. Both are derived from Bem's (1972) proposition that attitudes will follow self-perceptions of behavior only to the extent that external constraints on behavior are more salient than initial attitudes. In both cases, the extrinsic goal will *not* lead the hierarchy of goals during task engagement. First, the individual may be able to psychologically reduce the salience of the extrinsic goal while he is engaged in the task. He might, for example, be less dependent than most people on social approval and tangible rewards. Or, like Einstein (who engaged a friend to attend lectures for him), he might find ways of removing himself from situations where constraints are most salient. Second, the individual's intrinsic motivation may be so high that the extrinsic motivation is not primary. There is evidence that overjustification effects will not be obtained when initial interests are salient (Wood, 1982). Indeed, passionate interest in an activity is common in first-person accounts of the experience of creativity.

Allowing for these special cases, the intrinsic motivation hypothesis holds that, generally, extrinsic constraints will be detrimental to creative performance. In the following chapters, I will present evidence on this hypothesis and on other issues important to the development of a social psychology of creativity.

Update

The Original Model

Although the 1983 edition of this book focused on the social psychology of creativity, the componential model that it presented was intended as a comprehensive theory of creativity (Amabile, 1983a, 1983b). Its purpose was twofold: to provide a context in which social influences on creative behavior could be understood, and to advance the field of creativity research in general.

The model was one of the first to comprehensively take into account cognitive, personality, motivational, and social influences on the creative process, and it was the first to propose how each of these factors might influence different steps in the creative process. The other primary contribution of the model lay in the prominence it placed on two aspects that had been largely neglected by earlier theorists: the role of motivation in the creative process, and social-environmental influences on creativity.

Expansion, Refinement, and Revision of the Original Model

Revision of Terms

Figure A replicates the original graphical presentation of the componential model, with a few revisions. One change is that we have changed the terminology used for two elements in the model. We now use the term "Problem or Task Identification" for step 1 in the model because we find it more general than the original term, "Task Presentation." "Presentation" implies that an external source is responsible,

Figure A. Revision of the componential model of creativity. Broken lines indicate the influence of particular factors on others. Wavy lines indicate the steps in the process (where large variations in the sequence are possible). Only direct and primary influences are depicted.

but because we admit the possibility of either an external or an internal source, we feel that "identification" more adequately captures both possibilities. In other words, an individual may identify a particular problem as worthy of task engagement, or someone else may identify the problem and present it to the individual. This revision acknowledges the demonstrated importance of problem definition or "problem finding" in creativity (Getzels & Csikszentmihalyi, 1976).

We also changed "Creativity-Relevant Skills" to "Creativity-Relevant Processes." This component as described in the 1983 edition includes a cognitive style appropriate to the generation of new ideas, an implicit or explicit knowledge of heuristics for generating novel ideas, and a conducive work style. It depends on training, experience in idea generation, and personality characteristics. Because personality characteristics are not generally considered to be "skills," we have substituted the more general term "processes." Here, we use the term "processes" in the same sense that the term is used in the *Journal of Personality and Social Psychology* subsection, "Personality Processes and Individual Differences."

Our third change in terminology is the most important. We have added "Communication" to "Response Validation" in step 4 to signify that the working out and validation of an idea cannot stop in the problem solver's own head; if it did stop there, no observable product would be generated. In keeping with our operational definition of creativity, we cannot say that creativity exists unless the problem solver produces a product, articulates an idea, or in some way communicates the results of the process. This role of communication at the end of the creative process also appears in earlier theories of creativity (e.g., Stein, 1967).

Revision of Graphical Presentation

There are three other changes in our graphical presentation of the model. In the original version we used solid lines with arrows to connect the steps in the process. Although we stated that we were not proposing a strictly sequential process, the model has been misinterpreted as such. Recent theoretical statements in the literature reiterate the view that the creative process is nonsequential (e.g., Isaksen, Dorval, Noller, & Firestien, 1993). Thus, we replace the original straight-arrow lines with wavy lines. By this, we mean to imply that steps 1 through 5 may depict the most logical sequence in which the creative process will unfold, but it is by no means the only sequence. For example, it is quite likely that in the course of generating ideas (step 3), an individual may realize the need to return to step 2 (gathering additional information) or, perhaps, even step 1 (reconceptualizing the problem). Such a nonsequential process might continue through several iterations before any attempt is made at response validation and communication (step 4).

For the same reason, we have revised one of our outcome predictions. We originally suggested that in step 5, if people perceived some progress toward the problem-solving goal, they would likely return to step 1 (Problem Identification). However, given the apparently nonlinear nature of the creative process, we recognize that if they do decide to reenter the process, individuals may do so either by re-conceptualizing the problem (Problem Identification), gathering more information (Preparation), generating more ideas (Response Generation), or even by reworking or repackaging the original idea (Response Validation and Communication).

The most important change in our graphical presentation, however, is the prominent inclusion of the social environment in the figure. Although in describing the theory we discussed the influence of the social environment at great length, we failed to depict this factor in the figure. As a result, readers who rely on the figure sometimes fail to realize that social influences play a central role in the theory. As can be seen in Figure A, the theory proposes that the social environment has its primary influence on creativity by influencing task motivation. As described in the original articulation of the theory, extrinsic constraints in the environment can undermine intrinsic motivation, which, in turn, can lead to lower creativity. However, we recognize that the social environment can also directly influence the other components of creativity—for example, by providing access to education that will increase domain-relevant skills or creativity-relevant processes. For the sake of simplicity, only direct and primary influences are depicted in the figure.

Revision of the Intrinsic Motivation Hypothesis

The intrinsically motivated state is conducive to creativity, whereas the extrinsically motivated state is detrimental (Amabile, 1983a, p. 91). Some years ago we began calling this statement, which we had earlier termed the Intrinsic Motivation Hypothesis of Creativity (in the 1983 edition), the Intrinsic Motivation Principle of Creativity. We did so on the basis of mounting empirical evidence that intrinsic motivation is a crucial determinant of creativity across different domains for different types of subject populations. Because this seemed to be a general law of human behavior, we decided to refer to it as a principle.

However, at the same time that we have become more convinced of the central role of intrinsic motivation, we realize that the original statement of the intrinsic motivation hypothesis is inaccurate. As a result, we set out here to revise the statement.

We begin by offering more precise definitions of intrinsic and extrinsic motivation. Through the course of our recent research, we have come to believe that the best definitions of these constructs are the simplest. We define as *intrinsic* any motivation that arises from the individual's positive reaction to qualities of the task itself; this reaction can be experienced as interest, involvement, curiosity, satisfaction, or positive challenge. We define as *extrinsic* any motivation that arises from sources outside of the task itself; these sources include expected evaluation, contracted-for reward, external directives, or any of several similar sources. These definitions of intrinsic and extrinsic motivation differ from those in our 1983 edition in two ways. Our earlier definitions of these concepts were less focused, and they often equated extrinsic motivation with perceptions of constraint. Recent theoretical advances by Edward Deci and Richard Ryan have made clear that extrinsic motivation is often perceived as externally controlling but can, under some circumstances, instead be perceived as informational (Deci & Ryan, 1985).

Our recent research has confirmed our earlier notions concerning the nature of intrinsic and extrinsic motivation. In the 1983 edition, we proposed that an individual's task motivation includes two elements: "the individual's baseline attitude toward the task (the 'trait'), and the individual's perceptions of his reasons for undertaking the task in a given instance (the 'state')" (p. 76). The trait element is relatively stable and enduring; the state element is subject to influence from the immediate social environment. Our recent research has found that intrinsic and extrinsic motivational orientations do indeed have elements that are stable over months and years (Amabile, Hill, Hennessey, & Tighe, 1994).

However, this research has uncovered evidence that requires revision in one of our earlier statements about motivation. In the 1983 edition, we stated that "intrinsic and extrinsic motivation can be viewed as both a state and a trait (although this trait should not be thought of as general and pervasive, but specific to particular classes of activities)." In other words, the original statement proposed that motivation was specific to particular tasks (such as writing poetry) or perhaps to sets of similar tasks (such as writing). However, our empirical evidence suggests that intrinsic and extrinsic motivational orientations can indeed be thought of as general and pervasive orientations toward one's work or one's activities. Thus, although the mix of intrinsic and extrinsic motives for particular tasks at particular points in time can certainly vary within the individual, it does seem to be the case that intrinsic and extrinsic motivational orientations toward one's work are general across tasks and are relatively stable.

Our revision of the original statement of the intrinsic motivation principle unites two alternative models for the combination (or interaction) of intrinsic and extrinsic motivation. We briefly described these two models in the 1983 edition, referring to them as *hydraulic* and *additive*:

> It is important to consider the relationship between intrinsic and extrinsic motivation. Although many organizational theories of job satisfaction include the common assumption that the two forms of motivation are additive (e.g., Porter & Lawler, 1968; Vroom, 1964), social psychological theories propose that they interact, with high levels of extrinsic motivation precluding high levels of intrinsic motivation (e.g., Calder & Staw, 1975; Lepper et al., 1973). In this view, if a task is intrinsically interesting, the imposition of salient extrinsic constraints on task engagement will lead to the self-perception that one is performing that task primarily to attain the extrinsic goal. Intrinsic motivation will decrease accordingly. Although there is considerable empirical evidence to support this hydraulic view of motivation (cf. Calder & Staw, 1975), it is possible that, if we consider affective as well as cognitive consequences of task engagement and extrinsic constraint, we might find some conditions under which an additive model would apply.

In other words, the hydraulic model proposes that as extrinsic motivation increases, intrinsic motivation (and creativity) must decrease. The additive model proposes that extrinsic motivation can increase without any negative impact on intrinsic motivation (or creativity)—and perhaps with a positive impact. Although we do not know if affective mechanisms can fully account for the effects, we now have considerable evidence that extrinsic motivation need not undermine intrinsic motivation and creativity. Indeed, it appears possible that some types of extrinsic motivation may enhance creativity.

One piece of evidence suggesting an additive effect was reported in the 1983 edition. In a study that crossed reward with choice of task engagement, we found that the highest levels of creativity were produced by subjects who received a reward as a kind of bonus (Amabile, Hennessey, & Grossman, 1986). Clearly, in this circumstance the extrinsic motivator of reward did not have undermining effects. Our more recent research has also found that reward can lead to higher levels of creativity under some circumstances. In a series of training studies with children, those who had been taught to focus on intrinsic motivation and to cognitively distance themselves from extrinsic motivators performed more creatively when offered reward than when not offered reward, and they also performed more creatively than children who had not been trained (Hennessey, Amabile, & Martinage, 1989; Hennessey & Zbikowski, 1993).

In a study with professional artists, we found that commissioned work was significantly less creative than noncommissioned work but that this effect was largely due to the degree of constraint the artist felt in exactly how the work was to be done (Amabile, Phillips, & Collins, 1994). Moreover, we found that among the commissioned works, self-rated creativity on an artwork correlated positively with the degree to which the artists reported perceiving the commission as informational (i.e., providing information about their competence) or enabling (i.e., enabling them to do something exciting). And in the same study, artists' overall creativity (as rated by experts) correlated positively with both an intrinsic motivational orientation and an extrinsic motivational orientation on a personality instrument. (Due to our small sample size, only the intrinsic correlation was significant.) The particular intrinsic motivational orientation in question was challenge, and the extrinsic motivational orientation was recognition, which can be viewed as informational—the confirmation of one's competence by respected others.

Additional evidence of positive effects of certain extrinsic motivators comes from a series of nonexperimental studies in R&D laboratories. In those studies, we found that many of the extrinsic motivators that we studied experimentally do appear to undermine creativity: win-lose competition within an organization, expected negative evaluation of one's ideas, a concern with rewards, and constraint on how the work is to be done. On the other hand, we found several other factors that might be construed as extrinsic motivators—and indeed some of the *same* factors—operating as supports to creativity: reward and recognition for creative ideas, clearly defined overall project goals, and frequent constructive feedback on the work (Amabile, Conti, Coon, Lazenby, & Herron, in press; Amabile & N. Gryskiewicz, 1989; Amabile & S. Gryskiewicz, 1987).

In a recent theoretical paper we reconcile these motivation findings with our earlier research by using a conceptualization of *motivational synergy* (Amabile, 1993). This conceptualization proposes that certain types of extrinsic motivation—those we call "synergistic extrinsic motivators"—can combine positively with intrinsic motivation, particularly when initial levels of intrinsic motivation are high. Rewards that confirm competence without connoting control, or rewards that enable the individual to do exciting work can serve as synergistic extrinsic motivators.

We propose two mechanisms for these positive combinations of seemingly opposite types of motivation. According to the first, *extrinsics in service of intrinsics*, any extrinsic factors that support one's sense of competence or enable one's deeper involvement with the task itself, without undermining one's sense of self-determination (termed "synergistic extrinsic motivators"), should positively add to intrinsic motivation and should enhance creativity. These conceptualizations derive in part from Deci and Ryan's proposals concerning "informational" versus "controlling" extrinsic motivators (1985). According to the second mechanism, *the motivation-work cycle match*, synergistic extrinsic motivators may serve a special function at certain stages of the creative process. We propose that the first (problem identification) and third (response generation) stages of the creative process, where the *novelty* of the outcome is importantly determined, may require intrinsic motivation that is unencumbered by any significant extrinsic motivation. However, at those stages where the novelty of the work (though still important) is less crucial, the synergistic extrinsic motivators may serve to focus and energize the individual toward getting the job done in an *appropriate* way. Specifically, these external motivators may be useful in carrying the performance over the sometimes tedious hurdles of prior preparation (step 2) and careful validation and communication of ideas (step 4). Moreover, they are unlikely to significantly undermine intrinsic motivation for the work, particularly if intrinsic motivation is already strong.

These concepts of motivational synergy, and the various ways in which intrinsic and extrinsic motivation might have an impact on the creative process at different points, are detailed in Figure B. Note that in this figure motivation contributes to each step in the creative process. Obviously, we believe this to be true—even though in Figure A we connect motivation only to steps 1 and 3. We do so there for simplicity, depicting only the connections that we believe are most important for distinguishing creative (novel and appropriate) performance from good (appropriate) but ordinary performance.

Note also that in Figure B we have divided the influence of the social environment into two main categories. One category, social-environmental factors connoting control, will lead to nonsynergistic extrinsic motivation within individuals and will detract from intrinsic motivation. The other category consists of social-environmental factors supporting autonomy, competence, or task involvement. Certain of the influences in this category will directly enhance intrinsic motivation; others will lead to synergistic extrinsic motivation within individuals.

Figure B. Detail of the componential model: Mechanisms of social-environmental influence on creativity. Only direct and primary influences are depicted.

Thus, we propose a revision of the Intrinsic Motivation Principle of Creativity: *Intrinsic motivation is conducive to creativity; controlling extrinsic motivation is detrimental to creativity, but informational or enabling extrinsic motivation can be conducive, particularly if initial levels of intrinsic motivation are high.*

Range of Social-Environmental Influences

In the experimental, nonexperimental, and theoretical work that we have done over the past twelve years, we have considerably expanded our understanding of the range of social-environmental factors that can influence creativity. Table C presents a compilation of our categorization of these factors to date. In the table, we divide the factors in two ways. Vertically, they are divided according to positive and negative overall influences on creativity. The positive influences in Table C were referred to in Figure B as "social-environmental factors supporting autonomy, competence, or task involvement." All other things being equal, each of these factors should contribute positively to creative performance. Some of these, such as optimally challenging tasks, will do so by leading directly to higher levels of intrinsic motivation. (These are marked with an asterisk in Table C.) Other positive

Table C Social-Environmental Influences on Creativity

	Positive	Negative
General	*Autonomy/sense of control Sufficient resources *Importance/urgency in the work *Optimal challenge Recognition/reward that confirms competence Reward that enables intrinsically interesting work *Task matched to interests Sufficient task structure to support competent performance	Threatening critical evaluation connoting incompetence Expectation of critical evaluation Surveillance Contracted-for rewardconnoting Restricted choice/constraint control Arbitrary/unrealistic deadlines Competition with coworkers
Organizational	Recognition that failure in work can provide valuable information *Mechanisms for considering new ideas *High-level encouragement toward innovation *Immediate supervisor encouragement Coworker skill diversity Coworker openness to new ideas Rigid status structures Coworkers challenge ideas constructively *Emphasis on intrinsic motivators Competition with outside organizations Constructive work-focused feedback Clear strategic direction, with procedural autonomy Cooperation Collaboration	Lack of communication Lack of cooperation Emphasis on the status quo Emphasis on extrinsic motivators Win-lose competition within the organization Rigid procedures Apathy toward project from others in organization

*These positive influences likely have a direct impact on intrinsic motivation. The other positive influences likely serve as synergistic extrinsic motivators.

1. Organizational influences are proposed to operate primarily on individuals who work in organizational settings. Some of these factors may be more important to overall organizational innovation than to individual creativity specifically.

2. We do not suggest that these are a complete set of all social-environmental influences on creativity. Supporting data for many of these influences appear in the updates to Chapters 5–8.

3. A notable absence of the positive factors should have negative consequences on creativity, and a notable absence of the negative factors should have positive consequences.

4. The influences described are general; these factors can interact with other variables and with individual traits and skills. Some effects may be nonlinear, especially at the extremes.

influences, such as recognition and rewards that confirm competence, will lead to synergistic extrinsic motivation. It is likely that some of these positive influences will also have effects on the nonmotivational creativity components—domain-relevant skills, or creativity-relevant processes.

The negative influences will undermine intrinsic motivation and creativity. In Figure B, these were referred to as "social-environmental factors connoting control." These should serve to increase nonsynergistic extrinsic motivation and decrease the intrinsic motivation that is essential for creativity.

Horizontally, we divide the factors into those that should generally operate on individuals engaged in any creative activities and those that should only be salient influences in organizational settings where individuals work together on creative pursuits (or at least are dependent on the organization for support of their work). Moreover, although more research is required, it appears that some of the "organizational" factors more strongly influence individual creativity, but others more strongly influence overall organizational innovation (the successful implementation of the creative ideas generated by individuals or teams). For example, the positive organizational factor "immediate supervisor encouragement" most likely has its locus of influence on individual or team creativity, while the positive organizational factor "mechanisms for considering new ideas" most likely exerts influence on the innovation that might result from individual creativity. These ideas are detailed in a theoretical model of creativity and innovation in organizations that incorporates much of our original componential model of individual creativity (Amabile, 1988a, 1988b).

We do not propose that the list in Table C presents all possible social-environmental influences on creativity. It is, however, a considerably more complete compilation than we were able to provide in the 1983 edition; we expect that with future research the list will continue to grow.

The influences proposed here are general and should be observed on average. Each can, of course, interact with other social-environmental variables, and with individual traits and skills as well. Moreover, we suspect that some of the influences may be nonlinear; as such, their placement in the positive or the negative column would depend on their intensity.

Supporting data on the influences listed in Table C appear in our updates to Chapters 5–8.

Cognitive Mechanisms

In the 1983 edition, we suggested some cognitive mechanisms by which motivational state might impact creativity. Generally, these mechanisms centered on attention to the task and to aspects of the environment that might be relevant to the task as well as willingness and ability to explore alternative cognitive pathways in problem solving. More recently, we have proposed a metaphor to capture these mechanisms (Amabile, 1987a). It is the metaphor of a maze in which the maze represents the problem to be solved or the task to be completed. Exiting the maze is equivalent to arriving at a satisfactory solution to the problem or a satisfactory completion to the task. A straightforward *algorithmic approach* for solving the problem or doing the task is represented by a straight line in the maze going directly from entrance to exit. However, there are a number of alternative exits representing alternative problem solutions; these can only be reached by the more *heuristic approach* of deviating from the straight path by exploring the maze and by taking the risk of going into a dead end.

We propose that extrinsically motivated individuals, because they are motivated primarily by some task-extrinsic factors, will be more likely to rely on common, well-worked algorithms that they have learned for doing a particular task. In other words, they will be more likely to exit the maze as safely and surely as possible, and the result is unlikely to be novel. By contrast, intrinsically motivated individuals, because they enjoy the task itself and the process of searching for a new solution, will be more likely to explore the maze, attempting to find their way to one of the more novel exits.

We have recently conducted a study designed to investigate the cognitive mechanisms underlying the effects of intrinsic motivation on task performance (Ruscio, Whitney, & Amabile, 1995). Using think-aloud protocols and microcoding of subject task behaviors, we examined the impact of motivational state on task processing and the impact of task processing on judge-rated creativity of the final products in three domains—art, writing, and problem solving. Our behavioral coding and verbal protocol analysis yielded reliable measures that when empirically combined to form task-processing factors strongly predicted independent judges' ratings of product creativity in each domain. Several of the obtained factors, most notably *involvement in the task*, served as mediators of the positive influence of intrinsic motivation on creativity. Involvement in the task included an apparent absorption in and focusing on the work itself. This study allows us a first glimpse into the mechanisms by which motivation may have an impact on very specific task behaviors that lead to observable differences in the creativity of products.

Empirical Support for the Componential Model

Much of our research over the past twelve years, like the research reported in the 1983 edition, has examined the impact of particular social-environmental variables on creativity. In other words, it has focused on two links in the componential model as presented in Figure A: the link between social environment and task motivation, and the link between task motivation and response generation. This new research is reported in our updates to Chapters 5 through 8. However, we have also conducted research designed to examine other aspects of the model. For example, the original model proposed that creativity-relevant processes can operate quite generally, across tasks and even across domains to some extent. Recently, because we had conducted several different creativity studies on the same subject populations, we were able to examine correlations between creativity levels within a domain (such as different artistic creativity tasks) and across domains (such as artistic and verbal creativity tasks) (Conti, Coon, & Amabile, in press). Of the 36 correlations we computed, 35 are positive and many are statistically significant despite very small sample sizes. Nonetheless, there are systematic differences in the magnitude of these correlations. As predicted by the model, the correlations are higher within a domain and even higher within a domain in situations where task motivation is likely to remain constant. Nonetheless, the overall pattern of correlations suggests, contrary to recent suggestions in the literature (e.g., Baer, 1994), that there are some general creativity-relevant processes.

The first study to simultaneously examine several aspects of the model used an ecologically valid setting: a set of college writing classrooms (Hill, 1991; Hill, Amabile, Coon, & Whitney, 1994, Study 1). There were no manipulated variables. Instead, assessments were taken of the major components in the model: motivation (intrinsic and extrinsic), domain-relevant skill (technical quality of writing), creativity-relevant processes (innovative thinking style), and the social environment (as assessed by a new classroom-climate instrument). Partial support for the overall model was obtained. Writing creativity was predicted by domain-relevant skill, creativity relevant processes, and motivational orientation (with extrinsic motivation negatively predicting creativity). However, the data revealed no direct relationship between the social environment and motivation or the social environment and creativity (both of which have been found in our experimental work).

A second study obtained similar measures in a laboratory setting but added an experimental manipulation of expected evaluation for half of the subjects (Hill, Amabile, Coon, & Whitney, 1994, Study 2). This study, too, provided some support for the model. In the absence of a manipulated extrinsic constraint, writing creativity was significantly predicted by previously assessed domain-relevant skills, creativity-relevant processes, and motivational orientation. Interestingly, however, when subjects were working under the social constraint of expected evaluation, creativity was not directly predicted to a significant degree by the three basic components in the model. Instead, subjects' general motivational orientation (intrinsic and extrinsic) and task-specific motivation (interest in writing) significantly predicted their reported motivation in the experimental situation, which in turn significantly predicted the creativity of their writing in that situation. Thus, although our data support the inclusion of the basic components in the model, it is clear that future theoretical developments must take into account complex interactions between person-variables and situational-variables.

With another recent study in our laboratory we began a preliminary investigation of stages in the creative process. This study examined the role of planning on problem-solving creativity (Whitney, Ruscio, Amabile, & Castle, 1995). Subjects engaged in a structure-building task after being given instructions and 5 minutes to freely manipulate sample building materials (Play condition) or 5 minutes to simply look at sample materials (Planning condition). Control condition subjects began the experimental task immediately after receiving instruction. To use the terminology of the componential model as depicted in Figure A, the planning group was given more time than the control group for preparation (step 2) and response generation (step 3). The play group, too, was given more time than the control group for preparation (step 2) and response generation (step 3) but also had the opportunity to engage in response validation (step 4). We found that both the planning and the play groups produced structures that were judged as significantly more creative than those produced by the control condition. However, there were no differences between the planning and play conditions, suggesting that it is primarily preparation and response generation that makes the difference in this simple laboratory problem-solving task.

The componential model also proposes a feedback loop by which creative activity can indirectly lead to an increase in domain-relevant learning by leading to an increase in intrinsic task motivation (see Figure A, p. 113). A recent study in our laboratory addressed this issue (Conti, Amabile, & Pollak, 1995). Prior to reading a short instructional passage, subjects in this study were given either a creative pretask or a noncreative pretask on the topic covered in the passage. We found that overall, engagement in the creative pretask did lead to higher levels of both intrinsic motivation and long-term retention of the material learned. Moreover, participants who performed more creatively on the creative pretask tended to show better long-term retention than those who were less creative.

Thus, although the componential model leads to many propositions that have not yet been adequately tested, we have made some progress in recent years in examining aspects of the model that go beyond the linkage of social environment, motivation, and creativity of response. To a considerable degree, our recent research supports the basic model. Clearly though, much work remains to be done.

Comparison to Other Comprehensive Models

A number of theoretical advances have taken place in the field of creativity research since our original model was published in 1983. Most notably, other theorists have proposed comprehensive creativity models that include motivational and social variables along with cognitive and personality variables. Of the recently articulated theories, the one that is the most similar to our componential model (and indeed can be viewed as an elaboration of our model) is that of Sternberg and Lubart (1991). These theorists propose that creative individuals behave in a manner that is conceptually similar to that of the financial investor who attempts to "buy low and sell high." According to this "investment theory," creative persons are those who invest their energies in developing ideas that are initially low in currency because they are unusual but that will eventually be recognized and appreciated as highly valuable. Thus, this theory, like the componential model (Amabile, 1983a, 1983b, 1988a), rests on a social consensus operational definition of creativity: "a stock is valuable because investors collectively desire to possess it, and a product is creative because appropriate judges collectively agree on this evaluation" (1991, p. 3).

The investment theory builds upon the componential model (Amabile, 1983a, 1983b, 1988a) in describing a set of six components or "resources" that are deemed important for creativity. There are essentially two differences between the components of our componential model and those of the investment model. First, the investment model contains more components because it splits domain-relevant skill into the components of *intelligence* and *knowledge*; it splits creativity-relevant processes into the components of *intellectual style* and *personality*; and it includes the *environment* as a component at the same level as the others. (In our componential model, only intraindividual components directly influence the creative process; each of those components—but primarily motivation—is influenced by the environment.) Second, there is a subtle difference between the description of the motivational component in the investment theory and the description in our theory. The investment theory proposes that the essential motivation for creativity is *task-focused motivation*. It suggests that task-focused motivation is often, but not always, the same as intrinsic motivation. According to these theorists, this sort of task focus can also arise from extrinsic motivators that serve to increase the individual's concentration on the task.

The second primary difference between these two component-based theories concerns domain-specificity. Our model proposes that creativity-relevant processes are quite general across domains, that domain-relevant skills are operative within broad domains of tasks, and that motivation is often quite specific to particular tasks (in large part because it depends on the social context in which the task is carried out). In contrast, Sternberg and Lubart propose that the components of creativity are neither entirely domain-general nor entirely domain-specific. They suggest that some abilities and attributes may apply more to some domains than to others and that the convergence of these abilities and attributes will be difficult to predict a priori.

The investment theory proposes that the social environment impacts creativity in three ways. As noted above, the social context is deemed relevant to the evaluation of ideas. In addition, however, the theory proposes that the environmental context—both physical and social—can spark ideas. Finally, in a proposition similar to the intrinsic motivation hypothesis of creativity (Amabile, 1983a, 1983b), the investment theory proposes that the social environment provides a context in which creative ideas are nourished or suppressed; for example, constraints placed on activities are suggested as detriments to creativity. In a study with adults, including several different domains of creative activity, the investment theory has received partial empirical support (Sternberg & Lubart, 1991, 1993).

Another recent theory that bears considerable similarity to our componential model is Woodman and Schoenfeldt's (1990) "interactionist" model, which integrates personality, cognitive, and social psychological perspectives. These theorists suggest that creative behavior is produced by a complex interaction between the person and the situation. They define personal factors to include cognitive styles and abilities, personality traits, and characteristics of the organism as a whole, such as motivations and values. The situation is divided into broad contextual influences (including physical surroundings and cultural factors) and more interaction-oriented social influences (such as competition and social facilitation). Both situational and personal factors are influenced by antecedent conditions (such as early socialization, gender, and birth order) as well as by a feedback loop from the consequences of creative behavior. The primary difference between this model and our own is the explicit inclusion of the physical environment and broad cultural factors, as well as the specification of some antecedent conditions for the development of motivations, values, and personality traits.

Other theories, have, like our componential model, given prominence to social factors. However, in general these theories are less specific in their descriptions of the mechanisms by which social factors might influence creativity. For example, in his "ecological" model, Harrington (1990) asserts that the social system is intricately involved in the creative process by virtue of the role it plays in recognizing (or overlooking), creating (or destroying), and extending (or limiting) the creative potential of a particular act. In this view, creativity must be recognized as a product not only of the individual who generates an idea but also of both the objective and the subjective ecosystems. Harrington describes a "creative ecosystem" as providing the ingredients for creativity, including the presence of interesting, solvable problems, novel techniques and perspectives to apply to the problem, norms encouraging the sharing of ideas, avenues of communication between people with complementary abilities, and a variety of rewards to meet different motivations.

Other theories include a broad range of social influences starting at the broadest cultural level but, again, provide little detail on mechanisms of social influence on individual creativity. Simonton, in his largely cognitive "chance-configuration theory" (1989a), proposes that social factors play a role both in developing a person's creative potential and in determining acceptance of a creative idea. This theory considers social factors at the level of the family, the field, and society in general. In his "evolving systems" approach to creativity, Howard Gruber (1988; Gruber & Davis, 1988) proposes that the creative person is influenced by diverse social relationships, that the creative person is inextricably entwined with the historical, societal, and institutional context, and that the creative person is an active constructor of the social milieu.

Finally, in an "interactive framework" for studying creativity, David Feldman, Mihaly Csikszentmihalyi, and Howard Gardner (1994; Csikszentmihalyi, 1988; Csikszentmihalyi & Robinson, 1986) see the creative product as the interaction of three subsystems: individual, domain, and field. Social influences enter in primarily at the domain and the field levels. A domain, defined as an organized body of knowledge about a particular topic, serves as a context for creativity that was created by other thinkers and passes on structured information to the individual. A field, defined as the group(s) of people whose presence supports and influences the structure of the domain, is responsible for the selection and retention of ideas. Creative individuals not only produce ideas and communicate them to the field, but they also may bring pressure upon the field to transform the domain in some way. Like other theorists, Feldman, Csikszentmihalyi, and Gardner assert that the historical/social context of a discovery is crucial for understanding creativity.

Summary

In recent years, several theorists (including us) have elaborated upon and gone far beyond our original componential model. Formal proposals concerning the influence of social factors have extended beyond the immediate social environment to the historical context of the individual, the field, and the society. Moreover, important advances have been made by reversing perspective and considering the influence that creative behavior can have upon the social environment of a field, a society, or an entire culture.

Besides the cosmetic changes in the basic graphical presentation of our theoretical model, we have undertaken more substantive revisions as well. The most important is the revision of the intrinsic motivation principle. Although we still recognize the critical importance of intrinsic motivation to creativity, we have recently discovered that certain forms of extrinsic motivation—which we call synergistic extrinsic motivators—do not necessarily detract from intrinsic motivation and creativity. Rather, these motivators, such as rewards that enable the individual to undertake an exciting project, may actually increase creativity. We suggest that "pure" intrinsic motivation may be most crucial at those heuristic stages of the creative process where novelty is most needed (such as idea generation), but that synergistic extrinsic motivation may play a useful role if it appears at those more algorithmic stages of the process where outcome appropriateness is determined (such as idea validation).

Our current theoretical statement also includes a considerable expansion of the range of social-environmental influences that are considered. Although the original statement (Amabile, 1983a, 1983b) focused primarily on factors that can negatively influence an individual's creativity in any setting, our current presentation of factors includes both negative and positive influences in organizational as well as individual work settings.

Part Two
Social and Environmental Influences

5

Effects of Evaluation
on Creativity

Of the creative individuals whose first-person accounts were considered in Chapter 1, none appears to have been so strongly influenced by external constraints as was Sylvia Plath. And of those constraints that impeded her work, none was so devastating as evaluation—particularly competitive evaluation: "Yes, I want the world's praise, money, and love, and am furious with anyone . . . getting ahead of me" (Hughes & McCullough, 1982, p. 305). "I want . . . to feel my work good and well-taken. Which ironically freezes me at my work, corrupts my nunnish labor of work-for-itself-as-its-own-reward" (p. 305). In this chapter, I will present empirical evidence demonstrating that evaluation can, in fact, undermine creativity.

The intrinsic motivation hypothesis states that the intrinsically motivated state will be conducive to creativity, whereas the extrinsically motivated state will be detrimental. Intrinsic motivation is not a clearly defined concept. Indeed, as noted in the last chapter, many different (though compatible) descriptions of intrinsic motivation have been offered. Hebb (1955) and Berlyne (1960) suggested that enjoyable (intrinsically motivating) activities are those that present an optimal level of novelty. White (1959) and Harter (1978) proposed that a sense of competence and mastery are the primary features of intrinsic motivation. DeCharms (1968), Deci (1971), and Lepper and his colleagues (Lepper et al., 1973) suggested that a sense of control is important to intrinsic motivation: To the extent that individuals perceive their task engagement as externally controlled, they are extrinsically rather than intrinsically motivated. Each of these conceptions focuses on phenomenology—an individual's level of stimulation through novelty, an individual's feelings of mastery, an individual's feelings of control. Moreover, virtually all theorists concerned with intrinsic motivation have described that phenomenological state as marked by both deep involvement and playfulness.

There are, then, a number of features of task engagement that could contribute to intrinsic motivation: The individual is curious about or otherwise stimulated by features of the task; the individual gains a sense of competence from task engagement; the activity, as perceived by the individual, is free of strong external control; and the individual has the sense of engaging in play rather than work.

How might these different features of task engagement contribute to creativity in performance? According to the componential framework presented in the last chapter, the individual's baseline level of interest in the activity and prior success or failure (confirmation of competence or incompetence) influence the desire to engage in the activity again without external inducement. More directly relevant to the creative quality of performance, however, are the factors of external control and resulting task perceptions as work or play. Extrinsic constraints can contribute to uncreative performance in two ways. They can divert attention away from the task itself and task-relevant aspects of the environment by directing attention to progress toward the extrinsic goal. And they can make the individual reluctant to take risks, since those risks might impede attainment of that goal.

There is little previous empirical research on the effects of external evaluation on creativity. Nonetheless, there is some suggestive evidence in support of the intrinsic motivation hypothesis. In one clinical interview study (Garfield, Cohen, & Roth, 1969), undergraduate subjects who were judged to have an internal locus of evaluation scored higher on standard creativity tests than did subjects judged to have an external locus of evaluation. A similar study (Poole, Williams, & Lett, 1977) found that elementary school subjects who scored high on the Torrance Tests differed significantly on a locus-of-evaluation test from those who scored low; high creativity was associated with an internal locus of evaluation. Finally, in a study employing a more strictly experimental methodology (White & Owen, 1970), boys assigned to a classroom stressing self-evaluation were significantly more creative on a standard test than those assigned to classrooms stressing peer evaluation or teacher evaluation.

Some researchers, however, clearly contradict the hypothesis that external evaluation will undermine creativity. Most of the arguments and the evidence favoring evaluation have focused on competitive evaluation, in which experts evaluate products or responses and distribute rewards on that basis. For example, Torrance (1974; Torrance, Bruch, & Torrance, 1976) suggested that interscholastic problem-solving competitions can be used to foster creative development in school children. Osborn (1963) encouraged the use of competition to stimulate creative ideas in brainstorming, and Brown and Gaynor (1967) proposed that competition can contribute to creativity.

There is some empirical evidence to support these views. In his early studies (1964, 1965), Torrance found that competition (rewarding prizes to high scores) increased the fluency and flexibility of children's responses to his test items. Bloom and Sosniak (1981), in a study of extraordinarily talented pianists and mathematicians, found that competition in the form of recitals, contests, and concerts was quite common in the early lives of individuals who later went on to distinguish themselves in their talent fields. In a straightforward behavior-modification study (Goetz, 1981), preschool children who were given verbal praise for novelty in blockbuilding showed significant increases in novelty over baseline levels. Finally, Raina (1968) used a simple experimental design to assess the effects of competition on children's scores for the Product Improvement and Unusual Uses tests (Torrance, 1966). Children in the control group were given the standard instructions for these tests, which make no mention of competition. In the experimental group, however, children were told that their performance would be evaluated, with monetary prizes awarded to the three top scorers. To make this manipulation as salient as possible, the researchers displayed the money on the teacher's desk during test administration. In addition, the experimental-group children were told that the names of the winners would be displayed on the school bulletin board. The results showed a clear superiority of the experimental group children, who scored significantly higher on both fluency and flexibility.

Intrinsic Motivation, Creativity, and the Nature of the Task

The apparently contradictory results obtained in studies on effects of evaluation can be reconciled by considering the nature of the tasks employed. The conceptual definition of creativity states that a creative response is a novel and appropriate solution *to a heuristic task*. If the path to solution is clear and straightforward, the task is an algorithmic one, and responses to it simply cannot be considered creative. To allow responses that may be considered creative, the task must be open-ended to some degree. Some search for solution paths is required.

Virtually all of the studies demonstrating positive effects of evaluation and competition used tasks that can be considered algorithmic. As I argued in Chapter 2, many types of scores on the most popular creativity tests reflect algorithmic processes. In particular, "fluency" simply reflects the number of responses made, and "flexibility" reflects the number of different categories of responses made (often correlated with fluency). It is on precisely these two aspects of performance, however, that positive effects of evaluation and competition have been shown.

McGraw's (1978) theory proposes that extrinsic motivation will undermine performance on heuristic tasks, but enhance performance on algorithmic tasks. Thus, it should be expected that fluency and flexibility, as measured by standard creativity tests, will improve under conditions of extrinsic constraint. Children told they can do well by giving a large number of answers on a test will, not surprisingly, give a large number of answers—larger, perhaps, than children not competing for positive evaluations and prizes. In a similar vein, Wallach (1970) argues that higher training-group performance on a creativity test is to be expected if the training involves essentially telling children what they should do to perform well. He implies that, even if the test might not originally have been straightforward, the training rendered it so; whether such performance should be called "creative" is doubtful. To the extent that the path to correct (i.e., positively evaluated) performance is straightforward, then, evaluation and competition can be expected to enhance performance. This will not be the case, however, with heuristic tasks. On such tasks, the expectation of evaluation should work against the deep levels of attention and high degrees of intellectual playfulness required for creativity. My program of research on the effects of evaluation was designed to test these ideas.

The Basic Research Paradigm

Most of the research reported here and in the next chapter relied on a modified version of the standard overjustification paradigm. In that paradigm (e.g., Lepper, Greene, & Nisbett, 1973; Amabile, DeJong, & Lepper, 1976), subjects are randomly assigned to constraint or no-constraint conditions and presented with an intrinsically interesting task. Their subsequent interest to engage in that task is assessed under conditions in which the constraint is clearly absent. The paradigm I have used to assess the effects of extrinsic constraint on creative performance borrows much from overjustification research.

First, as in the overjustification paradigm, the task is an intrinsically interesting one. In addition, however, to make it appropriate for testing hypotheses about creativity, the task (1) is an open-ended (heuristic) one; (2) does not depend heavily on special skills; and (3) is one in which subjects actually make an observable product or a response that can be recorded and later judged on creativity (see Chapter 3).

Second, the subjects selected for most of these studies are "ordinary" individuals. Only individuals with extremely high levels of experience in the domain are excluded.

Third, just as subjects in the overjustification studies are not told that the experiment concerns intrinsic interest, subjects in these studies are normally not told that the experiment concerns creativity. Clearly, to have subjects aware of the purpose of these studies would be a serious mistake. Although the tasks were chosen so that the path to "correct" (i.e., creative) solutions is not clear and straightforward, subjects who knew the experiment concerned creativity might be able to generate algorithms for producing creative solutions.

Fourth, as in the overjustification studies, the experimental groups are placed under a salient extrinsic constraint—for example, the expectation of external evaluation—before they are presented with the task. The control groups are not. Certainly, in an experimental setting, even control groups work under some constraints. Thus, because the intrinsic motivation hypothesis is concerned with the presence or absence of constraint, it is important that these studies were conducted in a variety of settings, under a variety of conditions. These included university laboratories, classrooms in elementary schools, and a day-care center.

Although the classic overjustification studies focused on subsequent intrinsic interest in task engagement, the major dependent variable in my studies is the creativity of the products or responses. Other dependent variables may include other subjectively judged dimensions of the products or responses, and various measures of intrinsic interest in the task. The consensual assessment technique (see Chapter 3) is used to obtain measures of creativity and other aspects of the products.

Impact of Evaluation Expectation

Effects on Algorithmic and Heuristic Tasks

This initial study of evaluation expectation (Amabile, 1979) was designed to test the hypothesis that such constraint will undermine creative performance on heuristic tasks. The task used was the collage-making activity described in Chapter 3—a task for which the path to a "creative solution" is not clear and straightforward. For some subjects in constraint conditions, however, this task was rendered algorithmic: They were given specific instructions on how to make a collage that would be judged as creative. In this way, it was possible to test the hypothesized differential effects of constraint on heuristic and algorithmic tasks.

In accord with McGraw's (1978) theory, I predicted that subjects placed under constraint (evaluation expectation) for the heuristic collage-making task would show lower levels of both creativity and intrinsic interest in the task than would no-constraint controls. In addition, since McGraw suggests that *extrinsic* motivation will enhance performance on *algorithmic* tasks, I expected that the group placed under constraint but given explicit instructions on "being creative" would show higher levels of creativity than controls, but would show *lower* levels of intrinsic interest.

In addition to the constraint and instructions variables, a "focus" variable was included in this design. Some subjects within each level of evaluation expectation were asked to focus on the creativity of their art works. Some were asked to focus on the technical aspects; others were not given any particular focus. This variable was included to determine whether, in some unexpected way, subjects could generate algorithms for producing creative collages simply by knowing that the task called for creativity.

The subjects in this study were 95 women enrolled in an introductory psychology course at Stanford University. As a cover story, the female experimenter explained that this study was actually a pretest for an experiment to be done the following quarter. This alleged pretest was being run in order to identify activities that would affect most individuals' moods in certain predictable ways. The subject was told that she would randomly choose one of five different activities, and that, after engaging in the activity, she would complete a mood questionnaire. This cover story was used to ensure that subjects would be ignorant of the study's focus on creativity.

After the subject chose a number from 1 to 5, the experimenter consulted her "assignment sheet" and announced that that particular number corresponded to the art activity. At this point, the experimenter asked the subject if she was an artist or had done much collage work. If the subject answered in the affirmative, the session was terminated.[1] In introducing the art task, the experimenter stressed

---

[1] Only three subjects were eliminated on this basis, and they were replaced.

Table 5-1.   Experimental Design for Amabile (1979)[a]

Evaluation Expectation	Instruction				
	No Focus	Technical Focus	Specific Technical Focus	Creativity Focus	Specific Creativity Focus
Absent	C_1	C_2		C_3	
Present	E_1	E_2	E_2	E_3	E_4

Note. The letter in each box indicates whether a condition is control or experimental, and the subscripts link experimental groups to their appropriate controls.

[a]From Amabile, T. M. Effects of external evaluation on artistic creativity. *Journal of Personality and Social Psychology,* 1979, *37,* 221–233.

that the subject had complete freedom in using the materials to form a design, but that only the materials provided should be used. In addition, the subject was asked to make a design that conveyed a feeling of silliness, "as when a child is acting and feeling silly." Thus, extraneous sources of variability were reduced by (1) eliminating subjects with extreme levels of experience in the domain, (2) limiting the materials that subjects might use, and (3) providing them all with the same general theme for their work.

Following the general introduction, the instructions diverged to produce the eight treatment conditions. (Table 5-1 summarizes the experimental design.) Assignment of subjects to conditions had been predetermined by a randomized schedule, and up to this point, the experimenter was unaware of the subject's treatment condition. The experimenter now turned to the "manipulation" page in the subject's packet and read the crucial instruction. Subjects in the control conditions (nonevaluation-no focus, nonevaluation-technical focus, and nonevaluation-creativity focus) were told:

> There is one more important point that I should make clear before you begin. We won't be using your design as a source of data. We are not interested at all in the activity itself or what you do with the activity. We are *only* interested in the mood you report on the questionnaire. So we do not care about the design itself at all—its only purpose is to provide you with this experience so we can see how it affects your mood.

In addition, the subjects in the nonevaluation-technical focus condition were asked to concentrate on the technical aspects of the activity "for this particular mood induction," and subjects in the nonevaluation-creativity focus condition were asked to focus on the creative aspects.

The basic instructions for the five experimental groups (evaluation-no focus, evaluation-technical focus, evaluation-creativity focus, evaluation-specific technical focus, evaluation-specific creativity focus) were:

> There is one more important point that I should make clear before you begin. In addition to your questionnaire, we will be looking at your finished design as an important

source of data. We have five graduate artists from the Stanford Art Department working with us, and when this experiment is over, we will have them come in to judge each art work. They will make a detailed evaluation of your design, noting the good points and criticizing the weaknesses. And since we know that our subjects are interested in how they were evaluated, we will send you a copy of each judge's evaluation of your design in about two weeks.

In addition, subjects in the evaluation-technical focus condition were told that the judges would base their evaluation on how technically good the designs were. Subjects in the evaluation-creativity focus condition were told that the judges would base their evaluations on how creative the designs were. Those in the evaluation-specific technical focus condition were told that the judges would make their technical evaluation on the basis of six elements: (1) the neatness of the design; (2) the balance of the design; (3) the amount of planning evident; (4) the level of organization in the design; (5) the presence of actual recognizable figures or objects in the design; and (6) the degree to which the design expresses something to them. Finally, subjects in the evaluation-specific creativity focus condition were told that the judges would base their creativity evaluation on seven elements: (1) the novelty of the idea; (2) the novelty shown in the use of the materials; (3) the amount of variation in the shapes used; (4) the asymmetry in the design; (5) the amount of detail in the design; (6) the complexity of the design, and (7) the amount of effort evident. These components were those that had, in fact, clustered closely with pretest judges' ratings of technical goodness and creativity, respectively.

Each subject was left alone for 15 minutes to work on her collage. At the end of the session, the experimenter presented the subject with a "Mood Questionnaire" and an "Art Activity" questionnaire. The first was in keeping with the cover story. The second included a number of questions designed to assess the subjects' interest in and attitude toward the art activity. During a postexperimental debriefing, the subject was asked a series of questions designed to probe suspicions about the experimental situation, the tasks, or the instructions.[2]

The 95 collages were judged on 16 artistic dimensions by 15 artists. Details of the reliabilities of these judgments and of the factor analysis done on them can be found in Chapter 3, Study 2.

Creativity results. The interjudge reliability of creativity ratings of the 15 artist-judges was .79. Seven of the subjectively rated dimensions loaded high and positively on the creativity factor in factor analysis: creativity, novelty of material use,

---

[2] No subjects guessed that the study concerned creativity. Fifteen subjects, distributed evenly throughout the eight conditions, expressed suspicions about being watched during a 10-minute free-time period that elapsed between administration of the two questionnaires. Since the behavioral measure obtained during that period proved not to be useful, these subjects were retained, and their data appear in all analyses reported here.

novelty of idea, effort evident, variation of shapes, detail, and complexity. A composite creativity measure was formed by combining the normalized rating for each of these creativity dimensions.

Judge ratings on creativity and the six component creativity dimensions strongly support the hypothesis that evaluation expectation is detrimental to creativity. An overall analysis of variance of composite creativity scores was conducted for the seven groups excluding the evaluation-specific creativity focus group; this group was eliminated from the analysis because it alone was predicted to deviate from the pattern of evaluation groups being lower in creativity. The results of this analysis were statistically significant. Thus, a planned contrast was performed on these seven groups to test the hypothesis that control groups (nonevaluation) were judged higher on creativity than experimental groups (evaluation, excluding the specific creativity focus group). This contrast was strongly significant ($p < .001$). Means for the composite creativity measure are presented in Figure 5-1.

Confirmation of McGraw's (1978) hypothesis on the differential effects of constraint on heuristic and algorithmic tasks is provided by a series of paired comparisons between control groups and the relevant experimental groups. As expected, only when evaluation subjects were given specific instructions on how to make a creative design did they produce art works judged as significantly more creative than those of nonevaluation subjects. The mean rated creativity for this specific instructions group (evaluation-specific creativity focus) was significantly higher than that of the relevant control. In all other cases, the nonevaluation groups were significantly higher on judged creativity than the comparable evaluation groups.

Technical goodness results. The technical goodness of the art works—the degree of technical competence displayed by subjects in their work—was also examined. Based on the factor analysis, a composite technical goodness measure was formed, composed of organization, neatness, planning, and expression of meaning. For the no-focus groups (nonevaluation-no focus and evaluation-no focus) and the creativity focus groups (nonevaluation-creativity focus, evaluation-creativity focus, and evaluation-specific creativity focus), the evaluation groups were rated lower on technical goodness than their nonevaluation controls. Paired comparisons bear out this observation: (1) the nonevaluation-no focus group was rated significantly higher than the evaluation-no focus group; and (2) the nonevaluation-creativity focus group was rated significantly higher than both the evaluation-creativity focus group and the evaluation-specific creativity focus group. However, this pattern seems to be reversed for the three technical focus groups, with the nonevaluation control (nonevaluation-technical focus) being rated the lowest of the three, although it was significantly lower than only the specific technical focus group.

At first glance, it appears that the pattern of technical goodness results mimics the pattern of creativity results. With the exception of the evaluation group that was told exactly what to do (the specific instructions group in each case), nonevaluation

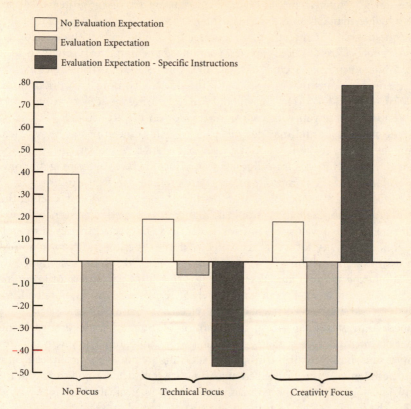

Figure 5-1.   Mean creativity of collages (Amabile, 1979).
Note. These numbers are the means of composites of six normalized components of creativity that clustered on the factor analysis of artist judgments.

groups were rated higher than evaluation groups. There is, however, one important difference between the creativity results and the technical goodness results. The creativity focus group that was told to expect evaluation, but was *not* told specifically what to do to receive a good evaluation (evaluation-creativity focus), was rated very low on creativity—significantly lower than its control. By contrast, however, the technical focus group that was told to expect evaluation, but was not told specifically what to do to receive a good evaluation (evaluation-technical focus), was *not* rated low on technical goodness. In fact, it was rated higher (though not significantly so) than its control group. This fits well with the notion that technical qualities of art works result from algorithmic processes that are not so severely affected by constraint as are the more heuristic processes that lead to creativity.

Intrinsic interest results. Several items on the Art Activity Questionnaire were intended to measure subjects' attitude toward the collage-making activity. A composite intrinsic interest measure was formed using six of those items. All six loaded higher than .50 on the intrinsic interest factor obtained in a factor analysis of questionnaire items, and they all correlated significantly with one another. These six items were: (1) "Did you view your engagement in the art activity as motivated more by intrinsic factors, like your own interest, or by extrinsic factors, like the experimenter's instructions?" (2) "Was the art activity more like work or more like leisure activity?" (3) "How playful did you feel during the activity session?" (4) "How satisfied were you with your performance on the art activity?" (5) "How much do you like your finished design?" and (6) "How much pressure did you feel during the activity session?" (This last item loaded high and negatively on the intrinsic interest factor, so it was subtracted from the other five in forming the composite.) Means for this composite measure are presented in Figure 5-2.

According to the predictions set out earlier, it was expected that, overall, the control groups (nonevaluation) would be higher in self-rated interest than the experimental groups (evaluation). In particular, it was expected that even though the specific creativity focus subjects might exhibit superior creativity in accord with their task instructions, their intrinsic interest would still be undermined by evaluation expectation. Thus, all eight groups should fit the pattern of lower interest under evaluation. This overall pattern of results was, in fact, obtained. An analysis of variance on all eight groups yielded a significant effect, as did a planned contrast testing the specific pattern of nonevaluation groups being higher on intrinsic interest than evaluation groups. In comparison with the creativity results, however, the intrinsic interest results are not as strong. Indeed, only two experimental-control paired comparisons are statistically significant: that for the two no focus groups (nonevaluation-no focus vs. evaluation-no focus), and that for the specific technical focus group and its control.

Despite the failure of specific comparisons, however, the overall planned contrast suggests that intrinsic interest was undermined by evaluation expectation in this study. This result is particularly important when the two specific focus groups are considered. Although the specific technical focus group was high on rated technical goodness, and the specific creativity instructions group was high on creativity, both of these groups were quite low on intrinsic interest. In other words, as predicted, the group that received specific creativity instructions did *not* exhibit a high level of intrinsic interest to match its high level of "creativity."

This study, then, demonstrates a negative effect of evaluation expectation on creativity. On the face of it, however, it also appears to demonstrate a *positive* effect of evaluation expectation if people are given specific instructions on how to "be creative." For two reasons, this high creativity of the specific creativity instructions group must be interpreted cautiously. On a practical level, it is unlikely that creativity in everyday performance could be enhanced by telling people exactly what constitutes a creative performance. The reason we value creative work so highly is that we cannot know beforehand just how to achieve a novel and appropriate response. On a theoretical level, the conceptual definition of creativity

Figure 5-2.   Mean self–ratings of intrinsic interest (Amabile, 1979).
Note. These numbers are the means of composites of six normalized measures of intrinsic
interest that clustered on the factor analysis of questionnaire items.

clearly disallows the consideration of the specific instructions task as "creative."
According to that definition, the task must be heuristic in order for the product of
task engagement to be considered creative. In this study, specific instructions on
how to make a collage that would be judged as "creative" rendered the task algorithmic. Thus, according to the conceptual definition, it is simply inappropriate to
assign the label "creative" to the performance of the specific creativity instructions
group. It *is* appropriate, though, to assign that label to the performance of the
nonevaluation groups since, for them, the task remained a heuristic one.

A Replication with Artistic Creativity

In order to firmly establish the finding that evaluation expectation has negative effects on adults' creativity, two replications were undertaken. In both, a simple two-
way factorial design was used: (1) subjects expected or did not expect evaluation
of their work, and (2) they worked either alone or in the presence of others. For
both of these replications, the purpose of and findings on the second variable will
be discussed in Chapter 7.

Subjects in the replication with artistic creativity (Amabile, Goldfarb, &
Brackfield, 1990, Study 2) were 40 undergraduate women enrolled in an introductory psychology course at Brandeis University. They participated in individual

sessions. Equal numbers of subjects were assigned randomly to one of four conditions: nonevaluation-no audience, nonevaluation-audience, evaluation-no audience, evaluation-audience. In this study, no subjects were told to focus on particular aspects of the collages. As in the previous study (Amabile, 1979), women with extremely high levels of experience in art were excluded, and subjects were told that the experiment examined the effects of various activities on mood.

The experimenter introduced the crucial manipulations as she presented the task. She told subjects in the evaluation-audience condition that their art works would be used as an important source of data in the experiment. She told them that, on the other side of a one-way mirror in the experimental room, four student-artists were waiting to watch subjects making their collages. These artists had supposedly been hired to make expert evaluations of their collage-making and their finished products, "noting the good points and criticizing the weaknesses." In addition, the experimenter told the subjects that they would see these evaluations before they left the experimental session.

Subjects in the evaluation-no audience condition received similar instructions. For them, however, a heavy curtain was drawn across the one-way mirror. They were informed that four student-artists waited in a conference room down the hall to view and inspect the finished collages. As in the evaluation-audience condition, subjects were told that the judges' expert evaluations would note the good points and criticize the weaknesses, and that they would see these evaluations before leaving.

Evaluation was not mentioned to subjects in the two nonevaluation conditions and, indeed, they believed (as did subjects in the earlier study) that the collages would not be used as a source of data. Subjects in the nonevaluation-audience condition were told that other subjects waited for a different experiment in the room on the other side of the one-way mirror. These other undergraduates were supposedly waiting in the dark for a vision experiment. Thus, although subjects in this condition believed that they would be seen while working on their collages, the audience would be relatively nonevaluative. Subjects in the nonevaluation-no audience condition were told nothing about an audience; for them, the one-way mirror was covered.

The reliability of 10 artist-judges' ratings of the collages was .93 for creativity. In support of the intrinsic motivation hypothesis, analysis of variance on the creativity judgments yielded a significant main effect of evaluation on creativity. The collages produced by the nonevaluation subjects were more creative than those produced by the evaluation subjects. There was a nonsignificant trend on the audience variable (to be discussed fully in Chapter 7), but there was no significant interaction between the two variables. Means for the creativity ratings are presented in Figure 5-3. The interjudge reliability of the technical goodness ratings was .91. There was no significant main effects or interactions on this variable.

Thus, the results of this study perfectly replicate the major finding of the earlier study on artistic creativity (Amabile, 1979). When given no particular focus

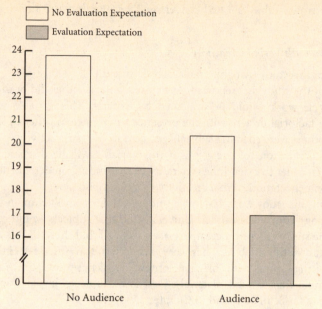

Figure 5-3.   Mean creativity of collages (Amabile, Goldfarb, & Brackfield, 1990, Study 2). *Note.* Highest possible value is 40, lowest is 0.

for their art works, subjects who expected an expert evaluation produced less creative work than subjects unconcerned about evaluation. Interestingly, there was no effect of evaluation on technical goodness in this study—a result that is in keeping with the suggestion that technical aspects of art work are largely algorithmic, while creative aspects are largely heuristic.[3]

Subjects' postexperimental questionnaire responses in this study yielded some intriguing results. Apparently, evaluation was quite salient to subjects in those conditions. When asked to rate the extent to which they felt anxious, evaluation subjects gave significantly higher self-ratings than did nonevaluation subjects. A similar main effect of evaluation held for subjects' responses to a question asking how concerned they were with possible evaluations of their work. In light of my suggestion that attention might mediate detrimental effects of constraint on creativity, one result from this questionnaire is of primary importance: Evaluation subjects reported significantly more distraction while working than did nonevaluation subjects. As might be expected, there was a significant negative correlation

---

[3] Neither this nor the earlier study (Amabile, 1979) provided clear evidence that technical goodness of the collages was *enhanced* by extrinsic constraint, as might be expected from McGraw's (1978) propositions on algorithmic and heuristic tasks. It could be, however, that technical proficiency on this simple collage-making task is quite easy to achieve and that adult subjects' baseline performance on the task is already high on this dimension.

($r = -.41$) between subjects' rated concern with evaluation and the creativity of their collages.

A Replication with Verbal Creativity

The design of this study (Amabile, Goldfarb, & Brackfield, 1990, Study 1) was similar to that of the study just reported. As before, subjects either did or did not expect that their work would be evaluated by experts. This variable was again crossed, in a factorial design, with the presence or absence of others. Here, however, those others were coacting subjects engaged in the same activity. (Again, the theoretical justification for inclusion of this variable will be discussed fully in Chapter 7.) In order to extend the generality of the finding on detrimental effects of evaluation expectation, verbal creativity was examined here.

Subjects in this study were 48 female undergraduates enrolled in an introductory psychology course at Brandeis University. So that subjects would remain ignorant of the study's focus on creativity, they were all told that this was an experiment on handwriting analysis. They were each to write an American Haiku poem as a handwriting sample with "original content" (which, presumably, would yield a better sample than copied material). Details of subjects' instructions for the Haiku-writing task can be found in Chapter 3.

Subjects in the evaluation conditions were told that the experimenter intended to relate handwriting features to poem content, and that both would be evaluated by expert judges. In addition, these subjects expected that they would receive a copy of the judges' evaluations of their poems. Those in the nonevaluation conditions were told that the experimenter was simply interested in the handwriting of an original work and was not at all concerned with the content of their poems. Evaluation of poem content was not mentioned. As a cross variable, either subjects were alone as they worked on their poems, or they worked in a room with three others. Each subject completed a postexperimental questionnaire designed to assess intrinsic interest.

Creativity of the poems was assessed according to the consensual assessment technique (see Chapter 3), yielding an interjudge reliability of .87 for the 10 poet-judges. In strong support of the intrinsic motivation hypothesis, and in good agreement with the earlier studies, there was a significant main effect of evaluation expectation on the creativity ratings. As illustrated in Figure 5-4, nonevaluation subjects wrote poems that were significantly more creative than those written by evaluation subjects. There was no main effect of the coaction variable, and no interaction between the two.

As in the collage studies, there were interesting results on the postexperimental questionnaire. As noted in Chapter 1, phenomenological accounts suggest that intrinsically motivated work is more satisfying than extrinsically motivated work. In keeping with this proposition, nonevaluation subjects reported feeling more satisfied with their poems than did evaluation subjects. In addition, there were two nonsignificant trends in the questionnaire data: (1) evaluation subjects, compared

Figure 5-4.   Mean creativity of poems (Amabile, Goldfarb, & Brackfield, 1990, Study 1).
Note. Highest possible value is 40, lowest is 0.

with nonevaluation subjects, reported that the task was more like work than like leisure; and (2) evaluation subjects scored higher in their self-rated concentration on the rules of American Haiku. As in the previous study, this result suggests the importance of attention to the task itself (rather than task constraints) in creative performance.

Impact of Actual Evaluation

In discussing the effects of reward on intrinsic motivation, Deci (1975) suggests that rewards can serve two distinct functions, which may affect intrinsic motivation differentially:

> Every reward (including feedback) has two aspects, a controlling aspect and an informational aspect which provides the recipient with information about his competence and self-determination. The relative salience of the two aspects determines which process will be operative. If the controlling aspect is more salient, it will initiate the change in perceived locus of causality process. If the informational aspect is more salient, the change in feelings of competence and self-determination process will be initiated. (p. 142)

Clearly, although these remarks are focused on the effects of rewards, they apply equally well to evaluation. Deci suggests that, to the extent that external evaluation of a person's work conveys external control over that work, intrinsic motivation will be undermined. And to the extent that external evaluation conveys competence information, intrinsic motivation will be enhanced. Implicit in these statements, of course, is the assumption that the evaluation is in fact positive. Intrinsic motivation theorists agree that failure will undermine intrinsic motivation—a key proposition in the componential framework of creativity (Chapter 4).

Actual evaluation, then, can have one of two effects on intrinsic motivation. First, as suggested by Karniol and Ross (1977), evaluative (or performance-contingent) rewards may enhance such motivation because they convey competence information. Deci (1975) agrees, but also suggests that performance-contingent rewards may undermine intrinsic motivation even more than task-contingent rewards if they are perceived as more controlling.

There is empirical evidence to suggest that both phenomena do, in fact, occur. Karniol and Ross (1977) found that, while performance-contingent rewards did not actually enhance intrinsic motivation above the level shown by nonrewarded controls, such informative rewards at least maintained motivation relative to a task-contingent reward condition (where the rewards were both nonevaluative and noninformative). In several experiments (Deci, 1971, 1972a; Deci, Cascio, & Krusell, 1973), Deci and his colleagues demonstrated consistently that male subjects show higher levels of intrinsic motivation after receiving positive feedback about their performance than after receiving no feedback. (As expected, the latter study also found that negative feedback decreased intrinsic motivation.)

On the other hand, Deci (1972b) has also demonstrated that performance-contingent rewards, which convey external control through the use of evaluation, *can* undermine intrinsic motivation relative to both task-contingent rewards and nonrewarded controls. Harackiewicz (1979) confirmed this finding in a particularly elegant experiment. Her results showed that performance-contingent rewards undermined interest more than task-contingent rewards which, in turn, undermined interest relative to a nonrewarded control. It is most interesting, in light of my earlier statements on the role of attention in creativity, that, compared to other subjects, the performance-contingent subjects in the Harackiewicz study recalled fewer aspects of the task that were not immediately relevant to solving the problem. For the purposes of the present discussion, however, it is important to point out that positive *feedback* in that study (whether it was initially expected or not) did enhance intrinsic motivation—independently of reward effects.

It appears, then, that the effects of evaluation on intrinsic motivation are complex. If the evaluation conveys external control over task engagement, then intrinsic motivation can be expected to decrease. If it conveys positive competence information, then intrinsic motivation can be expected to increase. According to the intrinsic motivation hypothesis of creativity, the creativity of immediate performance should show the same effects.

These hypotheses suggest a possible difference between *expected* evaluation and *actual* evaluation. With the performance (and any resultant feedback) yet to come, expected external evaluation can convey *only* external control over performance, thus undermining interest and creativity. This finding was demonstrated repeatedly in the studies reported earlier (Amabile, 1979, 1982a; Amabile, Goldfarb, & Brackfield, 1990). On the other hand, actual evaluation of performance can affect subsequent intrinsic motivation and creativity positively (if a feeling of competence is conveyed) or negativity (if controlling information is still more salient). One important determinant of the effect of actual evaluation might be the "size of the stakes" in the evaluation. If the external importance of the evaluation is made more salient than the information it communicates about competence, it is more likely that creativity will be adversely affected.

My colleagues and I (Berglas et al., 1979) set out to examine the effects of actual prior evaluation on children's subsequent creativity. In an attempt to study the impact of increasing the external-control aspects of the evaluation, we included a condition designed to raise its salience (the "size of the stakes"). Thus, some children were told that their doing well determined the potential job status of the experimenter. For others, no external event was contingent on their performance. It was expected that increasing the salience of evaluation would lead to greater creativity decrements. In addition, we decided to examine possible differential effects of *types* of positive evaluation. It seemed likely that evaluation directed at specific aspects of task performance (task-based evaluation) would convey more clear and salient competence information than would evaluation vaguely praising the performer (person-based evaluation). Thus, task-based evaluation should have a less detrimental effect on creativity than person-based evaluation.

This study employed a 2 × 2 factorial design with a separate control group. The subjects were 97 boys and girls in grades 2–6 at a private elementary school in eastern Massachusetts. All children made two art works. Experimental-group subjects received positive evaluation on their first art work, with half receiving task-based evaluation, and half receiving person-based. As a cross dimension, half of these subjects believed that the experimenter's welfare was in some way contingent on their performance, and half did not. After receiving their evaluations, the experimental-group subjects made the second art work—a collage that was subsequently rated on creativity. Control-group subjects simply made the two art works, with no evaluation and no information about external contingencies for their performance.

All children participated in individual sessions. At the beginning of each session, the experimenter explained that she was a student teacher and asked the children to listen to a tape-recording of instructions while she went to retrieve some needed materials. In this way, the experimenter remained blind to the instruction manipulation presented to the subjects. A condition of teacher-student *interdependence* was established by telling the children that the experimenter might get a job at another school if she showed that she could teach children at this school to make good art projects. A condition of teacher-student *independence* was established by telling the children that the experimenter was at their school merely to gain experience in teaching children to make good art projects prior to assuming a faculty position at another school.

When this introductory tape was finished, the experimenter returned and gave the subject the first art project—"Spin-Art." Each child made one spin-art design by placing a white card on a battery-powered turntable and, after sprinkling dots of colored ink anywhere on the card, turning on the motor for varying lengths of time. By this procedure, each child produced a unique design, depending on the amount, color, and placement of ink, and the duration of spinning to mix the colors.

Halfway through the spin-art period, and again following its completion, the experimenter administered the verbal reinforcement to experimental-group subjects. Half of the subjects received *task-based* praise, in which the experimenter described which physical aspects of the subject's project were good and why. The remaining experimental subjects were given *person-based* feedback, in which the experimenter told subjects that they appeared to be good artists. Following the second administration of feedback, subjects began work on the collage.

Subjective ratings of the creativity and technical goodness of the collages were obtained according to the standard consensual assessment technique. The inter-judge reliability of these ratings, over six judges, was .77 for creativity and .72 for technical goodness.

Means for the creativity scores are presented in Figure 5-5. It appears that, in fact, feedback based on specific information about task performance did lead to somewhat higher levels of creativity. In addition, there was some tendency for children who believed the experimenter was dependent on their performance to produce less creative collages. Neither of these main effects was significant by an analysis of variance, however, nor was their interaction.

The most striking pattern in the creativity results is the clear superiority of the control group over all four experimental groups. Although the orthogonal contrasts for the main effects and the interaction were nonsignificant, a planned contrast with the control group higher than the experimental groups *was* significant.[4] As in the earlier study of expected evaluation (Amabile, Goldfarb, & Brackfield, 1990, Study 2), there were no significant differences between conditions on the rated technical goodness of the collages.

Thus, although there might be some differences between types of positive evaluation in their effect on subsequent creativity, this study suggests that the overall negative effects of prior evaluation may be much more important. Certainly, all of the experimental-group children had received competence information about their artistic ability. At the same time, they most likely expected that their performance on the second activity—collage-making—would also be evaluated by the experimenter. This controlling aspect might have been more salient than the informational aspect of the feedback, regardless of whether it was person- or task-based.

---

[4] The weights used in this contrast were -1, -1, -1, -1, and +4.

Figure 5-5.   Mean creativity of collages (Berglas et al., 1981).
Note. Highest possible value is 40, lowest is 0.

Indeed, it may be that feedback on artistic pursuits is more likely to convey external control than is feedback on other types of tasks. Harackiewicz (1979) has suggested that activities such as games may be intrinsically motivating for the feelings of competence they produce. Feedback on these may more easily convey competence information and, in so doing, avoid an undermining of intrinsic motivation. On the other hand, activities such as drawing may be intrinsically motivating because they are enjoyable in their own right. Feedback on such activities may be most likely to convey control.

Summary

The studies presented in this chapter clearly demonstrate the negative effects that evaluation and evaluation expectation can have on creativity. This research points to a number of new conclusions about extrinsic constraint, intrinsic motivation, and creativity:

1. Although it has not been examined in previous intrinsic motivation research, the expectation of external evaluation should be included in the class of extrinsic constraints that comprises rewards, deadlines, and surveillance.
2. The expectation of evaluation can undermine creativity.
3. This effect will only hold if the task is a truly heuristic one; "creativity" will be enhanced by the expectation of evaluation if "creative" performance has been rendered algorithmic.

4. The undermining effect of evaluation holds for both adults and children, and for both artistic creativity and verbal creativity.
5. The technical aspects of performance do not appear to be adversely affected by the expectation of evaluation to the same degree as the creative aspects.
6. Actual evaluation, even if it is positive, may undermine future creative performance because it leads to expectations of future evaluation.

Update

Having spent several additional years conducting experimental and nonexperimental research and examining the growing body of research conducted by others, we now realize that the effects of expected evaluation on creativity are more complicated than we had originally proposed. Perhaps this should not be surprising, given that even in the 1983 edition we acknowledged that "the effects of evaluation on intrinsic motivation are complex." The complexity of evaluation effects on intrinsic motivation is borne out in several recent publications (e.g., Jussim, Soffin, Brown, Ley, & Kohlhepp, 1992; Harackiewicz, Abrahams, & Wageman, 1991). Creativity research over the past twelve years has yielded some replications of the negative effect of expected evaluation on creativity, some nonreplications, some partial replications, and even some evidence of positive effects of evaluation under certain conditions.

Some studies, using somewhat different methodologies from our original studies, have replicated those findings. In a study where children engaged in computer activities on which creativity could be assessed, those who were led to expect evaluation by either "the computer" or the experimenter produced less creative work than those not expecting evaluation (Hennessey, 1989). Other researchers have examined evaluation effects on creativity within the context of studies on social loafing. Typical social loafing studies have shown that subjects perform more poorly (i.e., they exert less effort) on noncreative tasks when they are working in group situations where their individual output cannot be evaluated, compared to situations where they work individually. However, when tasks calling for creativity are used (such as Unusual Uses tasks), it appears that participants whose outputs are pooled perform better—more "creatively"—than participants whose outputs can be evaluated (Bartis, Szymanski, & Harkins, 1988). Moreover, in social loafing studies, the potential for self-evaluation appears to have the same negative effect on creativity that the potential for external evaluation does (Szymanski & Harkins, 1992). Thus, there is considerable additional evidence that expected evaluation can indeed undermine creativity, even when the locus of evaluation is internal.

In our own laboratory, we have conducted some studies where evaluation failed to have a significant impact on creativity. For example, in one study subjects' motivational orientations (intrinsic or extrinsic, as assessed by a personality test) were crossed with the presence or absence of evaluation expectation. We found no effect of expected evaluation on creativity in that study. However, we had introduced an important variation into the procedure: we allowed subjects to decide for themselves how long they would spend working on their creativity task—a paper collage. Although we found no effect of evaluation on creativity, we did find a significant positive effect of evaluation on task persistence; subjects who expected evaluation spent significantly more time working on their collages. Moreover, we found that persistence and creativity were strongly positively correlated. This latter finding may have emerged because subjects who spend more time place more pieces on their collages, and judge-rated creativity tends to be correlated with the complexity of collages.

Other studies have partially replicated the negative effect of evaluation. In a study that preassessed subjects' shyness and experimentally manipulated evaluation expectation, there was no main effect of evaluation on poem-writing creativity (Cheek & Stahl, 1986). However, this study revealed that when faced with the prospect of receiving evaluative feedback, shy subjects performed substantially less creatively than those who were not shy. Thus, the effects of expected evaluation may depend on certain personality characteristics.

A number of our recent experiments have failed to find main effects of evaluation on creativity but have found intriguing interaction effects. For example, in one study where half of the subjects engaged in a creative preactivity related to the target activity and half engaged in a noncreative preactivity, the effect of evaluation depended on the subjects' preactivity condition (Conti, Amabile, & Pollak, 1995). Nonevaluation subjects did exhibit higher creativity than those expecting testlike evaluation, but only in the creative preactivity condition. All subjects in the noncreative preactivity condition exhibited relatively low creativity, even those who were not expecting evaluation.

In another study where the subjects were all computer science students and the creativity task involved computer programming, we obtained separate measures of the students' skill levels in computer programming (Conti & Amabile, 1995). Although, again, there was no main effect of expected evaluation in this study, we found that low-skill students wrote better programs when expecting evaluation, and high-skill students wrote better programs in the no-evaluation condition. Similar effects have emerged in a study where the subjects were advanced art students and the creativity task was a drawing activity (Pollak, 1992), and in a study where the subjects were poetry students and the creativity task was writing poetry. We have also found this skill level–evaluation interaction pattern in a study where introductory psychology students wrote a brief prose passage as their creative activity following a separate assessment of their skill in prose writing (Hill, Amabile, Coon, & Whitney, 1994). Half of the subjects expected public evaluation of their work immediately following the creative writing activity whereas the other half had no expectation of evaluation. Although there was no main effect of evaluation expectation on creativity, we found that low-skill subjects were more creative under evaluative conditions, but high-skill subjects were more creative under non-evaluative conditions.

Finally, in our nonexperimental research over the past several years, we have found some evidence of positive effects of evaluation on creativity. In interview studies where employees were asked to describe both high-creativity and low-creativity events from their work experience, we have found, as expected from our experimental research, that the prospect of threatening critical evaluation often co-occurs with low levels of creativity (Amabile & S. Gryskiewicz, 1987). However, these same studies show that informative, constructive feedback and evaluation that conveys positive recognition of creative work often co-occur with high levels of creativity. Similar findings have emerged in studies that used questionnaire measures to assess the presence or absence of particular social factors in the work environment (Amabile, Conti, Coon, Lazenby, & Herron, in press; Amabile & N. Gryskiewicz, 1989). In sum, these studies suggest that in real-world settings, creativity may be undermined by evaluation that conveys incompetence or threatens self-determination, but creativity may be supported by evaluation that is work-focused and constructive (even when negative), that provides information about performance improvement, or that conveys positive recognition of competence and valued work. These positive effects of evaluation may be due to the motivational synergy mechanisms described in the update to Chapter 4: extrinsics in service of intrinsics, and the motivation–work cycle match.

Clearly, much work needs to be done to untangle the complex effects of evaluation (and expected evaluation) on intrinsic motivation and creativity. Because negative evaluation effects have been found even under self-evaluative conditions, it appears that there is something more than threatened self-determination operating. It might be useful to explore the role of attentional mechanisms, and consider the possibility that a concern with evaluation might lead to a focus on more obvious aspects of the task or more algorithmic forms of task engagement. In addition, future research should examine the role of skill in the task domain, exploring the possibility that evaluation is more likely to be perceived as informational at low levels of skill, but as controlling at higher levels of skill. Finally, the informational value of evaluation should be studied more broadly, even beyond the context of skill-level studies, and attempts should be made to discover possible supportive functions of positive evaluation that go beyond competence information.

Summary

Research on the negative effects of evaluation on creativity has yielded some replications, some partial replications, and some failures to replicate. It appears that the negative effect depends on certain individual-difference traits, on initial interest in the activity, and on initial skill level. Some new findings from nonexperimental research suggest that evaluation can have positive effects on creativity when it is work-focused and constructive.

6
Effects of Reward and Task Constraint

One of the most fascinating and frustrating aspects of creativity is that, in some ways, it defies effort. Unlike most desirable behaviors that psychologists study, creative behavior cannot be achieved simply by trying. Even individuals who have previously distinguished themselves for outstanding creativity often fail to produce creative work, despite their best efforts. Indeed, these individuals—for example, writers suffering "writer's block"—often complain that the harder they try, the more meager their success. Recall the excerpt from Dostoevsky's letter that was presented in Chapter 1. There, he described the extreme difficulty he encountered in writing a commissioned novel: "I believe you have never written to order, by the yard, and have never experienced that hellish torture" (Allen, 1948, p. 231). These difficulties often seem to arise when people attempt to meet the demands of others—in other words, when they try for the wrong reasons.

This chapter will examine some ways in which people may make demands on the performance of others, and the effects that those demands can have on creativity. Each of these factors in some way conveys direct external control over task engagement: a lack of choice concerning whether to engage in a task, the offer of some type of reward for task engagement, and a lack of choice concerning how to engage in a task.

These factors, particularly the use of reward, have been the focus of heated controversy in psychology over the past two decades. Perhaps no independent variable has been more thoroughly studied by experimental psychology than reward. According to the classical Skinnerian position (e.g., Skinner, 1938), reinforcement is the heart of behavioral control. If desired behaviors (or successive approximations to them) are rewarded, the likelihood of those behaviors will increase. Beginning around 1970, researchers began to question seriously the assumption that reward will always enhance (or will at least maintain) all behaviors. Basing their conclusions largely on the overjustification research described in Chapter 4, intrinsic motivation theorists suggested that reward can undermine certain aspects of behavior under some conditions (e.g., deCharms, 1968; Deci, 1971; Lepper et al., 1973; McGraw, 1978). Specifically, they concluded that, for many behaviors, reward can decrease the likelihood that those behaviors will be performed under subsequent nonrewarded conditions. In addition, they suggested that reward can decrease enjoyment in the activity itself and can undermine certain noninstrumental aspects of task performance. Not surprisingly, these claims have been challenged by researchers working in the behaviorist tradition (e.g., Farr, 1976; Feingold & Mahoney, 1975; Hamner & Foster, 1975; Reiss & Sushinsky, 1975). Nonetheless, the phenomenon of lower intrinsic motivation following external reward has been well-documented empirically, and there is evidence that other external constraints are functionally equivalent to rewards in this respect (e.g., Amabile et al., 1976; Lepper & Greene, 1975).

According to self-perception theory (Bem, 1972), subjects in the overjustification studies do not begin with a clear and salient awareness of their intrinsic interest in the task. Because of this, subjects who perform the task in order to meet some extrinsic contingency "infer" that their task engagement was motivated only by the constraint, and not by their own interest. In other words, these subjects should see themselves as extrinsically motivated. This explanation suggests that subjects make use of the "discounting principle" applied to the schema for "multiple sufficient causes" (Kelley, 1973): An individual will discount one possible cause of a behavior if other, more salient or plausible causes are present. In the case of the intrinsic motivation studies, the external constraint is taken to be a more salient and plausible cause than the subjects' own interest in the task. Similarly, cognitive evaluation theory (Deci, 1975; Deci & Ryan, 1980) proposes that the presence of salient external constraints on performance cause a shift in the individual's perceived locus of causality from internal to external.

In focusing on attentional processes, the intrinsic motivation hypothesis of creativity shares with these theories an emphasis on the cognitive effects of external constraint. This hypothesis builds upon previous intrinsic motivation theories by proposing that, in undermining intrinsic motivation, rewards and other constraints will undermine the creativity of the immediate performance. I have already suggested (Chapter 4) that this undermining effect occurs, in part, because some of the individual's attention is diverted from the task itself and nonobvious aspects of the environment that might be used in achieving a creative solution.

There is reason to believe, however, that noncognitive processes can also play a role in the negative influence of constraints on interest and creativity. For example, it appears that young children do not apply this proposed cognitive analysis to their own behavior in situations of social constraint. Indeed, they may be incapable of doing so. In studies where children were explicitly requested to answer questions for which the discounting principle is applied by adults, virtually no children under the age of 7 were capable of using the discounting principle (DiVitto & McArthur, 1978; Karniol & Ross, 1976; Morgan, 1981; Smith, 1975). In one study where they did apply discounting correctly, they seemed to do so without any awareness of the general principle. Nonetheless, children of these ages do quite consistently show an undermining of intrinsic interest under conditions of social constraint (e.g., Lepper et al., 1973; Lepper & Greene, 1975; Ross, 1975).

It is possible that the negative effects of constraint on children's intrinsic interest might be primarily mediated by affective rather than cognitive mechanisms and that, if not primary, affective mechanisms might at least be important mediators for adults as well. In other words, the mechanism underlying this phenomenon might be dependent on "feeling," "emotion," or "arousal" in addition to (or even instead of) thought or rational analysis.

There is, in fact, evidence that the phenomenon has affective components in adults. In many of the intrinsic motivation studies (e.g., Amabile et al., 1976), adults who work under social constraints and subsequently display less interest in the task also express less retrospective satisfaction in and enjoyment of the task itself. It may be that people react negatively to a task as "work" when their behavior is controlled or appears to be controlled by socially imposed factors, and that they react positively to the task as "play" when there are no constraints on task engagement. In other words, negative affect may be generated by socially learned stereotypes of "work" as something unpleasant that one has to be coerced to do (e.g., Lepper & Greene, 1978a; McGraw, 1978; Morgan, 1981). This affective explanation of the phenomenon is consistent with the introspections of many highly creative individuals (see Chapter 1).

Thus, I suggest that the undermining of creativity under external constraint is mediated not only by cognitive processes (task judgments, self-judgments, and attention), but also by affective processes (feelings of displeasure with a task approached as "work"). Likewise, the conducive effect of intrinsic motivation on creativity may be mediated by feelings of pleasure in a task approached as "play." Thus, not only should factors that decrease the individual's enjoyment of a task undermine creativity, but factors that *increase* the individual's enjoyment should enhance creativity. It is even possible that, under some circumstances, certain types of reward might enhance enjoyment and, hence, creativity. This is an important and somewhat controversial point, and I will return to it later.

Previous Research

Negative Effects of Reward on Performance Quality

There is little previous research directly demonstrating a negative effect of reward on creativity, but some suggestive evidence does exist. A number of studies, for example, demonstrate effects on other qualitative aspects of immediate performance. In one (Garbarino, 1975), fifth- and sixth-grade girls acted as tutors to first- and second-grade girls. The older children were asked to teach a matching task to the younger girls in a single experimental session. The tutors were either promised a reward (a free movie ticket) if the younger child learned well, or were told nothing of reward. The dependent variables included a rich array of qualitative performance dimensions: the tutors' use of evaluation, hints, and demands; the learners' performance; the emotional tone of the interaction, including the instances of laughter between the children during the session; and the efficiency of the tutoring (learning per unit time spent). Overall, the rewarded tutors held sessions that were high-pressured and business-like, while the nonrewarded tutors held sessions that were relaxed yet highly efficient. Subjective ratings by two observers characterized the rewarded sessions as tense and hostile, and the nonrewarded sessions as warm and relaxed. Moreover, the rewarded sessions were marked by more demands from the tutors, more negative evaluative statements by the tutors, less laughter, and poorer learning by the learners.

Expected reward can also influence an individual's initial approach to a task. Shapira (1976) found that subjects expecting payment for success chose relatively easy puzzles to work on, whereas subjects expecting no payment chose much more challenging ones. Similarly, Pittman and his colleagues (Pittman, Emery, & Boggiano, 1982) found that nonrewarded subjects showed a strong subsequent preference for complex versions of a game, whereas rewarded subjects chose simpler versions. This effect obtained even though the groups had performed equally well on moderately complex versions of the game. Even monkeys, according to Harlow (Harlow, Harlow, & Meyer, 1950), will show less interest in solving puzzles and will perform less well after food rewards have been introduced.

Some studies have used tasks similar to those used in the creativity research reported later in this chapter. A number of researchers, for example, have asked children to draw pictures under rewarded or nonrewarded conditions (e.g., Greene & Lepper, 1974; Lepper, Greene, & Nisbett, 1973; Loveland & Olley, 1979). These studies have found that, for children who initially display a high level of interest in drawing, working for expected reward decreases subsequent interest. This decrement in interest persists for at least a week beyond the initial rewarded or nonrewarded drawing session. Furthermore, the globally assessed "quality" of these children's drawings is lower than that of nonrewarded children. Interestingly, some of these studies have also found that working for expected reward may *increase* the subsequent interest of children who were initially uninterested in the activity.

Other research has examined processes related to creative behavior as it is described in Chapter 4. Work on incidental learning is particularly relevant. In an early study (Bahrick, Fitts, & Rankin, 1952), subjects performed a tracking task either with or without the expectation of performance-contingent reward. Nonrewarded subjects were much more likely to correctly report a sequence of lights that had been flashing on the periphery of the visual field during the tracking task. Indeed, almost half of the rewarded subjects failed to notice the flashing lights at all, whereas virtually all of the nonrewarded subjects noticed them. In a conceptual replication of this study (Johnson & Thomson, 1962), rewarded subjects remembered significantly fewer nonsense syllables overheard during serial learning than did nonrewarded subjects. Finally, in a serial learning study (McNamara & Fisch, 1964), students learned words printed in upper case, one per card, in the center of index cards. Four additional words were typed in lower case at varying distances from the center of the cards. No mention was made of these words, and they were irrelevant to the central task as presented by the experimenter. Rewarded subjects recalled significantly fewer of these words than did nonrewarded subjects. In addition, those words the rewarded subjects did recall tended to appear closer to the center of the cards. Clearly, these results suggest a narrowing of attention to goal-relevant stimuli during engagement on externally rewarded tasks.

Studies of outstandingly creative persons provide little insight into the short-term effects of rewards and other extrinsic constraints on creative performance. In a massive archival study, Simonton (1977a) examined the relationship between creative productivity at various points in the lives of 10 classical composers (total number of works and total number of themes) and the social reinforcements they received during those periods (an honorary doctorate, a public monument erected in one's honor, membership in an honorary society, listing in a *Who's Who,* public celebration of one's birthday, knighting, a prize, a "key to the city," and a society founded in one's honor). The two variables were not significantly related. By contrast, in a study of Nobel laureates in science, Zuckerman (1967) found that productivity declined by a third after receipt of the award—from an average of 6.2 papers per year in the 5 years before the award to an average of 4.2 papers per year in the 5 years following it. The productivity of a control group of scientists (matched on age, field, and type of organizational affiliation) declined by only 12% during the same period. Neither of these studies, though, is ideal for a test of the intrinsic motivation hypothesis of creativity. For one thing, both studied individuals who undoubtedly had extraordinarily high levels of baseline intrinsic interest in their fields. In addition, Simonton's study examined relatively long-term relationships between variables, and Zuckerman's results could easily be explained by the increased extraneous demands on one's time following the Nobel prize.

Negative Effects of Reward on Creativity

There are a few studies that directly show a negative effect of reward or task constraint on creativity. In the only such study using standard creativity tests (Sanders, Tedford, & Hardy, 1977), volunteer subjects scored higher on three tests (though not significantly so) than subjects forced to participate for course credit. Virtually all of the studies showing an undermining effect have used relatively open-ended tasks. For example, Glucksberg (1962) gave subjects Duncker's (1945) candle problem. This task requires subjects to mount a candle on a vertical screen, using only the screen, the candle, a book of matches, and a box of thumbtacks. Solution of the problem requires subjects to "break set" by seeing that the thumbtack box can be used not only as a container but also as a platform for the candle. Subjects in the reward condition were told that they could win $5 if their solution time was in the top 25% and $20 if it was the single fastest solution time. Nonreward subjects, who received no such instructions, solved the problem significantly faster. In a conceptual replication (Glucksberg, 1964), subjects were told either that they could win $10 if their solution time was the fastest, or that the task was simply being pilot-tested to establish solution-time norms. The set-breaking problem involved seeing that a screwdriver could be used to complete an electrical circuit for which the available wires were too short. Again, nonrewarded subjects solved the problem significantly faster. Interestingly, when the correct solution was made obvious by providing a screwdriver that was perceptually similar to the wires and posts, reward had no significant detrimental effect. Indeed, reward led to somewhat faster solution times. This result, of course, fits well with McGraw's proposition that extrinsic constraint will undermine performance on heuristic tasks but enhance performance on algorithmic tasks (cf. Chapter 4).

McGraw and McCullers (1979) replicated Glucksberg's basic results, using another set-breaking task: Luchins's (1942) water jar problems. Each problem presents subjects with drawings of three water jars (A, B, and C) of different sizes. For each problem, subjects are to write an equation for using the three jars to measure out an exact amount of water. Each of the first nine problems in the series can be solved with the equation, B - A - 2C. Problem #10, the "set-breaking" problem, can only be solved with a different, simpler equation: A - C. Although there were no differences in solution time or error rates on the first nine problems, subjects who had been offered rewards for correct solutions took significantly longer to solve the tenth problem than did nonrewarded subjects. Surprisingly, there were no differences in this study between rewarded and nonrewarded subjects in their expressed interest in the water-jar task.

Another study, however, did find effects for both performance and expressed interest. Kruglanski et al. (1971) gave two open-ended creativity tasks (among several other tasks) to Israeli high school students who either had or had not been promised a reward for their participation. The reward was a tour of the Tel Aviv University psychology department. The creativity tasks, adapted from Barron (1968), required subjects to list as many titles as possible for a literary paragraph, and to use as many words as possible from a 50-word list in writing their own story. The originality ratings of these responses by two independent judges had good interjudge reliabilities (.92 and .87 for the two creativity tasks, respectively). There was a clear and statistically significant superiority of nonrewarded subjects on these measures. In addition, there were nearly significant differences between the two groups on two intrinsic interest measures: subjects' expressed enjoyment of the activities and their willingness to volunteer for further participation. There is, then, considerable evidence suggesting that reward and other forms of task constraint might be detrimental to creativity. Subjects offered rewards differ from subjects not offered rewards in their approach to open-ended tasks: Rewarded subjects prefer simpler, less challenging tasks; they approach their tasks with less enjoyment; they focus more narrowly on the attainment of the extrinsic goal; they sometimes express less interest in the task; they have more difficulty breaking set; and they may even produce work that is subjectively rated as less creative.

Positive Effects of Reward on "Creativity"

The intrinsic motivation hypothesis concerning reward and task constraint, however, faces some difficulty when the results of creativity-enhancement studies are considered (cf. Amabile, 1983). These studies, generally designed in the behavior modification tradition, were intended to show—and, for the most part, do show—positive effects of reward on creative performance. In reconciling these studies with the intrinsic motivation hypothesis, it will be important to consider the nature of the tasks used. In virtually every one of the creativity-enhancement studies, creative performance is assessed by standard creativity tests.

Research by Glover and Gary (1976) provides a good example. Using a standard behavior modification paradigm, these researchers first obtained baseline measures of the performance of eight children on the Unusual Uses test. Following five baseline sessions, the experimenter explained to the children each of the dimensions of creativity scored on this test: fluency (number of different responses); flexibility (number of different verb forms used in responses—e.g., *holding* various things in a tin can, *pounding* various things with the tin can); elaboration (number of words per response); and originality (statistical infrequency of the response). For the next several sessions, the class of eight children was divided into two teams. At the start of each session, the teams were told that the one with the most points each day would win extra recess time, cookies, and milk. Both could win if the lower score was within 80% of the higher score. For each of five consecutive days, the children were told that fluency would be rewarded; then flexibility was rewarded for five days, and so on. The pattern of results was striking. During the period that a particular response dimension was rewarded, scores on that dimension showed an increase over baseline. Following the reward period, they dropped back to the baseline levels. It is interesting to compare the magnitude of changes in the various dimensions. By far, the greatest increase occurred in elaboration (the number of words per response), followed by fluency (the number of responses) and flexibility (the number of verb forms). By far, the smallest increase was found in originality (the statistical infrequency of responses).

Other behavior-modification studies of creativity have obtained results that are generally similar to these:

1. Subjects told they would receive extra course credit for doing well on the Torrance Tests of Creative Thinking achieved significantly higher scores on fluency, flexibility, and originality than did nonrewarded subjects (Halpin & Halpin, 1973). The research report does not allow a determination of the relative magnitudes of differences on the three dimensions.
2. Offer of performance-contingent reward led to greater fluency and flexibility of ideas produced on the Torrance tests (Raina, 1968).
3. Fluency on the Wallach and Kogan tests has been increased by both tangible and verbal reward, compared to nonreward conditions (Milgram &

Feingold, 1977; Ward, Kogan, & Pankove, 1972). Originality on these tests has not shown similar effects.

4. Subjects participating in a "creativity workshop" which included reinforcement for the different dimensions of creativity achieved higher creativity-test scores than a control group. The only large difference, however, was on fluency (Glover, 1980).

5. Economically disadvantaged children who were promised a reward if they "worked hard" on a creativity test scored higher on fluency, flexibility, elaboration, and originality than those not promised a reward (Johnson, 1974). This effect was not found for economically advantaged children, however; indeed, for them, there was a trend in the opposite direction.

6. Fluency, flexibility, and elaboration in children's essays were enhanced by token and social reinforcement in one study (Campbell & Willis, 1978). No attempt was made in this study to enhance originality.

7. When children were offered extra candy and recess as prizes, their use of different adjectives, different action verbs, and different sentence beginnings in stories was increased (Maloney & Hopkins, 1973). Stories written after the reinforcement period were generally rated as more creative.

8. Subjects who were reinforced for making uncommon word associations produced more of them than did nonreinforced subjects (Locurto & Walsh, 1976).

These studies, then, seem to "add creativity to the growing list of behaviors amenable to behavior modification by means of contingency management" (Milgram & Feingold, 1977). In so doing, they seem to contradict the research showing that expected reward and other forms of task constraint will undermine creativity. This seeming contradiction can be resolved, however, by considering both the nature of the rewards and the nature of the tasks in the two groups of studies.

A Resolution of Contradictory Findings

There is, first, a theoretical explanation for the apparently contradictory findings on effects of reward. As noted in the last chapter, rewards that convey competence information to subjects may not undermine intrinsic motivation as much as rewards that convey only controlling information. In fact, informative rewards might actually enhance intrinsic motivation (Deci, 1975; Deci & Ryan, 1980). Many of the "token economy" studies, in which subjects are contingently rewarded over relatively long periods of time, convey continuous information to subjects about their performance. If the performance meets certain standards, subjects automatically receive rewards. Thus, if this informative aspect of reward becomes more important than its controlling aspect, subjects might not experience a decrement in intrinsic motivation.

There are also two ways in which the nature of the tasks used in reward studies can account for the apparently contradictory results. Intrinsic motivation theorists have maintained that it only makes sense to discuss an undermining of intrinsic motivation when the task is originally intrinsically interesting to subjects (e.g., Deci & Ryan, 1980; Lepper & Greene, 1978a). Similarly, McGraw (1978) has proposed that extrinsic constraints will undermine performance on tasks only when the individual's own interest in those tasks is enough to motivate engagement. Although there is some evidence that subjects find the open-ended tasks of problem-solving and storytelling intrinsically interesting, there is no evidence that subjects feel the same way about the standard creativity tests. Indeed, there might be little intrinsic interest in instruments that, like standard achievement and intelligence tests, are group-administered in classrooms. Interest in the creativity task, then, is one basic difference between the studies showing negative and positive effects of reward. Enhancement in performance is to be expected when intrinsic interest is initially low.

Most importantly, however, it is essential to consider differences in the algorithmic or heuristic nature of the tasks used in these studies (cf. McGraw, 1978). I argued in Chapters 4 and 5 that performance on a task can only be called "creative" if that task is heuristic rather than algorithmic. In other words, the task must be relatively open-ended, with no clear and straightforward path to solution. However, the tasks used by virtually all of the behavior modification studies do have relatively clear and straightforward paths to the "creative" solutions. In fact, in many of those studies, subjects were told precisely what sort of responses would be considered creative. Not surprisingly, as when subjects making collages were told precisely how to make a "creative" collage (Amabile, 1979), external constraint led to enhanced performance. The researchers designing the creativity-enhancement studies would, perhaps, argue that open-ended tasks would be inappropriate for use in their studies; it must, after all, be clear to subjects which aspects of performance are to be reinforced. This is precisely the point. To the extent that such aspects of performance are readily available to subjects, the task is inappropriate for a demonstration of creativity.

This argument is bolstered by an examination of the patterns of results obtained in the behavior modification studies. In most of them, the more strictly algorithmic aspects of assessed creativity were the most strongly influenced by reinforcement. Specifically, sheer quantity and variety of responses (fluency, flexibility, and elaboration) were much more strongly influenced than originality (statistical infrequency of responses). And where originality (statistical infrequency) of responses was enhanced by reward, subjects had been told explicitly that they should give unusual responses. In addition, the set-breaking studies (Glucksberg, 1962; 1964; McGraw & McCullers, 1979) showed a superiority of nonreward subjects on problems where the correct solution was not directly obvious. There was no such superiority, however, when the correct solution *was* obvious; in fact, under such circumstances, reward subjects sometimes performed better (Glucksberg, 1964).

Thus, the results of creativity-enhancement studies can be reconciled to the hypothesis that reward and other constraints will undermine creativity. Previous research, however, provides neither strong support for nor strong disconfirmation of that hypothesis. As noted in my review above, most of the supportive evidence is suggestive; very few studies have directly assessed the effect of reward on creativity with open-ended tasks. So that the conclusion could be drawn with greater certainty, I conducted two studies examining the effects of external reward on creativity.

Effects of Reward on Children's Creativity

Most studies that examine the effects of reward on intrinsic motivation use a paradigm in which subjects are promised some tangible reward before engaging in an activity, but the reward itself is delivered after the activity has been completed. Critics of overjustification research (e.g., Reiss & Sushinsky, 1975) have suggested that this methodology allows for alternative explanations of subsequent declines in task engagement. For example, they suggest that subjects are so distracted by anticipation of reward during the initial task engagement that their enjoyment of the activity is hampered. Thus, according to this explanation, later lack of interest in the activity occurs not because subjects came to see it only as a means to some external goal, but because their intrinsic enjoyment of the activity was directly blocked by the "competing response" of reward anticipation.

In this study of reward effects on children's creativity, Beth Hennessey and I used a paradigm that renders the competing response hypothesis untenable. The reward offered to children before task engagement was not a tangible gift to be delivered afterwards. Rather, it was an enjoyable activity—playing with a Polaroid camera—that children were allowed to do *before* the target activity. In other words, children in the reward condition promised to do the target activity in order to first have a chance to play with the camera. Children in the no-reward condition were simply allowed to play with the camera and then given the target activity; there was no contingency between the two. Since children in both conditions had already enjoyed the "reward" before the activity began, then, it is unlikely that any reward-related "competing responses" were operating.

In addition to the offer of reward, task labeling was introduced as a second independent variable in this study. This was done to test the possibility that simply viewing activities as "work" can lead to the same undermining effects on intrinsic motivation and creativity as being placed under extrinsic constraints. Earlier in this chapter, I suggested that overjustification effects might occur even if people do not go through the discounting analysis proposed by self-perception theory (Bem, 1972). That is, rather than cognitively discounting their own interest in an activity when some salient external goal is present, people (particularly children) might simply come to see such an activity as "work"—as something that is done only under external constraint. Thus, introducing a task to children as "work" might directly instantiate the task attitude that they are presumed to develop under conditions of social constraint.

The 58 boys and 57 girls who participated in this study were enrolled in Grades 1–5 at a private elementary school in eastern Massachusetts. Within each grade, children were randomly assigned to experimental condition according to a 2 × 3 factorial design: Two levels of reward (reward or no reward) were crossed with three levels of task label ("work" or "play" or no label). The children participated in individual sessions with a female experimenter who told them that she had different activities for them to do. The target activity for all children was the same— telling a story to a book without words. This book (Mayer, 1967) tells a story through 30 pages of pictures. The pictures are sufficiently ambiguous that, although the basic story line is clear, there is room for a great deal of flexibility in interpretation and description of events, reactions, and so on.

The experimenter began by telling children in the reward conditions that she would let them take two pictures with a Polaroid camera if they would promise to then tell her a story from the book. All children expressed enthusiasm for playing with the camera, and all did promise to do the target activity later. At this point, the experimenter asked children in the reward conditions to sign a contract stating their promise. Children in the no-reward conditions were simply told that the experimenter had two different things for them to do—taking pictures with a Polaroid camera, and telling a story from a book. No promise was requested, and no contract was presented. All children were then allowed to use the camera to take two photographs of interesting objects the experimenter had brought. These photographs were then labeled with the child's name and placed in a large album.

After the picture-taking session had ended, the experimenter reminded children in the reward conditions of their promise to tell a story. She then presented the storytelling task according to the appropriate label condition. To children in the "work" conditions, she presented the task as "something for you to work on." To those in the "play" conditions, she presented it as "something for you to play with." She used neither a work label nor a play label in presenting the task to children in the "no label" conditions. All children were asked to look through all the pictures in the book first, and then to start at the beginning with their story, "saying one thing" about each page. Just before the children began their storytelling, the experimenter again referred to the task as "work" or "play" for those in the labeling conditions. She made no remarks during the storytelling, although she did prompt children if they neglected to say something for a particular page.

These stories were tape-recorded and later transcribed. They were independently read and rated on creativity by three elementary school teachers who yielded an interjudge reliability of .91. The mean ratings for the six conditions are presented in Figure 6-1. It is clear from the pattern of means that, overall, children in the no-reward conditions told more creative stories than did children in the reward conditions. This main effect of reward is, in fact, statistically significant by analysis of variance. There was no significant effect of task label on creativity.

Given the clear superiority of nonrewarded children over rewarded children under "work" label and "play" label conditions, it is surprising that there was no

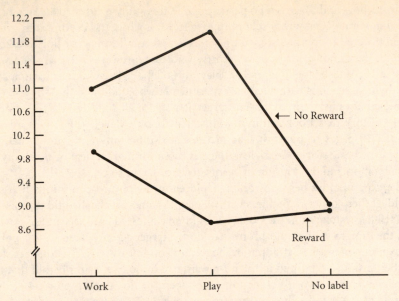

Figure 6-1.   Mean creativity of stories (Hennessey 1982).
Note. Highest possible value is 21, lowest possible is 3.

effect of reward when no task label was provided. It is inappropriate to draw conclusions from this deviant data point, however, since the interaction between reward and task label was not statistically significant.

Clearly, differential task labels had no effect on children's creativity. It is possible, of course, that the manipulation of task label in this study was too weak to produce any reliable effects. Perhaps the children did not attend to the experimenter's brief mention of the task as "work" or "play." It may be, however, that overjustification effects are *not* mediated by the adoption of the view that a task is "work." It may be that, instead, decreases in intrinsic motivation are mediated by discounting effects (as predicted by self-perception theory), or by negative affect resulting from perceptions of external control. Additional research will be needed to allow firm conclusions on the mediation of decreases in intrinsic motivation and creativity under extrinsic constraint.

This study, then, provides clear evidence that, at least under some circumstances, undertaking an activity as a means to an end can undermine creativity. It is important that this effect occurs even when nonrewarded subjects also experience the "reward," and even when the reward is delivered before the target activity. The only difference in the experiences of rewarded and nonrewarded children in this study was their *perception* of the reward as contingent or not contingent upon the target activity. Thus, it appears that the perception of a task as the means to an end is crucial to creativity decrements in task engagement.

The Interaction of Reward and Choice

Several intrinsic motivation theorists have proposed that, in order to undermine intrinsic interest, rewards must be salient (Ross, 1975) and perceived as a means to an extrinsic end (Calder & Staw, 1975; Deci, 1975; Kruglanski et al., 1971; Lepper et al., 1973; Ross, 1977; Staw, 1976). The second point is particularly important, and the study just reported provides some suggestive evidence in support of it. Other researchers have produced convincing demonstrations of the role of means-end contingency in undermining intrinsic interest. For example, in one of the earliest overjustification studies (Lepper et al., 1973), it was found that children who received an unexpected reward after engaging in a task displayed just as much subsequent interest in the task as did children who received no reward at all. At the same time, children in those two groups displayed significantly more subsequent interest than children in an expected-reward group. In other words, only those who had explicitly contracted to do the activity in order to obtain a reward showed a decrement in interest.

In another study (Kruglanski et al., 1972), subjects who received an unexpected reward after task engagement, but were induced to believe that they had been promised it in advance, showed significantly less subsequent interest in the task than those not rewarded at all. It is important that this effect was almost entirely accounted for by subjects in the unexpected-reward condition who actually did believe the experimenter when told that they had engaged in the task in order to obtain the reward.

Finally, in a study where experimental-group children engaged in one activity in order to have the chance to engage in another, they were later less interested in the first activity than were control-group children who simply engaged in both tasks (Lepper, Sagotsky, Dafoe, & Greene, 1982). This effect held regardless of which task was presented as the means and which was presented as the reward. Thus, it has been shown that rewards *will not* undermine interest if they are not seen as an end for which task engagement is the means. They *will* undermine interest if they are seen as an end for task engagement, even if subjects are led to believe after the fact that receiving them was contingent on task performance. And they will undermine interest even if they are no more "reward-like" than the task upon which they are contingent.

There is one additional method for demonstrating the crucial role of perceiving a task as a means to a reward—offering people a *choice* concerning task engagement. If people perceive themselves as freely choosing to do an activity for which a reward is offered, they might well adopt an extrinsic motivational orientation toward that activity. They should come to view the task as work, and their own engagement in the activity as motivated by that external reward. On the other hand, if people are simply presented with a task to do and told that they will be paid, with no choice in the matter, reward should not have this detrimental effect. This phenomenon was demonstrated in a recent study by Folger, Rosenfield, and

Hays (1978). Using a factorial design with two levels of choice and two levels of reward, these researchers obtained a clear interaction on the subjects' subsequent interest. Under conditions of high choice, rewarded subjects showed significantly less interest than nonrewarded subjects. By contrast, under conditions of no choice, rewarded subjects showed more interest.

In a recent study (Amabile, Goldberg, & Capotosto, 1982, Study 1), my students and I examined the interactive effects of reward and choice on artistic creativity. The subjects in this study were 60 undergraduate women recruited from an introductory psychology course at Brandeis University. All subjects were brought to the laboratory expecting to take part in a person perception experiment to partially fulfill a course requirement. About 10 minutes into the person perception task, the experimenter pretended that a videotape player was operating incorrectly, forcing her to terminate the experiment for which the subjects had come to the laboratory. She then presented the target activity (collage-making) as an alternative experiment the subject could do. The person perception task was used to ensure that reward subjects would perceive themselves as being rewarded for the target activity itself, and not simply for experiment participation.

In presenting the collage task, the experimenter delivered the independent-variable manipulation according to a 2 × 2 factorial design which crossed two levels of choice with two levels of reward. In the *no-choice, no-reward* condition, subjects were told:

> Well, I'm doing another study and I guess I can have you do that instead for the rest of the time. It involves spending about 15 minutes making a paper collage.

In addition to this, subjects in the *no-choice, reward* condition were told, "I'm paying subjects $2 in that study, so what I'll do is give you credit for the part you just did and you'll earn $2 for doing the second study." By contrast, instructions to the subjects in the *choice, no-reward* condition stressed the voluntary nature of further participation:

> Well, I'm doing another study and I guess I could have you do that instead for the rest of the time. It involves spending about 15 minutes making a paper collage. Would you be willing to do that?

Additionally, subjects in the *choice, reward* condition were told, "I can give you credit for the part you just did, and since I'm paying subjects for the second study, you can earn $2 if you'll agree to do the collage. Would you be willing to do that for $2?" All subjects in the choice conditions agreed to participate in the collage-making activity.

After presenting the standard collage materials (see Chapter 3), the experimenter placed $2 on the table in front of subjects in the reward conditions, in order to increase the salience of the reward. Subjects were left alone for 15 minutes to work on their collages, after which they were given a questionnaire containing several items designed to assess their interest in and enjoyment of the art

Figure 6-2. Mean creativity of collages (Amabile, Goldberg, & Capotosto, 1982, Study 1). *Note.* Highest possible value is 560, lowest possible is 0.

activity. The collages were subsequently rated on creativity by 14 artist-judges, according to the standard consensual assessment technique (see Chapter 3). The interjudge reliability of these ratings was .75.

Means for the creativity scores in each of the four conditions are presented in Figure 6-2. Clearly, the expected interaction between reward and choice was obtained. Subjects who chose to engage in the activity in order to obtain a reward exhibited the lowest creativity. On the other hand, those who earned a reward for doing the art activity with no choice in the matter exhibited the highest creativity. The two nonreward groups were intermediate. By paired comparisons, the choice-reward group was significantly lower than each of the three other groups. In addition, there was a significant main effect of choice on collage creativity. Subjects not given a choice concerning task engagement were significantly more creative than those given a choice. Clearly, though, this effect reflects significant differences obtained only for the reward groups. The no-choice and choice conditions are not significantly different when no reward is offered.

Of the items on the post-collage questionnaire, only one yielded a noteworthy effect. There was a nearly significant interaction between reward and choice on subjects' ratings of how pressured they felt while working on the collage ($p < .06$). For rewarded subjects, those who chose to do the activity felt more pressured than those not given a choice. By contrast, for nonrewarded subjects, those not given a choice felt more pressure than those given it. In fact, the subjects who felt the most pressure were those who chose to do the activity in order to obtain the reward; subjects who felt the least pressure were those who chose to do the activity with no mention of reward. This pattern closely complements the creativity pattern; higher levels of creativity are exhibited by those groups expressing lower levels of pressure.

Although there were no significant effects on other questionnaire measures of interest in and reaction to the collage task, the relationship between creativity and intrinsic interest or enjoyment was demonstrated by correlational data. Subjects' creativity scores correlated significantly and positively with their self-ratings of enjoyment in the art activity ($r = .32$) and their feelings of satisfaction with their collage ($r = .25$). In addition, there was a marginally significant correlation between creativity and expressed interest in the collage activity ($r = .17$, $p < .09$). Thus, there is some support in this study for the intrinsic motivation hypothesis of creativity: The intrinsically motivated state (marked by involvement in and playful enjoyment of the task) is conducive to creativity, but the extrinsically motivated state (marked by a lower level of involvement and enjoyment) is determental. These conclusions, of course, are only tentative, since higher levels of creativity could have led to greater satisfaction and enjoyment.

In demonstrating high creativity in no-choice-reward subjects, this study provides further evidence against the "competing response" explanation for overjustification effects (Reiss & Sushinsky, 1975). Since subjects in that condition expected the same reward as those in the choice-reward condition, any distraction caused by thinking about the reward should have been the same for both groups. According to the competing response hypothesis, then, intrinsic motivation and creativity should have been similar in the two groups. Clearly, this was not the case.

Thus, choice can be an important mediator of the effects of reward on creativity. As noted earlier, previous theories of intrinsic motivation suggest that subjects who perceive themselves as contracting to do a task in order to receive a reward will experience decrements in intrinsic motivation. By extension of the intrinsic motivation hypothesis of creativity, this effect should obtain for the creativity of the performance as well. This notion, however, can only explain the relatively low creativity of the choice-reward group. It cannot explain the extremely high creativity of the no-choice-reward group.

In their discussion of the interaction between reward and choice, some theorists (Folger et al., 1978; Kruglanski, 1978) suggest that high levels of intrinsic interest might be obtained under no-choice-reward conditions because subjects in those conditions experience positive affect. The same phenomenon could be operating in this study. Subjects in the no-choice-reward condition would not be extrinsically motivated, because they would have no reason to perceive the art activity as a means they chose to achieve some external end. They would, however, be expected to feel rather happy about making an unexpected $2 for 15 minutes' work, in addition to the experimental credit they expected to receive. This positive affect could be expected to add to the intrinsic interest that subjects already had in the collage-making activity, thus enhancing their creativity. By contrast, subjects in the reward-choice condition might have perceived themselves as extrinsically motivated, as having contracted to do the task in order to obtain a reward. Their feelings of being pressured while working support this explanation. This negative affect, this feeling of being pressured, could well have undermined their creativity.

Choice in Aspects of Task Engagement

Given the apparently crucial role of choice in intrinsic motivation and creativity, it is essential to consider the type of choice that is offered. People may be given a choice concerning task engagement itself, or they may be given a choice concerning aspects of task engagement. On the basis of the study just reported, it appears that choice about whether to engage in a task at all may have disparate effects on creativity; those effects may depend on the presence or absence of expected reward. Subjects who choose to engage in an activity for which a salient reward is offered may exhibit lower levels of creativity than subjects not given a choice at all. Thus, choice concerning task engagement will sometimes enhance creativity, and sometimes undermine it.

Choice concerning *how* to engage in an activity, however, should only enhance intrinsic motivation and creativity. It is unlikely that choosing some materials or methods of task engagement over others would cause subjects to see themselves as extrinsically motivated. It is most likely that such choices will enhance feelings of self-determination and intrinsic motivation (cf. Deci, 1980; Deci & Ryan, 1980); as a consequence, creativity should also increase.

Although, like other social-psychological variables, choice is predicted to influence motivation and creativity, there is an important difference between choice and other variables that researchers have examined for effects on intrinsic motivation. With rewards, deadlines, and evaluation, there is some external goal to be attained, some goal for which the task is the means. Subjects' perceptions of self-determination under these circumstances are manipulated through presentation of the task as the means to a goal. There is no such external goal, however, when choice is the independent variable. Instead, subjects' perceptions of self-determination in task engagement are manipulated directly.

There is some previous research to support the hypothesis that intrinsic motivation will be enhanced by perceptions of choice in aspects of task engagement. In one study (Zuckerman, Porac, Lathin, Smith, & Deci, 1978), subjects were given either a choice or no choice about which puzzles to try in an experimental situation and how long to work on each puzzle. Those in the no-choice group had been yoked to the choice-group subjects in the puzzles and time constraints they were given. Subjects given a choice showed higher levels of subsequent intrinsic interest in working on the puzzles than did no-choice subjects. These differences obtained even when analyses controlled for actual performance on the puzzles.

In a preliminary test of the effects of choice on creativity, Judy Gitomer and I conducted a simple, two-condition experiment with nursery school children (Amabile & Gitomer, 1984). The subjects were 14 boys and 14 girls, ages 2–6, enrolled in a day-care center. Prior to subject assignment to conditions, each of the four head teachers of the day care center was asked to complete a questionnaire assessing each child's skill, interest, and creativity in art activities. On this basis, each child was assigned a composite creativity prescore. The children were assigned randomly to condition, with the restriction that the groups be approximately equivalent on prescore, age, and sex distribution.

As intended, there were no significant differences between the choice and the no-choice conditions on age ($M = 3.14$ and 3.21, respectively) or on the creativity prescore ($M = 4.21$ and 4.70, respectively, with a higher number representing higher teacher-rated creativity). Furthermore, although there was a trend for girls to receive higher creativity ratings than boys, this difference was not significant.

The children participated in individual experimental sessions conducted in a separate room within the day care center. The female experimenter was a regular teacher's aide at the school. After seating the child at a small table, the experimenter presented 10 plastic boxes of collage materials. Each box contained a different kind of material (e.g., purple paper triangles, red lengths of braided yarn). The experimenter told all children that she would like them to make a design by pasting the materials onto a cardboard in any way they wished.

At this point, the instructions diverged for the two conditions. Children in the choice condition were told to choose any five of the ten boxes that they would like to use in making their collages. After they made their choices, the other five boxes were removed. For children in the no-choice condition, however, the experimenter chose five of the ten boxes and said that those were to be used in the collage-making. Again, the remaining boxes were removed. Each child in the no-choice condition had previously been randomly yoked with a child in the choice condition, such that the experimenter gave each no-choice child those boxes that had been picked by the corresponding child in the choice condition. Thus, this can be viewed as a matched-pairs design, with children matched on materials used.

All children were given approximately 10 minutes to complete their collages, although the experimenter did not mention a time limit at the outset. Instead, if the child was still working after 9 minutes had elapsed, she suggested that the child finish.

Two weeks after the initial sessions had been completed, a behavioral measure of subsequent intrinsic interest in the collage activity was obtained. On each of 3 days, leftover collage materials were made available for several hours as part of the array of usual art materials in the center. Each child's engagement in the collage activity during this free-choice period was timed.

The 28 collages were rated on creativity by eight artist-judges whose interjudge reliability was .79. As predicted, there was a substantial difference between conditions on collage creativity. Children in the choice condition made collages that were judged as significantly more creative ($M = 183.93$, on a scale from 0 to 320) than those made by children in the no-choice condition ($M = 144.57$). In addition, children in the choice condition spent more time (though not significantly more) with the collage materials during the free-play period ($M = 3.00$ minutes) than did children in the no-choice condition ($M = 2.07$ minutes).

This simple study makes an important point: People given a choice in certain aspects of task engagement will produce more creative work than people for whom the choice is made by someone else. The restriction of choice is unlike the constraints considered earlier, in some respects. With both evaluation and reward, subjects are presented with some external goal to be met; the target activity is the means to that goal. There is no such goal, however, with the restriction of choice. Instead, this constraint is only similar to the others in signalling external control over behavior. This, clearly, is in keeping with the intrinsic motivation hypothesis: If individuals see their task engagement as extrinsically motivated—externally controlled—they will be less creative than if they see task engagement as internally controlled.

Summary

The research presented in this chapter offers considerable support for the intrinsic motivation hypothesis of creativity. It suggests that widely differing external constraints will undermine creativity, as long as those constraints can lead people to view their work as extrinsically motivated rather than intrinsically motivated:

1. Contracting to do an activity in order to obtain a reward can be detrimental to creative performance on that activity. This effect obtains even if the reward is simply another activity, and even if the reward is delivered before the creative activity is begun.
2. Choice in whether to do a task can interact with the offer of reward for task engagement. Monetary reward given for a task about which the subject has no choice can enhance creativity (perhaps by inducing positive affect), but monetary reward offered to the subject in exchange for his consent to do the task can undermine creativity.
3. Choice in aspects of how to do a task can enhance creativity and intrinsic interest.
4. There is a consistent positive relationship between expressed interest in an activity and actual creativity of performance.

Update

Reward

Research on the effects of reward on human behavior continues to generate considerable interest and controversy both within and outside of academic psychology. In the 1983 edition, we reported some studies demonstrating negative effects of reward on creativity. (These studies were later published together in Amabile, Hennessey, & Grossman, 1986.) As we found in our evaluation research, the picture became more complex as we continued our empirical probing of the effects of reward and as other researchers carried out their own investigations.

Some recent research with task-contingent reward has provided clear conceptual replication of our original findings. In one study, children engaged in a computer line-drawing task that could be reliably assessed on creativity (Hennessey, 1989). Whether children were expecting reward delivered by the experimenter or reward delivered by the computer, they exhibited lower levels of creativity than children not expecting reward. Other research has demonstrated that reward can have negative effects on the performance of heuristic (complex) tasks such as block design and object assembly, which are similar to creativity tasks (Fabes, Moran, & McCullers, 1981).

However, one recent paper suggests that reward can increase creativity—as long as the reward is not overly salient and the rewarded "creative" behavior is divergent thinking (Eisenberger & Selbst, 1994). These researchers used an experimental paradigm that contrasted to ours in three important ways. First, the creative activities used were quite similar to those on standard creativity tests, where divergent thinking is equated with creativity. In our studies, subjects engage in real activities, such as writing prose, and actually produce work that can be rated on creativity by experts. Second, the children who participated in the studies were rewarded over several trials on a particular creativity test (the training task), and then generalizability to divergent thinking on another creativity test was examined within the same context (with the same experimenter). In our studies, there is a single administration of reward. Third, the rewards were performance-contingent rather than task-contingent. Subjects in the high-divergent condition were rewarded for producing many responses on the training task, and subjects in the low-divergent condition were rewarded for producing just a single response.

It is interesting that in these studies, higher levels of divergent thinking were exhibited under conditions of less salient (rather than more salient) reward. These findings are compatible with the body of psychological research demonstrating stronger negative effects of reward on intrinsic motivation as the salience of the reward increases (e.g., Ross, 1975). However, for many reasons, the results of these studies do not directly address the question of how reward affects creativity. Perhaps the most important reason has to do with the nature of the activities used. As we argued in the 1983 edition, it clearly *is* possible to increase algorithmic aspects of performance with reward, and the tasks used in these studies (listing words, or turning circles into pictures) appear to be much more algorithmic than the tasks used in the studies that show undermining effects of reward (making a paper collage or doing a free-form drawing on a computer). Indeed, in one of our own studies we elicited superior performance under extrinsic constraint when a heuristic task was modified into an algorithmic task (Amabile, 1979). Furthermore, because the training and the target tasks were administered by the same experimenter in the same situation, and because subjects had been trained to expect reward from that experimenter for certain kinds of responses, we question whether the "creative" behavior had truly "generalized." We wonder if the rewarded children in these experiments would have shown higher levels of creativity on an open-ended creativity task presented by a different experimenter in a different setting. We suspect not.

In our search for mechanisms by which reward might undermine creativity, and in our exploration for the boundaries of this effect, we uncovered considerable complexity. Recall that some of this complexity had already revealed itself in the research we reported in the 1983 edition. We had found that subjects who were given reward as a kind of "bonus" for task engagement without explicitly entering into a contract with the experimenter to do the task in order to receive the reward actually displayed higher levels of creativity than nonrewarded subjects (Amabile, Hennessey, & Grossman, 1986). Subsequently, we encountered a strikingly similar result in a decidedly different kind of experiment. Here, instead of studying how creativity might be killed—as we had in nearly all of the studies reported in the 1983 edition—we were studying ways to maintain creativity.

We entered into this inquiry because we wanted to see if it was possible to halt or resist the negative effects of reward that we had earlier found. In planning the research, we were guided by a biological analogy. If the extrinsic constraint of contracted-for reward can be considered a kind of germ or virus, might it be possible, we wondered, to immunize people against its negative effects on intrinsic motivation and creativity? Again drawing loosely from biological analogy, we thought this might be accomplished by doing two things: (1) strengthening intrinsic motivation, and (2) providing mild doses of extrinsic motivation along with "antibodies" (techniques) for fighting it.

The general paradigm was a simple one. In small groups, children watched one of two videotapes. Both tapes depicted an attractive boy and girl about their age talking with an adult. In the intrinsic motivation training tape, the two children talked about their schoolwork in highly intrinsically motivated terms. In addition, they presented cognitive techniques that they used in school for keeping extrinsic motivators in perspective. For example, when asked whether they ever think about the grades they're going to receive for their schoolwork, they replied that although they know that getting a good report card is important, and although they try to get good grades, grades are never the most important thing to them while they are working. In the control condition tape, the same children talked with the same adult about their favorite foods, favorite seasons of the year, and so on. The experimenter then led a discussion of the videotapes with the small groups, asking the children to reflect on any experiences and feelings they might have had that were similar to those expressed on the tape. The goal of this discussion was to help children in the intrinsic motivation training condition internalize the strong intrinsic motivation toward learning that was modeled on their videotape and practice the cognitive distancing techniques described.

A few days later, in a different room, a different experimenter worked with the children in individual sessions. First, she gave all children a paper-and-pencil test of intrinsic-extrinsic motivation toward schoolwork (Harter, 1981). Then, half of the children in each training condition were asked to do a creativity task in order to earn a reward; as in our earlier studies (reported in Chapter 6 of the 1983 edition), the reward was another activity and was completed before the target creativity task. The other half of the children in each training condition were simply given both activities to do.

Although the results differ somewhat across our different replications of this immunization study, the basic pattern is clear (Hennessey, Amabile, & Martinage, 1989; Hennessey & Zbikowski, 1993). The intrinsic motivation training children tend to report higher levels of intrinsic motivation toward learning on the paper-and-pencil test. And in general, the control group children exhibit a lower level of creativity under reward; this pattern replicates our earlier findings. Most importantly, however, the intrinsic motivation training children do not exhibit a lower level of creativity under reward. In contrast, they exhibit a *higher* level of creativity under reward.

This result appears conceptually similar to the high creativity of no-contract/reward subjects that we found in our earlier research. Moreover, this result fits well with the notions of motivational synergy that we presented in the update to Chapter 4. It appears that we have found a way (or perhaps we have found three ways) to produce an additive effect of intrinsic and extrinsic motivation: (1) positive affect produced by receiving a "bonus" reward in the absence of the kind of control that is suggested by contracted-for reward; (2) high levels of intrinsic motivation, particularly when that intrinsic motivation has been made salient; and (3) reduced salience of the extrinsic motivator, for example through cognitive distancing techniques.

Recall the tactic used by the poet Anne Sexton when her agent tried to involve her in the monetary details of a book contract. She asked him to take care of the matter because she did not want to focus on these things while she was trying to write. She said, "I am in love with money, so don't be mistaken, but first I want to write good poems. After that I am anxious as hell to make money and fame and bring the stars all down." More recently, the novelist Stephen King said of his own writing, "Money is great stuff to have, but when it comes to the act of creation, the best thing is not to think of money too much. It constipates the whole process" (King, 1990, p. xv).

Motivational synergy of certain types of reward in certain circumstances is also suggested by our nonexperimental research in organizations (Amabile, Conti, Coon, Lazenby, & Herron, in press; Amabile & N. Gryskiewicz, 1989; Amabile & S. Gryskiewicz, 1987). Our results in these studies suggest that reward can indeed have a negative effect on creativity when that reward is presented as a kind of "carrot" to induce people to do a particular piece of work. Interestingly, negative effects also seem to appear where people feel that they are not being generously and equitably compensated for their work. But our results also suggest that creativity can be supported by rewards that signal the positive value placed on creativity by the organization, and by rewards that enable people to engage in the sort of work they want to do. For example, one particularly positive form of reward appears to be additional freedom to create or choose one's next project or project team. This is what we mean by "extrinsics in service of intrinsics."

Another of our recent nonexperimental studies sheds additional light on some of the complexities of reward's effect on creativity. In that study, we had 29 professional artists from across the United States submit to us 10 randomly chosen commissioned works that they had done over the past 7 years, and 10 noncommissioned works (Amabile, Phillips, & Collins, 1994). In addition, each artist completed a detailed questionnaire about the conditions under which each artwork was done, his or her feelings about doing the artwork, and his or her own assessment of the work's creativity. Subsequently, all artworks were rated on creativity by expert artist judges who were blind to the artworks' commission status. Consistent with our earlier (experimental) results, we found that overall the commissioned works were rated as less creative than the noncommissioned works. Among the commissioned works, there was (as expected) a negative correlation between the work's creativity and the degree to which the artist reported feeling constrained by the commission. Interestingly, however, there was a *positive* correlation between the work's creativity (as assessed by the artist) and the degree to which the artist found the commission enabling—that is, the degree to which the commission enabled the artist to do something interesting or exciting—and the degree to which the artist found the commission informational about competence.

We can now summarize, according to our current state of knowledge, the conditions under which reward will have negative or positive effects on creativity. It appears that the effects will likely be negative when the reward is salient and the person perceives the reward "contract" as controlling or constraining. However, there are a set of conditions under which reward might be expected to have positive (or at least neutral) effects on creativity. Two of these (c and d) were suggested in the 1983 edition: (a) the reward is not salient relative to self-perceived intrinsic motivation because the reward is very small, or cognitive distancing techniques are used, or the salience of intrinsic motivation has been increased; or (b) the reward is perceived as more enabling than controlling (where enabling refers to the degree to which the reward or contract enables the individual to do something interesting or personally challenging); or (c) the reward is perceived as more informational about competence than controlling; or (d) the reward leads to positive affect in the absence of controlling implications (such as a "bonus" reward situation); or (e) the "reward" is perceived as equitable compensation for one's work in general (such as a person being paid a salary for one's job) rather than as reward for a particular task.

In considering what all of this implies for practical application, there are two points to note. First, we are discussing creativity, the production of novel and appropriate ideas to open-ended problems. Other, more straightforward aspects of performance, and performance on algorithmic tasks should be enhanced by reward (cf. McGraw, 1978). It is true that intrinsic motivation might be decreased under reward conditions on these sorts of tasks, but if reward can be maintained, then the algorithmic task performance should be maintained, and this lower level of intrinsic motivation might not have much practical consequence in the short run. Second, although the list of conditions under which reward might have positive effects is much longer than the list under which it should have negative effects, the conditions for negative effects may well be more common in most everyday situations.

Finally, as we consider the mechanisms of reward's negative effects, we turn once again to attentional explanations. When working under reward, people may pay less attention to fine details of the task and to aspects of the environment that may be useful in the task. However, it seems that this does not occur because (or only because) people are distracted by the reward they will receive or what they need to do to attain the reward. Several times we have found negative effects of contracted-for reward even when the reward was "consumed" before the target creative activity (e.g., Amabile, Hennessey, & Grossman, 1986). It may be that under reward conditions people simply feel less involved in the intrinsic aspects of the task, or they feel less positively toward it and thus engage their attention less deeply. This cognitive explanation is supported by the research that we reported in the Update to Chapter 4. In that research, we found that people who are less intrinsically motivated are less likely to demonstrate involvement during task engagement and that as a result they are less likely to produce creative work.

Constraint

In the 1983 edition, we included a discussion of the effects of constraint in the same chapter as our discussion of reward. Indeed, the two factors appear to be closely related. Our study with professional artists actually illuminates more about the effects of task constraint than it does about reward (Amabile, Phillips, & Collins, 1994). Although we did find a significant difference in creativity, with noncommissioned works being rated as more creative than commissioned works, the artist's reported perception of constraint while doing the artwork accounted for more of the variance in creativity than did the presence or absence of the commission. To be sure, there was much more perceived constraint in the commissioned than the noncommissioned works, and even the relatively nonconstrained commissioned works were rated somewhat lower on creativity than the noncommissioned works. Nonetheless, the role of constraint was clear and strong in this study. Combining across commissioned and noncommissioned works, creativity (as rated by the judges and by the artists themselves) correlated negatively with perceptions of constraint.

Other researchers have uncovered negative effects of constraint on creativity. In a study where children made paintings, they were given instructions for the painting task that differed in terms of their controlling implications (Koestner, Ryan, Bernieri, & Holt, 1984). The controlling instructions told children that they had to be neat in doing their paintings because those were the rules. The informational instructions acknowledged that children didn't always like to be neat but pointed out the importance of being neat in this situation so that other children could use the materials. The paintings done by children in the informational-limits condition were rated as more creative than those done by children in the controlling-limits condition. In a quite different study where fashion design students drew sample garment designs, those given choice in how they structured their work produced designs that were rated as more creative than did those not given such choice (Greenberg, 1992).

Nonexperimental studies have revealed that people who generally feel controlled or constrained in their daily environments may be less creative than those who feel more autonomous. Children's perceptions of autonomy in their classrooms tend to positively correlate with the children's intrinsic motivation and creativity (Picariello, 1994; Ryan & Grolnick, 1986). And the creativity of work groups within organizations correlates positively with the degree to which the members of those work groups report feeling that they have freedom in their work, a sense of autonomy and control over their own work and their own ideas (Amabile & S. Gryskiewicz, 1987; Amabile, Conti, Coon, Lazenby, & Herron, in press).

Summary

Although there have been some replications of the negative effect of reward on the performance of heuristic tasks, some promising positive effects of reward have also been discovered. These positive effects appear when intrinsic motivation is kept salient, when extrinsic motivation becomes less salient (or cognitively diminished), and when rewards signify competence or enable performance of interesting new activities—rather than signifying external control of behavior.

A considerable body of experimental and nonexperimental evidence suggests that constraint placed on task engagement has consistent negative effects on creativity.

7

Social Facilitation, Modeling, and Motivational Orientation

When asked about the influence his mentors had on his professional development, a Nobel laureate in physics recalled their importance, not so much as teachers, but as models of thinking and working:

> I knew the techniques of research. I knew a lot of physics. I had the words, the libretto, but not quite the music. In other words, I had not been in contact with men who were deeply imbedded in the tradition of physics: men of high quality. This was my first real contact with first-rate creative minds at the high point of their power. (Zuckerman, 1977, p. 123)

This chapter considers three social factors that appear to be important for creative behavior: (1) social facilitation (or social inhibition) brought about by the mere presence of others; (2) modeling, the imitation of observed behavior; and (3) motivational orientation, an individual's intrinsic or extrinsic approach to work. In contrast to Chapters 5 and 6, this chapter does not deal with social factors that are constraints on performance. With external evaluation, rewards, or restricted choice, one individual actively imposes some condition, goal, or restriction on the performance of another individual. With the social factors considered here, however, the outside-party influence on performance is more passive and usually less intentional: With social facilitation or social inhibition, the mere presence of others (as an audience or as coactors) is the source of influence; with modeling, the observed behavior of others can affect performance, even when those others are unaware that they are a source of influence; and motivational orientations toward work can be learned through the normal process of socialization.

Social Facilitation Theories: Implications for Creativity

Social facilitation effects were demonstrated in what was probably the first social-psychological experiment ever performed. Triplett (1898) had observed that, in bicycle races, faster times were almost always set by racers simultaneously competing against each other than by racers who rode alone, competing only against the clock. Among several possible explanations for this effect (most having to do with the specific physical activities involved in bicycling), Triplett considered "dynamogenesis." According to this theory, the presence of another cyclist arouses a "competitive instinct" and serves as an inspiration to greater effort. Triplett's experiment favored this explanation over the others; children asked to wind fishing reels in competition with others worked faster than those asked to perform the same task alone.

Allport (1924) used the term "social facilitation" to describe one of two factors that might cause this performance enhancement: "The first is social facilitation, which consists of an increase of response merely from the sight or sound of others making the same movements. The second is rivalry, an emotional reinforcement of movement accompanied by the consciousness of a desire to win." In his experiments, Allport found that simple tasks were performed better in groups of five coactors, but that more difficult tasks were performed better alone. There was one important qualification, however: Subjects who were highly proficient were not influenced by the presence of others.

Social facilitation research following the early work of Triplett and Allport generally demonstrated a facilitative effect of the presence of others on simple tasks and an inhibiting effect on difficult tasks (although both effects have been subsumed under the generic term "social facilitation"). For example, Travis (1925) found that an audience facilitated subjects' performance on a rotary pursuit task. Dashiell (1930) demonstrated that coaction facilitated performance on a simple task, as did "cognitive coaction," where subjects merely believed that others were working on the same task in other rooms. Husband (1931) found that an audience impaired performance in a complex finger maze. And Pessin (1933) showed similar effects for learning lists of nonsense syllables.

In 1965, Zajonc proposed a drive theory of social facilitation that was designed to explain both the facilitative and the inhibiting effects of the presence of others. According to this theory, the presence of other organisms, either as coactors or as passive observers, produces an increase in general arousal. This increased arousal energizes dominant responses at the expense of subordinate ones. Thus, if a dominant response is the correct response on a task, performance should be enhanced by the presence of others. If, however, the dominant response is incorrect, performance will be undermined.

A great deal of research conducted since 1965 has supported Zajonc's theory. In one study (Zajonc & Sales, 1966), a verbal learning paradigm was used to establish varying "habit strengths" for different words. That is, subjects saw some words frequently and others infrequently during the initial phase of the experiment. Later, these subjects were presented with a "pseudorecognition" task where meaningless patterns were presented for extremely brief periods of time. Subjects, believing these patterns to be words they had initially learned, were asked to read those words. The presence of an audience facilitated the dominant responses—the well-learned words—on this task.

Cottrell (1968) proposed evaluation apprehension as the immediate antecedent of the increase in drive produced by the presence of others: "It does not appear that the simple presence of others increases drive level. I believe the additional process involved is the anticipation of positive or negative outcomes" (p. 103). This proposition has been supported by some research. In the study mentioned earlier (Dashiell, 1930), coacting subjects who were told explicitly not to compete with one another performed similarly to those who worked alone. In a study specifically designed to test Cottrell's theory (Cottrell, Wack, Sekerak, & Rittle, 1968), subjects who performed a pseudorecognition task in the presence of potentially evaluative observers emitted more dominant responses than those who worked alone. Importantly, though, subjects who performed the task in the presence of nonevaluative (blindfolded) individuals emitted dominant responses at the same rate as those in the alone condition.

The proposition that evaluation apprehension is an essential feature of the social facilitation effect has been challenged, however. Some experiments have shown the effect with nonhuman species, such as cockroaches, where reactions similar to evaluation apprehension are unlikely (Zajonc, Heingarner, & Herman, 1969). In other research, dominant responses have been facilitated by the presence of others even when those responses are expressions of preference and, as such, cannot be construed as good or bad (Zajonc, Wolosin, Wolosin, & Loh, 1970).

There is some intriguing evidence, though, that evaluation expectation can add to the effects of the more generalized arousal that occurs even in the presence of a nonevaluative audience. Henchy and Glass (1968) compared the pseudorecognition task performance of subjects who worked alone with the performance of subjects in three other conditions: those who worked before an expert (evaluative) audience, those who worked before a nonexpert (nonevaluative) audience, and those who worked alone but expected subsequent expert evaluation. The results suggested that the mere presence of even a nonevaluative audience did increase the emission of dominant responses (over the level of the "alone" condition), but that adding the expectation of expert evaluation by the audience increased the frequency of dominant responses even further. Moreover, the actual presence of experts led to a higher rate of dominant responses than the simple expectation of future expert evaluation.

In sum, social facilitation research has shown that the mere presence of others—either as coactors or as an audience—can impair performance on poorly learned or complex tasks, but enhance performance on well-learned or simple tasks. Most of the evidence also suggests, however, that in humans the expectation of evaluation can augment these social facilitation effects (cf. Geen & Gange, 1977).

There is only one previous social facilitation study that used creative performance as a dependent variable. Matlin and Zajonc (1968) gave subjects a word association test to do either alone or in the presence of an audience. Not only did subjects give their associations more quickly in the presence of an audience, but they also gave more common associations when observed than they did when alone. With this exception, there is no previous research evidence on this question. Since so much potentially creative work is carried out in the presence (or the close proximity) of others, however, this area is an important one for the development of a comprehensive social psychology of creativity.

Within the creativity literature, there are conflicting notions about the effect that the presence of others will have on creativity. Osborn (1953), in defending the brainstorming procedures he proposed for enhancing creativity, suggested that a social facilitation effect occurs in group settings; individuals stimulate one another's thinking, leading to a larger number of unusual and acceptable ideas. These conditions, of course, are different from those used in social facilitation research, where subjects may work in the presence of others, but they do not work *with* others. Nonetheless, Osborn's assertion would suggest that working in the presence of others should at least do no harm to creativity. On the other hand, if it is true that the presence of others leads to increased arousal and, perhaps, to evaluation expectation, then creative performance should suffer under such conditions. As asserted in Chapter 4, creativity tasks are heuristic tasks; in Zajonc's terms, they are complex, difficult, or unfamiliar. Thus, if Zajonc's notions are correct, performance on such tasks should be undermined by the mere presence of others. In addition, as suggested by Cottrell and by the evaluation expectation research in Chapter 5, performance should be undermined even more by the presence of evaluative others.

Evidence on the Social Facilitation and Inhibition of Creativity

Psychological studies of outstandingly creative individuals provide little information on the role of the passive or active presence of others in creative performance. At least one sociological study, however, bears on this issue. In an exhaustive analysis of the work patterns and attitudes of winners of the Nobel prize, Zuckerman (1977) found that nearly two-thirds of the 286 laureates named between 1901 and 1972 were honored for work that they did collaboratively. By comparison, a smaller percentage of nonlaureate scientists were engaged in active collaboration. Certainly, collaboration cannot be considered as work done in the "mere presence" of others. Nonetheless, this result bears on the general question of whether other people have facilitative or inhibiting effects on creativity; it suggests that working with (as well as in the presence of) others can enhance creativity.

There are a number of alternative interpretations, however. Perhaps the most plausible is that modern science, more and more, *requires* collaborative work. It may be that the nature of problems in modern natural science is such that only work done by teams is likely to be successful. This suggestion is supported by evidence that, over time, the incidence of collaborative work in these sciences is increasing. During the first 25 years of the Nobel prize, 41% of the prize-winning work was collaborative. By 1972, 79% of the laureates were honored for collaborative work (Zuckerman, 1977). Thus, this sociological study provides only suggestive evidence for the facilitative effects of other people on individual creativity.

Nearly all of the psychological research in this area has compared group performance on creativity tests (where subjects generate ideas together) to the performance of subjects working as individuals. Most of the evidence from these studies suggests that subjects perform more poorly on idea-production tests when they work together than when they work alone. Although some results show that the quality of ideas might sometimes be better in group situations, there is overwhelming evidence that individuals produce fewer ideas overall in such situations (Stein, 1975). For example, in one study (Gurman, 1968), all subjects were trained in the principles of brainstorming (Osborn, 1953); these rule out criticism, encourage quantity of ideas without regard to quality, and seek the combination and improvement of ideas. Half of the subjects then worked in three-person groups, spending 5 minutes on each of several creativity problems. The other subjects worked individually on each of the creativity problems. The results showed unequivocally that, collectively, the subjects working individually (the "nominal groups") performed better than the real groups, both in the quantity and the judge-rated quality of the ideas. Other studies support the finding that real groups are less productive than "nominal groups" (e.g., Chatterjea & Mitra, 1976; Renzulli, Owen, & Callahan, 1974; Street, 1974).

There is little evidence that groups perform better than individuals. Indeed, only one study showed, in a relatively unambiguous way, that subjects working together (in dyads) produced more original responses on a creativity test than subjects working alone (El Dreny, 1979). Thus, overall, it appears that people perform better at idea-generation when they work as individuals.

A few studies have examined the impact of the mere presence of others on creativity test performance. Generally, these studies have shown either no effect of differential test administration, or a detrimental effect of group administration. For example, in one such experiment (Milgram & Milgram, 1976), elementary school children were given the Wallach-Kogan (1965) creativity tests either alone or in large groups. Nongifted children scored significantly higher under individual administration, but there were no differences between the two conditions for gifted children. These results recall those of Allport's (1924) early social facilitation study. In that study, most subjects performed simple tasks better, but difficult tasks more poorly, in the presence of others. Highly proficient subjects, however, showed no such differential effects.

The bulk of the evidence, then, suggests that subjects perform more poorly on creativity tests when they work as a group, and that some subjects may also perform more poorly on individual creativity tests if they must work in the presence of others. There are some important qualifications, however. Mere presence does not always have negative effects on the performance of open-ended tasks (e.g., Street, 1974). In addition, subjects who are highly skilled at a complex task may experience no decrement in performance under group conditions. This result fits well with the proposition in Chapter 4 that people for whom "creative" performance has become virtually algorithmic should not be adversely affected by the social factors that normally undermine creativity in others.

Thus, it appears that the detrimental effect of group performance on creativity is considerably more reliable than the detrimental effect of mere coaction. One plausible explanation for this discrepancy can be drawn from Cottrell's (1968) discussion of evaluation expectation. Since evaluation by other group members is always a possibility when subjects are working together (even if they have been told not to judge one another's ideas), it might be expected that these circumstances would have greater negative effects on creativity than merely working alongside others.

Virtually all of the research examining the effects of others' presence on creativity has relied on standard creativity tests. It is possible that, with truly openended tasks, even the mere presence of others would have reliable detrimental effects on creativity. Certainly, it would be expected that the presence of evaluative others will negatively influence performance on such tasks. My students and I (Amabile, Goldfarb, & Brackfield, 1990) set out to examine these possibilities in two studies using the consensual creativity assessment technique.

Both of these studies were described in Chapter 5, in my discussion of the effects of evaluation expectation on creativity. As noted there, the studies were designed to investigate social facilitation as well as simple evaluation effects. Study 1 utilized a 2 × 2 factorial design to examine verbal creativity (poem-writing); subjects did or did not expect evaluation, and they did or did not work alone. Evaluation subjects expected that their poems would be given detailed written evaluations by experts, and that these evaluations would be returned to them at a later time. Nonevaluation subjects believed that the content of their poems would not be evaluated. They were told that the poem would simply provide a handwriting sample. As a cross dimension, subjects either worked alone on their poems or they worked in the same room with three other subjects who sat at desks several feet apart.

Study 2 was designed to examine the effects of an evaluative audience on creativity and, in addition, to isolate the source of any such effects. Thus, in one condition, subjects believed they were being watched by a group of experts who were evaluating their work. In another, subjects worked only under evaluation expectation, with no belief that they were being watched. In a third condition, subjects believed that they were being watched by a nonexpert audience. Finally, in a control condition, subjects worked with neither an audience nor evaluation expectation.[1]

Specifically, in Study 2, evaluation-audience subjects believed that there was a small group of artists watching and evaluating their collage-making from the other side of a one-way mirror. Evaluation-no audience subjects believed that such a group of experts waited down the hall to review their work once it was finished. Nonevaluation-audience subjects believed that they were being watched by some students who were merely waiting for another experiment in the room on the other side of the one-way mirror. They believed that the collage-making was simply a

---

[1] This design is similar to that used by Henchy and Glass (1968), as described earlier, to study social facilitation effects on a pseudorecognition task.

mood induction task. Finally, nonevaluation-no audience subjects neither expected evaluation of their work nor believed that they were being watched. In both no-audience conditions, a heavy curtain was drawn across the one-way mirror.

According to the Zajonc (1965) model, the results should have shown a main effect of coaction in Study 1 and a main effect of audience presence in Study 2. According to the Cottrell (1968) model, the results should have shown only a main effect of evaluation expectation in both Study 1 and Study 2. According to a compromise suggested by Geen and Gange (1977), the studies should have shown two main effects. Both coaction and audience presence should undermine creative performance by increasing arousal. Furthermore, if the two effects are additive, an interaction might also be expected.

As illustrated in Figure 7-1, the results suggest that both evaluation expectation and the presence of others can undermine creativity, but only if the others are present as an audience. Both studies showed strongly significant main effects for evaluation, such that evaluation groups were less creative than nonevaluation groups. In Study 2, there was a nonsignificant trend ($p < .08$) for an audience main effect, such that subjects in the audience conditions were less creative. In Study 1, however, there was no effect of coaction on creativity. There was no interaction between the variables in either study.

These results tentatively suggest that the presence of others may disrupt an individual's creative performance only if those others are concentrating on the individual's work. In Study 1, each subject was involved in writing a poem at her own desk. Thus, it is unlikely that those in the coaction groups believed that any of the others was observing their performance. In Study 2, by contrast, the task was an easily observable one—collage-making. Moreover, subjects in the audience conditions in this study believed that the audience had nothing to do but watch them at their work. Under these conditions, apparently, the audience might undermine creativity. Certainly, this phenomenon may reflect evaluation effects; even a nonexpert audience, as in Study 2, can be seen as a source of evaluation. Apparently, what is important is the audience's *attention* to the individual's work—not the audience's expert status.

Modeling Influences on Creative Individuals

"I can tell you how to get a Nobel prize . . . have great teachers." This is how the Nobel laureate economist Paul Samuelson (1972, p. 155) summarized his views on the importance of mentors in creative development. The belief that creativity can, in part, be learned through association with great models is one shared by some psychologists, as well:

> Research of any importance and creative thought in general are not a matter of intellectual tricks and classroom-acquired procedures, but spiritual activities, tied to value systems and ways of life best acquired by living association. Creativity is perhaps best acquired by association with creativity. (Cattell & Butcher, 1968, p. 285)

Figure 7-1. Creativity means for two studies of social facilitation and evaluation expectation (Amabile, Goldfarb, & Brackfield, 1990).
Note. Highest possible value is 40, lowest possible is 0.

Thus, it is important to explore the possibility that, although the presence of evaluative others can inhibit creativity, the presence of actively creative others as models can enhance creativity.

Evidence of the importance of models in creative development comes from a variety of sources. For example, Bloom and Sosniak (1981) conducted lengthy interviews with dozens of individuals who have achieved international recognition in several fields. Their parents and some of their teachers were interviewed, as well. These researchers found strong evidence that most of these talented individuals had at least one model of achievement in the domain (often a parent) during childhood. In addition, many of these individuals sought out models, if only by reading about persons of outstanding accomplishment in the domain. Other studies have shown that parents' abilities and personality traits are at least moderately predictive of children's creativity (e.g., Domino, 1969). This evidence, which might be explained by modeling effects, will be discussed in more detail in the next chapter.

One of the richest sources of information on the professional socialization and development of highly creative people is Zuckerman's (1977) study of the 92 Nobel laureates who worked in the United States and who received their prizes between 1901 and 1972. This research strongly suggests the crucial role of modeling in at least some types of creativity. There is, first, substantial evidence that Nobel laureates are often trained by Nobel laureates or other members of the "scientific elite." Zuckerman uses the term "social inbreeding" to describe the statistic that more than half (48) of the 92 worked as graduate students, postdoctorates, or junior collaborators under other Nobel laureates.

There is, of course, an obvious explanation for these data. Nobel laureates, who are permanently eligible to nominate others for the prizes, may tend to nominate their own students. However, for two reasons, Zuckerman believes that this cannot adequately account for the high degree of association between laureates of different generations. First, the percentage of nominators who are laureates is quite small. In recent years, over a thousand nominators have been canvassed by the prize committee. Second, the social kinship among the scientific elite is a pattern that has held for centuries in a variety of fields. Thus, it is unlikely that the process of nomination alone accounts for the degree of association between laureates of different generations.

It is interesting to consider the ways in which potentially creative individuals are matched to influential models. Apparently, a two-way process is involved. On the one hand, future laureates showed a pronounced tendency to seek out the great masters to work with during their graduate and postdoctoral stages. On the other hand, it is clear that many outstanding scientists carefully selected young collaborators of talent. Fermi, for example, explicitly let it be known that he wanted to be approached by promising students; in the end, he had served as mentor to six laureates. Significantly, this process of master-apprentice selection often occurred *before* the masters had won their Nobel prizes (Zuckerman, 1977). Thus, even aside from the worldwide recognition associated with the Nobel prize, there was something notable in the masters' working style and achievements that drew promising young scientists to them. It is intriguing that the pattern was often repeated through several scientific generations. Former apprentices would, upon reaching maturity in their own careers, become mentors for other young scientists destined to become widely recognized for their work.

The consequences of such partnerships can be far-reaching. Certainly, some of the advantage that accrues to the apprentices comes from the sheer power that the master holds in the scientific community. Accomplished scientists are much more likely than others to have first-rate laboratory facilities, funds for research assistants and technicians, and connections enabling them to place their students in prestigious positions. As one chemist laureate said,

> I've accumulated over the years a lot of what I call wealth. Many, many connections. I keep them all extremely active. All for one purpose: to do my research and teaching better. Science in this day is a world-wide proposition. I have three worldwide empires which I can call on: research, teaching, and industry. [. . .] All of this is done for this reason, taking care of the students. There aren't many people "rich" enough to do that: rich in the sense of connections, power, financing for research, influence. (Zuckerman, 1977, p. 134)

Of greater interest for psychological theories on the modeling of creative behavior, however, are the less tangible benefits that the scientific apprentices gain.

Many of them agree that, more important than any other factors, their masters were models from whom they learned styles of thinking and working, matters of scientific taste, and standards for judging performance. For example, a laureate in chemistry describes the value of working with great scientists during one's period of scientific development:

> It's the contact: seeing how they operate, how they think, how they go about things. (Not the specific knowledge?) Not at all. It's learning a style of thinking, I guess. Certainly not the specific knowledge. . . . There were always people around who knew more than he did. It wasn't that. It was a method of work that really got things done. (Zuckerman, 1977, p. 122)

Throughout their statements, these laureates and many others make clear the major influence that they feel their masters had on them: modeling a "creative" style of thinking, a productive style of working, an esthetic sensibility capable of sensing the important problems that were ripe for research, a sense of self-confidence, and a set of high performance standards for one's own work. Clearly, in the terms proposed in Chapter 4, the models for these Nobel laureates were responsible for enhancing both the domain-relevant and creativity-relevant skills of their students.

Although there has been little empirical work on the role of modeling in the development of creativity, Simonton has done some meticulous archival research that addresses this issue. In one study, for example, a time-series analysis was done on creative products spanning 127 generations of European history (Simonton, 1975a). Achievements included works in science, philosophy, literature, musical composition, painting, sculpture, and architecture. Measures of creativity were computed by weighting the number of such accomplishments in each generation by the frequency with which the accomplishment was cited in histories, anthologies, and so on. Analyses of this dependent variable by a number of social and cultural independent variables revealed a significant effect of "role models." Creativity in any one generation is a positive function of prior creativity, with the previous two generations having about equal impact. In other words, the level of creative productivity in any given generation is significantly influenced by the level of creative productivity in the two preceding generations. These results suggest that creative models do have a positive effect on the development of creativity in observers.

Other results, however, complicate the picture. One study (Simonton, 1976b), rather than examining aggregate levels of creative productivity for entire generations, looked at the eminence achieved by 2,012 individual philosophical thinkers from 580 B.C to 1900 A.D. Overall, the results showed a *negative* relationship between a thinker's eminence and the availability of creative role models (eminent philosophers) during his developmental period. According to Simonton (1976b), when considered together with other results, these findings suggest that lesser thinkers require role models more than major thinkers do. While the earlier study included *all* creators in *all* fields for each generation, this latter study specifically examined each individual's achieved eminence.

A later study (Simonton, 1977b) also found that the direct relationship between role-model availability during development and later creative productivity was a negative one. Here, 696 classical composers were studied. The structural equation model that resulted from an analysis of musical eminence and several social variables revealed that the direct relationship between model availability and creative productivity was negative. However, modeling had an indirect positive influence on creativity. Role-model availability contributed positively to creative precociousness (recognized creative achievement at a young age) which, in turn, contributed positively to creative productivity.

What, then, do Simonton's studies suggest about the function of creative models in the lives of outstanding individuals? First, it is clear that a large number of creative models in one generation will stimulate general creative productivity in the next generation. At the individual level, however, the pattern of influence seems to be somewhat more complex. At the very highest levels of creative eminence, modeling may be relatively unimportant. In addition, although exposure to creative models may stimulate early high-level productivity, it may be important at some point to go beyond the examples set by one's masters:

> In the short run, role-model availability can have a beneficial effect on creative productivity by increasing creative precociousness, yet in the long run the effect may prove negative for those creators who fail to break away from their mentors. It is acceptable for a youth to imitate seniors, but to continue to do so into maturity is most damaging to the reputation of one's creative efforts. (Simonton, 1977b, p. 813)

These findings are provocative when considered within the componential framework of creativity. In Chapter 4, I considered (and rejected) the possibility that a person can have "too much knowledge," too many domain-relevant skills. I argued there that additional exposure to factual and technical knowledge in a domain can only make it more likely that new solutions and responses will be discovered. It is possible, however, for an individual to come to rely on "too many algorithms," too many standard methods for solving problems in a domain or for producing responses. Thus, it might be expected that when people learn facts, techniques, and creativity heuristics (domain-relevant and creativity-relevant skills) from models, their creativity can only be enhanced. If, however, they try to slavishly extract and follow response-generating algorithms from the behavior of their models, their own behavior will be judged as progressively less creative over time.

Experimental Studies of Modeling

Virtually all of the experimental research conducted on modeling effects in creativity has examined the impact of a model's behavior on the creativity-test performance of "ordinary" individuals, usually children. Most of these studies were devised as straightforward tests of the proposition from social learning theory (Bandura, 1969; Bandura & Walters, 1963) that individuals who do not perform a behavior, but are capable of doing so, are more likely to perform it after seeing a model—as long as the model is not punished for that behavior. The underlying assumption is that, even if it is difficult to identify and teach the behaviors that lead to creative performance directly, watching creative models can lead people to become more creative.

Many studies have in fact found positive effects of modeling on creativity test performance. In one study (Mueller, 1978), undergraduate women first did one form of a verbal test and one form of a figural test from the Torrance Tests of Creative Thinking. Experimental-group subjects then observed a live model giving either highly creative or highly uncreative responses to the figural test. Finally, all subjects completed alternate forms of the initial verbal and figural tests. The results were quite clear. Subjects who had observed the uncreative model showed less flexibility, originality, and elaboration on the figural posttest than did control subjects, while those who observed the creative model showed more. Although these results were quite strong on the direct generalization task (the figural test), the effect did not generalize to the verbal posttest.

Many different forms of modeling have been used. In one study, children watched filmed models giving responses to an unusual uses test or read a creativity-training booklet (Belcher, 1975). Later, they completed another unusual uses test. Modeling again appeared to have a positive effect. Although there were some differences between boys and girls, in general, the children who saw a model giving highly original answers performed better (higher originality and fluency) than children who saw a model giving unoriginal answers. This latter group in turn performed better than children who read a creativity-training booklet or who simply took the posttest.

In another study (Gary & Glover, 1975), children were first given an unusual uses test to obtain baseline measures. They were then placed in one of five experimental conditions. In Group 1, children heard an audiotape of a model giving 50 unusual responses to the question they themselves had initially answered. In Group 2, they heard only 5 unusual responses to that question. In Group 3, they heard a model read the responses they themselves had just given. In Group 4, they heard taped music for 5 minutes. In Group 5, they sat in silence for 5 minutes. On a posttest that was identical to the pretest, only children in Group 1 showed a clear improvement in originality over their baseline levels of performance.

Two modeling studies with adults used written materials to model creative performance. In the first of these (Harris & Evans, 1973), undergraduates read written responses to an unusual uses test that was supposedly taken by another subject. Those responses were either "convergent" (involved using a brick as building material) or "divergent" (involved using the brick for other purposes). Subjects who read the convergent responses made more such responses on later tests than did subjects who read the divergent responses. In the second study (Harris &

Evans, 1974), subjects who read divergent responses subsequently gave the most original answers to an unusual uses test. Those who had been given instructions to respond creatively scored the next highest, followed by those who had seen no model and, finally, by those who had seen convergent responses to the unusual uses test.

One study deserves mention even though it was not primarily designed to examine modeling influences on creativity (Feitelson & Ross, 1973). In this study, modeling was used in an attempt to increase children's "thematic play"—pretend play in which one theme is the source of activity. After initial sessions for assessing the children's baseline levels of thematic play and creativity, they participated in several sessions over a number of weeks in which one of four conditions was implemented: (1) play tutoring, in which an adult tutor encouraged children to combine play materials in new ways (partly by example); (2) toys only, in which the same play materials were available, but no direct tutoring was provided; (3) music tutoring, in which children spent the same amount of time being tutored on a musical instrument by the same adult who worked with the other groups; and (4) no intervention. In posttest sessions, the play-tutored group displayed significantly more thematic play that involved combining toys in new ways. In addition, that group scored higher on creativity-test measures of exploration, innovation, and originality.

Some modeling studies of creativity have had less positive results. For example, in one study, children watched a videotaped model who gave either low flexibility-low originality responses, high flexibility-low originality responses, or high flexibility-high originality responses to a creativity test. The impact of these modeling procedures depended in complex ways on sex, race, creativity subtest scores, and test used (Landreneau & Halpin, 1978). In another study, where children watched a videotaped model answering a creativity test, the most fluent and flexible responses on a posttest were given by children who had seen the model giving fluent but not original or flexible responses (Halpin, Halpin, Miller, & Landreneau, 1979). Interestingly, the most original responses were given by children who had not seen a model at all. The results were further complicated by significant effects of the children's race, locus of control, academic achievement level, and general self-esteem. Finally, in a study using similar stimuli, modeled fluency led to significant increases in the children's fluency and flexibility on the posttest, but modeled flexibility led to significant decreases in the children's fluency and flexibility (Zimmerman & Dialessi, 1973).

On the basis of most of the experimental evidence, and on the basis of the archival studies of Zuckerman and Simonton, it might seem reasonable to conclude that, at least in the short run, certain aspects of creative behavior can be learned through modeling. But this conclusion is premature for a number of reasons. First, although the Zuckerman study presented consistent anecdotal evidence and sociological data suggesting the positive impact of models on creative development, that study was limited to the natural sciences, and the evidence is open to alternative interpretations. Second, Simonton's research has uncovered some puzzling complexities in the relationship between early role-model availability and later creative achievement. Role models appear to positively influence creative precociousness which, in turn, can positively influence later productivity. However, the direct relationship between role-model availability and creative productivity is negative. In addition, the dependent variable in those studies was eminence rather than creativity; although the two are undoubtedly related, a perfect correspondence cannot be assumed. Third, the experimental evidence suggests clearly that performance will improve on tasks that are very close to the modeled activity, but that generalization to other tasks is quite rare. Finally, and perhaps most importantly, virtually all of the experimental evidence comes from studies that relied on creativity tests. On those tests, it may be easy for subjects to extract a simple algorithm for "creative" performance from a model's behavior. On more complex and open-ended (heuristic) tasks, however, modeling effects may be more difficult to find. Extensive modeling research with more heuristic tasks will be necessary before definite conclusions can be drawn about the short-range consequences of modeled creativity.

Motivational Orientation: A Theoretical Analysis

If early exposure to highly creative individuals can have a positive influence on creative development, one mechanism through which this influence operates might be the modeling of an intrinsic motivational orientation toward one's work—a view of that work as enjoyable and engaging in itself, as under the control of the individual's own interests, as both challenging and satisfying. This transmission could occur in different ways. The mentor might explicitly discuss the domain in intrinsic terms but, more likely, the mentor might simply behave in a manner that clearly displays a passionate involvement in the work for its own sake.

Because it might be an important mediator of many social influences on creativity, and because it is, theoretically, a crucial variable in its own right, motivational orientation merits close attention. It is difficult to find definitions of motivational orientation, although many theorists have used the concept in their work. Harter (1978, 1981) has delineated five aspects of classroom learning that she considers indicative of intrinsic or extrinsic motivational orientations: (1) learning motivated by curiosity versus learning in order to please the teacher, (2) incentive to work for one's own satisfaction versus working to please the teacher and get good grades, (3) preference for challenging work versus preference for easy work, (4) desire to work independently versus dependence on the teacher for help, and (5) internal versus external criteria for determining success or failure. Pittman and his colleagues (Pittman, Emery, & Boggiano, 1982) present a similar conceptualization of motivational orientation. They suggest that an intrinsic orientation leads to a preference for challenging, enjoyable tasks, whereas an extrinsic orientation leads to a preference for simple, predictable tasks.

Harter's conceptualizations are intended to describe a relatively stable, general intrinsic or extrinsic orientation toward classroom work. According to the componential model, however, in order to determine the likelihood of creative performance on any one task at any one time, it is important to examine the individual's task motivation toward that activity at that time. Intrinsic or extrinsic motivation may be quite specific to the particular task. Moreover, it may change considerably over time, depending on the initial level of intrinsic interest, the presence or absence of social constraints, and the individual's ability to deal with those constraints effectively. According to the intrinsic motivation hypothesis, it is motivational orientation that underlies the effects of evaluation expectation, restricted choice, and working for reward on creativity. With those effects, an underlying change in motivational orientation—from intrinsic to extrinsic—was presumed to underlie the observed decrements in creativity. Indeed, in some studies, relationships between creativity and motivational orientation were demonstrated in postexperimental self-reports. If it is possible to influence motivational orientation in the absence of any specific social constraints, and to demonstrate corresponding consequences for creativity, then the intrinsic motivation hypothesis and the place of task motivation in the componential framework will be strengthened considerably. According to the intrinsic motivation hypothesis of creativity, it should be possible to demonstrate an increase in creativity by an induced intrinsic orientation, and a decrease in creativity by an induced extrinsic orientation. To provide such a demonstration, I designed a study where both types of motivational orientation could be influenced, and subsequent effects on creative writing could be examined.

Motivational Orientation: An Empirical Demonstration

This study (Amabile, 1985) differed from those I reported in previous chapters in two important ways. First, there was no manipulation of social constraint (such as evaluation or reward) or of socially induced control state (being given choice about task engagement or aspects of task engagement). Second, the subjects in this study, unlike those in the previous studies, were individuals actively engaged in a creative pursuit in their daily lives. Furthermore, many of them had achieved some measure of recognition for their creativity. Thus, this study represents an important extension of previous results. It tests the intrinsic motivation hypothesis of creativity on bona fide creative individuals, and it does so in a direct way without the mediation of extrinsic constraint.

The subjects in this poetry-writing study were 72 creative writers, both undergraduates and graduate students, at Brandeis University and Boston University. So that prospective subjects would not know that the study specifically concerned creativity, they were told only that we wanted writers ("people who are actively involved in writing poetry or fiction") in order to study their "reasons for writing." Initial criteria for choosing subjects included: (a) completion of one or more ad-

vanced creative writing courses, or (b) publication of one or more works of poetry, or (c) publication of one or more works of fiction, or (d) spending an average of 4 or more hours of one's own time per week in writing poetry, or fiction.

To obtain information on these criteria, prospective subjects were given preliminary questionnaires to complete. Four measures were taken from this questionnaire: number of advanced writing courses taken, pieces of poetry published,
pieces of fiction published, and hours per week (of one's own time) spent on writing. In addition, responses to an open-ended question asking subjects to "give
other information on your involvement in writing" were rated by three judges on
the extent to which an extrinsic or an intrinsic orientation toward writing was exhibited. Subjects were eliminated if they did not fulfill at least one of the four initial criteria, or if they fell more than two standard deviations above the mean on
any of the measures (or on age).

Of the items on this preliminary questionnaire, two were considered most likely
to influence the creativity of subjects' poems—number of pieces of poetry published, and number of hours per week spent writing. These items had standard deviations approximately six times those of most of the other items. This weighting
of the two major items was allowed to stand; the weightings of the other items
were adjusted until they were equal to each other and to one-sixth of the weightings of each of the major items. The weighted scores for each subject were then
summed into an overall prescore to be used as a basis for roughly equating the
writing experience and interest of subjects in the three experimental conditions.

Subjects were randomly assigned to the conditions of the experiment—control,
intrinsic orientation, and extrinsic orientation—within certain restrictions. First,
there were an equal number of males and females in the conditions. Second, each
of the four female experimenters ran an approximately equal number of subjects
in each condition. Finally, means and variances on the prescores were approximately equal in the three conditions. Since there was no matching at the level of
subjects, however, this is best considered a quasiexperimental design.

The procedure for manipulating motivational orientation was adopted from a
methodology developed by Salancik (1975). This technique involves inducing an
extrinsic or intrinsic motivational orientation toward an activity simply by having
subjects rank-order extrinsic or intrinsic reasons for doing that activity. The underlying assumption is that, although particular rank-orderings of the reasons are
unimportant, the act of reading, concentrating on, and applying to oneself the extrinsic or intrinsic reasons for task activity can make that particular motivational
orientation salient or temporarily induce that orientation.

Using this technique in a study that is procedurally similar to mine, Seligman,
Fazio, and Zanna (1980) had the individual members of dating couples rank order
intrinsic reasons for dating their partner (such as, "I go with _____ because we
always have a good time together") or extrinsic reasons (such as, "I go out with
_____ because my friends think more highly of me since I began seeing
her/him"). Predictions for this study derived from attribution theory (Bem, 1972;

Kelley, 1967): If subjects attribute their interest in their dating partner to intrinsic reasons, they should experience themselves as being more in love than if they attribute their interest to extrinsic reasons. These predictions were strongly confirmed. Subjects who rank-ordered extrinsic reasons had lower scores on a postquestionnaire assessing love for their partner than did subjects in the intrinsic condition. Moreover, extrinsic subjects rated marriage to the dating partner as significantly less likely. Interestingly, subjects in a control condition, who did not rank order any reasons, scored very close to the intrinsic subjects on virtually all dependent measures. The researchers interpret this as indicating that the subjects' "natural cognitive set" toward their dating partners was intrinsic.

Using a similar procedure, experimental-group subjects in my study rank-ordered a list of reasons for being involved in writing. For some, these reasons were intrinsic. For others, they were extrinsic. In a pretest designed to develop a list of reasons that could reliably be considered intrinsic or extrinsic, a group of 20 Brandeis undergraduates were asked to identify 30 different reasons for writing as intrinsic, extrinsic, or neither/both. These subjects consistently identified seven of the reasons as intrinsic:

— You get a lot of pleasure out of reading something good that you have written.
— You enjoy the opportunity for self-expression.
— You achieve new insights through your writing.
— You derive satisfaction from expressing yourself clearly and eloquently.
— You feel relaxed when writing.
— You like to play with words.
— You enjoy becoming involved with ideas, characters, events, and images in your writing.

Seven other reasons were consistently rated as extrinsic:

— You realize that, with the introduction of dozens of magazines every year, the market for freelance writing is constantly expanding.
— You want your writing teachers to be favorably impressed with your writing talent.
— You have heard of cases where one best-selling novel or collection of poems has made the author financially secure.
— You enjoy public recognition of your work.
— You know that many of the best jobs available require good writing skills.
— You know that writing ability is one of the major criteria for acceptance into graduate school.
—Your teachers and parents have encouraged you to go into writing.

Subjects participated in the study individually. When they arrived at the laboratory, the experimenter first asked them to write a Haiku poem on a "Snow" theme. This initial creativity measure was collected as a means of further testing the initial equivalence of the three groups. Following this, all subjects were given a short story to read. Control subjects read the story for 15 minutes and then completed a questionnaire on their impressions of the story and the author. Experimental-group subjects, however, read the story for only 10 minutes before completing the questionnaire. Then, they spent about 5 minutes rank-ordering either the intrinsic or the extrinsic reasons for writing. Finally, all subjects wrote a second Haiku poem on the theme of "Laughter" and then completed a questionnaire on their reaction to the poem-writing activity.[2]

Twelve poet-judges rated the poems on creativity, with an interjudge reliability of .82 on the "Snow" poems and a reliability of .78 on the "Laughter" poems. As expected, there were no overall differences between conditions on the creativity of the initial poems subjects wrote: control, $M = 18.18$ (40-point scale); intrinsic, $M = 18.76$; extrinsic, $M = 18.19$ ($F < 1$). On the poem written after the independent variable manipulation, however, there was a statistically significant effect of condition. As illustrated in Figure 7-2, the creativity of subjects in both the control condition and the intrinsic condition was fairly high. The creativity of subjects in the extrinsic condition, however, was markedly lower. Indeed, creativity in this condition was significantly lower than that in both the control condition and the intrinsic condition.

This clear confirmation of prediction adds considerable strength to the intrinsic motivation hypothesis. This study demonstrates that, even in the absence of specific extrinsic constraints, if extrinsic goals are simply made salient to subjects, their creativity may be undermined. It does appear, however, that an *increase* of intrinsic motivation may be more difficult to obtain than a decrease. The mean creativity of the second poem for subjects in the intrinsic condition was not significantly higher than that of subjects in the control condition. Perhaps the similarity of the intrinsic and control conditions in this study should not be surprising, given the high level of involvement that these subjects already showed in their writing. This situation may be analogous to that uncovered by Seligman and his colleagues (1980), who found that increasing the salience of intrinsic reasons for dating one's partner did not increase the reported love that subjects felt for that partner.

Considering the high levels of initial interest in writing that my subjects demonstrated, the decrease in creativity in the extrinsic condition is particularly impressive. Although the effects of the extrinsic manipulation would only be expected to be temporary, it is nonetheless startling that spending barely 5 minutes reading and ranking extrinsic reasons for writing could have a significant impact on the creativity of creative writers.

---

[2] To ensure that the extrinsic manipulation had no long-lasting detrimental effects, we gave all extrinsic-condition subjects the intrinsic questionnaire after completion of the second poem. In addition, all subjects were given a thorough "process" debriefing (Ross, Lepper, & Hubbard, 1975).

Figure 7-2.   Mean creativity of poems by creative writers (Amabile 1985).
Note. Highest possible value is 40, lowest possible is 0.

Summary

Social-psychological factors can have important effects on creativity beyond the previously discussed influences of extrinsic constraints such as evaluation and control variables such as choice. On the basis of sociological, archival, and experimental research, several tentative conclusions can be drawn:

1. When people try to solve problems as a group, they may produce fewer ideas than they would individually; it is unclear whether the quality of ideas is consistently affected.
2. When people work individually on creativity tests in the presence of others, their performance may be impaired.
3. When people work individually on open-ended creative activities in the presence of others, there may be little impact on creativity unless those others are in a position to observe and possibly evaluate the performance. At this point, however, evidence on the effects of attentive observers on creativity is only suggestive.
4. Feelings of being evaluated undermine creativity, whether the work is done in group or individual settings.
5. An exposure to creative models early in one's professional development can have a positive impact on early creative achievement, although extended imitation of the model might, in the long run, undermine creativity.

6. Exposure to models can improve performance on creativity tests, but only if the modeled behavior is very similar to the performance assessed.
7. Motivational orientation toward one's work (which could be socially transmitted through modeling) has an important impact on creativity. A general extrinsic orientation toward an activity can lead to lower levels of creativity than a general intrinsic orientation.

Update

Unlike the social factors considered in Chapters 5 and 6, the factors reviewed here—social facilitation, modeling, and motivational orientation—do not operate as direct constraints or controls on behavior. Rather, their influence is relatively indirect or passive: the presence of others, the behavior of others as models, and the adoption of an intrinsic or extrinsic motivational orientation. Each of these may operate to support or undermine creative behavior.

Social Facilitation

Few researchers over the past decade have considered the question of the facilitation or inhibition of creativity by the mere presence of other individuals. However, one program of research (mentioned in the Chapter 5 update) has examined creativity in situations of pooled group output. In these "social loafing" studies, subjects were given a creativity task to do under group conditions where their individual performance was either identifiable or nonidentifiable (Bartis, Szymanski, & Harkins, 1988; Szymanski & Harkins, 1992). Although the quantity of output was generally higher in identifiable conditions, subjects produced more creative work in the group condition where their individual output was not identifiable. Although this effect can be viewed in terms of the evaluation expectation that subjects most likely felt when their work was public, it can also be seen as a kind of social facilitation afforded by the de facto anonymity (and thus the evaluation protection) of a group situation.

Modeling

Although there is little new empirical research on the effect of modeling on creative behavior, several scholars have suggested the importance of modeling in various creativity domains. For example, McKeachie (1983) proposes that the role of teacher as model is an important determinant of motivation and creativity in the learning of music. Harrington (1990) argues that modeling played a part in the invention of the computer, where each of a series of workers learned from and elaborated upon the work of predecessors. Similarly, Weber and Perkins (1989) suggest that previous inventions provide heuristics and prototypes for future inventions, and they argue that models of highly creative work are needed for effective idea generation. Finally, the work of Savolaninen (1990) demonstrates that computers may be used to model certain creativity skills for children.

Motivational Orientation

Recent research from our laboratory indicates that the effect of induced motivational orientation on creativity may be more complex than was suggested by the original experiment (Amabile, 1985). In that experiment, experienced creative writers (poets, fiction writers, and playwrights) wrote haiku poems in our laboratory after being exposed to one of three motivational orientation inductions. The induction was a relatively passive one, where the subjects read and rank-ordered intrinsic reasons for being a writer or extrinsic reasons for being a writer (or did a filler task in the control condition). These extrinsic reasons were primarily ones that, in our current terminology, we would call "nonsynergistic extrinsic motivators" (e.g., "You have heard of cases where one best-selling novel or collection of poems has made the author financially secure"). We found that the extrinsic induction led to significantly lower creativity than either the intrinsic induction or the control condition. We hypothesized that the intrinsic induction may have failed to produce higher levels of creativity due to a ceiling effect. Because we selected only subjects who were committed to spending several hours of their own time each week on writing, their initial intrinsic motivation may have been sufficiently high that no brief laboratory manipulation was likely to increase it.

In our first attempt to replicate and extend those results, we had nonexpert subjects (introductory psychology students) do a creative writing task after a passive motivational induction in which they simply read intrinsically or extrinsically motivated statements that others had written. There were no differences between conditions. In our second attempt, we had nonexpert subjects (again, introductory psychology students) do a creative writing task after an active motivational induction in which they were instructed to write either intrinsically or extrinsically motivated statements about writing. Again, there were no differences. We were particularly surprised by this second failure to replicate, especially because the active induction was intended to make the motivational orientation both salient and easily internalized.

However, one study has provided some evidence of the effectiveness of motivational induction manipulations with undergraduate populations (Greer & Levine, 1991). In that study, subjects wrote a haiku poem after being exposed to an intrinsic motivation induction drawn from the original study (Amabile, 1985), or a fantasy induction with guided imagery on the poem topic, or no induction (in the control condition). Both induction techniques led to significantly higher levels of judge-rated creativity compared to the control condition. It is intriguing that in contrast to the original study, this study demonstrated a significant impact of an intrinsic motivational orientation induction. Unfortunately, it is impossible to compare our finding of the effectiveness of an extrinsic induction in reducing creativity, because this study did not attempt to induce extrinsic motivation.

The immunization studies with children, reported in the update to Chapter 6, do provide some information about motivational induction (Hennessey, Amabile, & Martinage, 1989; Hennessey & Zbikowski, 1993). In those studies, where only intrinsic induction was used, children either did or did not receive training designed to focus them on their own intrinsic interest in learning. We found evidence in one of the immunization studies that this induction actually increased children's intrinsic motivation toward learning as assessed by a standard method (Harter, 1981). Moreover, one of the studies yielded a main effect of the intrinsic motivation training on subsequent creativity.

On the basis of the original motivational induction study, we concluded that simply having a motivational state made salient could have an impact on creativity, even in the absence of specific extrinsic motivators at that point in time. Now it appears that that conclusion must be qualified. It may be more subtle and fragile than we had originally believed, and it may more reliably obtain with experts or with individuals who have an ongoing involvement in the target domain. Perhaps individuals who feel particularly invested in a task domain are more likely than others to internalize the intrinsic or the extrinsic motives that are brought to their attention. For example, it is likely that people who identify themselves as writers have actually experienced strong intrinsic motives and strong extrinsic motives to engage in writing. Perhaps, when asked to spend a few moments reflecting on only one set of those motives, they may be more likely to call up other instances of such motives from their own experience—thus strengthening a very brief and relatively trivial laboratory manipulation.

Some recent biographical studies have provided additional support for our contention that intrinsic motivation is essential for creativity and that extrinsic motivation may be detrimental. In one study, Thematic Apperception Tests (TATs) of art students were examined for intrinsic and extrinsic motivational themes (Carney, 1986). Those with higher levels of extrinsic imagery tended to drop out of the profession if they were not immediately successful after school. By contrast, those whose imagery focused more on the joy of making art and the value of self-discovery tended to persist; they were also more likely to be successful eventually. In another study where teenagers were interviewed, higher levels of lifelong intrinsic motivation were evident in the teens identified as "creative" than in their less-creative peers (Heinzen, Mills, & Cameron, 1993).

The strongest direct evidence we have collected over the past twelve years on the importance of intrinsic motivation in creativity comes from nonexperimental research. Recognizing that our theory required us to examine stable traitlike motivational orientation in addition to temporary, situationally-induced motivation, we set out to develop a personality inventory to assess intrinsic and extrinsic motivational orientation in adults. This Work Preference Inventory (WPI) has two primary scales, Intrinsic and Extrinsic Motivation. The Intrinsic scale is further subdivided into two secondary scales, Enjoyment (being strongly motivated by curiosity and by self-expression, getting so absorbed in the work that everything else is forgotten, preferring to figure things out for oneself, preferring to set one's own goals, wanting to learn from one's own work, feeling that it is important to enjoy what one does) and Challenge (preferring new, difficult, complex problems; not being satisfied by straightforward tasks; preferring work that stretches one's abilities). Similarly, the Extrinsic scale is subdivided into two secondary scales, Compensation (being motivated by the monetary compensation for one's work, and being keenly aware of one's income, or grade point, goals) and Outward Orientation (being motivated by recognition, being sensitive to others' opinions of one's work and one's ideas, judging one's success relative to other people, and preferring work with clear goals and procedures). All of the primary and secondary WPI scales have acceptable psychometric properties (Amabile, Hill, Hennessey, & Tighe, 1994).

Through several years of WPI research with hundreds of college students and working adults, we have found little consistent evidence that extrinsic motivational orientation is correlated with product creativity (on verbal, artistic, and problem-solving tasks). We did discover that compared to a normative adult population, a sample of professional artists scored significantly lower on the extrinsic secondary scale of Compensation (Amabile, Phillips, & Collins, 1994). And compared to the normative population, a sample of high-level corporate scientists scored significantly lower on the extrinsic secondary scale of Outward Orientation (Amabile, Hill, Hennessey, & Tighe, 1994). However, when we correlate actual product creativity levels with WPI extrinsic scales, most of the correlations are close to zero, a few are negative, but some are positive as well. For example, in our study of professional artists, there was a positive (though nonsignificant) correlation between the artist's expert-rated creativity and Outward Orientation—the degree to which the individual is generally oriented toward recognition from other people (Amabile, Phillips, & Collins, 1994). These findings are in keeping with our recently revised Intrinsic Motivation Principle of Creativity, which recognizes the possible value of synergistic extrinsic motivators. It is likely that the extrinsic motivators that consistently attract some people in their work will often be the positive motivators that provide information value or that enable task engagement rather than the nonsynergistic motivators that lead people to feel externally controlled.

Our most consistent creativity findings with the WPI reveal a positive relationship between intrinsic motivation and creativity. In a study of student artists, both expert-rated creativity and instructor-rated creativity correlated strongly and positively (and significantly) with the students' scores on the intrinsic motivation scales (Pollak, 1992). In the study of professional artists, expert-rated creativity not only correlated positively with extrinsic motivation, as noted above, but it also correlated positively with the intrinsic motivation secondary scale of Challenge (Amabile, Phillips, & Collins, 1994). Finally, both the professional artists and the high-level corporate scientists scored significantly higher than the normative population on the intrinsic secondary scale of Enjoyment (Amabile, Hill, Hennessey, & Tighe, 1994).

Thus, our recent nonexperimental research, as well as the research of other scholars, supports the basic argument that intrinsic motivation is conducive to creativity. The story on extrinsic motivation is less straightforward. It appears that although certain forms of extrinsic motivation are detrimental to intrinsic motivation and creativity, other forms are either neutral or may actually enhance creativity under some circumstances. These findings are consistent with the revised Intrinsic Motivation Principle of Creativity and the statements made there about synergistic extrinsic motivators (see the Update to Chapter 4).

Summary

New empirical evidence from research with adults suggests that focusing on extrinsic motives may undermine creativity only for experts or others who are invested or involved in the particular domain. However, recent research with both children and adults also suggests that focusing on intrinsic motives may increase intrinsic motivation and creativity. Moreover, for some groups, certain types of extrinsic motivation may positively relate to creativity.

As a personality trait, intrinsic motivation is positively related to creativity in a variety of domains.

Thus, taken together, the results of several studies support the basic tenets of the revised Intrinsic Motivation Principle of Creativity. Intrinsic motivation does appear to be essential for creativity, and certain forms of extrinsic motivation may have no impact, or even a positive impact, on creativity.

8

Other Social and Environmental Influences

The factors considered in Chapters 5–7 are usually directed specifically at the creative activity. For example, evaluation is focused on a particular product or response, or a task-specific reward is imposed, or choice on a given task is restricted. As indicated by the writings of creative persons reviewed in Chapter 1, however, even mundane social events that are not directed toward the creative activity can have an important impact on creativity. Charles Dickens, for example, lamented the disruptions of his work environment caused by ordinary social demands:

> "It is only half-an-hour"—"It is only an afternoon"—"It is only an evening," people say to me over and over again; but they don't know that it is impossible to command one's self sometimes to any stipulated and set disposal of five minutes—or that the mere consciousness of an engagement will sometimes worry a whole day. (Allen, 1948, p. 230)

In this chapter, I will consider several social-environmental factors whose effects on creativity appear to be less task-specific than those discussed in previous chapters: educational environments, work environments, family influences, and societal, political, and cultural influences. In addition, I will discuss several other factors that might have an impact on creativity: prior activity, play and fantasy, and the physical environment. Although, strictly, these cannot be considered social-environmental influences, the social environment can play a role in their instantiation; thus, they should be included in a social psychology of creativity.

Educational Environments

Of all the social and environmental factors that might influence creativity, most can be found in some form in the classroom. Moreover, not only is the incidence of such factors perhaps highest in educational environments, but it is probably easiest to control them there, as well. Thus, despite the many difficulties inherent in conducting psychological research in school settings (cf. Amabile & Stubbs, 1982), such inquiry is particularly important for the social psychology of creativity. Many investigators have, in fact, examined the impact of various facets of educational environments on creativity. Virtually all of this research has focused on elementary school children.

Peers

Some studies have investigated the impact of children's classmates on their creativity. One practical issue that often arises when teachers must decide how to deal with outstandingly creative children concerns ability grouping: Is it best to form heterogeneous classes or to separate children into homogeneous ability levels for instruction? An early investigation of this issue revealed that, in homogeneous groupings, superior students engaged in many more creative activities and felt more positively about school in general (Drews, 1961). Later studies (e.g., Marjoribanks, 1978) support the conclusion that educating outstanding children in separate groups can be generally beneficial for their creative development. As suggested by the research reviewed in Chapter 7, these positive effects may be due to a mutual modeling of both creativity heuristics and intrinsic motivational orientations.

There is some suggestive evidence that peer pressure in classrooms can undermine creativity. Torrance (1967, 1968) documented a consistent drop in creativity test scores after the third year of elementary school—what he terms the "fourth grade slump." In identifying possible causes for this temporary decline, Torrance pointed to evidence of increased tendencies for children to conform with their peers at about the fourth grade. According to the theoretical notions discussed in Chapter 4, this increased conformity pressure would be expected to reduce children's willingness to take risks in exploring new paths to solutions.

Teacher Characteristics and Behavior

Although many theorists suggest the importance of modeled creativity, there is almost no research on the effects of teacher characteristics on the creativity of their pupils. In one study, where the Torrance Tests were administered to teachers and students in Grades 3–5, the results were mixed (Baker, 1979). Of five verbal creativity measures, three demonstrated superiority of the children whose teachers scored high on creativity. However, of five nonverbal creativity measures, two showed a superiority of children whose teachers scored low on creativity.

Another study, although not directly examining creativity, points to teacher attitudes that might be conducive to children's creativity (Deci, Nezlek, & Sheinman, in press). In that study, teachers' beliefs in the importance of student autonomy correlated significantly and positively with their students' preference for challenge, curiosity, and desire for independent mastery. In addition, this study showed that, when children see their own teacher as more intrinsically oriented toward work, they perceive themselves as more competent and more intrinsically motivated. Thus, children's intrinsic motivation (and, hence, creativity) might be enhanced by teacher attitudes toward autonomy and self-direction in work.

The effects of specific teacher behaviors on children's creativity have also received little research attention. One study examined the so-called "Pygmalion effect," in which teacher expectations about students' performance may actually influence that performance (Rosenthal, Baratz, & Hall, 1974). Children in Grades 1–6 at a black inner-city school were given an IQ test and an open-ended drawing test at the beginning of the school year. Teachers were then given the names of approximately 20% of the children in their classes and told that those children would show unusual gains in creativity during that year. In fact, these names were randomly chosen. The same tests were again administered at the close of the school year. For the fifth grade only, those children who had been designated as "creative bloomers" did show significantly higher gains in judge-rated creativity than did the control children. There were no differences at the other grade levels.

Although these results are quite inconclusive, the study did provide intriguing data on the teacher characteristics that were conducive to children's gains in creativity during the school year (regardless of the experimental manipulations). Those teachers whose pupils showed the greatest gains in creativity were rated by classroom observers as significantly more likeable, more interested in children, more satisfied, more enthusiastic, more courteous, more business-like, more professional, and more encouraging at the beginning of the school year. These correlational data, although only suggestive, do point to some teacher characteristics that should be considered in future research.

Another study examined differential teacher perceptions of and behaviors toward creative and uncreative children (Evans, 1979). In that study, four teachers in preschool and primary school were asked to nominate the three most creative and the three least creative children in their classes. Although the initial proportions of girls and boys in the classes were virtually identical, there were clear sex differences in teachers' nominations and teachers' behaviors toward the nominated children. At both ends of the continuum, many more boys were nominated than girls. In other words, boys were often seen at the extremes of creative ability. Girls were seen as more uniformly moderate in creative abilities. In addition, classroom observers' ratings revealed that these teachers were more likely to give encouragement to the "most creative" boys than the "most creative" girls.

Finally, in their research on highly creative and highly intelligent adolescents, Getzels and Jackson (1962) found that creative children are often viewed as bothersome by their teachers. These researchers suggest that creative children, because of their playfulness, humor, and independence, may be difficult for teachers to control. As a result, these children may frequently fall into the teacher's disfavor.

Overall Classroom Climate

Apart from investigations of specific teacher characteristics and behaviors, several attempts have been made to study other, more globally defined aspects of classroom environments that might influence creativity. One study, for example, found that children in public schools scored significantly higher on creativity tests than did children in parochial schools (Check, 1969). Most of this "general classroom climate" research, however, has focused on the distinction between "open" and traditional classrooms.

Perhaps the most difficult aspect of reviewing research on open classrooms is the variability in definitions of "openness." Silberman (1970) has described this quality as "less an approach or method than a set of shared attitudes and convictions about the nature of childhood, learning, and schooling" (p. 208). Openness, although sometimes identified with the use of large open rooms for classes, is most often viewed as "a style of teaching involving flexibility of space, student choice of activity, richness of learning materials, integration of curriculum areas, and more individual or small-group than large-group instruction" (Horwitz, 1979, pp. 72–73). Other researchers have focused on the open classroom as an atmosphere for developing critical inquiry, curiosity, exploration, and self-directed learning, without grading or authoritative teaching (Ramey & Piper, 1974; Sullivan, 1974). These researchers describe traditional classrooms in strict contrast to open classrooms: Examinations, grading, and authoritative teaching are common; large group instruction is the norm, and a carefully prepared curriculum is followed with little variation (Ramey & Piper, 1974; Sullivan, 1974).

One study included a frequency count of the number of hours per week spent on various classroom activities in open and traditional classes (Sullivan, 1974). The most frequent activities in a traditional classroom were group reading and math drill, while the most frequent activities in the open classroom were creative writing, group projects, and independent reading. Thus, open classrooms generally contain less structure, fewer teacher-initiated constraints on performance, and more individualized effort. Since many of the differences between open and traditional classrooms concern extrinsic constraint, the intrinsic motivation hypothesis of creativity would lead to predictions of higher creativity among children in open classrooms.

In a review of studies that examine the relationship between open education and creativity, Horwitz (1979) reported finding no studies that unequivocally favored traditional classrooms. Of the 33 studies reviewed, 12 indicated that children in open classrooms were more creative, 10 obtained mixed results, and 11 found no significant differences. Nonetheless, there are a few studies that do suggest a superiority of traditional classrooms on some measures. For example, in a study that used teacher self-reports to categorize classrooms as open or traditional (Ward & Barcher, 1975), there were no differences between classes for low-IQ children; for high-IQ children, however, those in the traditional classrooms had higher figural creativity scores. Another study, using loosely operationalized definitions of "open" and "traditional," examined three grades in each of two different school systems. Figural creativity was higher in the open system, but verbal creativity was higher in the traditional system (Ramey & Piper, 1974). Using a somewhat more rigorous rating procedure, other researchers (Thomas & Berk, 1981) found that classroom environments categorized as intermediate or informal facilitated greater gains in creativity than classroom environments categorized as formal.

Most of the evidence does favor open classrooms. In perhaps the best-known studies of open education and creativity, Haddon and Lytton (1968) tested over

200 British children, half from formal and half from informal primary schools. The two groups were matched on verbal reasoning quotient and socioeconomic status. Using a variety of creativity tests, these researchers discovered a consistent superiority of children in the informal classes. In a follow-up investigation which included nearly three-fourths of the original sample (Haddon & Lytton, 1971), results revealed that the children from the open classrooms retained their superiority in divergent thinking 4 years after they had left primary school. Other researchers have obtained similar results. Goyal (1973) found that children in open classrooms scored higher on fluency, flexibility, and originality than did children in intermediate classrooms who, in turn, scored higher than children in traditional classrooms. Open classroom children have also been shown to score higher on open-ended design-making tests (McCormick, Sheehy, & Mitchell, 1978) and on originality and fluency in a puzzle-solving test (Hyman, 1978). It is particularly interesting that the puzzle-solving differences appeared after children had been in their different classrooms only 8 months.

Finally, Sullivan (1974) found that children in open classrooms scored significantly better on two of four Guilford tests than children in traditional classrooms. In addition, on a story-telling task, open classroom children used more vivid language and greater variety in sentence structure. Interestingly, on self-rating questionnaires, there were several significant differences in the reported working styles of children in the two classrooms. Those in the open classrooms rated themselves as significantly more likely to do their homework alone, make things without help from others, leave something unfinished because they become interested in something else, ask for help in following directions, prefer to have no set plans for the school day, and build something as they go along (rather than planning everything in advance).

There is, then, qualified support for the prediction that relatively informal classroom environments will facilitate creativity more effectively than traditional, restrictive classroom environments. There are a number of difficulties, however, in attempting to determine what these results mean. Primarily, of course, there are methodological problems to consider. The operational definitions of "open" and "traditional" are not clear and consistent. Much of the research does not control for students' socioeconomic status and intelligence. And, rather than using open-ended measures of creativity, most of the studies rely on creativity tests. In addition, reporting biases may be operative. It is likely that most individuals who study differences in creativity between open and traditional schools do, in fact, ideologically favor open schools. Thus, negative or mixed results may be given less prominence in this literature.

Keeping these limitations of the classroom data in mind, however, explanations can be offered for any superiority that open classrooms do in fact enjoy. Clearly, one viable explanation is that intrinsic task motivations are encouraged by the relative lack of extrinsic constraints in the open classrooms. Children, instead of concerning themselves with pleasing the teacher, doing better than other students, winning good grades, or meeting deadlines, may instead concentrate their efforts on playful and innovative exploration with materials and ideas. Another explanation is that, because many of the activities that children frequently do in open classrooms (such as creative writing) are similar to those used during testing, these children have acquired a set of creativity-relevant skills that are easily applied on the creativity tests.

College Environments

Although most of the research on educational environments has focused on elementary schools, some investigators have studied college environments that might be conducive or detrimental to creativity. Occasionally, these studies look at global effects of the college experience on creativity-test performance. For example, in a study that used both cross-sectional and longitudinal designs (Eisenman, 1970), student nurses showed significant decreases in originality with advancement in class standing from freshman to senior year. These results were interpreted as consistent with views of nursing school as socializing passive acceptance of rules and routines. It is possible, of course, that similar results would apply to the general college population.

In an investigation of college teaching styles that facilitate or inhibit creativity, Chambers (1973) asked several hundred creative psychologists and chemists to describe the teachers who had the greatest facilitating and inhibiting influences on their creative development. The results were compiled into two lists, one rank-ordering the ten most important facilitating factors, and another rank-ordering the eight most important inhibiting factors. Facilitating factors (in order of importance) were: (1) treated students as individuals; (2) encouraged students to be independent; (3) served as a model; (4) spent considerable amount of time with students outside of class; (5) indicated that excellence was expected and could be achieved; (6) enthusiastic; (7) accepted students as equals; (8) directly rewarded student's creative behavior or work; (9) interesting, dynamic lecturer; and (10) excellent on one-to-one basis. Inhibiting factors (again in order of importance) were: (1) discouraged students (ideas, creativity, etc.); (2) was insecure (hypercritical, sarcastic); (3) lacked enthusiasm; (4) emphasized rote learning; (5) was dogmatic and rigid; (6) did not keep up with field; generally incompetent; (7) had narrow interests; and (8) not available outside the classroom. Other data collected in this study revealed that the teachers seen as most important for creative scientific development were usually professors on the graduate, rather than the undergraduate, level. In addition, the most creative scientists reported being most favorably influenced by graduate school professors who were more interested in research than in teaching. Overall, the respondents revealed that their most important contacts with the facilitating teachers occurred not in the classroom but in less formal settings, such as the laboratory, the office, or the home.

In an important set of studies by Hyman (1960, 1964), subjects evaluated other persons' solutions to a problem. They were asked either to list positive features and advantages of those solutions, or to list weaknesses and faults. Later, when giving their own solutions to the problem, subjects making the previous evaluations under a positive set were more creative than those making previous evaluations under a negative set. Thus, although these studies did not directly examine teaching methods, the results suggest that teachers who encourage positive, constructive criticism may foster creativity.

More global aspects of the college environment have also been investigated. In a study of 36 American colleges, Thistlethwaite (1959a, 1959b) formed "productivity" scores for each school in the natural sciences and the humanities-social sciences. The index of natural science productivity, for example, was defined as the discrepancy between a college's expected rate of producing natural science PhD's (as predicted from its enrollment of National Merit Scholars) and its actual rate of undergraduates who later went on to receive such degrees. Using this method, the productivity measure was computed by counting those alumni in the classes of 1943–1949 who had gone on to receive doctorates in the fields mentioned. It was found that women's colleges ranked low on both indices, that land-grant colleges were unusually productive in the natural sciences, and that Catholic colleges were significantly less productive than Protestant and nondenominational colleges, which did not differ. This latter result is consistent with Zuckerman's (1977) finding that Catholics are vastly underrepresented in the population of Nobel laureates, while Protestants are represented at about expected levels, and Jews are vastly overrepresented.

Of greater interest, however, are the measures of social climate that correlate with a school's productivity in the two areas. Those measures were obtained by asking students at the 36 schools to rate their college on several true-false items (The College Characteristics Index). Among the more interesting items that correlated positively with productivity in the natural sciences were: (1) students frequently do things on the spur of the moment here; and (2) hazing, teasing, and practical joking are fairly common. Some negatively correlated items were: (1) students ask permission before deviating from common policies or practices; (2) professors usually take attendance in class; (3) when students get together they seldom talk about science; (4) students think about dressing appropriately and interestingly for different occasions; (5) faculty members and administrators see students only during scheduled office hours or by appointment; (6) instructors clearly explain the goals and purposes of their courses; and (7) religious worship here stresses service to God and obedience to His laws.

Among the more interesting items that correlated positively with productivity in the arts, humanities, and social sciences were: (1) there is a lot of emphasis on preparing for graduate work; (2) there is a lot of interest here in poetry, music, painting, sculpture, architecture, etc.; (3) there would be a capacity audience for a lecture by an outstanding philosopher or theologian; (4) if a student fails a course he can usually substitute another one for it rather than take it over; and (5) student pep rallies, parades, dances, carnivals, or demonstrations occur very rarely.

Some negatively correlated items on this measure were: (1) students are more interested in specialization than in liberal education; (2) modern art and music get little attention around here; (3) religious worship here stresses service to God and obedience to His laws; (4) there is a lot of apple-polishing around here; (5) most students have little interest in round tables, panel meetings, or other formal discussions; (6) hazing, teasing, and practical joking are fairly common; and (7) faculty members and administrators see students only during scheduled office hours or by appointment.

These results must be considered with caution for a number of reasons. First, the data were collected over two decades ago on people who graduated from college over three decades ago. Second, the validity of the self-report measure has not been established. And, finally, any correlations might simply be indications of student or faculty self-selection. Still, the patterns revealed in this research are generally consistent with the findings on open classrooms at lower educational levels. In addition, these results agree in one important respect with those on characteristics of college professors who facilitate creativity (Chambers, 1973): Productivity in both the sciences and the arts is positively affected by ample student-faculty contact outside of the classroom.

Work Environments

In contrast to the large volume of studies on the influence of educational environments, there is almost no empirical research on the effects of work environments on creativity. One large-scale study did examine the relationship between social-psychological factors in the workplace and fulfillment of creative potential (Andrews, 1975). The subjects in this research were 115 scientists working in research organizations, each of whom had been director of a research project dealing with social-psychological aspects of disease. These medical sociologists held doctorates or master's degrees in psychology, sociology, or medicine. The research reports resulting from the projects were submitted to experts in medical sociology who rated them on "innovativeness—the degree to which the research represents additions to knowledge through new lines of research or the development of new theoretical statements of findings which were not explicit in previous theory" (p. 122).

Each subject completed extensive questionnaires on the social-psychological environment during the course of the project and, in addition, each took the Remote Associates Test (Mednick & Mednick, 1966). The RAT presents subjects with several sets of three words and asks them to supply the term for each set which is associated in some way with each of the other three. (For example, the answer to the item, "rat-blue-cottage" is "cheese.") This measure of the subjects' ability to make unusual but appropriate associations was taken as a measure of creative potential. Correlations between RAT scores and actual innovativeness were taken as indicators of the degree to which the various working conditions facilitated or inhibited the fulfillment of creative potential in these researchers.

A number of social-psychological factors discriminated researchers who exhibited positive correlations from those who exhibited negative correlations between creative ability and actual innovativeness. Four social-psychological factors seemed most important in facilitating the realization of creative potential: (1) high responsibility for initiating new activities, (2) high degree of power to hire research assistants, (3) no interference from administrative superior, and (4) high stability of employment. In those cases where all four of these factors were present, the correlation between RAT performance and innovativeness of the project was +.55. This correlation steadily decreased as fewer of the factors were present, until it reached -.97 in those cases when none of the factors was found.

Although this correlational evidence must be interpreted cautiously, it does suggest facilitative and inhibitory social-psychological effects of the work environment on creativity. In the main, these results agree well with the theoretical propositions presented in Chapter 4. The best atmospheres appear to be those with little extrinsic constraint, little interference with work, and little cause for concern with problems (such as unemployment) that are extrinsic to the research problem itself.

Family Influences

A great deal of research has examined the influence of family characteristics and parental behaviors on creative development.[1] Roe's (1952) finding that a disproportionately large number of eminent scientists are firstborns and only children led several researchers to study the influence of *birth order* on creativity. Later research has confirmed that firstborns are overrepresented in many realms of creative achievement. For example, a higher proportion of classical music composers are firstborns or only children than would be expected from base-rates in the general population (Schubert, Wagner, & Schubert, 1977). In studies where noneminent individuals are given creativity tests, however, the results are not nearly so clear-cut. Some have found a positive relationship between birth order and creativity, showing that firstborns are more creative (e.g., Eisenman & Schussel, 1970; Helson, 1968; Lichtenwalner & Maxwell, 1969; Weisberg & Springer, 1961), others have reported no relationship (Cicirelli, 1967; Datta, 1968; Dewing & Taft, 1973; Joesting, 1975), and still others have uncovered negative relationships (Eisenman, 1964; Staffieri, 1970).

Miller and Gerard (1979) have attempted to reconcile these results by suggesting that firstborns excel at creative tasks requiring an achievement orientation (such as science), whereas later-borns excel at tasks that are more artistic in nature. There are, however, many studies whose data do not fit this pattern. Another intriguing

---

[1] Many of the factors discussed in this section are considered in detail in an excellent review by Miller and Gerard (1979).

solution to these inconsistencies has been offered by Albert (1980), who suggests that it is not birth order per se that influences later creative achievement, but any special position within the family. Certainly, first birth order is one form of special family position. However, according to Albert, other family positions can produce psychological effects that are equally important: being the only son of a family, being the oldest son, becoming the oldest surviving son during childhood, being the last child or the last son, or being a child who loses a parent early in life.

There are some data to support Albert's explanation. Of 31 Nobel laureates studied, 74% occupied one of the special family positions listed above; in another group of 62 eminent scientists, 76% occupied special family positions (Albert, 1980). Furthermore, in comparison with an average of 8% of the general population that suffers early parental death, the figures are 26% for a sample of eminent scientists, 24% for a sample of eminent French and English poets, and 55% for a sample of eminent English writers and poets (Albert, 1980). In general, on the basis of a few studies with noneminent individuals, it does appear that father absence is positively correlated with creative performance; this finding might be mediated by parents' age at the time of the child's birth (Miller & Gerard, 1979). With caution, though, the data on family position and parental loss can be taken as evidence that a family constellation which places special attention and emphasis on a child can foster that child's creativity.

Parental characteristics and behavior should be even more closely related to children's creativity than family constellations. This does, in fact, appear to be the case. There is ample evidence, for example, that children tend to be more creative when their parents feel personally secure and relatively unconcerned about conforming to society's behavioral inhibitions or rules on status and roles (Miller & Gerard, 1979). In a study of high school boys and their fathers (Grant & Domino, 1976), the fathers of highly creative boys showed less conventional sex-role stereotyping on a number of measures than the fathers of uncreative boys. In addition, they scored significantly higher on the femininity scale of the California Psychological Inventory. In another study of high school boys (Domino, 1969), mothers of those in the highly creative group were less inhibited, less concerned about making a good impression, and relatively unresponsive to social demands.

Obviously, parental behaviors directed specifically at the child can also be extremely important to development, including creative development. In their study of talented mathematicians and composers, Bloom and Sosniak (1981) discovered that the parents were usually intensely involved in the child's talent development from the beginning. They offered enthusiasm and encouragement and, in some cases, themselves served as models of passionate involvement in the talent field. Moreover, as the child's talent became increasingly evident, they expended large amounts of money and effort in finding the best possible tutors for those children and in working with those tutors in the child's early learning.

But what of more mundane child-rearing matters, such as discipline and warmth in the home? Considerable evidence suggests that families most likely to foster creativity in children are characterized by a low level of authoritarianism and restrictiveness, an encouragement of independence, and a somewhat cool interpersonal distance between parents and children (Miller & Gerard, 1979). For example, in his study of creative architects, MacKinnon (1962) found many family characteristics that fit this general pattern: (a) the parents displayed respect for their children and confidence in the children's ability to do the right thing; (b) often the father, and even the mother, exhibited a lack of intense closeness with the children; there was, overall, a lack of strong positive or negative emotion; (c) the mothers often led autonomous, active lives; and (d) although there was an emphasis on developing a personal code of conduct, there was often little attention paid to formal religious practice.

Other studies have supported the conclusions that the parents of creative children are not only low in authoritarianism (Bayard de Volo & Fiebert, 1977) and disciplinary restrictiveness (Datta & Parloff, 1967; Getzels & Jackson, 1961; Parish & Eads, 1977), but also low in strong overt expressions of warmth (Drevdahl, 1964; Siegelman, 1973). Indeed, in one study, low maternal warmth was associated with higher creativity, and being a "Daddy's girl" appeared to lead to particularly low levels of creativity in women (Halpin, 1973).

Virtually all of the research on family influences examines the impact of an individual's *childhood* family on subsequent creativity. It is also interesting, however, to consider possible impacts of an individual's *adulthood* family on the fulfillment of creative potential. One study that examined this issue (Torrance, 1972b) was a 12-year follow-up of men and women who had been tested for creativity in elementary school and high school. Although there were generally good correlations between predicted and actual levels of creative achievements, there were interesting sex differences. The number of children that the subjects had was negatively related to their adult creative performance. This effect was much more pronounced for women. In addition, the more creative women were more likely to be simultaneously involved in family and career, while the less creative women limited their involvement to their families.

Societal, Political, and Cultural Influences

By far, the largest systematic program of research in the social psychology of creativity is that conducted over the past 8 years by D. K. Simonton. All of Simonton's research is archival, using sophisticated statistical procedures to discern correlations and causal patterns between social variables and the originality or productivity of musicians, writers, artists, philosophers, and scientists throughout history. Some of this research has examined creators as individuals, while the rest has grouped creators into generations and examined aggregate trends. All of the work has been characterized by a particularly careful attention to the operational definition of independent variables (social, political, cultural, and individual factors) and dependent variables (originality, productivity, eminence, and fame).

A detailed description of one of Simonton's studies will serve to illustrate his general approach to the social psychology of creativity. In this study (1977a), the lives of 10 classical composers were examined in detail to determine the influence on musical productivity of the composer's age, social reinforcements, biographical stress, war, and political disturbances. So that abundant information on the lives of the composers would be readily available, Simonton chose the 10 most eminent classical composers (according to a reliable archival source). In rank order of eminence, these composers were Bach, Beethoven, Mozart, Haydn, Brahms, Handel, Debussy, Schubert, Wagner, and Chopin. For the purposes of this multivariate time-series analysis, each composer's life was divided into 5-year intervals and the dependent measures were computed for each interval; the first such period for any composer was the period in which he began to compose.

On the basis of theories in personality, social psychology, and creativity, Simonton set down six hypotheses for this study: Creative productivity per unit time is (1) a curvilinear inverted-U function of age; (2) a positive linear function of social reinforcement; (3) a curvilinear inverted-U function of biographical stress; (4) a negative linear function of war intensity; and (5) a negative linear function of internal disturbances. (6) The proportion of major creative products relative to minor creative products per time unit is a positive linear function of age.

Two measures of the composers' productivity were taken. First, a count was made of the total number of *works,* and these works were then weighted according to the number of movements, the size of the instrumental or vocal ensembles required for performance, and the structural complexity of the musical forms. By this scheme, for example, masses and operas were weighted most heavily, while dances, marches, and revisions of arrangements received the smallest weightings. Finally, each of the weighted works was assigned to the 5-year time period in which it was composed. The second measure of productivity was based on the total number of *themes.* Instrumental and vocal themes were determined by reference to a musical dictionary that lists over 18,000 themes, covering virtually every classical composition ever phonographically recorded. Using this source, the number of themes that a composer wrote in each 5-year period was determined. Not surprisingly, since larger works tend to have more musical themes, this measure correlates highly (.64) with the weighted total of works. Nonetheless, because some large works (such as fugues) have relatively few themes, the two measures are certainly not equivalent.

The independent variables in this study were defined as follows:[2]

> *Age.* The age of the composer at the onset of each 5-year period was used. In the statistical analyses, two transformed age variables were included, both based on deviations from the overall mean age.

---

[2] In practice, of course, when correlational analyses are being considered, the identification of some variables as "independent" and others as "dependent" is largely arbitrary. The distinctions used here and in Table 8-1 are based on Simonton's own manner of discussing these variables in most cases.

Biographical stress. Based on contemporary scales for determining stress caused by life changes, a scale appropriate for these archival data was constructed. Some of the life changes included on this scale, along with their corresponding weights, were: job change (20), beginning and/or end of a reciprocated love affair (30), detention in jail or exile to avoid arrest (63), and death of spouse (100). Total points accumulated for each 5-year period (determined by consulting numerous biographical sources) were tabulated; again, transformed variables were used in the statistical analyses.

Physical illness. A scale assigning points to various types of physical illnesses was developed, and point totals for each 5-year period were computed by reference to the biographical sources. Serious injuries, for example, received 2 points each, while total blindness or deafness received 10 points per year.

Social reinforcement. For each 5-year period, one point was assigned for each of several honors bestowed on the composer: honorary doctorate, public monument erected in his honor, membership in an honorary society, listing in a *Who's Who,* public celebration of his birthday, knighting, prize, "key to the city," or a society founded in his honor.

Competition. A biographical dictionary of composers, assigning each a number of stars (0–3) according to eminence, was used to compute this value. Competition for each composer for a given 5-year period was computed by assigning one point for each other composer who was alive and at least 20 years old during that period, with one extra point for each star assigned to those composers.

War intensity. The intensity of wars involving the composer's nation of permanent residence was computed for each 5-year period. "Nation" was defined in a cultural-linguistic, rather than a political, sense. The nations of these 10 composers, then, were Germany-Austria, England, France, Italy, and Russia. One point was assigned for each year that the nation was at war, with one extra point for each battle, siege, invasion, city or fortress captured, territorial conquest, or raid, as listed in an encyclopedia of military history.

Internal disturbances. The number of internal revolutions, revolts, riots, coups d'etat, and the like, was tabulated for the composer's nation of permanent residence during each 5-year period. Each such episode was weighted according to social area, duration, size of the masses involved, and intensity. For both this measure and the war intensity measure, the final 5-year period of the composer's life did not include events occurring after his death.

In carrying out the multivariate cross-sectional time-series analysis, several control variables were included. These controlled for a number of features of the composers' biographies: (1) Many composers did not begin composing at exactly the first year of their first 5-year period; (2) many composers died before the close of their last 5-year period; (3) general time-wise trends in musical composition can obscure the patterns of interest here; and (4) dating of compositions may sometimes be inexact, with biographers tending to assign round-number dates.

The analyses uncovered some intriguing information on social and political influences. There was a negative relationship between thematic productivity and number of competitors, although the same association was not found for the total number of works produced. In other words, the more competitors and the more eminent those competitors, the fewer different themes these composers produced. Equally interesting, several of the social and political variables *failed* to demonstrate any influence on creative productivity: social reinforcement, biographical stress, war intensity, and internal political disturbances.

In addition, analyses of the age variables produced results of interest. For both measures of productivity, an inverted-backward-J function was revealed: Productivity rose to a peak throughout the composer's lifetime and then fell, but the decline never reached the low levels characteristic of the early career. Interestingly, social reinforcements awarded to these composers followed a J-function of age; they received more awards early and late in their careers than they did at midcareer, with most coming late. As might be expected, physical illness was negatively related to both total and thematic productivity.

On the basis of these results, Simonton accepted only the hypothesis that creative productivity is a curvilinear inverted-U function of age. All of the others were rejected.

This study illustrates the basic approach of Simonton's work: the specification of hypotheses about creativity on the basis of existing psychological theories, the gathering of historical information about a group of creators, the operationalization of dependent variables (creativity or productivity) and independent variables (social, political, cultural, and individual factors), and the appropriate statistical analyses of those data to test the hypotheses. In addition to those described earlier (creative productivity as measured by total weighted works and total themes), this research has included several different operationalizations of dependent variables. The first two listed below, discursive and presentational creativity, were computed on entire generations of creators. The others were computed for individuals:

> *Discursive creativity* (Simonton, 1975a, 1975b). This was the number of creators in a given generation involved in science, philosophy, literature, and musical composition. A weighted measure of discursive creativity was also used, with weighting based on the achieved eminence of the creators according to frequency of citation in archival sources.

> *Presentational creativity* (Simonton, 1975a, 1975b). This was the number of creators in a given generation involved in painting, sculpture, and architec-

ture. A weighted measure of presentational creativity was also used, with weighting again based on the achieved eminence of the creators.

Eminence. In one study (Simonton, 1976a), eminence of 301 geniuses in Cox's (1926) sample was based on her initial rankings. In another (1977b), a study of classical composers, eminence was the total of six individual measures: (1) the percentage of time that the composer's music is performed; (2) the rank of the composer according to a standard source; (3) the rating given to the composer in another standard source; (4) the composer's inclusion in or exclusion from standard archival sources such as encyclopedias; (5) and (6) the presence and level of attention given to the composer in two other sources.

Versatility (Simonton, 1976). In analyses of Cox's (1926) data, versatility was computed by assigning points to each creator's achievements within and outside of his major field of eminence.

Repertoire melodic originality (Simonton, 1980a, 1980b). This is defined as "the unusual sound of a melody in comparison to the entire repertoire of music listening" (1980b, p. 974). Statistically, this measure is based on an analysis of the first six notes of each musical theme studied. The measure of originality was based on both the rarity of the notes used and the rarity of all of the two-note transitions among the six notes. Rarity was computed in relation to the entire repertoire of all composers studied, which included 15,618 classical themes.

Zeitgeist melodic originality (Simonton, 1980b). This is defined as "the degree to which the structure of a given theme departs from contemporaneously composed themes" (1980b, p. 974). The method of assessment is similar to that used for repertoire melodic originality, except that the computation was done in relation to those themes composed contemporaneously with a given work.

The independent variables studied by Simonton represent an equally broad range, including several social, political, cultural, and individual variables. And the list of subject populations included in this research is equally impressive. The major variables and results of Simonton's research are summarized in Table 8-1.

Of most interest to the social psychology of creativity, of course, are the effects of social, political, and cultural variables on creativity. Individual-level variables examined by Simonton, such as the creator's age, are also included in the table.

In his own review of most of these studies (1978), Simonton drew a broad conclusion about sociocultural influences on creativity: Although several social factors during a creator's developmental period (childhood, adolescence, and early adulthood) influence later creativity, virtually no social factors during the actual productive period have an impact. During the developmental period, several variables are influential:

Table 8-1.   Summary of D. K. Simonton's Research

Substantive Variable	Sample or Population	Relationship or Function	Source
		Social	
Social reinforcements	10 classical composers	Productivity is not affected by social reinforcements	1977a
Competitors	10 classical composers	Thematic productivity is negatively influenced by number of contemporary competitors	1977a
Role-model availability	127 generations of European creators	Discursive creativity is a positive function of previous two generations' creative productivity	1975a
	696 classical composers	Creative precociousness is a positive function of role-model availability in the field	1977b
	696 classical composers	Creative productivity is a negative direct function of role-model availability in the field	1977b
Formal education	301 geniuses (Cox)	Eminence is an inverted-U function of formal education for creators	1976
	301 geniuses (Cox)	Versatility is positively related to formal education	1976
Father's status	301 geniuses (Cox)	Eminence has no relationship to father's professional status	1976
		Political	
Political fragmentation	127 generations of European creators	Both discursive and presentational creativity are a positive function of prior political fragmentation[a]	1975a
Imperial instability	127 generations of European creators	Discursive creativity is a positive function of prior imperial instability[b]	1975a
Political instability	127 generations of European creators	Discursive creativity is a negative function of prior political instability[c]	1975a
War	127 generations of European creators	Creativity (discursive and presentational) is not affected by war	1975a
	12,761 important discoveries	Medical discoveries have a negative contemporaneous relationship with casualties in war	1976
	10 classical composers	Productivity is unrelated to war intensity	1977a
	404 years of European scientific creativity	Creativity is discouraged by balance-of-power wars fought close to home, but encouraged by those fought far away	1977c

Table 8-1.   Summary of D. K. Simonton's Research (*continued*)

Substantive Variable	Sample or Population	Relationship or Function	Source
Internal political disturbances	10 classical composers	Productivity is unrelated to internal political disturbances	1977a
Cultural persecution	127 generations of European creators	Creativity (discursive and presentational) is not affected by cultural persecution	1975a
		Individual	
Age	420 literary creators	Poetry is produced at a younger age than prose	1975c
	10 classical composers	Thematic productivity is an inverted backwards J-function of age	1977a
	15,618 musical themes	Repertoire melodic originality is an inverted backwards J-function of age	1980a
	15,618 musical themes	Zeitgeist melodic originality increases with composer's age	1980a
	5,046 melodic themes	Melodic originality is an inverted backwards J-function of age	1980b
Life span	301 geniuses (Cox)	Eminence is a U-function of life span for creators	1976
Creative precociousness	696 classical composers	Creative productivity is a positive function of creative precociousness	1977b
Physical illness	10 classical composers	Thematic productivity is negatively affected by physical illness	1977a
Stress	10 classical composers	Productivity is unaffected by biographical stress	1977a
	5,046 melodic themes	Melodic originality is a positive function of biographical stress	1980b

[a]Political fragmentation is the number of independent states existing in a given generation of European history (a generation being defined as an arbitrarily delimited 20-year period).

[b]Imperial stability is the number of popular revolutions, revolts, and rebellions per independent state in a given year (European history).

[c]Political instability is computed by totaling the number of political assassinations and coups d'etat, adding points for each battle, each government overthrown, each external power brought in, and each claimant to the same power position (European history).

Formal education. Formal education contributes positively to a creator's eminence up to a point. Beyond that point, higher levels of formal education are associated with lower levels of eminence.

Role-model availability. As noted in the last chapter, the influence of this variable is quite complex. When aggregate analyses are done, they demonstrate a positive influence. Specifically, the total number of creative individuals in a given generation is a positive function of the number of creative individuals in the parent and grandparent generations. However, an examination of influences at the individual level reveals that positive influences of models are mediated by creative precociousness. The more creative models available during the individual's developmental period, the more likely he is to produce notable work at an early age. This early productivity, in turn, has positive effects on later productivity and eminence. However, perhaps because an individual may adopt a too-faithful imitation of models, the direct effect of model availability on individual creative productivity (if not mediated by precociousness) is actually negative.

Political fragmentation. A larger number of independent states during the developmental period of the creator is positively related to later achieved eminence. This relationship might obtain because the number of independent states indicates the degree of cultural diversity in a nation; cultural diversity might be generally conducive to creativity.

Civil disturbances. Again perhaps resulting from increased cultural diversity, popular revolts, rebellions, and revolutions in the developmental period of the creator appear to be a stimulus to later creative eminence, especially when these disturbances are directed against large empire states.

Political instability. Instability in the form of assassinations and coups d'etat during the developmental period tend to have a negative impact on later creativity. Simonton (1978) suggests that during such unstable times, young persons learn to believe that the world is unpredictable. Such a belief in unpredictability can be detrimental to active productivity.

Only one sociocultural variable during adulthood appears to be related to creative productivity. Balance-of-power wars fought close to home tend to discourage the individual's creative productivity, but such wars fought far away actually appear to stimulate it (Simonton, 1977c). Two nonsocial variables in adult life also have significant impacts on creativity: age and physical illness. As noted earlier, productivity increases over the life span up to a maximum, and then exhibits a partial decline. Physical illness has a generally negative effect on productivity.

A Comparison of Research Strategies and Conclusions

Simonton's research methods differ widely from my own, and his conclusions are, in some cases, divergent from those I have drawn. For example, although he concludes that social reinforcement is unrelated to creativity, I found that the relationship is sometimes positive and sometimes negative. Because of these differences, it is important to compare the two approaches on a number of dimensions: the subjects studied, the temporal span of the predicted effects, the independent variables examined, and the operational definitions of creativity.

An important advantage of Simonton's method is that it studies individuals who are undeniably outstanding—eminent scientists, artists, musicians, and creators in other fields. Thus, conclusions drawn from his research apply to creative achievement at the highest levels. By contrast, because my research primarily studies "ordinary" children and adults, my conclusions are applicable to lower levels of creativity. While there is no a priori reason to expect that conclusions based on one population will not be applicable to the other, such applicability does remain to be demonstrated. Moreover, there are theoretical reasons in some cases for expecting that the two groups will, in fact, differ in their response to certain social-psychological variables. For example, as I argued in Chapter 4, people working at the highest levels of a field might be relatively immune to the negative effects of extrinsic constraint because of their intense intrinsic interest in the domain.

There is little overlap between the sociocultural independent variables studied by Simonton (e.g., war, cultural persecution, education, competitors, and social reinforcements) and the social variables that I have studied (e.g., evaluation, reward for performance, and motivational orientation). Even the variables that appear similar have, in fact, been operationalized quite differently. For example, my study of rewards had children do a task either with or without the explicit understanding that the task was a means to a specific reward. In Simonton's study, on the other hand, social reinforcement was defined as any honor that came to a composer following outstanding accomplishments. It is unlikely that composers viewed these honors as rewards for which particular compositions were to be written.

Perhaps more importantly, these independent variables are studied across vastly different time periods. While my research most often involves independent variable manipulations lasting less than 20 minutes, the variables studied by Simonton may have an impact over a period of many months or years. Moreover, I examine the short-term effects of these variables on the creativity of tasks performed immediately following the independent variable manipulations. Simonton's research, however, examines the life-span impact of social variables and, furthermore, studies the impact of such variables over many generations.

Finally, differences in the operational definitions of creativity are apparent. In one study on melodic originality (1980a), Simonton was careful to point out that such originality should not be equated with creativity. Defining creativity as a quality that can only be assessed by the reliable reaction of observers, Simonton equated the creativity of a musical theme in that study with the *fame* that it had achieved. In other studies, Simonton has implicitly or explicitly equated creativity with the eminence or overall productivity of the individual. While these definitions are certainly not incompatible with my own (see Chapter 2), measures of a creator's eminence or productivity might be influenced by factors besides the reliable subjective assessment of the creator's work.

Given the different foci of my research and Simonton's, there are few points of either agreement or disagreement in our findings. One possible point of disagreement does emerge: I found that expected reward for performance can, under some circumstances, be detrimental to creativity. Simonton found, however, that social reinforcements (honors, prizes, and the like) were unrelated to creative productivity.

A number of explanations can be offered for this apparent contradiction. First, the operational definitions of creativity differed considerably. Second, as just noted, social rewards in my studies were expected and contingent on performance. It is likely that many of the rewards tabulated in Simonton's study were unexpected or were, at least, not seen as expected rewards for particular pieces of work. Third, my studies found that, while rewards undermined creativity under some circumstances, they actually enhanced it under others. Such complex effects might well cancel out in statistical analyses over long periods of time. Finally, it may be that, while rewards can undermine the creative performance of less talented individuals, highly creative people may be immune to such influences because of their high levels of initial interest in their work or because their creativity has become largely algorithmic (see Chapter 4).

In sum, it is important to realize that, as Simonton (1975a) pointed out, both experimental and archival studies of the social psychology of creativity are necessary. The former can be most useful for discovering specific, short-term influences on particular tasks. The latter can be most useful for discovering global, long-term influences on the entire body of an individual's work.

Other Influences on Creativity

Some creativity researchers have investigated factors that, although not strictly social-psychological, may vary as a function of the social environment. A person's activities prior to task engagement, which may have an impact on subsequent creativity, are often determined by other people. The same applies for a person's opportunity to engage in play or fantasy before task engagement. And, clearly, the physical environment—which may influence creative productivity—is often affected by social factors. Research on the influence of prior activity, play and fantasy, and the physical environment on creativity is still in preliminary stages. The work reviewed here, then, must be taken as only suggestive of issues that need to be addressed in the future.

Prior Activity

Stimuli present in the immediate environment can, conceivably, influence an individual's performance on a creativity task. Some researchers have set out to examine the effects of stimuli that are directly relevant to the subsequent creativity task. Sobel and Rothenberg (1980) showed pairs of pictorial slides to artists as a means of stimulating artistic expression. For example, some artists saw a slide of five nuns walking before the steps of St. Peter's cathedral, and a slide of five horsemen in bright uniforms galloping toward the viewer. For half of the subjects, these slides were presented side by side on a screen. For the others, the slides were superimposed. Following the slide presentation, the subjects were asked to draw anything they wished. Results showed that the "creative combination" of superimposed slides stimulated drawings that were judged as significantly more creative than the separate presentation.

Other studies have also examined the effects of prior cognitive activities that are somehow related to the subsequent creativity task. In one (Nash, 1975), small groups of first-grade children were given one of the "product improvement" tasks from the Torrance Tests of Creative Thinking—producing interesting and unusual ideas for improving a toy elephant. Prior to this, they had participated in one of four "warm-up" activities. One treatment involved 20 minutes of free play; another involved 20 minutes of listening to humorous and dramatic stories about lions in the jungle; and a third involved physically acting out the things a lion in the jungle might do if feeling happy, angry, or sad. A control group received no treatment. Both of the "lion" treatment groups performed significantly better than the control group on originality in the elephant product improvement task, and the acting-out group was significantly more flexible, as well. Although it is not possible to determine why these prior activities increased creativity. Nash (1975) interpreted these results as evidence that the effective treatments led children to become less inhibited and restricted in their thinking about jungle animals.

Many theorists have suggested a close association between creativity and humor. For example, Levine (1969) states that, in order to indulge in humor, "one must be free from the constraints of rational thoughts and decisions" (p. 16). Interestingly, this description of the necessary conditions for humor is remarkably similar to theoretical descriptions of the necessary conditions for creativity. Indeed, Koestler (1964) includes humor with science and art as the three basic areas of creative thought.

Nonetheless, empirical research on the relationship between creativity and humor is rare. Some personality studies have yielded suggestive results. Getzels and Jackson (1962), for example, found that a keen sense of humor was one of the most important features distinguishing highly creative adolescents from those who were less creative. Similarly, Treadwell (1970) found a positive correlation between creativity and sense of humor in college undergraduates. In one of the few empirical studies examining the impact of humor on creativity (Ziv, 1976), Israeli high school students listened to a recording of a popular Israeli comedian before completing some of the Torrance Tests of Creative Thinking. Although there was no direct connection between the comedian's material and the test requirements, students who had listened to the recording scored significantly higher on fluency, flexibility, and originality than students who had not. There are, of course, several possible explanations for this finding. These results do suggest, though, that prior exposure to humor may be conducive to creativity.

In addition to work on the effect of special types of cognitive stimuli on creativity, there has been some research on the general effects of stimulating or monotonous time periods prior to task engagement. One study (Maddi, Charlens,

Maddi, & Smith, 1962) found that subjects who had spent a free-time period or a period with different types of novel stimulation showed more novelty in their TAT stories than did subjects who had spent a period of monotony just prior to writing the stories.

There is another set of findings, however, that appears to contradict these. In two similar studies (Maddi, 1965; Maddi, Propst, & Feldinger, 1965), it was found that the most novel TAT stories were written by subjects who had spent their waiting period sitting quietly in the waiting-room office, rather than walking about randomly manipulating objects. There are a number of alternative explanations for these results; for example, those walking about the waiting room might have been anxious about their ability to perform the upcoming experimental tasks. However, it is interesting to consider the possibility that, although relatively passive prior cognitive stimulation might be beneficial to creativity, active cognitive engagement in unrelated activities might be detrimental.

Ellen Langer and I conducted a study to investigate this possibility. The participants in this study were 93 male and female undergraduates at Brandeis University. For all subjects, the creativity task was an adaptation of Luchins's (1942) water jar problems. For each problem, subjects were given drawings of three water jars of different sizes and were asked to write an equation for using these jars to measure out an exact amount of water. The first five problems are all solved by the same equation: Jar B - Jar A - 2(Jar C). The next two are "set-breaking" problems, however; they can be solved either by the familiar algorithm or by another, simpler one: Jar A - Jar C. Following this is a problem that can *only* by solved with the simpler equation and, finally, two more problems that can be solved by either method. Thus, following the five initial set-making problems, there are four set-breaking problems that can be solved by the old or the new method (interspersed with one problem that can only be solved by the new method).

Before working on the water jar problems, subjects did one of four cognitive tasks according to a 2×2 factorial design: type of task (alphabet or counting) and task difficulty (easy or difficult). For the easy alphabet task, subjects were given several typed lines of letters and asked to cross out every *e*. For the difficult alphabet task, subjects were given similar sets of typed lines and told:

> Go backwards through the alphabet in your head and cross out every other letter (for example, find a *z* and cross it out, then find an *x*, and so on). When finished going through the alphabet backwards once, continue on the lines of letters, going backwards through the alphabet again by 3s. Then go backwards by 4s, and so on.

For the easy counting task, subjects were asked to count backwards mentally from 9000 to 0 by 50s. For the difficult counting task, subjects were asked to count backwards mentally from 2000 to 1000 by 35s and write down the number they reached that is closest to 1000. Then, they were to continue counting backwards, this time by 85s, until they reached the number closest to 600. The difficult and easy tasks had been pretested and had been found to take approximately the same amount of time.

We obtained striking effects of prior cognitive activity on subsequent ability to break set. As illustrated in Figure 8-1, subjects who had done the difficult tasks were significantly less likely to break set on the four critical problems than were subjects who had done the easy tasks. There was no effect of type of task, and no interaction. Thus, it appears that prior engagement on an unrelated taxing cognitive activity can impair performance on tasks that require set-breaking perceptions.

Play and Fantasy

In Chapter 4, I suggested that high levels of creativity are only possible in an intrinsically motivated state, when the individual approaches the task with an intellectual playfulness and a deep level of involvement. Several other theorists have proposed that play (and the social conditions that facilitate play) can have beneficial effects on creativity. Piaget (1951, p. 155) referred to play as "a source of creative imagination." Some theories of play propose that playful activity enhances flexibility and novel adaptation (Bruner, 1972; Lieberman, 1977; Piaget, 1951; Sutton-Smith, 1972). And Gordon (1961), who initiated the popular creativity-training program "Synectics," asserts the essential role of play in the creative process:

> Not all play is creative, but . . . all creativity contains play.
> "Play" in the creative process means the activity of floating and considering associations *apparently* irrelevant to the problem at hand. (p. 110)
> Play . . . involves the willingness to manipulate words, concepts, everyday and technical assumptions, together with playing with apparently irrelevant objects and things. (p. 121)

Thus, previous theorists have suggested that play is an important component of creative behavior and, moreover, that prior playful activity can lead to playfulness and creativity during task engagement. There is, however, little naturalistic evidence that playful behavior is an important precursor or component of creativity in outstanding individuals, or that play in daily activities can enhance creativity in ordinary people. Interviews with highly talented composers and mathematicians do suggest that most of their early contact with the talent domain was relatively unstructured and "playful" (Bloom & Sosniak, 1981). And some personality studies have found a relationship between playfulness (as an enduring trait) and creativity. For example, a number of researchers have identified playfulness as a characteristic distinguishing creative children and adolescents from their less creative age-mates (e.g., Getzels & Jackson, 1962; Lieberman, 1965; Torrance, 1961; Wallach & Kogan, 1965).

Most of the research attempting to link play to creativity, however, has involved either laboratory training in play or opportunities to engage in play, followed by creativity testing. In a study described in the previous chapter, children who were

Figure 8-1.   Mean number of problems solved with the set–breaking solution.

trained in play showed more creativity following the training than did children in
several control groups (Feitelson & Ross, 1973). Other research showed that children allowed to engage in make-believe play with a set of objects showed more
originality on alternate-uses tests than did children in control conditions or children asked to imitate an experimenter's activities with the play objects (Dansky &
Silverman, 1973, 1975; Li, 1978). In an even more impressive demonstration of
the facilitative effects of play on creativity (Smith & Dutton, 1979), 4-year-old
children in one condition were allowed time to play with blocks and sticks before
the testing session began. Children in other conditions either received training on
how to join the blocks and sticks or they proceeded directly to testing. The tests
required children to reach a marble using only the blocks and sticks available. The
first test required joining two sticks with a block, and the second required joining
three sticks with a block. Although both the play and training groups performed
better than the control group on the first test, the play group surpassed the others
in solving the more difficult problem.

Most of the researchers who conducted these studies assumed that free play or
make-believe play facilitated creativity not only because play gave children the opportunity to discover new properties of objects, but also because play stimulated
fantasy which, in turn, made creativity more likely. In a study designed to test this
assumption (Dansky, 1980), preschool children were first unobtrusively observed
and classified, on the basis of those observations, as "players" (spontaneously engage in make-believe play) or "nonplayers." They were then exposed to one of three
treatment conditions: free play with a set of objects, imitation of an experimenter's

actions with the objects, or straightforward problem-solving with the objects. Free play enhanced ideational fluency above the levels of the other two conditions, but only for those children who habitually engaged in make-believe play.

These results suggest that engaging in fantasy might, in itself, lead to increases in creativity. Few studies have examined this possibility directly, but some naturalistic investigations have studied possible relationships between creativity and the presence of imaginary companions in childhood. One study, which tested subjects in childhood and used a type of Rorschach and an unusual uses test as measures of creativity, found no differences between children who had imaginary companions and those who did not (Manosevitz, Fling, & Prentice, 1977). However, it might be argued that these creativity measures were too broad and should not have been expected to show strong influences of the child's ability to imagine a novel person, animal, or mythical creature. Another study included a measure more likely to be sensitive to fantasy (Schaefer, 1969b). Here, it was found that adolescents exhibiting high levels of literary creativity were significantly more likely to report childhood imaginary companions than were matched controls.

A link between creativity and fantasy is suggested by the results of other studies. In investigations of adults (Singer & Schonbar, 1961) and children (Singer, 1961), those who daydream more frequently have been found to produce more novel stories. (These results are uncontaminated by differences in intelligence.) And there is some evidence that a correlation between hypnotizability and creativity may be due to a common reliance on fantasy in both processes (Bowers, 1979).

Margaret Stubbs and I investigated the relationship between short-term fantasy and creativity in a correlational study of 47 young children (Stubbs & Amabile, 1979). We administered Barron's Movement Threshold Inkblot Test (1955b) as a measure of fantasy ability. This test presents 28 inkblots in which it becomes progressively easier to see human movement. Singer (1973) has found that the ability to see human movement on this test predicts other scores on imaginative ability. In this study, we found significant correlations between this test and both collage-making creativity ($r = .55$) and creativity on an unusual uses test ($r = .61$).

Finally, in a fantasy-training study, Hershey and Kearns (1979) conducted an 8-week program for elementary school children. Half of the children were randomly assigned to 1 hour of training in relaxation and guided fantasy per week, while the other children participated in an hour of arithmetical exercises. At the end of the program, the training group scored significantly higher on fluency, flexibility, and originality on the Torrance Tests than did children in a control group.

The Physical Environment

Although there is little research on the effects of physical surroundings on creativity, folklore does suggest that some creative individuals required particularly exotic physical environments in which to work. It is said that Schiller kept rotting apples in his desk drawer because the aroma helped him concentrate on writing poetry, and that de la Mare constantly kept a cigarette burning while writing (Spender, 1952). Dr. Johnson required a purring cat, an orange peel, and plenty of tea to drink while he worked. Zola insisted on working in artificial light. Both Carlyle and Proust tried to build soundproof working rooms for themselves (McKim, 1972, p. 32).

Despite a dearth of evidence on the optimal conditions of light, sound, smell, and taste for creative performance, there is a small literature on the effects of visual cues in the physical environment. La Greca (1980) found, for example, that children use environmental scanning in answering questions to creativity tests. When asked to think of unusual uses for an object, for instance, the more successful subjects will often scan the room they are in for clues to responses. Besides providing specific answers to test items, cue-rich environments might simply provide a level of cognitive stimulation necessary for subjects to engage their domain-relevant and creativity-relevant skills. In a study where some subjects endured 3 days of sensory deprivation (darkness and silence), their subsequent creativity test performance was worse than that of controls (Fuerst & Zubek, 1968).

The effect of cues in the physical environment may, however, depend importantly on subjects' ability to use them. Children in one study (Ward, 1969) took a creativity test in either a barren experimental room or a room that was rich in objects and pictures providing clues to possible responses. The cue-rich environment led to higher ideational fluency only for those subjects who had scored high on a creativity pretest. In another study (Friedman et al., 1978), children taking a creativity test in an "enriched" environment scored higher than those tested in a barren environment, but only if they had been given explicit instructions to use the environmental cues. Thus, it appears that the physical environment can provide visual stimulation for creative performance (or, at least, for performance on creativity tests), but only if subjects already know or can be taught how to use cues in the environment effectively.

Summary

Several diverse literatures have been reviewed in this chapter, covering a wide range of social-psychological variables that might influence creativity, plus several other variables that are indirectly relevant to a social psychology of creativity. Although a number of methods have been used, most of these studies have employed some type of correlational technique. The list of variables examined in these investigations has included both global environmental features (such as open vs. traditional classrooms) and more narrowly defined social factors (such as birth order).

Because of the widely differing approaches taken to studying these variables, it is difficult to draw firm conclusions or even to summarize the findings succinctly. Nonetheless, it is possible to outline some of the clearer patterns:

1. Open classrooms, with more individualized instruction and less emphasis on teacher control, may be more conducive to creativity than traditional classrooms.

2. College environments that are most conducive to creativity include teachers who give individualized attention to students outside of class, serve as models of creative activity, and encourage students to be independent.

3. Work environments most conducive to the fulfillment of creative potential may include: a high level of worker responsibility for initiating new activities, a low level of interference from administrative superiors, and a high stability of employment.

4. Children who enjoy a special family position (as a result of either birth order or some other circumstance) tend to perform more creatively than children who do not.

5. Creativity in children may be enhanced when parents are personally secure and relatively unconcerned about conforming to society's behavioral inhibitions or rules on status and roles.

6. Families likely to foster creativity in children are characterized by a low level of authoritarianism and restrictiveness, an encouragement of independence, and a somewhat cool interpersonal distance between parents and children.

7. Formal education contributes positively to a creator's eminence up to a point; beyond that point, higher levels of formal education are associated with lower levels of eminence.

8. The larger the number of creators in one generation, the larger will be the number of creators in the next.

9. The more available role models in his field, the more likely it is that an individual will show early creative achievement in that field. However, prolonged adherence to role models may reduce creative productivity.

10. Political fragmentation and civil disturbance in an individual's youth are positively related to adult productivity, yet political instability in an individual's youth contributes negatively to creative productivity.

11. A higher number of competitors in a creator's field may lead to lower levels of individual productivity in some domains.

12. Engaging in playful activities can increase subsequent creativity, especially if the objects of play are involved in the subsequent task.

Update

In this chapter update we consider the social contexts in which people learn, work, and live, contexts that may have broad effects on many aspects of behavior, including creativity. We also consider several possible influences that may be partially determined by social forces (prior activity, play, fantasy, and affective state), as well as one social factor—competition—that was not discussed in the 1983 edition.

Educational Environments

Although there has been essentially no new research on the effects of "open" classrooms, probably because such school environments have fallen out of favor over the past decade, some recent work is informative about the impact of classroom environments on creativity. In a study described in the update to Chapter 6 (Koestner, Ryan, Bernieri, & Holt, 1984), children did paintings after being given instructions about neatness. Some of the children, randomly assigned, received controlling instructions laying out the rules for neatness. The rest of the children were given neatness instructions in an informational way that acknowledged their reluctance to follow rules and stressed the reasons for neatness. The paintings made by children in the informational condition were rated as more creative than those made by children in the controlling condition. These results were interpreted in terms of the importance of autonomy for intrinsic motivation and creativity. Richard Ryan and Wendy Grolnick (1986) suggest that children's perceptions of their classroom environment, which include their perceptions of autonomy in the classroom, can significantly affect their intrinsic motivation and performance. Although these researchers propose large individual differences between children in their perceptions of autonomy, even within a classroom, other research has uncovered systematic between-classroom differences in autonomy perceptions (Picariello, 1994). There may also be systematic between-group differences depending on children's ages; Beth Hennessey (1989) found that the creativity of older children was more adversely affected by extrinsic constraints than was the creativity of younger children.

Some recent research has examined children's perceptions of teachers' warmth in the classroom in addition to perceptions of autonomy. The findings are quite consistent. Children who perceive greater warmth in their teachers also display higher levels of intrinsic motivation and creativity (Picariello, 1992; Ryan & Grolnick, 1986). These studies find large individual differences between children within classrooms on perceptions of teachers' warmth, suggesting that, to some extent, the "classroom climate" is different for each child. Such differences could be due to the children's individual characteristics, personalities, and motivational orientations, and to different interaction patterns between the teacher and individual children.

Work Environments

Our own research program over the past several years has investigated the impact of work environments on the creativity of adults at work and on the level of innovation produced by an organization. In this research we define creativity as the production of novel and appropriate ideas by individuals or small groups of individuals working closely together. We define innovation as the successful implementation of creative ideas by an organization.

In order to begin studying creativity and the factors that influence it in work organizations, we found it necessary to expand our methods outside the laboratory-based experimental methods we had relied upon in our earlier work. Although the findings of this organizational research do echo and complement our previous work, they extend far beyond what we were able to discern when studying single variables in controlled laboratory settings. Our empirical research on creativity and innovation in organizations began with an interview study of 129 R&D scientists from several different companies (Amabile & S. Gryskiewicz, 1987; Amabile, 1988a). The critical-incident technique used in the interviews called for participants to describe in detail two significant events from their work experience: one that exemplified high creativity, and one that exemplified low creativity. Content analyses of transcripts of both classes of stories revealed a powerful finding: Despite conventional wisdom on the importance of personal characteristics in creativity our interviewees made more comments describing the work environments than they did describing the personal characteristics of the "main characters" in their stories. This finding held regardless of whether the story described high or low creativity, and it also held regardless of whether the interviewee was a main character in the story. Clearly, it appeared that the work environment must not be ignored if we are to fully understand creative behavior in organizations.

The content analyses revealed 9 qualities of environments that served to promote creativity (which we termed Environmental Stimulants), and 9 qualities of environments that served to inhibit creativity (which we termed Environmental Obstacles). We present them here rank-ordered by the percentage of R&D scientists who mentioned them in their event descriptions. The same factors were found in later samples of bank and railroad employees, although there was some reordering in the rankings.

Environmental Stimulants to Creativity

1. Freedom: freedom in deciding what to do or how to accomplish the task; a sense of control over one's own work and ideas.

2. Good Project Management: a manager who serves as a good role model, is enthusiastic, has good communication skills, protects the project team from outside distractions and interference, matches tasks to workers' skills and interests, and sets a clear direction without managing too tightly.

3. Sufficient Resources: access to necessary resources, including facilities, equipment, information, funds, and people.

4. Encouragement: management enthusiasm for new ideas, creating an atmosphere free of threatening evaluation.

5. Various Organizational Characteristics: a mechanism for considering new ideas, a corporate climate marked by cooperation and collaboration across levels and divisions, an atmosphere where innovation is prized and failure is not fatal.

6. Recognition: a general sense that creative work will receive appropriate feedback, recognition, and reward.

7. Sufficient Time: time to think creatively about the problem, to explore different perspectives rather than having to impose an already-determined approach.

8. Challenge: a sense of challenge arising from the intriguing nature of the problem itself or its importance to the organization (internalized by the individual as a personal sense of challenge).

9. Pressure: a sense of urgency that is internally generated from competition with outside organizations or from a general desire to accomplish something important.

Environmental Obstacles to Creativity

1. Various Organizational Characteristics: inappropriate reward systems in the organization; excessive red tape; a corporate climate marked by a lack of cooperation across divisions and levels; little regard for innovation in general.

2. Constraint: lack of freedom in deciding what to do or how to accomplish the task; a lack of a sense of control over one's own work and ideas.

3. Organizational Disinterest: a lack of organizational support, interest, or faith in a project; a perceived apathy toward any accomplishments coming from the project.

4. Poor Project Management: a manager who is unable to set clear direction, who has poor technical or communication skills, who controls too tightly, or who allows distractions and fragmentation of the team's efforts.

5. Evaluation: inappropriate or inequitable evaluation and feedback systems; unrealistic expectations; an environment focused on criticism and external evaluation.

6. Insufficient Resources: a lack of appropriate facilities, equipment, materials, funds, or people.

7. Time Pressure: insufficient time to think creatively about the problem; too great a workload within a realistic time frame; high frequency of "fire fighting."

8. Overemphasis on the Status Quo: reluctance of managers or coworkers to change their way of doing things; an unwillingness to take risks.

9. Competition: interpersonal or intergroup competition within the organization fostering a self-defensive attitude.

As a tool to allow more standardized, quantitative measures of work environment factors that might influence creativity positively or negatively, we developed a questionnaire instrument called "KEYS: Assessing the Climate for Creativity" (formerly "The Work Environment Inventory" [WEI]) (Amabile, 1987b, 1990, 1995; Amabile, Burnside, & S. Gryskiewicz, 1995). This 78-item questionnaire asks employees to rate their perceptions of their current work environment. The 78 items are scored according to 10 scales; these scales are combinations of the Environmental Stimulants and Environmental Obstacles to Creativity identified in our earlier interview study, as well as environmental influences on creativity identified in our earlier empirical and theoretical research. Of the 10 scales, 6 assess Environmental Stimulants, 2 assess Environmental Obstacles, and 2 assess work outcomes—Creativity and Productivity.

KEYS Scales for Assessing Environmental Stimulants to Creativity

1. *Organizational Encouragement* (15 items): an organizational culture that encourages creativity through the fair, constructive judgment of ideas; reward and recognition for creative work; mechanisms for developing new ideas, an active flow of ideas; and a shared vision of what the organization is trying to do. Sample item: "People are encouraged to solve problems creatively in this organization."

2. *Supervisory Encouragement* (11 items): a supervisor who serves as a good work model, sets goals appropriately, supports the work group, values individual contributions, and shows confidence in the work group. Sample item: "My supervisor serves as a good work model."

3. *Work Group Supports* (8 items): a diversely skilled work group in which people communicate well, are open to new ideas, constructively challenge one another's work, trust and help one another, and feel committed to the work they are doing. Sample item: "There is free and open communication within my work group."

4. *Freedom* (4 items): freedom in deciding what work to do or how to do it; a sense of control over one's work. Sample item: "I have the freedom to decide how I am going to carry out my projects."

5. *Sufficient Resources* (6 items): access to appropriate resources, including funds, materials, facilities, and information. Sample item: "Generally, I can get the resources I need for my work."

6. *Challenging Work* (5 items): a sense of having to work hard on challenging tasks and important projects. Sample item: "I feel challenged by the work I am currently doing."

KEYS Scales for Assessing Environmental Obstacles to Creativity

1. *Organizational Impediments* (12 items): an organizational culture that impedes creativity through internal political problems, harsh criticism of new ideas, destructive internal competition, an avoidance of risk, and an overemphasis on the status quo. Sample item: "There are many political problems in this organization."

2. *Workload Pressure* (5 items): extreme time pressures, unrealistic expectations for productivity, and distractions from creative work. Sample item: "I have too much work to do in too little time."

KEYS Scales for Assessing Work Outcomes

1. *Creativity* (6 items): a creative organization or unit where a great deal of creativity is called for and where people believe they actually produce creative work. Sample item: "My area of this organization is innovative."

2. *Productivity* (6 items): an efficient, effective, and productive organization or unit. Sample item: "My area of this organization is effective."

Psychometric Characteristics and Utility of KEYS

KEYS has undergone considerable statistical development over a period of twelve years, and in general, the psychometric characteristics are strong (Amabile, Burnside, & Gryskiewicz, 1995). A few other instruments have been developed to assess the climate for creativity in work organizations. The Siegel Scale for Support of Innovation (Siegel & Kaemmerer, 1978) includes some of the same elements addressed by KEYS, but the database consists primarily of teachers and students. The Climate for Innovation Questionnaire (Ekvall, Arvonen, & Waldenstrom-Lindblad, 1983) is similar to KEYS in many respects, but it focuses more specifically on interactions within the work group and does not include larger, organization-wide influences. The Climate for Creative Productivity Index (Witt & Beorkrem, 1988) was developed to test our theory of creativity (Amabile, 1983a, 1983b, 1988a, 1988b). Although research with this inventory has demonstrated adequate convergent and discriminant validity, its database is limited and further research will be required to determine whether the psychometric characteristics are acceptable. We believe KEYS promises to be a useful tool for empirical and applied work on creativity and innovation in organizations because of its extensive database and strong psychometric characteristics. Future research should be directed at determining the most appropriate application arenas for KEYS and the other instruments that have been developed for studying the climate for creativity.

Perhaps the most important study that we have completed with KEYS is a study in which independent assessments of project creativity were obtained so that the work environments of projects rated high in creativity could be contrasted with the work environments of projects rated low in creativity (Amabile, Conti, Coon, Lazenby, & Herron, in press). (For all projects, creativity was both possible and desirable.) Members of the project teams of both types of projects filled out KEYS to describe the work environment surrounding that project. The high-creativity projects scored higher on the KEYS Stimulant scales, and the low-creativity projects scored higher on the KEYS Obstacle scales. Moreover, as might be expected, the high-creativity projects were rated higher on both of the outcome scales, Creativity and Productivity.

Although all of the work environment dimensions did differ between the high- and the low-creativity projects, some dimensions appear to carry more weight than others. In this study, the most important environmental aspects for creativity and innovation (in terms of effect sizes) appeared to be Challenging Work, Organizational Encouragement of Creativity, Work Group Supports, and Organizational Impediments to Creativity. The aspects that appeared to carry the least weight were Sufficient Resources and Workload Pressure. Moderate effect sizes were obtained by Freedom and Supervisory Encouragement of Creativity.

In another recent study we set out to determine how the environment for creativity and innovation might change in an organization that is undergoing rapid transition (Amabile & Conti, 1995). As part of another study at this high-tech electronics company, we had previously gathered KEYS data on the work environment. We returned to the company several months later, after a major (30%) downsizing had been announced, and proceeded to collect KEYS data at three additional points in time: halfway through the downsizing, just as the downsizing had ended, and four months after the end of the downsizing. The results showed a striking pattern. All of the Environmental Stimulants to Creativity declined during the downsizing but appeared to rebound as the downsizing came to an end. Although Workload Pressure remained unchanged during the downsizing, the Environmental Obstacle of Organizational Impediments increased significantly; however, this factor declined as the downsizing ended. Importantly, both Creativity and Productivity (as assessed by KEYS) declined during the downsizing. However, only Productivity had rebounded to a significant degree by four months after the downsizing. Potentially longer-term effects on creativity were suggested by a decline in the percapita invention disclosures logged by the company's engineers during the downsizing.

Additional questionnaire and interview data collected as part of the downsizing study allow some insight into mechanisms by which these negative effects might have occurred. Although the degree of actual downsizing experienced in an individual's department did not relate strongly to perceptions of the work environment or reported work behaviors, the degree of *anticipated* downsizing did strongly relate to such perceptions and behaviors. The most important aspects in determining perceptions and behaviors appeared to be the trustworthiness and frequency of the communication experienced and the degree of stability in one's own work group.

Other Research on Work Environments

Other researchers have discovered aspects of work environments that appear to affect creativity and innovation. Our finding of the positive impact of freedom or autonomy echoes a result obtained in a study of 200 R&D managers in eight semiconductor companies (Abbey & Dickson, 1983) where independence among R&D personnel was identified as a key determinant of success. Various organizational supports have appeared in other findings. In a survey of 77 strategic business units, the presence of innovation norms emerged as the single most important predictor of the effectiveness of entrepreneurial strategy (Russell & Russell, 1992). Using a methodology similar to that used in our high-creativity/low-creativity critical incidents study (Amabile & S. Gryskiewicz, 1987), another study examined the treatment of new ideas in high-technology and health-services organizations by gathering data from several hundred managers (Delbecq & Mills, 1985). A general innovation sequence was identified, consisting of: idea generation, preliminary analysis, decision to adopt, and implementation. Several features of successful innovations were identified, including: the earmarking of special funds for highly experimental research and development, the formal consideration of innovators' ideas followed by feasibility studies, consideration of marketing issues in the early stages of decisionmaking about an idea, substantial modification of most original ideas prior to final adoption, adequate funding and consistent monitoring of such projects, and initial small-scale implementation of the new idea.

Finally, it has been found that innovation within organizations has additional benefits aside from the creation of new products, services, and processes. In a study of 288 bank employees, the degree of innovation within a group was a significant negative predictor of turnover among employees in the group (McFadden & Demetriou, 1993). In a similar study of 314 nurses, job satisfaction was significantly predicted by innovation (Robinson, Roth, & Brown, 1993).

Family Influences

Recent research on the effects of home environments and families on creativity has supported the findings surveyed in the 1983 edition. For example, a study that used the Torrance Tests of Creative Thinking as its measure of children's creativity revealed that mothers of highly creative 8-year-old children were less emotionally involved with their children, less likely to be perceived as overprotective, and less likely to deny their feelings of hostility toward the children (Michel & Dudek, 1991). Moreover, the mothers of these children were more self-confident, more accomplished in their own work, and more "self-realized" in their homes; these measures of the mothers were obtained through interviews. Another study that used a paper-and-pencil creativity test found that college students who received the highest creativity scores tended to come from homes that were characterized as "adaptive" according to results of a questionnaire designed to assess family styles (Gardner & Moran, 1990).

One of the more comprehensive studies of family backgrounds in recent years was carried out by John Dacey (1989). He identified a set of 56 "creative" families as those in which either a parent (N = 27) or an adolescent was characterized as highly creative according to their accomplishments. For the parents, this meant that they were identified as being in the top 5% of their profession by members of that profession. For the adolescents, it meant that they were identified by staff members as being in the top 5% of creative students in their school system. These 56 families were contrasted with a comparison sample of 20 other families selected because no one in them was identified as creative. Data were collected through interviews and questionnaires. Results suggested that: (a) although the parents of creative adolescents refrained from imposing specific rules on them, they did set forth and model clear sets of values; (b) sense of humor is important in creative families; (c) in the creative families, imagination and honesty are more highly valued than good grades and good health; (d) the creative families tend to live in more unusual types of houses; (e) in the creative families, virtually all of the parents have well-developed interests outside of work; and (f) children in the creative group had suffered more traumas (causing grief, anger, or both) than children in the comparison group. Although it is difficult to specify particular social influences for these effects, many of these factors appear to support autonomy, intrinsic engagement in activities, and the practice of creativity-relevant skills.

A study of the relationship between the age intervals of children in a family and the children's creativity revealed a positive relationship (Radio-Gaynor & Runco, 1992). That is, the greater the spacing between children in the family, the higher the children's creativity. Another study reinforced the finding of earlier research that only children tend to score higher on divergent-thinking tests than do those who have siblings (Runco & Bahleda, 1987). After only children, the next highest scores were obtained by eldest, then youngest, then middle children. Interestingly, among people who had siblings, those who had more siblings scored higher in divergent thinking than those who had only one. Although these findings on birth order and family constellation do not identify specific source of influence, it is likely that the phenomena stem at least in part from social dynamics within the family.

Social, Political, and Cultural Influences

Dean K. Simonton has continued to lead this subfield of the social psychology of creativity using historiometric methods and archival data to examine factors such as international war, external threat, political instability, and civil disturbances. (For a review of his early work on these factors, see Simonton, 1988.) Although some of his recent work has studied the positive impact of mentors, collaborators, and successors (Simonton, 1992), Simonton has focused less on specific social influences and more on the broad social and cognitive effects that are expressed as changes in creativity across the life span. For example, he has documented and examined a general decline in creative productivity in the latter half of career life (Simonton, 1991). This research discovered that the average rate of creative output in the 70s falls to about half the rate of output in the peak years of the 30s and 40s. However, there is a great deal of variability between disciplines and between individuals in these fluctuations (Simonton, 1990). The quantity and quality of creative output across the life span are strongly correlated, and there is evidence of a "swan song" phenomenon whereby musical composers' final works achieve high levels of aesthetic quality and popularity (Simonton, 1989b).

Other Influences on Creativity

Prior activity, play, fantasy, and affective states are not, strictly speaking, social influences. However, they may be partially determined by social forces, and they may have an impact on creativity. Thus, they are relevant to a comprehensive consideration of creativity in context.

Prior Activity

In a recent laboratory study we examined the impact of prior creative activity on subsequent creativity, motivation, and learning (Conti, Amabile, & Pollak, 1995).

Prior to reading a short instructional passage, psychology students were given either a creative pretask or a noncreative pretask on the topic covered in the passage. The topic was psychological theories of dreaming, and the noncreative pretask involved simply copying over a printed dream report using a key to make substitutions for certain words. By contrast, the creative pretask involved writing down "interesting and unusual questions that you would like to ask a panel of experts on dreaming." In addition, subjects were given one of three sets of instructions: task-focused (emphasizing intrinsic involvement in the subsequent learning task), test-focused (emphasizing external evaluation of learning outcomes), or task/test-focused (combining the previous two instructions). After reading the instructional passage, subjects answered questions assessing immediate retention, wrote a creative essay, and responded to a questionnaire assessing intrinsic and extrinsic motivation. Subjects' long-term retention was assessed five days later with a surprise telephone quiz. We found that creative task engagement was an effective means of enhancing creativity—but only for those subjects who were not expecting evaluation of their work. Interestingly, we also found that prior creative activity had a positive impact on intrinsic motivation and learning. Overall, engagement in the creative pretask led to higher levels of both intrinsic motivation and long-term retention of the material learned. Moreover, participants who performed more creatively on the creative pretask tended to show better long-term retention than those who were less creative.

Play and Fantasy

Several recent studies have examined the impact of a particular type of prior activity on subsequent creativity—engaging in play. For example, in one study, elementary-school children engaged in either flexible ("playful") or highly structured art, drama, and playground activities (Berretta & Privette, 1990). Then, all children completed the Torrance Tests of Creative Thinking. Those children who participated in the flexible play experiences scored significantly higher than children who participated in the highly structured activities. Other studies have found similar effects (cf. Meador, 1992).

One researcher has suggested that the positive effects of play on associative fluency (which is the typical measure of creativity in these studies) arise not from a "playful disposition" but from exploration (Pellegrini, 1984–85). Specifically, compared to free play with an object, guided exploration of the object is proposed to better facilitate subsequent novel associations because it allows for prior consideration of more object attributes in a given period of time.

Fantasy, which may be considered a component of play, has long been proposed as a stimulant to creativity. One recent experiment found that fantasy induction led to increased creativity in poetry writing by college students (Greer & Levine, 1991). Other research has examined fantasy as an individual-difference trait. In several studies of undergraduates, a measure of fantasy proneness correlated positively with measures of fantasy, imagination, and creativity (Lynn & Rhue, 1986, 1988).

Affect

Several studies over the past decade have demonstrated that people show higher levels of associative fluency when they are in positive affective states; for example, subjects who watched films designed to induce a happy mood made more unusual associations on subsequent verbal tasks (Isen, 1987; Isen & Daubman, 1984; Isen, Johnson, Mertz, & Robinson, 1985). In explaining the results of one of our own studies, we speculated that subjects who received a "bonus" reward might have been more creative in part because their moods had been elevated by the experience. On the basis of these findings, it is reasonable to assume that situations that induce positive affect will lead to higher levels of creativity. However, in several attempts in our own laboratory, we have failed to show significant effects of positive mood induction. These studies used a variety of carefully pretested mood-induction techniques such as listening to music or watching films, and a variety of artistic and verbal creativity tasks. In a study in our laboratory, subjects in positive mood conditions wrote stories that were rated as *less* creative than did subjects in either negative or neutral conditions (Tighe, 1992). Thus, the effects of mood on creativity remain unclear.

Competition

Competition can be considered as a combination of several social factors: evaluation, reward, and an additional win-lose aspect that is unique to competitive situations. In two of our studies we have found that competition has a negative effect on creativity. In the first, elementary-school-age girls made collages in two different group situations (Amabile, 1982). In the competition condition, the children were told that the adult experimenters would award three attractive prizes to the creators of the three "best" collages at the end of the session. In the noncompetition condition, they were told that the three prizes would be raffled off at the end of the session. Expert judges' subsequent ratings of the collages revealed that those made by girls in the noncompetition condition were significantly more creative than those made by girls in the competition condition.

In the second study, adults worked in a large-group setting on a set of water-jar problems (Amabile, 1987a). These problems, which at first appear to be relatively complicated addition and subtraction problems, are all solved by the same equation—except for the final problem (Luchins, 1942). The final problem can be solved either by the familiar equation or by a novel equation that is considerably simpler. Half of the participants in this study received problem booklets that included competitive instructions promising a prize to the individual who "did the best job" on the problems. The other half received instructions encouraging them to have fun with the problems. Participants in the competitive condition were less likely to discover the novel solution for the final problem and were more likely to make errors in the problems. In addition, they were less likely to try solving some riddles that were included at the end of the booklet "to amuse yourself with if you finish before time is called."

Some recent research with children has suggested that the effects of competition on creativity may be more complex than we had originally believed. In two studies where boys and girls made collages in competitive or noncompetitive situations, the results suggest that the detrimental effect of competition on creativity may apply more to girls than to boys (Conti, Collins, & Picariello, 1995). Indeed, it appears that boys may even show higher levels of creativity on this artistic activity under competitive conditions. Moreover, in non-experimental studies of creativity in work organizations, within-group competition appears to be associated with low levels of creativity, but between-group competition appears to be associated with high levels of creativity (Amabile, 1988a; Amabile & S. Gryskiewicz, 1987). Clearly, additional research is needed to explore the conditions under which competition will undermine creativity, the conditions under which it may enhance creativity, and the mechanisms by which these effects might operate.

Summary

A considerable body of literature has gathered in the past twelve years on broad social influences upon creativity in schools, work organizations, families, and societies. Research on school children has pointed to the importance of perceptions of autonomy in their creativity in educational settings. Research on adults in work organizations has led to the discovery of a set of environmental factors that undermine creativity; many of these factors are consistent with those uncovered in previous experimental research. This research in organizations has also led to the discovery of a set of environmental factors that support creativity. An additional, methodological outcome of the research has been the development of a new tool (KEYS) for quantitatively assessing perceptions of the work environment along dimensions that appear to have an impact on creativity. Family environments conducive to creativity seem to be marked by autonomy supports, encouragement of intrinsic engagement in activities, and practice of creativity-relevant processes.

Prior creative activity can have a positive impact on learning, intrinsic motivation, and subsequent creativity, in the absence of extrinsic pressures. Similarly, engaging in playful activities or fantasy can have a positive effect, possibly by the active engagement of creativity-relevant processes.

Win-lose competition between peers has a negative effect on creativity. However, this effect may depend on some individual-difference variables such as gender or gender roles. Moreover, competition with outside groups may have a positive effect on the creativity of work teams.

Part Three
Implications

9
Implications for Enhancing Creativity

Although this certainly was not my initial aim, most of my research has uncovered methods for destroying creativity: making external evaluation salient, offering task-contingent rewards, imposing surveillance, making extrinsic motives salient. Other research on social-psychological factors, especially research using open-ended creativity tasks, has found similar effects. In this chapter, I will discuss the ways in which this research on the intrinsic motivation hypothesis and other social-psychological research on creativity can be used instead to maintain and enhance creativity.

In itself, the preponderance of undermining effects is informative. There are at least two plausible explanations for this phenomenon. First, of course, it may be that creativity *cannot* be enhanced, that the most one can do is to avoid undermining baseline levels of creativity. A second explanation is that it may simply be easier, methodologically, to arrange experimental situations in which creativity will be undermined than to arrange experimental situations in which creativity will be enhanced. At least, this may be true in studies where the independent variable is of brief duration. According to the componential conceptualization of creativity, domain-relevant skills, creativity-relevant skills, and task motivation are all necessary for creative performance. Domain-relevant skills and creativity-relevant skills are difficult or impossible to influence within short spans of time, since these components include such elements as knowledge in the domain, technical skills, facility with creativity heuristics, working styles, cognitive styles, and personality traits. Task motivation, on the other hand, can be manipulated more easily for most individuals engaging in most tasks. And, as previous research demonstrates (see Lepper & Greene, 1978b), it is much easier to undermine task motivation than to enhance it.

Task motivation, more than the other components, is subject to direct and immediate social-psychological influences. As I suggested in Chapter 4, however, such influences might, through their effect on task motivation, even extend to domain-relevant skills and creativity-relevant skills. Over time, a high level of intrinsic motivation toward a task could motivate learning of both types of skills. Over time, a high level of intrinsic motivation could also increase the probability that the creativity heuristics of risk-taking and playful exploration will be applied.

Thus, over long periods of time, conducive social-psychological conditions could contribute to measurable improvements in creative abilities. Such improvements would not be noticeable, however, over brief periods of observation. In studies of relatively brief duration, only direct task-motivational influences should be noticeable.

Thus, the theoretical conceptualizations presented in Chapter 4 and developed throughout the succeeding chapters suggest that creativity can, indeed, be enhanced. The development of domain-relevant skills and creativity-relevant skills can be stimulated by high levels of intrinsic motivation. Task motivation, though perhaps more easily undermined, might be enhanced by particular social-psychological factors.

Suggestions on improving creativity come from two sources: direct training programs designed to increase creativity through cognitive interventions, and various studies of social and environmental influences in naturalistic and experimental settings.

Direct Attempts: Creativity-Training Programs

Many creativity-training programs rely primarily on cognitive rather than social-psychological methods, but they deserve scrutiny because they are the most visible and frequent cited evidence on the possibility of enhancing creative performance. Dozens of such programs have been devised. I will describe the most popular ones and a sample of others that represent the range of approaches to creativity training.

Brainstorming

Originated by Alex Osborn in 1938 as a method for improving group problem-solving in an advertising firm, brainstorming is probably the most widely used program designed specifically to enhance creativity. Osborn (1963) suggests that the creative process involves two steps—idea generation and idea evaluation. Idea generation can be further subdivided into fact-finding (problem definition and preparation) and idea-finding (combination of and extrapolation from old ideas). According to Osborn, brainstorming is most useful for idea-finding.

The most important principle of brainstorming is the *deferment of judgment.* During brainstorming, no member of the group may criticize an idea, including the individual who suggested the idea. The second principle is that quantity breeds quality; the more ideas generated, the higher the probability that some of them will be original and useful. These principles are the basis for four rules that Osborn laid down for brainstorming sessions: (1) Criticism is ruled out. (2) "Free-wheeling" is welcomed. (3) Quantity is wanted. (4) Combination and improvement are sought. In the prototypical brainstorming session, approximately 12 participants of equal administrative rank are chosen. From these, a leader is selected to state the problem under consideration in a specific, workable manner, and to ensure that the brainstorming rules are followed throughout the session. A recording secretary notes all ideas that are generated. In sum, a brainstorming group is encouraged to generate as many unusual ideas on a problem as possible, combining or improving previous ideas wherever feasible, and refraining from judgment of any sort.

Although most creativity-training programs have not been thoroughly evaluated, a great deal of research attention has been directed toward evaluating brainstorming. (See Stein, 1975, for a review.) On some points, the research findings are clear. Brainstorming does generally result in a larger number of ideas than do procedures that admit judgment during idea-generation. At the same time, however, the quality of ideas does not show noticeable improvement. In addition, it seems that group brainstorming is not any more effective than individual brainstorming. Indeed, nominal groups (collections of individuals working alone with deferment of judgment) usually produce more ideas than actual groups. It is unclear, however, whether nominal or actual groups produce higher-quality ideas. Both the quantity and quality of ideas produced by a group can be improved (a) by first having each individual privately consider information and possible solutions to the problem, and (b) by having group members take turns offering suggestions during brainstorming (Stein, 1975).

Synectics

Developed by William Gordon in 1944, synectics is a creativity-stimulation program whose title is taken from the Greek word for joining together different and apparently irrelevant elements (Gordon, 1961). Also intended primarily as a group process, synectics is guided by two principles: (1) make the strange familiar (i.e., take a new problem and transform it into something familiar by the use of metaphor and analogy), and (2) make the familiar strange (i.e., take something commonplace and find new ways of viewing it through analogy). Like brainstorming, synectics uses deferment of judgment during idea generation. In synectics sessions, however, there is generally more use of emotion to generate ideas, and there is greater external direction of ideas. Specifically, participants are instructed to use four types of analogy: (1) *personal analogy,* in which the individual imagines himself to be the object with which he is working; (2) *direct analogy,* in which facts, knowledge, or technology from one domain are used in another; (3) *symbolic analogy,* in which images are used to describe the problem; and (4) *fantasy analogy,* in which the individual expresses his wishes for ideal, though fantastic, solutions to the problem. Although there is some evidence that the use of personal analogy enhances the effects of typical brainstorming procedures, there is no systematic research on the effectiveness of synectics as a program in itself.

Creative Problem Solving

Creative Problem Solving is an eclectic training program developed by Sidney Parnes (1967). The program comprises both individual and group techniques, including brainstorming and the use of checklists for generating new ideas from old ones. Over several sessions, participants in the program are taught to follow five stages of problem-solving: *fact finding,* or the gathering of information about a problem; *problem finding,* or the clear formulation of a specific problem to be solved; *idea finding,* or the generation of possible solutions; *solution finding,* or the evaluation of the generated solutions; and *acceptance finding,* or the selling of the final solution to others. In generating ideas, participants are taught to use a checklist of verbs for building upon previous suggestions: put to other uses, adapt, modify, magnify, minify, substitute, rearrange, reverse, and combine. In addition, they use forced relationships—ideas that combine two or more disparate notions. For the most part, evaluation studies of Creative Problem Solving are limited to informal demonstrations that trained individuals do indeed use deferment of judgment and do, at times, produce more and better ideas than untrained individuals.

Other Programs

Some programs have been designed specifically for use with schoolchildren. For example, the Purdue Creativity Training Program (Feldhusen, Treffinger, & Bahlke, 1970) consists of a series of tape-recorded presentations and stories integrated with creative problem-solving exercises. The presentations are persuasive statements and instructions on creative thinking, each followed by stories about famous inventors, discoverers, and leaders. The creativity exercises give children practice in increasing fluency, flexibility, and originality in writing and drawing. The Productive Thinking Program (Covington, Crutchfield, Davies, & Olton, 1972) presents children with 16 preprogrammed instructional units, each consisting of a mystery story that guides the children through problem-solution using a number of different techniques. Both programs have been found to be effective in improving scores on standard creativity tests.

A program developed with adults involves training in the use of self-instructional statements about creative behavior (Meichenbaum, 1975). Participants are taught to say these statements to themselves before and during problem-solving. The self-statements are based on three distinct theoretical approaches to creativity: creativity as a mental ability to manipulate information, creativity as an ability to engage in controlled regression to playful, child-like modes of thinking, and creativity as a product of attitudinal and personality characteristics:

MENTAL ABILITY SELF-STATEMENTS
Size up the problem; what is it you have to do?
You have to put the elements together differently.
Use different analogies.
Do the task as if you were Osborn brainstorming or Gordon doing Synectics training.
Elaborate on ideas.

Make the strange familiar and the familiar strange.
You're in a rut—okay, try something new.
How can you use this frustration to be more creative?
Take a rest now; who knows when the ideas will visit again.
Go slow—no hurry—no need to press.
Good, you're getting it.
This is fun.
That was a pretty neat answer; wait till you tell the others!

REGRESSION SELF-STATEMENTS
Release controls; let your mind wander.
Free-associate, let ideas flow.
Relax—just let it happen.
Let your ideas play.
Refer to your experience; just view it differently.
Let your ego regress.
Feel like a bystander through whom ideas are just flowing.
Let one answer lead to another.
Almost dreamlike, the ideas have a life of their own.

ATTITUDINAL AND PERSONALITY SELF-STATEMENTS
Be creative, be unique.
Break away from the obvious, the commonplace.
Think of something no one else will think of.
Just be freewheeling.
If you push yourself you can be creative.
Quantity helps breed quality.
Get rid of internal blocks.
Defer judgments.
Don't worry what others think.
Not a matter of right and wrong.
Don't give the first answer you think of.
No negative self-statements.
(Meichenbaum, 1975, p. 132)

This program was tested in a study where experimental-group subjects participated in six sessions designed to acquaint them with the rationale for the specific statements as well as the methods for remembering and using them. Subjects in the training group showed significant increases in originality and flexibility on standard creativity tests, but control-group subjects showed no such improvements.

Methodological and Conceptual Issues

Although these creativity-enhancement programs and most other such programs
have achieved some success in improving scores on creativity tests, some critics
have pointed to a number of methodological and conceptual problems inherent
in that research (e.g., Mansfield, Busse, & Krepelka, 1978). First, in many of the
evaluation studies, it may be that subjects were simply more persistent or expended more effort on the posttests than on the pretests. Second, after training,
subjects may have a clearer idea of the sorts of responses that are required on creativity tests. Indeed, in some programs, the posttests are virtually identical to the
materials used during training. These conditions would, of course, render the creativity tasks algorithmic and would invalidate any change scores. Third, evaluators
of many programs do not assign individual subjects randomly to conditions.
Finally, evaluation studies have generally made no effort to control for simple intervention effects, sometimes called Hawthorne effects.

Conceptual issues further limit the strength of conclusions that can be drawn
from studies of these programs. Given the problems with standard creativity tests
that were noted in Chapter 2, performance on such tests is not necessarily indicative
of real-world creative performance. In addition, most creativity-training programs
do not lend themselves well to a thorough theoretical analysis; rarely are they based
on clearly identifiable theories of creativity. Furthermore, even when unequivocal
positive results are found, their interpretation is problematic because of the shotgun
approach taken by most of the programs. Understandably, these programs are designed to use all of the procedures and approaches that their designers believe will
enhance creativity. As a consequence, however, the programs are poor arenas for
identifying the specific processes that are most conducive to creativity.

These creativity-training programs focus largely on cognitive procedures for
enhancing creativity, providing participants with methods and rules of thumb
that can be generally applicable to the generation of new ideas. Thus, they are
most informative about the creativity-relevant skills component of creative performance. For this reason, the programs have limited relevance for a social psychology of creativity. There is, however, one important implication. A crucial feature in the success of brainstorming appears to be the deferment of judgment.
Deferred judgment is also an integral part of synectics training, and figures
prominently in Creative Problem Solving and the self-instructional technique reviewed. To the extent that the findings on the deferment of judgment are reliable
and meaningful, these results can be taken as further support of the undermining
effects of salient external evaluation on creativity.

A Review of Social Influences on Creativity

The research that is most relevant to a consideration of social-psychological
methods for enhancing creativity was described in Chapters 5–8. Although, as I

noted earlier, most of my own research has illuminated factors that undermine creativity, some of that research and some research by other investigators does provide evidence of creativity enhancement by social-psychological means.

Choice (Chapter 6). The evidence on choice about how to perform a task suggests that such choice may enhance creativity. Children who were given a choice about materials to use in their work exhibited significantly higher creativity than did children who had the choice made for them. Although this result can be interpreted as an undermining by externally made choice or an enhancement by self-made choice (or both), the important point for practical application is that free choice in task engagement leads to higher creativity than constrained choice.

Reward (Chapter 6). One study demonstrated a clear enhancement of creativity when subjects were offered a salient monetary reward for doing a task, but only if they had no choice in the matter. This suggests that, as long as people do not see themselves as doing an activity *in order to* gain a reward, the reward might lead to positive affect, higher enjoyment of the activity, and, hence, greater creativity.

Motivational Orientation (Chapter 7). Creative writers given an intrinsic orientation toward writing were significantly more creative than those given an extrinsic orientation. Since the intrinsic condition was not significantly higher than the control condition, however, it is appropriate to say only that extrinsic motivation undermined creativity here. It is important to consider the possibility that a ceiling effect was operating in this study, since all subjects had initially expressed high levels of intrinsic interest in writing. Thus, it may be possible to introduce an intrinsic orientation that will enhance the creativity of persons who do not initially have an extraordinarily high level of interest in the domain.

Modeling (Chapter 7). The experimental evidence on modeling is not conclusive. Some studies have demonstrated improvements on creativity tests following modeled creative responses, but few have shown similar effects on more open-ended measures. Naturalistic studies provide evidence that is intriguing but equally complex. First, a large number of creative individuals in one generation appears to stimulate creativity in the next generation. Second, although exposure to creative models early in life appears to lead to precocious creativity, long-term dependence on models may undermine creativity in adulthood. Outstanding creative scientists often point to significant modeling influences that mentors had on their early professional development.

Stimulation (Chapter 8). Physical environments that are engineered to be cognitively and perceptually stimulating can enhance creativity, but active cognitive engagement in one task can undermine creativity in a later, unrelated task.

Play and fantasy (Chapter 8). For children, at least, playful and fantasy-oriented activities prior to task engagement can lead to higher levels of creativity.

Interpersonal detachment (Chapter 8). Although encouragement from important individuals can bolster creativity, a certain interpersonal detachment between parents and their children, or between teachers and their students, may also be helpful. This phenomenon might result from the increased independence and relative lack of external control that accompany such relationships.

This research, then, suggests methods for enhancing creativity. It is equally important, however, to consider methods for avoiding the undermining of creativity. My studies and the studies of others have uncovered several social-psychological conditions that should be avoided if creativity is to be maintained.

Constrained choice (Chapter 6). Just as free choice in how to do a task might enhance creativity, constrained choice can undermine it.

Reward (Chapter 6). Although high unexpected reward might sometimes enhance creativity, it seems more likely that reward will most often be detrimental. In two studies, reward undermined the creativity of subjects who explicitly chose to engage in the rewarded task.

Evaluation (Chapter 5). Several studies have demonstrated that expected external evaluation can lead to decreases in creativity; in addition, actual prior evaluation, even if it is positive, can lead to similar decreases.

Peer pressure (Chapter 8). There is some evidence that conformity pressure from peers can lead to at least temporary decrements in creativity.

Surveillance (Chapter 7). Being seen by others while engaging in an easily-observable performance might undermine the creativity of that performance. Similar effects might not be obtained, however, when the task is not easily observed or when there are others present in the room who are engaged in their own work.

Implications for Education and Child-rearing

These major findings on the impact of social factors and training programs on creativity can be translated into tentative suggestions for maintaining and enhancing creativity in a variety of settings. In this section and the next, I will outline several such suggestions. Although these are stated as simple prescriptions, it should be understood that each of them must be qualified by complexities in the research findings and by the need for further research. Thus, these suggestions are the best that can be made, given the current state of the art in creativity research.

In Chapter 2, I proposed a continuity from low to high levels of creativity, and a basic commonality between creative performances in different domains. Thus, I offer these implications as applicable in most cases to all levels and all types of creativity. These suggestions include both general factors, which may be influenced by social agents, and factors that are directly social. Research evidence on each point can be found in the chapters listed.

General Factors

Skills to teach (Chapter 8). Parents and teachers should provide environments that are perceptually and cognitively stimulating, and should teach children to scan the environment, while working on problems, for cues that might be relevant to problem-solution.

When children show special aptitudes, the means for talent development should be provided. These means could include access to special teachers and special materials, as well as provisions of time and freedom for the child to develop the talent.

Teaching methods (Chapter 8). People taught to make positive, constructive evaluations of problem solutions may themselves be more creative in solving those problems than people taught to make negative criticisms. This suggests that teachers should not only train students' critical facilities; perhaps more importantly, they must train students' abilities to identify and use the positive aspects of their own work and the work of others.

Teacher behaviors (Chapter 8). Students who score high on creativity tests, who produce unusual responses to questions, and who display a keen sense of humor might be disadvantaged in many classrooms. Because their behavior can be considered nonconforming and unpredictable, they may be viewed as intractable and irritating by their teachers. Thus, it may be important for teachers to recognize that at least some difficult behaviors of children are manifestations of creativity-relevant skills. In general, teachers at all levels of education who wish to encourage creativity should be enthusiastic, professional, encouraging, and available to students outside of class.

Peer influences (Chapter 8). It may benefit highly talented children to be taught separately from their more average peers. In addition, it may increase the creativity of all children if they can be taught to resist peer pressure toward conformity.

Dangers of education (Chapter 8). Although formal education is essential for high levels of creativity in most domains, an excessively extended formal education might be detrimental. This phenomenon could occur if continued formal exposure to organized knowledge in a domain leads to an over-reliance on established algorithms, or if it leads to a slavish imitation of models.

Social Factors

Socialization (Chapters 7 and 8). There appear to be many ways in which everyday child-rearing practices can contribute to or undermine creativity. For example, a deemphasis of traditional sex roles may be conducive to creative development. In general, families that express little concern for societal conventions appear most likely to promote creativity in children. Along with this disregard for arbitrary conventions, however, adherence to consistent moral and ethical principles can be helpful. Parents wishing to foster creativity in their children should display low levels of authoritarianism and, at the same time, should try to avoid an overly close affectional bond that the child might find smothering. In other words, creativity might best be promoted by respect for and confidence in the child, along with a secure but somewhat distant affection that allows the child a measure of independence from parental evaluation.

There is little parents can do to ensure special birth orders for children, unless it is to have only one child. Instead, they might attempt to achieve the equivalent of "special family position" for each child by providing both responsibilities and opportunities that meet the child's particular skills, interests, and needs.

Generous exposure to models of creative achievement early in life may enhance children's level of creativity. In addition, highly creative mentors during undergraduate and graduate training can be extremely influential in creative development. Nonetheless, as they mature, students should be encouraged to go beyond the modeled behavior they have observed.

Finally, exposure to cultural diversity throughout development—either through travel or through other means—can enrich and elevate the capacity for creative behavior.

Work attitudes (Chapter 7). Children should be encouraged to adopt an intrinsic orientation toward their work. That is, parents and teachers should frequently comment upon the enjoyable aspects of such activities, the inherent satisfaction of engaging in them, and the pleasure of watching one's own work unfold. In addition, when possible, attempts should be made to eliminate the strict dichotomy between work and play.

Control (Chapters 5–8). Under most circumstances, a high degree of choice in aspects of task engagement will be beneficial to creativity. Thus, children should be allowed as much freedom as possible in deciding on specific problems to attack, materials to use, methods of approach, and subgoals. Issues of choice concerning whether to engage in tasks are somewhat more difficult. Generally, choice will enhance intrinsic motivation and, hence, creativity. If, however, children perceive themselves as choosing to do a task in order to gain a reward, their intrinsic motivation and creativity might be undermined.

Although it is not possible or desirable to eliminate surveillance and evaluation of performance for children and adolescents, these factors should be made unobtrusive and nonsalient. Indeed, it might be beneficial to teach children self-observation and self-evaluation, in order to avoid a concentration and dependence upon the external evaluation that can undermine creativity.

It appears that teachers who exert a high level of control in their classrooms foster lower levels of intrinsic motivation in their children than do teachers who encourage a high level of self-determination and self-control. Specifically, teachers' acceptance of autonomy in their pupils is positively related to their pupils' preference for challenge, curiosity, and desire for independent mastery. In addition, when children see their own teacher as more intrinsically oriented toward work, they perceive themselves as being more competent and more intrinsically motivated. Thus, creativity may best be maintained and enhanced by classroom teachers who encourage independence and self-direction in their children.

Finally, classrooms that include some relatively unstructured instructional time, with individualized and self-directed learning in an informal atmosphere, are more likely to promote creativity than strictly traditional classrooms.

Reward (Chapter 6). In most cases, salient rewards that are explicitly contracted for as payment for an activity will undermine intrinsic interest in and creativity on that activity. Nonetheless, rewards that are unusually high, can be seen as bonuses for performance, or clearly convey positive performance information rather than controlling information, might not be damaging to children's creativity. In fact, such rewards might enhance it under some conditions.

Individual differences. The recommendations I have made assume that children have an initially high level of intrinsic interest in their work. Clearly, however, this is often not the case. If intrinsic interest is initially present, efforts should be made to avoid undermining it and, where possible, to enhance it. If there is little initial interest, however, it might be necessary to use constraints such as the offer of reward to engage children in an activity (cf. Lepper & Greene, 1978a). This might be the only way for them to gain the skills necessary for competent performance of the activity and the exposure necessary for them to develop an intrinsic interest. Then, as interest develops, extrinsic constraints can be withdrawn or made less salient. Thus, in both home and school settings, it is important to tailor the use of social control to the individual child's level of interest and ability.

Implications for the Arts, the Sciences, and Industry

Many of the recommendations that can be made for child-rearing and education are equally applicable, with modification, to adult creativity in the arts, the sciences, and industrial organizations. There are, however, some important differences in application. Perhaps primary among these is the inescapable emphasis upon external reward in adult pursuits. Industrial organizations are, by definition, profit-centered. And even individuals in the arts and sciences must be concerned with earning enough money to subsist. At the same time, creativity is highly desirable in each of these settings. Research demonstrating negative effects of external constraint would seem to suggest that creativity will be harmed by the job-like nature of these pursuits. Indeed, it might appear likely that adults will be more creative in their nonprofessional pursuits or hobbies than they can ever be in their professions. But, as I suggest below, if payment is a routine, nonsalient aspect of the work environment, and if the professional climate is one that alleviates monetary concerns and fosters an intrinsic motivational orientation, then creativity should be enhanced.

There may be other ways in which the application of social-psychological principles will be different for children's creativity and adults' creativity. Simonton (1978) has suggested that creativity is much less subject to social and environmental influences during adulthood than it is during childhood. The influences that his research examines, however, are global and extended in time—the influence of cultural diversity on lifetime creative productivity, for example. There are other social factors, however, that can have more specific and temporally restricted effects. For example, the expectation of evaluation of a piece of work can undermine intrinsic motivation for and creativity on that particular project. Thus, although persistent social influences in childhood might have wide-ranging effects on later creativity, social-environmental factors in adulthood can have an impact on the immediate creativity of specific performances.

Although there is only a modest amount of research on stimulating creativity in the sciences and industrial organizations, there is even less on stimulating creativity in the arts. Thus, the recommendations made here concerning the arts are, to a large extent, extrapolations from research in other settings. As with the recommendations for children, these are divided into general factors which may be influenced by social agents, and factors that are directly social.

General Factors

Stress (Chapter 8). Although a concern over the outcome of a project can motivate effort, stress and pressure that are unrelated to the project itself will most likely undermine creative performance. In other words, the fewer extraneous difficulties people must cope with in their work, the more likely they are to perform creatively. For example, job security appears to be extremely important in fostering creativity in adults. And physical illness, perhaps the most common source of stress, can seriously undermine creative productivity.

External Support (Chapter 8). F. Scott Fitzgerald often complained that many of his short stories and screenplays were "trash" that he wrote only for income and that these endeavors diverted him from his best and most creative writing (Graham, 1976). Because it is helpful for creators to be freed of excessive concern about supporting themselves, creativity will likely be stimulated by generous support of outstanding individuals and their work from government and private sources.

Creativity heuristics (Chapters 4 and 9). Deliberate attempts should be made to identify, learn, and use effective creativity heuristics. Since these, for the most part, are not domain-specific, they can be regarded as general rules of thumb that guide problem-solving, invention, and artistic creation. Some of the most frequently cited creativity heuristics include: (a) Rearrange the elements of the problem; take a break; rough out a plan for a solution in terms of just the important elements before attempting to work out a solution in detail; think in terms of classes of elements rather than particular elements; if you are unable to get all the way to a goal, look for a way to reduce the difference between your present position and the goal (Anderson, 1980). (b) Allow yourself to consider "intermediate impossibles": in generating ideas, be less concerned with the validity of an idea and more concerned with its value in setting off further ideas (deBono, 1971). (c) Use concentrated, massed work sessions rather than scattered, distributed work sessions; warm up prior to idea-generating sessions by playing with the same idea in a number of different ways; avoid overlearning of response algorithms (Mednick, 1962). (d) Try something counterintuitive (Newell et al., 1962). (e) Make the familiar strange and the strange familiar (Gordon, 1961). (f) Generate hypotheses by analyzing case studies, use analogies, account for exceptions, and investigate paradoxical incidents (McGuire, 1973). (g) Play with ideas (Wickelgren, 1979).

Personality (Chapter 4). Personality research has consistently uncovered a set of traits that seem to be characteristic of notably creative persons. These traits include, for example, independence, sensitivity, and preference for complexity. Some theorists suggest that if people can adopt these characteristics they will be more likely to produce creative work: "It seems reasonable to assume that creativity can be stimulated if individuals are helped to become more like those persons who are known to be creative" (Stein, 1974, p. 7). There are conceptual problems with this approach, however. First, it is not clear that these personality characteristics cause creative behavior. They may simply co-occur with it, or they may in fact result in part from consistent creative activity. Second, the definition of traits appears to preclude the possibility that they can be changed: "Since a trait approach to creativity assumes that the traits to be measured will express themselves under most existing environmental conditions, it follows by definition that these traits should not be easily influenced by training" (Feldman, 1980, p. 93). Finally, even if traits can be viewed as relatively enduring but partially changeable dispositions toward behavior, there are no straightforward methods for modifying the personality toward greater creativity.

Social Factors

Control (Chapters 5–8). For scientific research, and perhaps for other types of creative endeavor as well, it is best to have little financial or conceptual interference from administrative superiors. In general, greater measures of self-control over one's work should lead to higher levels of creativity. This includes choice of methods for completing a task, as well as choice of tasks in which to engage. The exception, of course, is that creativity can be undermined if individuals perceive themselves as choosing to engage in a task in order to earn some salient reward.

Reward (Chapter 6). Certainly, adults cannot engage in their professions without some substantial tangible rewards. There are ways, however, in which the negative impact on creativity of working for rewards can be minimized. First, the salience of rewards can be reduced. Second, rewards can be presented as indications of good performance and not merely used as a method of controlling behavior. Third, very high rewards can occasionally produce positive affect that might lead to increased creativity, but perhaps only if such rewards are seen as unexpected bonuses.

Play at work (Chapters 7 and 8). A generous level of freedom, in terms of time and resources, can encourage people to play constructively at their work—to combine ideas in new ways that might not seem immediately useful in generating products or solutions. Creativity can be further fostered by a clearly intrinsic motivational orientation toward work. Intrinsically satisfying aspects of the work should be emphasized in training and in working environments, and extrinsic motivations should be discouraged.

Organizational climates (Chapter 8). Experts on organizational innovation have noted ways in which overall organizational climate can inhibit or encourage creativity. Inhibiting factors include: (a) a fear of failure, which results in a reluctance to take risks; (b) a preoccupation with order and tradition; (c) a failure to see one's own strengths and the strengths of others in the organization; (d) an over-reliance on ineffective algorithms; (e) a reluctance to assert one's own ideas; (f) a reluctance to play; and (g) an excessive use of salient reward (Campbell, 1977). Conditions cited as favorable to organizational innovation include: (a) a climate conducive to new ideas; (b) an organizational structure flexible enough to bend with whatever strain innovation may bring; (c) an established process for developing new ideas into products; and (d) support for innovation from the highest levels of management (Jaoui, 1980).

Work settings (Chapter 7). In general, low levels of surveillance of work and low levels of evaluation expectation are most likely to encourage intrinsic motivation and creativity. Furthermore, perhaps because working in groups includes elements of surveillance and evaluation by others, individual idea-generation may be more productive in many situations than group idea-generation.

Individual differences. Just as it is important to consider individual differences in children's interest and skill in determining appropriate levels of social control, it is also important to consider individual differences in response to constraints among adults. As I suggested in Chapter 4, some individuals might be particularly resistant to the negative effects of extrinsic constraints on their intrinsic motivation and creativity—for example, individuals who have developed methods for cognitively distancing themselves from the constraints, or individuals who initially have such high levels of intrinsic interest that this interest cannot be easily undermined. In addition, as with children, initial levels of skill and motivation must be considered. Under some circumstances, extrinsic constraints must be used in order to motivate task engagement. Certainly, only by engaging in an activity can people develop the necessary skills and, subsequently, the intrinsic interest that is necessary for high levels of creativity.

Update

As evidenced by our studies attempting to immunize children against the negative effects of extrinsic motivators on creativity and by our research focus on educational settings and work settings over the past twelve years, we have increasingly attended to the maintenance and enhancement of creativity. Although many of our findings are directly relevant to social psychological considerations, some are related only indirectly. For example, we have found that people will be more creative in their work when they perceive that work as positively challenging (Amabile & S. Gryskiewicz, 1987; Amabile & N. Gryskiewicz, 1989; Amabile, Conti, Coon, Lazenby, & Herron, in press). Certainly there is a social psychological element to this phenomenon; people are more likely to feel positively challenged by the work if their managers match their projects to their skill levels and if others in the organization view the projects as important. However, the phenomenon also depends to some extent on nonsocial factors: the nature of the work and the individual's skills.

Thus, although Chapter 9 in the original edition of this book focused primarily on social psychological variables, we will take a somewhat broader approach here.

Enhancing the Components of Creativity

In Chapter 4 we reiterated the role of domain-relevant skills in creativity, and the feedback process through which creative success might enhance intrinsic motivation, which, in turn, might lead to increased learning of domain-relevant skills (see Figure A, page 113). Indeed, some recent research has demonstrated this feedback process (Conti, Amabile, & Pollak, 1995). In addition, the componential model and our immunization studies suggest that creativity can also be supported by environments that support intrinsic motivation during the initial learning of domain-relevant skills. Such environments: (a) frequently focus learners on their increase in competence; (b) emphasize the joy of discovery; and (c) allow learners considerable autonomy in the learning process (Amabile, 1989).

Much of the creativity literature continues to focus on creativity-relevant processes. One of our own recent studies falls into this category; we found that in the absence of evaluation pressure, simply engaging in a creative activity before learning can enhance creativity in the use of the learned material (Conti, Amabile, & Pollak, 1995). However, the vast majority of studies on creativity-relevant processes examine the explicit teaching of creative-thinking techniques. The original edition of this book noted several conceptual and methodological concerns with many creativity-training programs, including: practice effects, increased persistence after training, reliance on creativity tests, training directed specifically at tests, lack of appropriate control groups, and difficulty specifying mechanisms of improvement in particularly broad programs. Other researchers have since elaborated upon many of these concerns (Feldhusen & Clinkenbeard, 1986).

Nonetheless, creativity-training programs continue to increase in popularity, and some research suggests that certain of these programs may be effective in enhancing creativity-relevant processes. In a metanalysis of nearly 100 studies of major long-term creativity-training programs, Rose and Lin (1984) reported on the Osborn-Parnes Creative Problem Solving program (Parnes, 1967), the Purdue Creativity Training Program (Feldhusen, Treffinger, & Bahlke, 1970), the Productive Thinking Program (Covington, Crutchfield, Davies, & Olton, 1972), other creative thinking programs, various school-based programs, and a variety of special techniques (such as transcendental meditation). Overwhelmingly, the Creative Problem Solving program accounted for a higher percentage of the variance in total creativity scores (approximately 40%) than did the other programs (which varied from approximately 11% to 28%). Not surprisingly, given that most of the techniques are primarily verbal in nature, most of the programs accounted for more variance in verbal creativity test scores than in figural scores. Other studies on creativity training have found that brainstorming can be effective in increasing idea generation under some circumstances (Comadena, 1984; Necka, 1984; Thornburg, 1991), and that Synectics training may be effective only in a favorable social climate and only in the case of a well-defined problem (Necka, 1984).

A variety of other techniques have been tested for enhancing effects on creativity. These techniques share the goals of the creativity-training programs but do not use explicit training in creativity-relevant processes. Rather, they involve various activities that are presumed to facilitate engagement of creativity-relevant processes. Each has been found (usually in single studies) to enhance creativity scores: hypnosis (Raikov, 1992); humor (Ziv, 1988); relaxation/isolation environments (such as flotation isolation) (Forgays & Forgays, 1992; Suedfeld, Metcalfe, & Bluck, 1987); long-term and short-term exercise programs (Gondola, 1986); music (Burns, 1988); alcoholic beverages (Brunke & Gilbert, 1992); and divergent methods for participating in everyday activities (Cropley, 1990).

Although some of these techniques (such as humor) might operate through social psychological processes to some extent, they most likely operate largely through direct cognitive mechanisms. Likewise, most of the creativity-training programs rely primarily on cognitive mechanisms such as learning to take new perspectives on problems. Nonetheless, there are social aspects even in these programs, especially Creative Problem Solving (CPS), which is the most effective of these methods. In CPS, trainees are taught to defer judgment during idea generation—a method for reducing the extrinsic constraint of evaluation expectation.

As we argued in Chapter 4, social psychological processes are most relevant to the third component of creativity, intrinsic task motivation. Because extrinsic constraints can directly undermine intrinsic motivation and creativity, the most obvious method for enhancing creativity, based on our own research, is to reduce the emphasis on extrinsic constraints in the social environment. Research on these constraints was reviewed in Chapters 5–8: evaluation, surveillance, contracted-for reward, task constraint, and competition. Where these extrinsic motivators are a necessary part of the social environment (and they often are), attempts should be made to reduce their salience or to change their character. For example, teachers might reduce the salience of grade evaluations by simply talking about grades less in the classroom. They might also emphasize the informational nature of these evaluations—as guides to the development of stronger skills—rather than their controlling nature. The effectiveness of this technique of reducing the importance of or reinterpreting extrinsic motivators was demonstrated in our immunization studies (Hennessey, Amabile & Martinage, 1989; Hennessey & Zbikowski, 1993).

The immunization studies tested a second technique that might be useful in maintaining intrinsic task motivation: increasing its salience. Children's intrinsic motivation and creativity might be enhanced if their parents and teachers engage them in discussions about the intrinsic excitement and joy of learning; adults' intrinsic motivation and creativity at work might be enhanced if their managers established environments in which people could freely exchange their ideas and explore mutual interests in the work.

Our new theoretical conceptions of motivational synergy (Chapter 4) also have implications for enhancing the motivational component of creativity (Amabile, 1993). There are at least two means by which extrinsic motivators, rather than detracting from creativity, can add to it. First, according to a mechanism termed *extrinsics in service of intrinsics*, any extrinsic factors that support one's sense of competence without undermining one's sense of self-determination should positively contribute to intrinsic motivation. These are the "synergistic extrinsic motivators." As suggested by Deci & Ryan (1985), reward, recognition, and feedback that confirm competence, as well as feedback that provides important information on how to improve competence, should have such effects. In addition, extrinsic motivators that serve to directly increase one's involvement in the work itself should also operate in service of intrinsic motivation. For example, overall project goals that orient a person toward the nature of the task to be accomplished should add to rather than detract from intrinsic motivation and creativity; so should enabling rewards—rewards that involve more time, freedom, or resources to pursue exciting ideas. (The MacArthur Foundation "genius" grants serve as an example of this type of reward.) Similarly, performance feedback should enhance intrinsic motivation and creativity if it is informational—constructive, non-threatening, and work-focused rather than person-focused.

The second motivational synergy mechanism is the *motivation–work cycle match*. As noted in Chapter 4, overall creative performance is likely to be optimized if intrinsic motivation is most salient at those stages of the creative process where novel thinking is most crucial—the problem identification stage, and the idea generation stage. However, synergistic extrinsic motivators may play a facilitative role at those stages where novelty is less important—the preparation and idea-validation stages. For example, some scientists report great excitement during the idea generation and early validation stages of working on particularly complex problems. However, their engagement in the process sometimes flags if difficulties are encountered during the slow and tedious process of working out the fine details to fully develop, validate, and clearly communicate the idea. (Just think of how painful the doctoral dissertation can be in the final stages!) Some extrinsic motivators, such as clear deadlines or the promise of external reward and recognition, may do little harm at these stages because flexible, novel thinking is no longer the dominant mode. Indeed, these motivators, as long as they leave the sense of self-determination intact, should serve to keep the individual engaged in the work. Moreover, these extrinsic motivators may actually enhance the appropriateness or value of the work by attuning the individual to outcome requirements.

In considering means for enhancing creativity, it is important not only to consider each of the separate components of creativity (domain-relevant skills, creativity-relevant processes, and intrinsic task motivation) but also to consider their intersection. Imagine that the components are represented as three partially overlapping circles. Our multiplicative model suggests that creativity will be highest in that area where the three components share their greatest overlap—that is, where the individual's domain-relevant skills overlap with the individual's strongest intrinsic interests and creative-thinking processes. In other words, people are most likely to be creative within their "creativity intersection." Identifying this intersection can, in itself, be an important step toward enhancing creativity. This can be particularly important for gifted individuals, who are likely to have strong skills in many different domains, and who may also have high levels of creative thinking skills. These individuals should strive, and should be helped by their mentors, to discover where their strongest interests lie. It is in those areas of greatest passion that their greatest creativity is likely to emerge.

Supporting Children's Creativity

Most of the implications that we have outlined for enhancing creativity should apply to both children and adults. However, there are certain techniques and approaches that may be particularly appropriate for children. These are discussed in some detail elsewhere (Amabile, 1989); we will summarize them here as guidelines for parents and teachers.

Encourage autonomy by avoiding excessive, anxious control of children's activities and by respecting each child's individuality. Maintain a loving relationship with the child but avoid a smothering emotional closeness; encourage independence as the child grows. Autonomy and independence can be supported in the socialization process by emphasizing values (guiding principles) for behavior rather than rules, and by teaching children the reasoning behind these values.

Focus children on intrinsic rather than extrinsic motivation in a number of ways. In the formal educational process, highlight learning achievements rather than the external indicators such as grades and competitive awards. Emphasize the intrinsic joy of learning and focus children on their own development of competence and knowledge. Emphasize the value of taking the risk to challenge oneself beyond current skill levels; highlight the informational value of mistakes. Give precedence to intangible over tangible rewards and present rewards as bonuses rather than bribes. Use rewards to confirm the child's competence and to celebrate the child's creativity rather than to control the child's behavior. Avoid placing children in competitive situations for learning and for creative activities. Teach children that they can always learn and improve their skills, that developing competence is more important than showing how smart they already are. Help them to acknowledge but cognitively distance themselves from the extrinsic motivators that they encounter in school and other situations.

Creativity-relevant processes can be developed in children by modeling independent, interested creative activity. In addition, expose children to special experiences that might stimulate creativity, such as travel or introductions to people engaged in various types of creative activity. Encourage creative exploration of tasks and activities; encourage questioning and curiosity.

Finally, children can be helped to discover their creativity intersection by exploring a variety of activities so that they might identify their strongest intrinsic interests.

Supporting Creativity in Work Organizations

Our research in organizations over the past twelve years has led to several suggestions for maintaining and stimulating creativity and innovation in the work of adults. These suggestions too are detailed elsewhere (Amabile, 1988a; Amabile, Conti, Coon, Lazenby, & Herron, in press). They are summarized here as suggestions for managers and organizational leaders.

It is important to maintain a balance between clear motivating direction in the work and individual autonomy in conducting the work. Present a clear strategic direction for projects and for the organization overall but allow as much operational autonomy as possible to employees in the day-to-day carrying out of their projects. Clearly communicate a vision of the organization as creative and innovative.

Rewards can be used to support creativity, but considerable skill is required to do so effectively. Recognize and reward good creative efforts, even when the ultimate result may not have been profitable. Use rewards that confirm the individual's (or the team's) competence and the value of the individual's (or the team's) work. Use rewards that enable individuals to pursue work that they are interested in or challenged by. Avoid using rewards as bribes or controlling factors.

There are a number of ways in which the evaluative atmosphere and the reception of ideas can be managed to support creativity. Encourage frequent work-focused feedback (as opposed to person-focused criticism) among peers as well as from supervisors. Discourage excessively critical evaluations of new ideas. Avoid emphasis on maintaining the status quo; embrace a degree of risk.

An open, supportive interaction norm between groups will help to avoid the competition and infighting that can be destructive to creativity.

Provide logistical and tangible support for innovation by reducing red tape and approval layers and by committing sufficient resources for innovative projects.

An optimal degree of pressure or positive tension for creativity can be achieved by emphasizing the importance, even the urgency, of projects where creativity is desired, but avoiding extreme time pressures.

Match people to projects according to their interests and their skills so that interests are maximally engaged and skills are optimally challenged for further development.

Because so much work in contemporary organizations can be accomplished only through collective action, the development and management of work teams play a crucial role in creativity. Form work teams that combine diverse backgrounds and skills. Facilitate communication, collaboration, and idea support among and between work teams as well as constructive challenging of new ideas.

Demonstrate that creativity and innovation are valued by focusing communications within the organization on the excitement and potential of the ideas being generated and the work being accomplished.

Summary

The various suggestions for supporting and stimulating creativity that have been made in this chapter all stem from the implications of the theory presented in Chapter 4 and the research presented in Chapters 5–8. Although some focus on developing domain-relevant skills and creativity-relevant processes, most concentrate on establishing a social environment in homes, in schools, and in work organizations that will support intrinsic motivation and active engagement with creative activities. The evidence suggests that much can be done to enhance and maintain creativity by establishing stimulating, supportive, and positively challenging environments.

10

Toward a Comprehensive Psychology of Creativity

The literature of social influences on creativity contains a curious finding. Not only does first birth order seem to foster creativity, but early death of a parent seems to function in the same way (Albert, 1980). On the average, in the general population, about 8% of people lose a parent through death before they are 16 years old. By contrast, as reported in Chapter 8, the percentages are 26% for eminent scientists (Roe, 1952) 30% for historical geniuses (Cox, 1926), and 55% for eminent English poets and writers (Brown, 1968). The incidence of early parental loss is similarly high for individuals who have achieved eminence in domains not typically considered "creative." For example, 34% of American presidents and 35% of British prime ministers suffered such loss (Albert, 1980).

The similarity between birth order and early parental loss in impact on creative achievement is intriguing, but even more intriguing is the similarity between these data and the data on parent loss among deviant individuals. In comparison with 8% in the general population, 22% of male prisoners in one study had lost a parent before they were 16 (Brown, 1968); the percentages range from 24% to 40% in other studies of male prisoners, female prisoners, delinquent boys, and delinquent women (Andry, 1963; Brown, 1968; Cortes & Gatti, 1972; Glueck & Glueck, 1934).[1]

Apparently, early parent loss through death does not have a consistent relationship to later creative achievement. Albert (1980) has suggested two major determinants of whether this event in childhood will lead to eminence or to anti-social deviance: (1) the presence of giftedness, special talents, and high aptitudes in the child, and (2) the interest taken by a particular adult in the development of those qualities in the child. In other words, the direction of the effect is most likely mediated by other social factors and by individual differences in the children themselves—specifically, differences in domain-relevant skills, creativity-relevant skills, and task motivation.

---

[1] There are clear differences between types of early parent loss in their effects on adult behavior patterns. Although loss through death is associated with both extremely positive and extremely negative outcomes, as reported here, parent loss through other causes—separation, divorce, or mental illness—has a consistently detrimental effect (Santrock, 1972).

Evidence that individual differences can mediate the effects of social factors on creativity also comes from a more traditional social-psychological study. As reported in Chapter 6, Loveland and Olley (1979) examined the effects of external reward on children's interest in and performance on an art activity. Before the start of the experimental manipulations, children were classified as either high or low in interest in drawing on the basis of the amount of free time they spent in this activity. This variable interacted significantly with the reward manipulation. Children who were initially interested in drawing did more work, but work of poorer quality, under rewarded than under nonrewarded conditions. Later, the rewarded children in this group showed much less interest in drawing than did the nonrewarded children. With those who showed low initial interest, however, this pattern was reversed. These children also drew more pictures when they were rewarded for drawing, but these pictures were not of poorer quality than those done by nonrewarded low-interest children. In addition, the low-initial-interest children actually gained interest in drawing under rewarded conditions.

Studies on early parent death are naturalistic investigations of a significant social event and its effects on creativity. The reward study uses a traditional experimental paradigm to examine a specific, circumscribed social constraint and its effects on intrinsic interest. Yet, despite their disparate methodologies and aims, these studies have the same implications for a social psychology of creativity. It is not enough to simply study the impact of particular social factors on intrinsic motivation and creativity. A complete understanding of these factors and their effects on creativity can only be achieved by integrating the social psychology of creativity with the insights and methods of personality and cognitive psychology.

Social Psychology of Creativity: Current Status

By any measure—volume of research publications, number of investigators engaged in research, historical span—the social psychology of creativity is the least developed area in creativity research. The systematic study of the impact of social factors on creative performance has been virtually ignored until quite recently. To be sure, sociological and naturalistic correlational studies of the impact of "social environments" on creativity do have a long history. These studies provide evidence on the relationship between naturally occurring social environments and creative behavior. They do not, however, isolate particular social factors and examine their impact on creativity in carefully controlled settings.

As reviewed in Chapter 8, some correlational research has uncovered patterns of results that appear with sufficient consistency and clarity that they can be used as the basis for general principles. For example, special family positions (such as birth order) and early family relationships appear to contribute to adult creativity in fairly predictable ways. Early exposure to cultural diversity, either through traveling, moving frequently, or living in a society that is culturally diverse, are other factors that appear to have a reliable, positive influence on creativity. Educational environments that encourage autonomy and self-directed learning may foster creativity; self-direction seems to be equally important in adult work environments. Finally, this research tradition has led to the conclusion that exposure to a creative model in a particular domain can increase the likelihood that a young person will do outstanding creative work in that domain.

Although research on social environments has uncovered these general principles, however, it has not contributed directly to a theoretical model of creativity. Because of the nature of the factors examined, the methods employed, and the data obtained, it is virtually impossible to specify psychological mechanisms for the operation of these factors. There is no common theoretical framework that motivates these inquiries and, moreover, there is little possibility that their results alone can lead to the formulation of such a framework.

For the purposes of developing a theoretical basis for the social psychology of creativity, it is empirical research on specific social factors (rather than globally defined social environments) that will be most useful. Simonton's research (reviewed in Chapter 8) provides an essential conceptual bridge between the work on global social environments and my experimental research on specific social factors. Simonton's work does examine social-environmental factors that operate at the level of the family and society but, at the same time, it carefully isolates those factors in order to specify exactly the nature of their relationship to creative productivity. Nonetheless, in order to derive and test consistent theoretical models of the operation of particular social factors on creativity, correlational investigations must be coupled with experimental research.

The hypothesis most thoroughly tested by an experimental social-psychological approach to creativity is the intrinsic motivation hypothesis of creativity, as outlined in Chapter 4. In its simplest form, this hypothesis states that the intrinsically motivated state will be conducive to creativity, but the extrinsically motivated state will be detrimental. This hypothesis applies only to heuristic tasks, where the problem does not have a clear and straightforward path to solution. Opposite effects would be expected on algorithmic tasks, which do have a clear path to solution. On these tasks, extrinsic motivation should not impair performance, and might actually enhance it.

Although there remain a number of unanswered questions, the intrinsic motivation hypothesis has received firm support in the results of several studies. This support comes from four types of evidence. First, people who have worked under the imposition of salient extrinsic constraints generally produce work that is lower in creativity than that produced by people who have worked in the absence of such constraints. These constraints include external evaluation of work or the expectation of such evaluation, offer of reward contingent upon task performance, surveillance of work, and restricted choice in task engagement. Second, people placed in conditions designed to enhance intrinsic motivation—such as free choice in aspects of task engagement—generally produce work that is higher in creativity than that produced by people not working under such conditions.

Third, in many studies demonstrating these effects, there are significant correlations between subjects' expressed intrinsic interest in their work and the rated creativity of that work. Finally, in a study designed to directly manipulate intrinsic and extrinsic orientation toward a task, effects on subsequent creativity were consistent with the intrinsic motivation hypothesis.

This principle, then, can serve as the theoretical foundation for a social psychology of creativity: Social factors that enhance an individual's motivation to engage in an activity for its own sake will also enhance creative performance on the activity; factors that undermine that motivation, or factors that make more salient the motivation to engage in the activity for some external goal, will undermine creativity.

Perhaps the most important point to be made about the intrinsic motivation principle is that it proposes the functional equivalence of many social factors which seem quite disparate. Expecting to be evaluated on task performance functions in the same way as having choice of task engagement constrained, being watched while performing the task, receiving positive evaluations on previous work, contracting to receive an attractive reward for task performance, and being led to think about extrinsic reasons for doing a task. Similarly, working with the expectation that task performance will not be evaluated functions in the same way as being given free choice on aspects of task engagement and being led to think about the intrinsic value of doing the task. Clearly, despite the superficial differences between these various factors, their psychological impact on performance appears to be the same. The intrinsic motivation principle specifies what the nature of that impact must be in order to affect the motivation for creativity.

Social Psychology of Creativity: Future Directions

The preliminary empirical work that has been done on the social psychology of creativity should be expanded in several directions. The first, and most straightforward, extension of this research will be the investigation of social constraints for which data is still lacking. For example, since competition is such a prominent feature of many educational and working environments, it will be important to examine thoroughly the impact of competition and competitive evaluation on intrinsic motivation and creativity. Similarly, deadlines and other types of time constraints should be studied.

A second issue for consideration by social-psychological creativity research is the interaction between classes of social factors. One study that examined different types of prior positive evaluation found suggestive, but nonsignificant, differences in their effects on creativity. It may be that stronger manipulations of these variables will reveal, for example, that specific, informative evaluation is more conducive (or less detrimental) to creativity than vague praise. In addition, further work needs to be done on the effects of reward on creativity. The study on reward and task label revealed a significant superiority of nonreward groups over reward groups, but this difference was not found if subjects had not been given a task label (either "work" or "play"). Another study revealed that explicitly contracting for a reward for task engagement can undermine creative performance; by contrast, however, simply receiving the same reward without explicitly contracting for it seemed to enhance creativity. Thus, more work is needed to determine the specific conditions under which tangible reward will and will not undermine creativity.

Third, future research is necessary to identify the precise mechanisms by which extrinsic constraints can hinder creativity. More studies should explicitly examine subjects' subsequent intrinsic interest in the target activities, in order to determine whether differences in intrinsic motivation do consistently accompany differences in creativity. There should be a closer investigation of the ways in which intrinsic and extrinsic motivational states influence heuristic and algorithmic aspects of task performance. And, in addition to confirming the existence of motivational differences related to performance differences, future research should attempt to uncover the mechanisms by which social constraints can produce those motivational differences. Do people indeed discount their own interest in a task under extrinsic constraint? Is their attention diverted away from the task itself and toward concerns about the extrinsic goal? Do people simply feel less attracted to activities they view as "work"?

Fourth, for both theoretical and practical reasons, attempts should be made to alter these social constraints so that they might actually enhance creativity. Where restricted choice can undermine creativity, clear and salient free choice in activities might enhance it. Where external evaluation can be detrimental to creativity, self-evaluation or competence-bolstering external evaluation might be conducive. In addition, there is suggestive evidence from one study that calling subjects' attention to intrinsic reasons for working might enhance creativity; this possibility must be explored further.

Fifth, the temporal span of experimental social-psychological studies on creativity must be expanded. Most studies, to this point, have included independent and dependent variables of relatively brief duration. It will be important to determine whether the nature of longer-range effects will be comparable.

Finally, experimental research in the social psychology of creativity must continue to move beyond investigations of extrinsic constraints. This research, for example, should determine the circumstances under which modeling will have positive and negative effects on creativity. It is possible that modeling might lead to a slavish imitation of response algorithms under some circumstances, but to a properly applied set of creativity heuristics under others. Another potentially important impact of modeling is the imparting of an intrinsic (or extrinsic) motivational orientation toward one's work.

Similarly, effects of the mere presence of others on creativity should be examined, along with effects of having active, collaborative co-workers.

Finally, future research should continue the tradition of studying global social environments—families, classrooms, workplaces, societies, and cultures. As these are studied more extensively, however, they should also be studied more *intensively*. Efforts should be directed toward isolating specific features of these environments that influence creativity positively or negatively, as well as interactions between them.

In all of this future work, an attempt must be made to formulate consistent theoretical statements that will account for the effects of social and environmental factors on creativity. It is probably unreasonable to expect that a single unifying theoretical statement can be articulated that will account for all such effects—the effects of social constraints and motivational orientations, the effects of working in the presence of others, of observing creative others, of working in environments that are visually rich or visually impoverished or cramped or noisy. There is no need to expect all such behaviors to be accounted for by one explanatory mechanism; there is a need, however, for all such explanatory mechanisms to fit well together into a model of social-psychological influences on creativity.

Integrating Theoretical Perspectives

A pair of questions opened this book: How is creative performance different from ordinary performance? What conditions are most favorable to creative performance? Some answers to these questions have begun to emerge, many of them coming from the social psychology of creativity: Conditions that are most conducive to creativity include conditions free of salient extrinsic constraints on performance, conditions that encourage self-direction, and conditions where intrinsic reasons for engaging in activities are stressed over extrinsic reasons. Creative performance is different from ordinary performance in that it can be undermined by the offer of reward, the expectation of evaluation, and other social factors that have traditionally been seen as facilitating performance.

Clearly, though, these statements must be qualified by the knowledge that other factors can interact with social factors to mediate these effects. And these statements must be supplemented by statements on the impact of social and nonsocial factors on noncreative aspects of performance. Finally, as an ultimate goal for all creativity research, all such statements must fit into an integrated theoretical model of creative behavior.

Throughout the history of psychological research on creativity, ideologically divergent lines of work have remained almost completely separate. The dominant tradition, personality and individual-difference research, has proceeded fairly independently of the other separate areas—cognitive and social-environments research. Each line of research has been guided by a different fundamental assumption: The important determinant of creative behavior is a constellation of personality traits, preferences, and attitudes; the important determinant of creative behavior is a set of cognitive skills, both innate and learned techniques of creative thinking; the important determinant of creative behavior is a conducive social environment which supports and stimulates creative effort.

Each of these approaches has, of course, produced information useful to understanding the nature of creativity. For example, personality research has revealed a clearly defined group of personality characteristics that are often found in outstandingly creative individuals, such as a high level of independence, a resistance to conformity pressure, and a preference for complexity. Cognitive research has identified certain random-search qualities of creative thinking and has specified particular heuristics that can contribute to the effective generation of creative ideas. In short, these separate psychologies of creativity, though proceeding on their own independent empirical courses, have still made significant progress.

Ultimately, however, progress in creativity research will depend upon a unifying theoretical conceptualization of creative behavior. The componential framework presented in Chapter 4 may be useful in this regard, for a number of reasons. First, it includes all classes of factors that have been shown to affect creativity, as well as those that have been suggested but have yet to be investigated. Thus, it may serve a heuristic function in guiding future research on specific factors. Second, it suggests a sequence for the creative process and proposes the primary influences that each of the major components will have at each stage of the sequence. Not only should research on specific factors and classes of factors examine their impact on final levels of creativity, but it should examine their impact at each stage. Third, the componential framework suggests that the components of factors influencing creativity will, over the long term, exert mutual influence. These mutual influences may be the most fruitful area for future research. Finally, perhaps the most important contribution of the componential framework is the prominence given to task motivation. This component, though clearly significant in influencing creative performance, has been largely neglected in previous theoretical statements.

At this point, there are already a number of specific questions that go beyond a simple social psychology of creativity to embrace a more integrative approach: How are other aspects of performance (such as technical correctness) affected by changes in domain-relevant skills, creativity-relevant skills, and task motivation? In which domains are such aspects closely tied to creativity, and in which domains are they independent? How do the social and cognitive effects of formal education contribute to creativity? What personality variables mediate the effects of social factors on creativity? How do creativity-relevant skills develop, and what role does task motivation or general motivational orientation play? How do initial levels of interest, domain-relevant skills, and creativity-relevant skills mediate the effects of social factors on creativity?

Whatever resemblance a comprehensive theory of creativity will ultimately bear to the componential framework I have presented, such a theory must include a set of distinct components of abilities, characteristics, and conditions that can each independently influence creativity but can also interact. It appears that social-psychological factors are most important in their influence on task motivation which, in turn, affects initial stages of engaging in a task and the novelty and complexity of solutions generated. It is the task of future research to determine the extent to which social-psychological factors can interact with the other components.

The nature of creativity is such that a complete and useful theory of creativity cannot be a single, simple theoretical statement. Rather, it will be a complex model involving many classes of factors that contribute to the final creativity of a product or response. The painstaking effort required to formulate such a model is more than justified by the theoretical and practical importance of the result.

Update

The final chapter of the first edition of this book argued that "a complete understanding of [social] factors and their effects on creativity can only be achieved by integrating the social psychology of creativity with the insights and methods of personality and cognitive psychology." In the past dozen years, along with other researchers in the field we have tried to move toward that integration. In the process, we have shifted our focus from understanding social influences on creativity to understanding creativity more broadly.

The social psychology of creativity is no longer a neonate. It now has a twenty-year history, and significant progress has been made in basic knowledge about social influences on creativity and in the integration of social psychological with personality and cognitive variables. Many of these findings grew from the "future directions" outlined in the 1983 edition, but several stemmed from the pursuit of new questions that have arisen since that time.

Research Advances

In the Updates to Chapters 3–8 we described the major new findings in the field. Although most of these are directly relevant to the social psychology of creativity, a number of them address broader issues about the creative process and the entire range of factors that might influence it.

A number of methodological advances have contributed to the development of the field. New methods for assessing creativity have been developed, and the consensual assessment technique for creativity has been refined and expanded. New behavioral observation and verbal protocol analysis techniques promise to be useful for further study of the creative process. A methodological outcome of the research in work organizations has been the development of a new tool (KEYS) for quantitatively assessing perceptions of the work environment along dimensions that appear to have an impact on creativity.

Considerable empirical support has been found for several aspects of the componential theory of creativity that were previously untested. Research has demonstrated the crucial role of each of the three components of individual creativity (domain-relevant skills, creativity-relevant processes, and intrinsic task motivation) as well as the relative generality of creativity-relevant processes. Preliminary cognitive research has begun to reveal the mechanisms by which motivation exerts its influence on creative performance. We have attempted to begin separating out the stages of the creative process. And one study clearly demonstrated the feedback loop postulated in the original model whereby creativity can lead to increased intrinsic motivation and learning of domain-relevant skills.

New findings have emerged on several of the specific social-environmental factors discussed in the 1983 edition, particularly evaluation, reward, and constraint, and on one factor not discussed in the earlier edition—competition. Research on the negative effects of evaluation on creativity has yielded some replications, some partial replications, and some failures to replicate. It appears that the negative effect may depend on certain individual-difference traits, on initial interest in the activity, and on initial skill level. Some exciting findings from non-experimental research suggest that evaluation can have positive effects on creativity when it is work-focused and constructive.

Although there have been some replications of the negative effect of reward on the performance of heuristic tasks, some promising positive effects of reward have also been discovered. These positive effects appear when intrinsic motivation is kept salient, when extrinsic motivation becomes less salient (or cognitively diminished), and when rewards signify competence or enable performance of interesting new activities—rather than signifying external control of behavior.

We now have considerable experimental and nonexperimental evidence that constraint placed on task engagement has consistent negative effects on creativity.

Win-lose competition between peers has a negative effect on creativity. However, this effect may depend on some individual-difference variables such as gender. Moreover, competition with outside groups may have a positive effect on the creativity of work teams.

Recent research has provided general support for the Intrinsic Motivation Principle of Creativity. Several studies have produced clear evidence that as a personality trait, intrinsic motivation is positively related to creativity in a variety of domains. Moreover, experimental evidence suggests that focusing on intrinsic motives may actually increase intrinsic motivation and creativity. However, recent research also suggests that focusing on extrinsic motives may undermine creativity only for experts or others who are invested or involved in the particular domain.

Nonexperimental research in real-world settings has illuminated the influence of social factors on creativity in school, at work, and at home. Research on school children has pointed to the importance of perceptions of autonomy for their creativity in educational settings. Research on adults in work organizations has led to the discovery of a set of environmental factors that undermine creativity; many of these factors are consistent with those uncovered in previous experimental research. This research in organizations has also led to the discovery of a set of environmental factors that support creativity. Family environments conducive to creativity seem to be marked by autonomy supports, encouragement of intrinsic engagement in activities, and practice of creativity-relevant processes.

Finally, research has revealed that prior creative activity can have a positive impact on learning, intrinsic motivation, and subsequent creativity in the absence of extrinsic pressures. Similarly, engaging in playful activities or fantasy can have a positive effect, possibly by the active engagement of creativity-relevant processes.

Next Steps in Research

Perhaps it is unusual for psychological researchers to continue to focus their attention on a particular problem area for over twenty years. We have done so because every new study we undertake in creativity reveals a new set of fascinating and challenging questions. We outline here only those that we currently consider the most intriguing theoretically or the most pressing for practical application.

Several questions remain about the specific social factors of evaluation, reward, competition, and time.

Evaluation. What individual traits and motivations might immunize individuals against the potential negative effects of external evaluation on their creativity? What are the mechanisms by which such immunization operates? Why might highly skilled individuals be more susceptible to the undermining effects of evaluation? What are the critical components of evaluative communications that can render them supportive of or detrimental to intrinsic motivation and creativity?

Reward. If the impact of reward on creativity depends on the salience of intrinsic and extrinsic motivation, how can intrinsic motivation be kept salient (and extrinsic motivation be diminished) over long periods of time? How, specifically, can rewards be presented so that they signify competence rather than external control? Under what conditions will rewards be perceived as enabling rather than controlling?

Competition. If it is reliably demonstrated that local competition undermines creativity but competition between isolated groups supports creativity, by what mechanisms might these effects occur? What are the boundaries across which competitors are perceived as "local"?

Time. How does time pressure influence creativity? Although previous research (Amabile, DeJong, & Lepper, 1976) demonstrated that deadlines reduce intrinsic motivation, creativity research has not demonstrated consistent negative effects. Indeed, under some conditions the effect might be positive (Amabile, Conti, Coon, Lazenby, & Herron, in press; Amabile & S. Gryskiewicz, 1987).

A number of research questions focus on motivation and the ways in which intrinsic and extrinsic motivation might affect creativity. Is stable, personality-trait motivational orientation (intrinsic or extrinsic) more strongly predictive of creativity than situation-specific state motivation? What is the relationship between trait and state motivation? What is the nature of "synergistic" extrinsic motivators, and how do they influence creativity? Do intrinsic and extrinsic motivation exert different influences at different stages of the creative process? Are they differentially important at different stages? Will it be possible to clearly identify different stages of the creative process in naturalistic studies?

Although much is now known about general social influences in real-world settings, more detailed information is required for the specification of comprehensive methods for maintaining and enhancing creativity. What are the specific daily social-environmental events that influence adults' work motivation and overall perceptions of the work environment, ultimately influencing their creativity? What are the specific daily social-environmental events that influence children's motivation and overall perceptions of the classroom environment, ultimately influencing their creativity? What social conditions and cognitive activities will be most conducive to the active engagement of creativity-relevant processes?

Finally, our preliminary research on mechanisms has only begun to address a question that is crucial for future development of creativity theory: What are the specific cognitive and affective mechanisms by which social factors and motivational orientations affect creative behavior?

Theoretical Advances

The componential model of creativity proposed in the 1983 edition highlighted a creativity component—intrinsic task motivation—and a class of creativity influences—social-environmental factors—that had been largely neglected in the prior literature. Moreover, it was the first model to propose specific links between the components of creativity and the stages of the creative process. The model presented in this update (Chapter 4) follows closely from that original model, with some important modifications and expansions. These changes resulted from new empirical findings and from refinements in our conceptualization of creativity.

As points of clarification, we have now included an explicit recognition of the nonlinear nature of the creative process, we have added the social environment to the graphical depiction of the model, and we have changed the name of "creativity-relevant skills" to the broader "creativity-relevant processes."

More important, we have begun to bridge the gap between our conceptual and operational definitions of creativity. And we have expanded the range of social-environmental influences considered by the theory. In particular, we have considered how the creativity of teams (as well as individuals) can be influenced by the work environments of organizations. In a model detailed elsewhere, we have integrated individual and organizational influences into a more comprehensive model of creativity and innovation in these settings (Amabile, 1988a).

Based in large part on our recent studies of thoughts and behaviors during the creative process, we have begun to formulate a more detailed specification of the cognitive mechanisms by which motivation might influence creative performance.

Most important, however, we have revised the Intrinsic Motivation Principle of Creativity, which stood as the cornerstone for the social psychology of creativity. Although our current theoretical statement still gives primacy to the critical positive role of intrinsic motivation, it acknowledges that under certain circumstances, certain types of extrinsic motivation can add to rather than detract from creativity. We believe that investigations of such synergistic combinations of intrinsic and extrinsic motivation will yield some of the most exciting new insights—and new questions—about creativity in the coming decades.

Much still remains to be done if we hope to achieve a truly comprehensive theoretical model of creativity. We must move beyond individual psychology, as we have tried to do with our recent work on the creativity of individuals and teams in organizations, and as other theorists have tried to do in their consideration of the influence of domains, fields, social forces, and historical forces on the creative productivity of entire cultures and subcultures (e.g., Csikszentmihalyi, 1988; Csikszentmihalyi & Robinson, 1986; Feldman, Csikszentmihalyi, & Gardner, 1994; Gardner, 1988; Gruber, 1988; Gruber & Davis, 1988; Harrington, 1990; Simonton, 1989a). We must consider the impact of social influences not only on the individual's creative work but also on the ultimate acceptance and success of that creative work; in other words, we must consider innovation as well as creativity. Finally, we must look at creativity not only as a dependent variable but as an independent variable, considering the impact of creativity on the individual and the society.

Conclusion

Changing the title of a book is a decision that cannot be taken lightly. *The Social Psychology of Creativity* has become *Creativity in Context* in recognition of the qualitative change that has been brought about by the new theoretical and empirical work described in this update. Although this work is still firmly grounded in the immediate social context and in social psychological processes, work over the past twelve years has represented more than a continuing accumulation of evidence on the same questions. Rather, it has broadened the perspective on creativity to a more comprehensive examination of influences and a more integrative set of explanations—leading, we hope, to even broader investigations and ever more useful integrations. In that sense, the new title is both a description of current knowledge and a wish for future advances.

References to the 1983 Edition

Adams, J. C. The relative effects of various testing atmospheres on spontaneous flexibility: A factor of divergent thinking. *Journal of Creative Behavior,* 1968, *2,* 187–194.

Albert, R. S. Family positions and the attainment of eminence: A study of special family experiences. *Gifted Child Quarterly,* 1980, *24,* 87–95.

Allen, W. *Writers on writing.* London: Phoenix House, 1948.

Allport, F. H. *Social psychology.* Boston: Houghton-Mifflin, 1924.

Amabile, T. M. Effects of external evaluation on artistic creativity. *Journal of Personality and Social Psychology,* 1979, *37,* 221–233.

Amabile, T. M. Children's artistic creativity: Detrimental effects of competition in a field setting. *Personality and Social Psychology Bulletin,* 1982, *8,* 573–578. (a)

Amabile, T. M. Social psychology of creativity: A consensual assessment technique. *Journal of Personality and Social Psychology,* 1982, *43,* 997–1013. (b)

Amabile, T. M. Social psychology of creativity: A componential conceptualization. *Journal of Personality and Social Psychology,* 1983, *45,* 357–377.

Amabile, T.M. Motivation and creativity: Effects of motivational orientation on creative writers. *Journal of Personality and Social Psychology,* 1985, *48,* 393–399.

Amabile, T. M., DeJong, W., & Lepper, M. Effects of externally imposed deadlines on subsequent intrinsic motivation. Journal of Personality and Social Psychology, 1976, 34, 92–98.

Amabile, T. M., & Gitomer, J. Children's artistic creativity: Effects of choice in task materials. *Personality and Social Psychology Bulletin,* 1984, *10,* 209–215.

Amabile, T. M., Goldberg, N., & Capotosto, D. *Effects of reward and choice on adults' artistic creativity.* Unpublished manuscript, Brandeis University, 1982.

Amabile, T. M., Goldfarb, P., & Brackfield, S. C. Social influences on creativity: Evaluation, coaction, and surveillance. *Creativity Research Journal,* 1990, *3,* 6–21.

Amabile, T. M., & Stubbs, M. L. (Eds.). *Psychological research in the classroom.* Elmsford, N.Y.: Pergamon, 1982.

Amabile, T. M., & Zingmond, R. *Deadlines, type A syndrome, and creativity.* Unpublished manuscript, Brandeis University, 1982.

Anderson, B. F. *The complete thinker.* Englewood Cliffs, N.J.: Prentice-Hall, 1980.

Andrews, F. M. Social and psychological factors which influence the creative process. In I. A. Taylor & J. W. Getzels (Eds.), *Perspectives in creativity.* Chicago: Aldine, 1975.

Andry, R. G. *The short-term prisoner.* London: Stevens & Sons, 1963.

Bahrick, H. P., Fitts, P. M., & Rankin, R. E. Effects of incentive upon reactions to peripheral stimuli. *Journal of Experimental Psychology,* 1952, *44,* 400–406.

Bain, A. *The senses and intellect* (3rd ed.). New York: Appleton, 1874.

Baker, M. Teacher creativity and its relationship to the recognition of student creativity. *Creative Child & Adult Quarterly,* 1978, *3,* 106–115.

Baker, M. Teacher creativity and its effect on student creativity. *Creative Child & Adult Quarterly,* 1979, *4,* 20–29.

Bandura, A. *Principles of behavior modification.* New York: Holt, Rinehart, & Winston, 1969.

Bandura, A., & Walters, R. H. *Social learning and personality development.* New York: Holt, Rinehart, & Winston, 1963.

Barron, F. The disposition toward originality. *Journal of Abnormal and Social Psychology,* 1955a, *51,* 478–485.

Barron, F. Threshold for the perception of human movement in inkblots. *Journal of Consulting Psychology,* 1955b, *19,* 33–38.

Barron, F. Creative vision and expression in writing and painting. In *Conference on the creative person.* Berkeley: University of California, Institute of Personality Assessment and Research, 1961.

Barron, F. Creativity. In A. Deutsch (Ed.), *The encyclopedia of mental health* (Vol. II). New York: Franklin Watts, 1963.

Barron, F. The psychology of creativity. In T. Newcomb (Ed.), *New directions in psychology* (Vol 2). New York: Holt, Rinehart, & Winston, 1965.

Barron, F. *Creativity and personal freedom.* New York: Van Nostrand, 1968.

Bastos, L. D. An evaluation of the Torrance tests of creative thinking. *Dissertation Abstracts International,* January 1974, *34,* 3976–3977.

Bayard De Volo, C. L., & Fiebert, M. S. Creativity in the preschool child and its relationship to parental authoritarianism. *Perceptual & Motor Skills,* 1977, *45,* 170.

Belcher, T. L. Modeling original divergent responses: An initial investigation. *Journal of Educational Psychology,* 1975, *67,* 351–358.

Bem, D. Self-perception theory. In L. Berkowitz (Ed.), *Advances in experimental social psychology* (Vol. 6). New York: Academic Press, 1972.

Berglas, S., Amabile, T. M., & Handel, M. *Effects of evaluation on children's artistic creativity.* Unpublished manuscript, Brandeis University, 1981.

Bergman, J. Energy levels: An important factor in identifying and facilitating the development of giftedness in young children. *Creative Child & Adult Quarterly,* 1979, *4,* 181–188.

Berkowitz, W. R., & Avril, G. J. Short-term sensory enrichment and artistic creativity. *Perceptual & Motor Skills,* 1969, *28,* 275–279.

Berlyne, D. E. *Conflict, arousal, and curiosity.* New York: McGraw-Hill, 1960.

Berlyne, D. E. *Structure and direction in thinking.* New York: Wiley, 1965.

Berman, L. M. *Overinclusion and the creative product: An investigation of psychotic populations.* Unpublished honors thesis, Brandeis University, 1981.

Biller, H. B., Singer, D. L., & Fullerton, M. Sex-role development and creative potential in kindergarten-age boys. *Developmental Psychology,* 1969, *1,* 291–296.

Birch, H. G. The role of motivational factors in insightful problem-solving. *Journal of Comparative Psychology.* 1945, *38,* 295–317.

Bloom, B. S. Report on creativity research at the University of Chilcago. In C. Taylor (Ed.), *The 1955 University of Utah research conference on the identification of creative scientific talent.* Salt Lake City: University of Utah Press, 1956.

Bloom, B. S., & Sosniak, L. A. Talent development vs. schooling. *Educational Leadership,* 1981, 86–94.

Boersma, F. J., & O'Bryan, K. An investigation of the relationship between creativity and intelligence under two conditions of testing. *Journal of Personality,* 1968, *36,* 341–348.

Boring, E. Great men and scientific progress. *Proceedings of the American Philosophical Society,* 1950, *94,* 339–351.

Bowers, P. Hypnosis and creativity: The search for the missing link. *Journal of Abnormal Psychology,* 1979, *88,* 564–572.

Brackfield, S. C. *Audience effects on artistic creativity.* Unpublished honors thesis, Brandeis University, 1980.

Brill, A. A. (Ed.). *The basic writings of Sigmund Freud.* New York: Random House, 1938.

Brown, F. Bereavement and lack of a parent in childhood. In E. Miller (Ed.), *Foundations of child psychiatry.* Oxford, England: Pergamon, 1968.

Brown, G. I., & Gaynor, D. Athletic action as creativity. *Journal of Creative Behavior,* 1967, *2,* 155–162.

Bruner, J. The conditions of creativity. In H. Gruber, G. Terrell, & M. Wertheimer (Eds.), *Contemporary approaches to creative thinking.* New York: Atherton Press, 1962.

Bruner, J. S. The nature and uses of immaturity. *American Psychologist,* 1972, *27,* 687–708.

Calder, B., & Staw, B. Self-perception of intrinsic and extrinsic motivation. *Journal of Personality and Social Psychology,* 1975, *31,* 599–605.

Campbell, D. P. *Take the road to creativity and get off your dead end.* Allen, Texas: Argus, 1977.

Campbell, D. Blind variation and selective retention in creative thought as in other knowledge processes. *Psychological Review,* 1960, *67,* 380–400.

Campbell, J. A., & Willis, J. Modifying components of creative behavior in the natural environment. *Behavior Modification,* 1978, *2,* 549–564.

Carlsmith, J. M., Ellsworth, P., & Aronson, E. *Methods of research in social psychology.* Reading, Mass.: Addison-Wesley, 1976.

Cashdan, S., & Welsh, G. S. Personality correlates of creative potential in talented high school students. *Journal of Personality,* 1966, *34,* 445–455.

Castle, C. A statistical study of eminent women. *Columbia University contributions to philosophy and psychology,* 1913, *22,* 1.

Cattell, J. McK. A statistical study of eminent men. *Popular Science Monthly,* 1903, *62,* 359–377.

Cattell, R. B. The personality and motivation of the researcher from measurements of contemporaries and from biography. In C. W. Taylor (Ed.), *The Third (1959) University of Utah Research Conference on the Identification of Creative Scientific Talent.* Salt Lake City: University of Utah Press, 1959, 77–93.

Cattell, R. B., & Butcher, H. J. *The prediction of achievement and creativity.* New York: Bobbs-Merrill, 1968.

Cattell, R. B., & Eber, H. *Handbook for the sixteen personality factor questionnaire.* Champaign, Illinois: IPAT, 1968.

Chambers, J. A. Relating personality and biographical factors to scientific creativity. *Psychological Monographs,* 1964, *78,* (7, Whole No. 584).

Chambers, J. A. College teachers: Their effect on creativity of students. *Journal of Educational Psychology,* 1973, *65,* 326–334.

Chatterjea, R. G., & Mitra, A. A study of brainstorming. *Manas,* 1976, *23,* 23–28.

Check, J. F. *An Analysis of differences in creative ability between white and negro students, public, and parochial, three different grade levels, and males and females. Final Report.* Washington, D.C.: Office of Education, 1969.

Child, D., & Croucher, A. Divergent thinking and ability: Is there a threshold? *Educational Studies,* 1977, *3,* 101–110.

Christensen, R. R., Guilford, J. P., & Wilson, R. C. Relations of creative response to working time instructions. *Journal of Experimental Psychology,* 1957, *53,* 92–98.

Cicirelli, V. G. Sibling constellation, creativity, IQ, and academic achievement. *Child Development,* 1967, *38,* 481–490.

Condry, J. Enemies of exploration: Self-initiated versus other-initiated learning. *Journal of Personality and Social Psychology,* 1977, *35,* 459–477.

Cortes, J. B., & Gatti, F. M. *Delinquency and crime: A biopsychosocial approach.* New York: Seminar Press, 1972.

Cottrell, N. B. Performance in the presence of other human beings: Mere presence, audience, and affiliation effects. In E. C. Simmel, R. A. Hoppe, & G. A. Milton (Eds.), *Social facilitation and imitative behavior.* Boston: Allyn & Bacon, 1968.

Cottrell, N. B., Wack, D. L., Sekerak, G. J., & Rittle, R. H. Social facilitation of dominant responses by the presence of an audience and the mere presence of others. *Journal of Personality and Social Psychology,* 1968, *9,* 245–250.

Covington, M. V., Crutchfield, R. S., Davies, L., & Olton, R. M. *The productive thinking program.* Columbus: Charles E. Merrill, 1972.

Cox, C. *Genetic studies of genius, Vol. II. The early mental traits of three hundred geniuses.* Stanford, California: Stanford University Press, 1926.

Cropley, A. *Creativity.* Longmans, Green, 1967.

Crutchfield, R. S. Conformity and character. *American Psychologist,*1955, *10,* 191–198.

Crutchfield, R. S. Personal and situational factors in conformity to group pressure. *Acta Psychologica,* 1959, *15,* 386–388.

Crutchfield, R. S. The creative process. In *Proceedings of the Conference on "The Creative Person,"* University of California Alumni Center, Lake Tahoe, 1961, VI–1–VI–16.

Crutchfield, R. Conformity and creative thinking. In H. Gruber, G. Terrell, & M. Wertheimer (Eds.), *Contemporary approaches to creative thinking.* New York: Atherton Press, 1962.

Csikszentmihalyi, M. *Beyond boredom and amxiety.* San Francisco: Jossey-Bass, 1975.

Csikszentmihalyi, M. Intrinsic rewards and emergent motivation. In M. Lepper, & D. Green (Eds.), *The hidden costs of reward.* Hillsdale, N.J.: Lawrence Erlbaum Associates, 1978.

Dansky, J. Make-believe: A mediator of the relationship between play and associative fluency. *Child Development,* 1980, *51,* 576–579.

Dansky, J., & Silverman, I. Effects of play on associative fluency in preschool-aged children. *Developmental Psychology,* 1973, *9,* 38–43.

Dansky, J., & Silverman, I. Play: A general facilitator of fluency. *Developmental Psychology,* 1975, *11,* 104.

Dashiell, J. F. An experimental analysis of some group effects. *Journal of Abnormal and Social Psychology,* 1930, *25,* 190–199.

Datta, L. E. Birth order and potential scientific creativity. *Sociometry,* 1968, *31,* 76–88.

Datta, L. E., & Parloff, M. B. On the relevance of autonomy: Parent-child relationship and early scientific creativity. *Proceedings of the 75th Annual Convention of the American Psychological Association,* 1967, *2,* 149–150.

Davis, G. A., & Rimm, S. Characteristics of creatively gifted children. *Gifted Child Quarterly,* 1977, *21,* 546–551.

Davis, G. A., & Subkoviak, M. J. Multidimensional analysis of a personality-based test of creative potential. *Journal of Educational Measurement*, 1975, *12*, 37–43.

deBono, E. *Lateral thinking for management*. New York: American Management Association, 1971.

deCharms, R. *Personal causation*. New York: Academic Press, 1968.

Deci, E. Effects of externally mediated rewards on intrinsic motivation. *Journal of Personality and Social Psychology*, 1971, *18*, 105–115.

Deci, E. Intrinsic motivation, extrinsic reinforcement, and inequity. *Journal of Personality and Social Psychology*, 1972, *22*, 113–120. (a)

Deci, E. The effects of contingent and noncontingent rewards and controls on intrinsic motivation. *Organizational Behavior and Human Performance*, 1972, *8*, 217–229. (b)

Deci, E. *Intrinsic motivation*. New York: Plenum, 1975.

Deci, E. L. *The psychology of self-determination*. Lexington, Mass.: D. C. Heath, Lexington Books, 1980.

Deci, E. L., Cascio, W. F., & Krussell, J. *Sex differences, Positive feedback, in intrinsic motivation*. Paper presented at the meeting of the Eastern Psychological Association, Washington, D.C., May 1973.

Deci, E. L., Nezlek, J., & Sheinman, L. Characteristics of the rewarder and intrinsic motivation of the rewardee. *Journal of Personality and Social Psychology*, in press.

Deci, E. L., & Ryan, R. M. The empirical exploration of intrinsic motivational processes. In L. Berkowitz (Ed.), *Advances in experimental social psychology*. New York: Academic Press, 1980.

Dennis, W. Creative productivity between the ages of 20 and 80 years. *Journal of Gerontology*, 1966, *21*, 106–114.

Dentler, R. A., & Mackler, B. Originality: Some social and personal determinants. *Behavioral Science*, 1964, *9*, 1–7.

Dewing, K. The reliability and validity of selected tests of creative thinking in a sample of seventh-grade West Australian children. *British Journal of Educational Psychology*, 1970, *40*, 35–42.

Dewing, K., & Taft, R. Some characteristics of the parents of creative twelve-year olds. *Journal of Personalilty*, 1973, *41*, 71–85.

DiVitto, B., & McArthur, L. Z. Developmental differences in the use of distinctiveness, consensus, and consistency information for making causal attributions. *Developmental Psychology*, 1978, *14*, 474–482.

Dixon, J. Quality versus quantity: The need to control lfor the fluency factor in originality scores from the Torrance tests. *Journal for the Education of the Gifted*, 1979, *2*, 70–79.

Domino, G. Maternal personality correlates of sons' creativity. *Journal of Consulting & Clinical Psychology*, 1969, *33*, 180–183.

Domino, G. Assessment of cinematographic creativity. *Journal of Personality and Social Psychology*, 1974, *30*, 150–154.

Drevdahl, J. E. Some developmental and environmental factors in creativity. In C. Taylor (Ed.), *Widening horizons in creativity*. New York: Wiley, 1964.

Drews, E. M. A critical evaluation of approaches to the identification of gifted students. In A. Traxler (Ed.), *Measurement and evaluation in today's schools*. Washington, D.C.: American Council on Education, 1961.

DuCette, J., Wolk, S., Friedman, S. Locus of control and creativity in black and white children. *Journal of Social Psychology*, 1972, *88*, 297–298.

Duncker, K. On problem solving, *Psychological Monographs*, 1945, *58*, no. 270.

Einstein, A. Autobiography. In P. Schilpp, *Albert Einstein: Philosopher-scientist*. Evanston, Illinois: Library of Living Philosophers Inc., 1949.

Eisenman, R. Birth order and artistic creativity. *Journal of Individual Psychology*, 1964, *20*, 183–185.

Eisenman, R. Creativity change in student nurses: A cross-sectional and longitudinal study. *Developmental Psychology*, 1970, *3*, 320–325.

Eisenman, R., & Schussel, N. R. Creativity, birth order, and preference for symmetry. *Journal of Consulting & Clinical Psychology*, 1970, *34*, 275–280.

Eisner, E. A typology of creative behavior in the visual arts. *American Educational Research Journal*, 1965, *2*, 125–136.

El Dreny, H. The influence of dyadic interaction on originality, states of feeling and attention. *Creative Child & Adult Quarterly*, 1979, *4*, 93–98.

Ellison, R. L. *The relationship of certain biographical information to success in science*. Master's thesis, University of Utah, Salt Lake City, 1960.

Evans, T. D. Creativity, sex-role socialisation and pupil-teacher interactions in early schooling. *Sociological Review*, 1979, *27*, 139–155.

Farnsworth, R. R. *The social psychology of music*. Ames, Iowa: Iowa State University Press, 1969.

Farr, J. L. Task characteristics, reward contingency, and intrinsic motivation. *Organizational Behavior and Human Performance*, 1976, *16*, 294–307.

Feingold, B. D., Mahoney, M. J. Reinforcement effects on intrinsic interst: Undermining the overjustification hypothesis. *Behavior Therapy*, 1975, *6*, 367–377.

Feitelson, D., & Ross, G. S. The neglected factor: Play. *Human Development*, 1973, *16*, 202–223.

Feldhusen, J. F., Treffinger, D. J., & Bahlke, S. J. Developing creative thinking: The Purdue Creativity Program. *Journal of Creative Behavior*, 1970, *4*, 85–90.

Feldman, D. H., Marrinan, B. M., & Hartfeldt, S. D. Transformational power as a possible index of creativity. *Psychological Reports*, 1972, *30*, 335–338.

Feldman, D. *Beyond universals in cognitive development*. Norwood, N.J.: Ablex, 1980.

Folger, R., Rosenfield, D., & Hays, R. P. Equity and intrinsic motivation: The role of choice. *Journal of Personality and Social Psychology*, 1978, *36*, 557–564.

Friedman, F., Raymond, B. A., & Feldhusen, J. F. The effects of environmental scanning on creativity. *Gifted Child Quarterly*, 1978, *22*, 248–251.

Fuerst, K., & Zubek, J. P. Effects of sensory and perceptual deprivation on a battery of open-ended cognitive tasks. *Canadian Journal of Psychology*, 1968, *22*, 122–130.

Gakhar, S., & Luthra, S. The test-retest reliability of Torrance tests of verbal creative thinking in a sample of ninth and tenth grade Indian children. *Journal of the Indian Academy of Applied Psychology*, 1973, *10*, 48–52.

Galton, F. *Hereditary genius*. London: MacMillan, London, & Appleton, 1870.

Garbarino, J. The impact of anticipated reward upon cross-age tutoring. *Journal of Personality and Social Psychology*, 1975, *32*, 421–428.

Garfield, S. J., Cohen, H. A., & Roth, R. M. Creativity and mental health. *Journal of Educational Research*, 1969, *63*, 147–149.

Gary, A. L., & Glover, J. Eye color and sex: Their relationship to modeled learning. *Psychotherapy: Theory, Research & Practice*, 1975, *12*, 425–428.

Geen, R. G., & Gange, J. J. Drive theory of social facilitation: Twelve years of theory and research. *Psychological Bulletin,* 1977, *84,* 1267–1288.

Gergen, K. J. *Toward transformation in social knowledge.* New York: Springer-Verlag, 1982.

Getzels, J. W. Problem-finding and the inventiveness of solutions. *Journal of Creative Behavior,* 1975, *9,* 12–18.

Getzels, J., & Csikszentmihalyi, M. *The creative vision: A longitudinal study of problem-finding in art.* New York: Wiley-Interscience, 1976.

Getzels, J. W., & Jackson, P. W. Family environment and cognitive style: A study of the sources of highly intelligent and of highly creative adolescents. *American Sociological Review,* 1961, *26,* 351–359.

Getzels, J., & Jackson, P. *Creativity and intelligence: Explorations with gifted students.* New York: Wiley, 1962.

Ghiselin, B. Ultimate criteria for two levels of creativity. In C. Taylor & F. Barron (Eds.), *Scientific creativity: Its recognition and development.* New York: Wiley. 1963.

Ghiselin, B., Rompel, R., & Taylor, C. W. A creative process check list: Its development and validation. In C. W. Taylor (Ed.), *Widening horizons in creativity.* New York: Wiley, 1964.

Glover, J. A. Risky shift and creativity. *Social Behavior & Personality,* 1977, *5,* 317–320.

Glover, J. A. A creativity-training workshop: Short-term, long-term, and transfer effects. *Journal of Genetic Psychology,* 1980, *136,* 3–16.

Glover, J., & Gary, A. L. Procedures to increase some aspects of creativity. *Journal of Applied Behavior Analysis,* 1976, *9,* 79–84.

Glover, J. A., & Sautter, F. Relation of four components of creativity to risk-taking preferences. *Psychological Reports,* 1977, *41,* 227–230.

Glucksberg, S. The influence of strength of drive on functional fixedness and perceptual recognition. *Journal of Experimental Psychology,* 1962, *63,* 36–41.

Glucksberg, S. Problem-solving: Response competition and the influence of drive. *Psychological Reports,* 1964, *15,* 939–942.

Glueck, S., & Glueck, E. T. *Five hundred delinquent women.* New York: Knopf, 1934.

Goetz, E. M. The effects of minimal praise on the creative blockbuilding of three year olds. *Child Study Journal,* 1981, *11,* 55–67.

Golann, S. E. Psychological study of creativity. *Psychological Bulletin,* 1963, *60,* 548–565.

Goolsby, T. M., & Helwig, L. D. Concurrent validity of the Torrance tests of creative thinking and the Welsh figural preference test. *Educational & Psychological Measurement,* 1975, *35,* 507–508.

Gordon, W. *Synectics: The development of creative capacity.* New York: Harper & Row, 1961.

Gough, H. G. *The California Psychological Inventory.* Palo Alto, Calif.: Consulting Psychologists Press, 1957.

Gough, H. G. A creative personality scale for the adjective check list. *Journal of Personality & Social Psychology,* 1979, *37,* 1398–1405.

Gough, H. G., & Heilbrun, A. B., Jr. *The adjective check list manual.* Palo Alto, Calif.: Consulting Psychologists Press, 1965.

Goyal, R. P. Creativity and school climate: An exploratory study. *Journal of Psychological Researches,* 1973, *17,* 77–80.

Graham, S. *The real F. Scott Fitzgerald.* New York: Grosset & Dunlap, 1976.

Grant, T. N., & Domino, D. Masculinity-feminity in fathers of creative male adolescents. *Journal of Genetic Psychology,* 1976, *129,* 19–27.

Greene, D., & Leeper, M. Effects of extrinsic rewards on children's subsequent intrinsic interest. *Child Development,* 1974, *45,* 1141–1145.

Gruber, H. E., & Barrett, P. H. *Darwin on man: A psychological study of scientific creativity.* New York: E. P. Dutton, 1974.

Guilford, J. P. Creativity. *American Psychologist,* 1950, *5,* 444–454.

Guilford, J. P. The structure of intellect. *Psychological Bulletin,* 1956, *53,* 267–293.

Guilford, J. P. Intellectual resources and their values as seen by scientists. In C. W. Taylor & F. Barron (Eds.), *Scientific creativity: Its recognition and development.* New York: Wiley, 1963.

Guilford, J. P. *The nature of human intelligence.* New York: McGraw-Hill, 1967.

Gurman, E. B. Creativity as a function of orientation and group participation. *Psychological Reports,* 1968, *22,* 471–478.

Haddon, F. A., & Lytton, H. Teaching approach and the development of divergent thinking abilities in primary schools. *British Journal of Educational Psychology,* 1968, *38,* 171–180.

Haddon, F. A., & Lytton, H. Primary education and divergent thinking abilities: Four years on. *British Journal of Educational Psychology,* 1971, *41,* 136–147.

Halpin, G., & Halpin, G. The effect of motivation on creative thinking abilities. *Journal of Creative Behavior,* 1973, *7,* 51–53.

Halpin, G., Halpin, G., Miller, E., & Landreneau, E. Observer characteristics related to the imitation of a creative model. *Journal of Psychology,* 1979, *102,* 133–142.

Halpin, W. G. A study of the life histories and creative abilities of potential teachers (Doctoral dissertation, University of Georgia, 1972). *Dissertation Abstracts International,* 1973, *33,* 3382A.

Hamner, W. C., & Foster, L. W. Are intrinsic and extrinsic rewards additive: A test of Deci's cognitive evaluation theory of task motivation. *Organizational Behavior and Human Performance,* 1975, *14,* 398–415.

Harackiewicz, J. M. The effects of reward contingency and performance feedback on intrinsic motivation. *Journal of Personality and Social Psychology,* 1979, *37,* 1352–1363.

Harlow, H. F. Learning and satiation of response in intrinsically motivated complex puzzle performance by monkeys. *Journals of Comparative Physiological Psychology,* 1950, *43,* 289–294.

Harlow, H., Harlow, M., & Meyer, D. Learning motivated by a manipulation drive. *Journal of Experimental Psychology,* 1950, *40,* 228–234.

Harris, M. B., & Evans, R. C. Models and creativity. *Psychological Reports,* 1973, *33,* 763–769.

Harris, M. B., & Evans, R. C. The effects of modeling and instructions on creative responses. *Journal of Psychology,* 1974, *86,* 123–130.

Harter, S. Effectance motivation reconsidered: Toward a developmental model. *Human Development,* 1978, *21,* 34–64.

Harter, S. A new self-report scale of intrinsic versus extrinsic orientation in the classroom: Motivational and informational components. *Developmental Psychology,* 1981, *17,* 300–312.

Hattie, J. A. Conditions for administering creativity tests. *Psychological Bulletin,* 1977, *84,* 1249–1260.

Hebb, D. O. Drives and the CNS. *Psychological Review,* 1955, *62,* 243–254.

Heist, P. (Ed.). *The creative college student: An unmet challenge.* San Francisco: Jossey-Bass, 1968.

Heist, P., & Yonge, G. *Manual for the omnibus personality inventory—Form F.* New York: The Psychological Corporation, 1968.

Helson, R. Childhood interest clusters related to creativity in women. *Journal of Consulting Psychology,* 1965, *29,* 352–361.

Helson, R. Effects of sibling characteristics and parental values on creative interest and achievement. *Journal of Personality,* 1968, *36,* 589–607.

Helson, R., & Crutchfield, R. Mathematicians: The creative researcher and the average Ph.D. *Journal of Consulting and Clinical Psychology,* 1970, *3,* 250–257.

Henchy, T., & Glass, D. C. Evaluation apprehension and the social facilitation of dominant and subordinate responses. *Journal of Personality and Social Psychology,* 1968, *10,* 446–454.

Hennessey, B. *Effects of reward and task label on children's creativity in three domains.* Unpublished manuscript, Brandeis University, 1982.

Hershey, M., & Kearns, P. The effect of guided fantasy on the creative thinking and writing ability of gifted students. *Gifted Child Quarterly,* 1979, *23,* 71–77.

Higgins, E. T., & Chaires, W. M. Accessibility of interrelational constructs: Implications for stimulus encoding and creativity. *Journal of Experimental Social Psychology,* 1980, *16,* 348–361.

Hilgard, E., & Bower, G. *Theories of learning* (4th ed.). Englewood Cliffs, N.J.: Prentice-Hall, 1975.

Hocevar, D. A comparison of statistical infrequency and subjective judgment as criteria in the measurement of originality. *Journal of Personality Assessment,* 1979, *43,* 297–299. (a)

Hocevar, D. The unidimensional nature of creative thinking in fifth grade children. *Child Study Journal,* 1979, *9,* 273–278. (b)

Hocevar, D. Ideational fluency as a confounding factor in the measurement of originality. *Journal of Educational Psychology,* 1979, *71,* 191–196. (c)

Hocevar, D. Measurement of creativity: Review and critique. *Journal of Personality Assessment,* 1981, *45,* 450–464.

Hogarth, R. *Judgement and choice.* Chichester: Wiley, 1980.

Holland, J. L. Test reviews. *Journal of Counseling Psychology,* 1968, *15,* 297–298.

Holland, J. L., U Astin, A. W. *The prediction of academic, artistic, scientific, and special achievement among undergraduates of superior scholastic aptitude.* Evanston, Ill.: National Merit Scholarship Corp., 1961.

Holton, G. On trying to understand scientific genius. *American Scholar,* 1972, *41,* 95–110.

Horwitz, R. A. Psychological effects of the open classroom. *Review of Educational Research,* 1979, *49,* 71–85.

Hughes, T., & McCullough, F. (Eds.). *The journals of Sylvia Plath.* New York: Dial, 1982.

Hunt, J. McV. Intrinsic motivation and its role in psycholological development. In D. Levine (Ed.), *Nebraska Symposium on Motivation* (Vol. 13). Lincoln: University of Nebraska Press, 1965.

Husband, R. W. Analysis of methods in human maze learning. *Journal of Genetic Psychology,* 1931, *39,* 258–277.

Hyman, R. *Some experiments in creativity.* New York: General Electric, 1960.

Hyman, R. Creativity and the prepared mind: The role of information and induced attitudes. In C. W. Taylor (Ed.), *Widening horizons in creativity.* New York: Wiley, 1964.

Hyman, R. B. Creativity in open and traditional classrooms. *Elementary School Journal,* 1978, *78,* 266–274.

Institute for Behavioral Research in Creativity. *Alpha Biographical Inventory.* Greensboro, N. Car.: Prediction Press, 1968.

Ironson, G. H., & Davis, G. A. Faking high or low creativity scores on the adjective check list. *Journal of Creative Behavior,* 1979, *13,* 139–145.

Jackson, P., & Messick, S. The person, the product and the response: Conceptual problems in the assessment of creativity. *Journal of Personality,* 1965, *33,* 309–329.

Jaoui, H. *Creativity and management.* Paper presented at Creativity Week III, Center for Creative Leadership, Greensboro, North Carolina, 1980.

Joesting, J. Relationship of two tests of creativity to freshman English grades, school activities, and number of absences for black college students. *Psychological Reports,* 1975, *37,* 69–70.

Johnson, R., & Thomson, C. Incidental and intentional learning under three conditions of motivation. *American Journal of Psychology,* 1962, *75,* 284–288.

Johnson, R. A. Differential effects of reward versus no-reward instructions on the creative thinking of two economic levels of elementary school children. *Journal of Educational Psychology,* 1974, *66,* 530–533.

Jordan, L. A. Use of canonical analysis in Cropley's "A five-year longitudinal study of the validity of creative tests." *Developmental Psychology,* 1975, *11,* 1–3.

Kaltsounis, B., & Higdon, G. School conformity and its relationship to creativity. *Psychological Reports,* 1977, *40,* 715–718.

Karniol, R., & Ross, M. The development of causal attributions in social perception. *Journal of Personality and Social Psychology,* 1976, *34,* 455–464.

Karniol, R., & Ross, M. The effects of performance relevant and performance irrelevant rewards on children's intrinsic motivation. *Child Development,* 1977, *48,* 482–487.

Kasperson, C. J. An analysis of the relationship between information sources and creativity in scientists and engineers. *Human Communication Research,* 1978, *4,* 113–119. (a)

Kasperson, C. J. Psychology of the scientist: XXXVII. Scientific creativity: A relationship with information channels. *Psychological Reports,* 1978, *42,* 691–694. (b)

Katona, G. *Organizing and memorizing.* New York: Columbia University Press, 1940.

Kazelskis, R. The convergent, divergent and factorial validity of the Torrance figural test of creativity. *Southern Journal of Educational Research,* 1972, *6,* 123–129.

Kelley, H. Attribution theory in social psychology. In D. Levine (Ed.), *Nebraska Symposium on Motivation,* Vol. 15. Lincoln: University of Nebraska, 1967.

Kelley, H. The processes of causal attribution. *American Psychologist,* 1973, *28,* 107–128.

Kimble, G. *Hilgard and Marquis' conditioning and learning* (2nd ed.). New York: Appleton-Century-Crofts, 1961.

Klein, P. S. Effects of open vs. structured teacher-student interaction on creativity of children with different levels of anxiety. *Psychology in the Schools,* 1975, *12,* 286–288.

Koestler, A. *The act of creation.* New York: Dell, 1964.

Korb, R., & Frankiewicz, R. G. Strategy for a priori selection of judges in a product-centered approach to assessment of creativity. *Perceptual & Motor Skills,* 1976, *42,* 107–115.

Kosslyn, S. M. *Image and mind.* Cambridge: Harvard University Press, 1980.

Kruglanski, A. W. The endogenous-exogenous partition in attribution theory. *Psychological Review,* 1975, *82,* 387–406.

Kruglanski, A. W. Endogenous attribution and intrinsic motivation. In M. Lepper & D. Greene (Eds.), *The hidden costs of reward*. Hillsdale, N.J.: Erlbaum, 1978.

Kruglanski, A. W., Alon, S., & Lewis, T. Retrospective misattribution and task enjoyment. *Journal of Experimental Social Psychology*, 1972, *8*, 493–501.

Kruglanski, A. W., Friedman, I., & Zeevi, G. The effects of extrinsic incentive on some qualitative aspects of task performance. *Journal of Personality*, 1971, *39*, 606–617.

Kruglanski, A. W., Stein, C., & Riter, A. Contingencies of exogenous reward and task performance: On the "minimax" principle in instrumental behavior. *Journal of Applied Social Psychology*, 1977, *7*, 141–148.

Kuhn, T. S. The essential tension: Tradition and innovation in scientific research. In F. Barron & C. W. Taylor (Eds.), *Scientific creativity: Its recognition and development*. New York: Wiley, 1963.

La Greca, A. M. Can children remember to be creative? An interview study of children's thinking processes. *Child Development*, 1980, *51*, 572–575.

Landreneau, E., & Halpin, G. The influence of modeling on children's creative performance. *Journal of Educational Research*, 1978, *71*, 137–139.

Langer, E. Rethinking the role of thought in social interaction. In J. Harvey, W. Ickes & R. Kidd (Eds.), *New directions in attribution research*. Hillsdale, N.J.: Lawrence Erlbaum Associates, 1978.

Langer, E., & Imber, L. When practice makes imperfect: Debilitating effects of overlearning. *Journal of Personality and Social Psychology*, 1979, *37*, 2014–2024.

Lax, E. *On being funny: Woody Allen and comedy*. New York: Manor Books, 1975.

Lehman, H. *Age and achievement*. Princeton, N.J.: Princeton University Press, 1953.

Lepper, M., & Greene, D. Turning play into work: Effects of adult surveillance and extrinsic rewards on children's intrinsic motivation. *Journal of Personality and Social Psychology*, 1975, *31*, 479–486.

Lepper, M., & Greene, D. Overjustification research and beyond: Toward a means-end analysis of intrinsic and extrinsic motivation. In M. Lepper & D. Greene (Eds.), *The hidden costs of reward*. Hillsdale, N.J.: Lawrence Erlbaum Associates, 1978. (a)

Lepper, M., & Greene, D. (Eds.), *The hidden costs of reward*. Hillsdale, N.J.: Lawrence Erlbaum Associates, 1978. (b)

Lepper, M., Greene, D., & Nisbett, R. Undermining children's intrinsic interest with extrinsic rewards: A test of the "overjustification" hypothesis. *Journal of Personality and Social Psychology*, 1973, *28*, 129–137.

Lepper, M. R., Sagotsky, G., Dafoe, J. L., & Greene, D. Consequences of superfluous social constraints: Effects on young children's social inferences and subsequent intrinsic interest. *Journal of Personality and Social Psychology*, 1982, *42*, 51–65.

Levine, J. *Motivation in humor*. New York: Atherton, 1969.

Lewis, H., & Mussen, P. *Criteria for evaluation of children's artistic creativity. Final Report*. University of California, Berkeley, February 1967.

Li, A. K. Effects of play on novel responses in kindergarten children. *Alberta Journal of Educational Research*, 1978, *24*, 31–36.

Lichtenwalner, J. S., & Maxwell, J. W. Te relationship of birth order and socio-economic status to the creativity of preschool children. *Child Development*, 1969, *40*, 1241–1247.

Lieberman, J. N. Playfulness and divergent thinking: An investigation of their relationship at the kindergarten level. *Journal of Genetic Psychology*, 1965, *107*, 219–224.

Lieberman, J. N. *Playfulness: Its relationship to imagination and creativity.* New York: Academic, 1977.

Locurto, C. M., & Walsh, J. F. Reinforcement and self-reinforcement: Their effects on originality. *American Journal of Psychology,* 1976, *89,* 281–291.

Loveland, K., & Olley, J. The effect of external reward on interest and quality of task performance in children of high and low intrinsic motivation. *Child Development,* 1979, *50,* 1207–1210.

Lowell, A. *Poetry and poets.* Boston: Houghton Mifflin, 1930.

Luchins, A. Mechanization in problem solving: The effect of Einstellung. *Psychological Monographs,* 1942, *54* (6, Whole No. 248).

Lynch, M. D., & Edwards, T. M. The Miniscat: Its development and some evidence of its validity. *Educational and Psychological Measurement,* 1974, *34,* 397–405.

Mach, E. On the part played by accident in invention and discovery. *Monist,* 1896, *6,* 161–175.

MacKinnon, D. W. The nature and nurture of creative talent. *American Psychologist,* 1962, *17,* 484–495.

MacKinnon, D. W. Personality and the realization of creative potential. *American Psychologist,* 1965, *20,* 273–281.

MacKinnon, D. W. IPAR's contribution to the conceptualization and study of creativity. In I. Taylor & J. Getzels (Eds.), *Perspectives in creativity.* Chicago: Aldine, 1975.

Maddi, S. R. Motivational aspects of creativity. *Journal of Personality,* 1965, *33,* 330–347.

Maddi, S. R., Charlens, A. M., Maddi, D. A., & Smith, A. J. Effects of monotony and novelty on imaginative productions. *Journal of Personality,* 1962, *30,* 513–527.

Maddi, S. R., Propst, B. S., & Feldinger, I. Three expressions of the need for variety. *Journal of Personality,* 1965, *33,* 82–98.

Maddi, S. The strenuousness of the creative life. In I. Taylor & J. Getzels (Eds.), *Perspectives in creativity.* Chicago: Aldine, 1975.

Malone, T. W. Toward a theory of intrinsically motivating instruction. *Cognitive Science,* 1981, *4,* 333–369.

Maloney, K. B., & Hopkins, B. L. The modification of sentence structure and its relationship to subjective judgments of creativity in writing. *Journal of Applied Behavior Analysis,* 1973, *6,* 425–433.

Manosevitz, M., Fling, S., & Prentice, N. M. Imaginary companions in young children: Relationships with intelligence, creativity and waiting ability. *Journal of Child Psychology and Psychiatry and Allied Disciplines,* 1977, *18,* 73–78.

Mansfield, R. S., Busse, T. V., & Krepelka, E. J. The effectiveness of creativity training. *Review of Educational Research,* 1978, *48,* 517–536.

Manske, M. E., & Davis, G. A. Effects of simple instructional biases upon performance in the unusual uses test. *Journal of General Psychology,* 1968, *79,* 25–33.

Marjoribanks, K. The statification of socialisation processes: A further analysis. *Educational Studies,* 1978, *4,* 105–110.

Matlin, M. W., & Zajonc, R. B. Social facilitation of world associations. *Journal of Personality and Social Psychology,* 1968, *10,* 455–460.

Mayer, M. *A boy, a dog, and a frog.* New York: Dial Press, 1967.

McClelland, D. C. The calculated risk: An aspect of scientific performance. In C. W. Taylor (Ed.), *The 1955 University of Utah Research Conference on the Identification of Creative Scientific Talent.* Salt Lake City: University of Utah Press, 1956.

McCormick, M., Sheehy, N., & Mitchell, J. Traditional versus open classroom structure and examiner style: The effect on creativity in children. *Child Study Journal*, 1978, *8*, 75–82.

McDermid, C. D. Some correlates of creativity in engineering personnel. *Journal of Applied Psychology*, 1965, *49*, 14–19.

McGraw, K. The detrimental effects of reward on performance: A literature review and a prediction model. In M. Lepper & D. Greene (Eds.), *The hidden costs of reward*. Hillsdale, N.J.: Lawrence Erlbaum Associates, 1978.

McGraw, K., & McCullers, J. Evidence of a detrimental effect of extrinsic incentives on breaking a mental set. *Journal of Experimental Social Psychology*, 1979, *15*, 285–294.

McGuire, W. The yin and yang of progress in social psychology: Seven koan. *Journal of Personality and Social Psychology*, 1973, *26*, 446–456.

McKim, R. H. *Experiences in visual thinking*. Monterey, Calif.: Brooks/Cole, 1972.

McNamara, H. J., & Fisch, R. I. Effect of high and low motivation on two aspects of attention. *Perceptual and Motor Skills*, 1964, *19*, 571–578.

Mednick, M. T., Mednick, S. A., & Jung, C. C. Continual association as a function of level of creativity and type of verbal stimulus. *Journal of Abnormal and Social Psychology*, 1964, *69*, 511–515.

Mednick. S. The associative basis of the creative process. *Psychological Review*, 1962, *69*, 220–232.

Mednick, S. A., & Mednick, M. T. *Manual: Remote Associates Test. Form I*. Boston: Houghton-Mifflin, 1966.

Meichenbaum, D. Enhancing creativity by modifying what subjects say to themselves. *American Educational Research Journal*, 1975, *12*, 129–145.

Milgram, R. M., & Feingold, S. Concrete and verbal reinforcement in creative thinking of disadvantaged children. *Perceptual and Motor Skills*, 1977, *45*, 675–678.

Milgram, R. M., & Milgram, N. A. Group versus individual administration in the measurement of creative thinking in gifted and nongifted children. *Child Development*, 1978, *49*, 385–388.

Milgram, R. M., & Rabkin, L. Developmental test of Mednick's associative hierarchies of original thinking. *Developmental Psychology*, 1980, *16*, 157–158.

Miller, B. C., & Gerard, D. Family influences on the development of creativity in children: An integrative review. *Family Coordinator*, 1979, *28*, 295–312.

Morgan, M. The overjustification effect: A developmental test of self-perception interpretations. *Journal of Personality and Social Psychology*, 1981, *40*, 809–821.

Mozart, W. A. A letter, 1789. In E. Holmes, *The life of Mozart and his correspondence*. London: Chapman & Hall, 1878.

Mueller, L. K. Beneficial and detrimental modeling effects on creative response production. *Journal of Psychology*, 1978, *98*, 253–260.

Murphy, R. T. Investigation of a creativity dimension. *Dissertation Abstracts International*, 1972, *33*, 2328–2329.

Nash, W. R. The effects of warm-up activities on small group divergent problem-solving with young children. *Journal of Psychology*, 1975, *89*, 237–241.

Newell, A., Shaw, J., & Simon, H. The processes of creative thinking. In H. Gruber, G. Terrell & M. Wertheimer (Eds.), *Contemporary approaches to creative thinking*. New York: Atherton Press, 1962.

Newell, A., & Simon, H. *Human problem solving*. Englewood Cliffs, N.J.: Prentice-Hall, 1972.

Nicholls, J. G. Creativity in the person who will never produce anything original and useful: The concept of creativity as a normally distributed trait. *American Psychologist,* 1972, *27,* 717–727.

Nunnally, J. *Psychometric theory.* New York: McGraw-Hill, 1967.

Oates, J. C. Stories that define me. *New York Times Book Review,* July 11, 1982, pp. 1; 15–16.

Okoh, N. Bilingualism and divergent thinking among Nigerian and Welsh school children. *Journal of Social Psychology,* 1980, *110,* 163–170.

Osborn, A. F. *Applied imagination.* New York: Scribner's. 1953.

Osborn, A. *Applied imagination: Principles and procedures of creative thinking.* New York: Scribner's, 1963.

Owens, W. A., Schumacher, C., & Clark, J. The measurement of creativity in machine design. *Journal of Applied Psychology,* 1957, *41,* 297–302.

Parish, T. S., & Eads, G. M. College students' perceptions of parental restrictiveness/permissiveness and students' scores on a brief measure of creativity. *Psychological Reports,* 1977, *41,* 455–458.

Parnes, S. *Creative behavior guidebook.* New York: Scribner's, 1967.

Parnes, S. J. A program for balanced growth. *Journal of Creative Behavior,* 1975, *9,* 23–29.

Parnes, S. J., & Meadow, A. Development of individual creative talent. In C. W. Taylor & F. Barron (Eds.), *Scientific creativity.* New York: Wiley, 1963.

Pessin, J. The comparative effects of social and mechanical stimulation on memorizing. *American Journal of Psychology,* 1933, *45,* 263–270.

Piaget, J. *Play, dreams and imitation in childhood.* New York: Norton, 1951.

Pittman, T. S., Cooper, E. E., & Smith, T. W. Attribution of causality and the overjustification effect. *Personality and Social Psychology Bulletin,* 1977, *6,* 228–233.

Pittman, T. S., Emery, J., & Boggiano, A. K. Intrinsic and extrinsic motivational orientations: Reward-induced changes in preference for complexity. *Journal of Personality and Social Psychology,* 1982, *42,* 789–797.

Poincare, H. *The foundations of science.* New York: Science Press, 1924.

Pollert, L. H., Feldhusen, J. F., Van Mondfrans, A. P., & Treffinger, D. J. Role of memory in divergent thinking. *Psychological Reports,* 1969, *25,* 151–156.

Poole, M. E., Williams, A. J., & Lett, W. R. Inner-centeredness of highly creative adolescents. *Psychological Reports,* 1977, *41,* 365–366.

Porter, L., & Lawler, E. E. *Managerial attitudes and performance.* Homewood, Ill.: Free Press, 1968.

Prentky, R. A. *Creativity and psychopathology.* New York: Praeger, 1980.

Preston, J. H. A conversation with Gertrude Stein. In B. Ghiselin (Ed.), *The creative process.* Berkeley: University of California Press, 1952.

Quinn, E. Creativity and cognitive complexity. *Social Behavior and Personality,* 1980, *8,* 213–215.

Raina, M. K. A study into the effect of competition on creativity. *Gifted Child Quarterly,* 1968, *12,* 217–220.

Ramey, C. T., & Piper, V. Creativity in open and traditional classrooms. *Child Development,* 1974, *45,* 557–560.

Reiss, S., & Sushinsky, L. W. Overjustification, competing responses, and the acquisition of intrinsic interest. *Journal of Personality and Social Psychology,* 1975, *31,* 1116–1125.

Renzulli, J. S., Owen, S. V., & Callahan, C. M. Fluency, flexibility, and originality as a function of group size. *Journal of Creative Behavior,* 1974, *8,* 107–113.

Rimm, S. GIFT: An instrument for the identification and measurement of creativity. *Dissertation Abstracts International,* 1976, *37,* (5-A) 2804.

Rimm, S., & Davis G. A. GIFT: An instrument for the identification of creativity. *Journal of Creative Behavior,* 1976, *10,* 178–182.

Rimm, S., U Davis, G. A. Five years of international research with GIFT: An instrument for the identification of creativity. *Journal of Creative Behavior,* 1980, *14,* 35–46.

Rivlin, L. G. Creativity and the self-attitudes and sociability of high school students. *Journal of Educational Psychology,* 1959, *50,* 147–152.

Roe, A. A psychologist examines sixty-four eminent scientists. *Scientific American,* 1952, *187,* 21–25.

Roe, A. A psychological study of eminent psychologists and anthropologists and a comparison with biological and physical scientists. *Psychological Monographs,* 1953, *67* (2, Whole No. 352).

Rogers, C. Towards a theory of creativity. *ETC: A Review of General Semantics,* 1954, *11,* 249–260.

Rosenthal, R., Baratz, S., Hall, C. M. Teacher behavior, teacher expectations, and gains in pupils' rated creativity. *Journal of Genetic Psychology,* 1974, *124,* 115–121.

Ross, L., Lepper, M., & Hubbard, M. Perseverance in self-perception and social perception: Biased attributional processes in the debriefing paradigm. *Journal of Personality and Social Psychology,* 1975, *32,* 880–892.

Ross, M. Salience of reward and intrinsic motivation. *Journal of Personality and Social Psychology,* 1975, *32,* 245–254.

Ross, M. The self-perception of intrinsic motivation. In J. H. Harvey, W. J. Ickes, & R. F. Kidd (Eds.), *New directions in attribution research* (Vol. 1). Hillsdale, N.J.: Erlbaum, 1977.

Roweton, W. E., et al. Indices of classroom creativity. *Child Study Journal,* 1975, *5,* 151–161.

Ryan, B. A., & Winston, A. S. Dimensions of creativity in children's drawings: A social-validation study. *Journal of Educational Psychology,* 1978, *70,* 651–656.

Salancik, G. *Retrospective attribution of past behavior and commitment to future behavior.* Unpublished manuscript, University of Illinois, 1975.

Samuelson, P. A. Economics in a golden age: A personal memoir. In G. Holton (Ed.), *The twentieth century sciences: Studies in the biography of ideas.* New York: Norton, 1972.

Sanders, S. J., Tedford, W. H., & Hardy, B. W. Effects of musical stimuli on creativity. *Psychological Record,* 1977, *27,* 463–471.

Santrock, J. W. Relation of type and onset of father absence to cognitive development. *Child Development,* 1972, *43,* 455–469.

Schaefer, C. E. The prediction of creative achievement from a biographical inventory. *Educational and Psychological Measurement,* 1969, *29,* 431–437. (a)

Schaefer, C. E. Imaginary companions and creative adolescents. *Developmental Psychology,* 1969, *1,* 747–749. (b)

Schank, R., & Abelson, R. *Scripts, plans, goals, and understanding.* Hillsdale, N.J.: Erlbaum, 1977.

Schubert, D. Intelligence as necessary but not sufficient for creativity. *Journal of Genetic Psychology,* 1973, *122,* 45–47.

Schubert, D. S. Increase of creativity by prior response to a problem. *Journal of General Psychology,* 1977, *96,* 323–324.

Schubert, D. S., Wagner, M. E., & Schubert, H. J. Family constellation and creativity: Firstborn predominance among classical music composers. *Journal of Psychology,* 1977, *95,* 147–149.

Seligman, C., Fazio, R. H., & Zanna, M. P. Effects of salience of extrinsic rewards on liking and loving. *Journal of Personality and Social Psychology,* 1980, *38,* 453–460.

Sexton, L. G., & Ames, L. *Anne Sexton: A self-portrait in letters.* Boston: Houghton Mifflin, 1977.

Shapira, Z. Expectancy determinants of intrinsically motivated behavior. *Journal of Personality and Social Psychology,* 1976, *39,* 1235–1244.

Siegelman, M. Parent behavior correlates of personality traits related to creativity in sons and daughters. *Journal of Consulting and Clinical Psychology,* 1973, *40,* 43–47.

Silberman, C. E. *Crisis in the classroom: The remaking of American education.* New York: Random House, 1970.

Simon, H. Scientific discovery and the psychology of problem solving. In *Mind and cosmos: Essays in contemporary science and philosophy.* Pittsburgh: University of Pittsburgh Press, 1966.

Simon, H. Understanding creativity. In J. C. Gowan, G. D. Demos, & E. P. Torrance (Eds.), *Creativity: Its educational implications.* New York: Wiley, 1967. (a)

Simon, H. Motivational and emotional controls of cognition. *Psychological Review,* 1967, *74,* 29–39. (b)

Simon, H. Information-processing theory of human problem solving. In W. K. Estes (Ed.), *Handbook of learning and cognitive processes, Vol. 5: Human information processing.* Hillsdale, N.J.: Lawrence Erlbaum Associates, 1978.

Simonton, D. K. Sociocultural context of individual creativity: A transhistorical time-series analysis. *Journal of Personality and Social Psychology,* 1975, *32,* 1119–1133. (a)

Simonton, D. K. Interdisciplinary creativity over historical time: A correlational analysis of generational fluctuations. *Social Behavior and Personality,* 1975, *3,* 181–188. (b)

Simonton, D. K. Age and literary creativity: A cross-cultural and transhistorical survey. *Journal of Cross-Cultural Psychology,* 1975, *6,* 259–277. (c)

Simonton, D. K. Biographical determinants of achieved eminence: A multivariate approach to the Cox data. *Journal of Personality and Social Psychology,* 1976, *33,* 218–226. (a)

Simonton, D. K. Philosophical eminence, beliefs, and Zeitgeist: An individual-generational analysis. *Journal of Personality and Social Psychology,* 1976, *34,* 630–640. (b)

Simonton, D. K. Creative productivity, age, and stress: A biographical time-series analysis of 10 classical composers. *Journal of Personality and Social Psychology,* 1977, *35,* 791–804. (a)

Simonton, D. K. Eminence, creativity, and geographical marginality: A recursive structural equation model. *Journal of Personality and Social Psychology,* 1977, *35,* 805–816. (b)

Simonton, D. K. *Techno-scientific activity and war: A yearly time-series analysis.* Unpublished manuscript, 1977. (c)

Simonton, D. K. The eminent genius in history: The critical role of creative development. *Gifted Child Quarterly,* 1978, *22,* 187–195.

Simonton, D. K. Multiple discovery and invention: Zeitgeist, genius, or chance. *Journal of Personality and Social Psychology,* 1979, *37,* 1603–1616.

Simonton, D. K. Thematic fame and melodic originality in classical music: A multivariate computer-content analysis. *Journal of Personality,* 1980, *48,* 206–219. (a)

Simonton, D. K. Thematic fame, melodic originality, and musical Zeitgeist: A biographical and transhistorical content analysis. *Journal of Personality and Social Psychology,* 1980, *38,* 972–983. (b)

Simpson, E. Eliot and friends. *The New York Times Book Review,* January 24, 1982, pp. 11; 27.

Singer, J. L. Imagination and waiting ability in young children. *Journal of Personality,* 1961, *29,* 396–413.

Singer, J. L. *The child's world of make-believe.* New York: Academic Press, 1973.

Singer, J. L., & Schonbar, R. A. Correlates of daydreaming: A dimension of self-awareness. *Journal of Consulting Psychology,* 1961, *25,* 1–6.

Skinner, B. F. *The behavior of organisms: An experimental analysis.* New York: Appleton-Century-Crofts, 1938.

Smith, M. C. Children's use of the multiple sufficient cause schema in social perception. *Journal of Personality and Social Psychology,* 1975, *32,* 737–747.

Smith, P. K., & Dutton, S. Play and training in direct and innovative problem solving. *Child Development,* 1979, *50,* 830–836.

Sobel, R. S., & Rothenberg, A. Artistic creation as stimulated by superimposed versus separated visual images. *Journal of Personality and Social Psychology,* 1980, *39,* 953–961.

Souriau, P. *Theories de l'invention.* Paris: Hachette, 1881.

Spearman, C. *The abilities of man.* New York: Macmillan, 1927.

Speller, K. G., & Schumacher, G. M. Age and set in creative test performance. *Psychological Reports,* 1975, *36,* 447–450.

Spence, K. *Behavior theory and conditioning.* New Haven: Yale University Press, 1956.

Spender, S. The making of a poem. In B. Ghiselin (Ed.), *The creative process.* Berkeley: University of California Press, 1952.

Staffieri, J. R. Birth order and creativity. *Journal of Clinical Psychology,* 1970, *26,* 65–66.

Staw, B. M. *Intrinsic and extrinsic motivation.* Morristown, N.J.: General Learning Press, 1976.

Stein, M. I. Creativity and culture. In R. L. Mooney & T. A. Razik (Eds.), *Explorations in creativity.* New York: Harper, 1967.

Stein, M. I. Creativity. In E. F. Borgatta & W. W. Lambert (Eds.), *Handbook of personality theory and research.* Chicago: Rand McNally, 1968.

Stein, M. I. *Stimulating Creativity* (Vols. 1 and 2). New York: Academic Press, 1974 and 1975.

Sternberg, R. J. Component processes in analogical reasoning. *Psychological Review,* 1977, *84,* 353–378. (a)

Sternberg, R. J. *Intelligence, information processing, and analogical reasoning: The componential analysis of human abilities.* Hillsdale, N.J.: Erlbaum, 1977. (b)

Sternberg, R. J. Isolating the components of intelligence. *Intelligence,* 1978, *2,* 117–128.

Sternberg, R. J. The nature of mental abilities. *American Psychologist,* 1979, *34,* 214–230.

Stone, B. G. Relationship between creativity and classroom behavior. *Psychology in the Schools,* 1980, *17,* 106–108.

Street, W. R. Brainstorming by individuals, coacting and interacting groups. *Journal of Applied Psychology,* 1974, *59,* 433–436.

Stubbs, M. L., & Amabile, T. M. *Explaining the relationship between fantasy and creativity.* Paper presented at the Third Annual Conference on the Fantasy and Imaging Process, New York, November, 1979.

Stubbs, M. L. *Methodological improvements in exploring the relationship between fantasy and creativity.* Unpublished manuscript, Brandeis University, 1981.

Sullivan, J. Open-traditional—what is the difference? *Elementary School Journal,* 1974, *74,* 493–500.

Sutton-Smith, B. *Play: The mediation of novelty.* Address presented to the Scientific Congress, fur die Spiele der XX Olympiade, Munich, 1972.

Taylor, C., & Barron, F. *Scientific creativity: Its recognition and development.* New York: Wiley, 1963.

Taylor, D. W. Toward an information processing theory of motivation. In M. R. Jones (Ed.), *Nebraska Symposium on Motivation: 1960.* Lincoln: University of Nebraska Press, 1960.

Taylor, D. W. Variables related to creativity and productivity among men in two research laboratories. In C. W. Taylor & F. Barron (Eds.), *Scientific creativity: Its recognition and development.* New York: Wiley, 1963.

Taylor, W., & Ellison, R. Predicting creative performances from multiple measures. In C. W. Taylor (Ed.), *Widening horizons in creativity.* New York: Wiley, 1964.

Tchaikovsky, P. A letter, 1878. In R. Newmarch, *Life and letters of Peter Ilich Tchaikovsky.* London: John Lane, 1906.

Thistlethwaite, D. L. College environments and the development of talent. *Science,* 1959, *130,* 71–76. (a)

Thistlethwaite, D. L. College press and student achievement. *Journal of Educational Psychology,* 1959, *50,* 183–191. (b)

Thomas, N., & Berk, L. Effects of school environments on the development of young children's creativity. *Child Development,* 1981, *52,* 1153–1162.

Thurstone, L., & Chave, E. *The measurement of attitude.* Chicago: University of Illinois Press, 1929.

Torrance, E. P. Priming creative thinking in the primary grades. *Elementary School Journal,* 1961, *62,* 139–145.

Torrance, E. P. *Guiding creative talent.* Englewood Cliffs, N.J.: Prentice Hall, 1962.

Torrance, E. P. *Role of evaluation in creative thinking.* Cooperative Research Project No. 725, University of Minnesota, 1964.

Torrance, E. P. *Rewarding creative behavior: Experiments in classroom creativity.* Englewood Cliffs, N.J.: Prentice-Hall, 1965.

Torrance, E. P. *The Torrance tests of creative thinking: Norms-technical manual.* Lexington, Mass.: Personnel Press, 1966.

Torrance, E. P. *Understanding the fourth grade slump in creative thinking: Final report.* Athens: Georgia University, December 1967.

Torrance, E. P. A longitudinal examination of the fourth grade slump in creativity. *Gifted Child Quarterly,* 1968, *12,* 195–199.

Torrance, E. P. Predictive validity of the Torrance tests of creative thinking. *Journal of Creative Behavior,* 1972, *6,* 236–252. (a)

Torrance, E. P. Career patterns and peak creative achievements of creative high school students twelve years later. *Gifted Child Quarterly,* 1972, *16,* 75–88. (b)

Torrance, E. P. Interscholastic brainstorming and creative problem solving competition for the creatively gifted. *Gifted Child Quarterly,* 1974, *18,* 3–7.

Torrance, E. P. et al. *Rewarding creative thinking.* Minneapolis: University of Minnesota, 1960.

Torrance, E. P., Bruch, C. B., & Torrance, J. P. Interscholastic futuristic creative problem solving. *Journal of Creative Behavior,* 1976, *10,* 117–125.

Torrance, E. P., & Khatena, J. What kind of person are you? *The Gifted Child Quarterly,* 1970, *14,* 71–75.

Travis, L. E. The effect of a small audience upon eye-hand coordination. *Journal of Abnormal and Social Psychology,* 1925, *20,* 142–146.

Treadwell, Y. Humor and creativity. *Psychological Reports,* 1970, *26,* 55–58.

Triplett, N. The dynamogenic factors in pacemaking and competition. *American Journal of Psychology,* 1898, *9,* 507–533.

Trowbridge, N., & Charles, D. C. Creativity in art students. *Journal of Genetic Psychology,* 1966, *109,* 281–289.

van Mondfrans, A. P., Feldhusen, J. F., Treffinger, D. J., & Ferris, D. R. The effects of instructions and response time on divergent thinking test scores. *Psychology in the Schools,* 1971, *8,* 65–71.

Vroom, V. *Motivation and work.* New York: Wiley, 1964.

Walberg, H. J. Varieties of adolescent creativity and the high school environment. *Exceptional Children,* 1971, *38,* 111–116.

Wallach, M. A. Creativity. In P. H. Mussen (Ed.), *Carmichael's Manual of child psychology* (Vol. 1). New York: Wiley, 1970.

Wallach, M. A. *The creativity-intelligence distinction.* New York: General Learning Press, 1971.

Wallach, M., & Kogan, N. *Modes of thinking in young children.* New York: Holt, Rinehart & Winston, 1965.

Wallas, G. *The art of thought.* New York: Harcourt, Brace, 1926.

Wallen, N. E., & Stevenson, G. M. Stability and correlates of judged creativity in fifth grade writings. *Journal of Educational Psychology,* 1960, *51,* 273–276.

Walster, E., Aronson, V., Abrahams, D., & Rottman, L. Importance of physical attractiveness in dating behavior. *Journal of Personality and Social Psychology,* 1966, *4,* 508–516.

Ward, W. C. Creativity and environmental cues in nursery school children. *Developmental Psychology,* 1969, *1,* 543–547.

Ward, W. C. Creativity (?) in young children. *Journal of Creative Behavior,* 1974, *8,* 101–106.

Ward, W. C., & Barcher, P. R. Reading achievement and creativity as related to open classroom experience. *Journal of Educational Psychology,* 1975, *67,* 683–691.

Ward, W. C., Kogan, N., & Pankove, E. Incentive effects in children's creativity. *Child Development,* 1972, *43,* 669–676.

Watson, J. D. *The double helix.* New York: Atheneum, 1968.

Watson, J. *Behaviorism.* London: K. Paul, 1928.

Weisberg, P. S., & Springer, K. J. Environmental factors in creative function. *Archives of General Psychiatry,* 1961, *5,* 554–564.

Wertheimer, M. *Productive thinking.* New York: Harper & Row, 1945.

Wertheimer, M. *Productive thinking.* New York: Harper & Row, 1959.

White, K., & Owen, D. Locus of evaluation for classroom work and the development of creative potential. *Psychology in the Schools,* 1970, *7,* 292–295.

White, R. Motivation reconsidered: The concept of competence. *Psychological Review,* 1959, *66,* 297–323.

Whiting, C. *Creative thinking.* New York: Reinhold, 1958.

Wickelgren, W. A. *Cognitive psychology.* Englewood Cliffs, N.J.: Prentice-Hall, 1979.

Wilner, M. S. *The differential effects of assessment context on factors of divergent thinking abilities and creativity: IQ relationship in sixth-grade boys.* Unpublished doctoral dissertation, University of Houston, 1974.

Winer, B. *Statistical principles in experimental design.* New York: McGraw-Hill, 1971.

Wolfe, T. *The story of a novel.* New York: Scribner's, 1936.

Wood, W. Retrieval of attitude-relevant information from memory: Effects on susceptibility to persuation and on intrinsic motivation. *Journal of Personality and Social Psychology,* 1982, *42,* 798–810.

Zajonc, R. B. Social facilitation. *Science,* 1965, *149,* 269–274.

Zajonc, R. B., Heingarner, A., & Herman, E. M. Social enhancement and impairment of performance in the cockroach. *Journal of Personality and Social Psychology,* 1969, *13,* 83–92.

Zajonc, R. B., & Sales, S. M. Social facilitation of dominant and subordinate responses. *Journal of Experimental Social Psychology,* 1966, *2,* 160–168.

Zajonc, R. B., Wolosin, R. J., Wolosin, M. A., Loh, W. D. Social facilitation and imitation in group risk-taking. *Journal of Experimental Social Psychology,* 1970, *6,* 26–46.

Zervos, C. Conversation with Picasso. In B. Ghiselin (Ed.), *The creative process.* Berkeley: University of California Press, 1952.

Zimmerman, B. J., & Dialessi, F. Modeling influences on children's creative behavior, *Journal of Educational Psychology,* 1973, *65,* 127–135.

Ziv, A. Facilitating effects of humor on creativity. *Journal of Educational Psychology,* 1976, *68,* 318–322.

Zuckerman, H. Nobel laureates in science: Patterns of productivity, collaboration, and authorship. *American Sociological Review,* 1967, *32,* 391–403.

Zuckerman, H. *Scientific elite: Nobel laureates in the U.S.* New York: The Free Press, 1977.

Zuckerman, M., Porac, J., Lathin, D., Smith, R., & Deci, E. L. On the importance of self-determination for intrinsically motivated behavior. *Personality and Social Psychology Bulletin,* 1978, *4,* 443–446.

References to the Updates

Note: References not found here are included in the References for the 1983 Edition.

Abbey, A., and J. W. Dickson. 1983. R & D work climate and innovation in semiconductors. *Academy of Management Journal* 26:362–368.

Amabile, T. M. 1982. Children's artistic creativity: Detrimental effects of competition in a field setting. *Personality and Social Psychology Bulletin* 8:573–578.

_____. 1983a. *The social psychology of creativity.* New York: Springer-Verlag.

_____. 1983b. Social psychology of creativity: A componential conceptualization. *Journal of Personality and Social Psychology* 45:357–377.

_____. 1985. Motivation and creativity: Effects of motivational orientation on creative writing. *Journal of Personality and Social Psychology* 48:393–399.

_____. 1987a. The motivation to be creative. In *Frontiers in creativity research: Beyond the basics,* edited by S. Isaksen. Buffalo, N.Y.: Bearly Limited.

_____. 1987b. *The work environment inventory,* version 3. Greensboro, N.C.: Center for Creative Leadership.

_____. 1988a. A model of creativity and innovation in organizations. Vol. 10 of *Research in organizational behavior,* edited by B. M. Staw and L. L. Cummings. Greenwich, Conn.: JAI Press, 123–167.

_____. 1988b. From individual creativity to organizational innovation. In *Innovation: A crossdisciplinary perspective,* edited by K. Gronhaug and G. Kaufmann. Oslo: Norwegian University Press.

_____. 1989. *Growing up creative.* Buffalo, N.Y.: Creative Education Foundation.

_____. 1990. *The work environment inventory,* version 4. Greensboro, N.C.: Center for Creative Leadership.

_____. 1993. Motivational synergy: Toward new conceptualizations of intrinsic and extrinsic motivation in the workplace. *Human Resource Management Review* 3:185–201.

_____. 1995. *KEYS: Assessing the climate for creativity.* Greensboro, N.C.: Center for Creative Leadership.

Amabile, T. M., R. M. Burnside, and S. S. Gryskiewicz. 1995. *User's guide for KEYS: Assessing the climate for creativity.* Greensboro, N.C.: Center for Creative Leadership.

Amabile, T. M., and R. Conti. 1995. What downsizing does to creativity. *Issues and Observations* 15:1–6. Greensboro, N.C.: Center for Creative Leadership.

Amabile, T. M., R. Conti, H. Coon, J. Lazenby, and M. Herron. Assessing the work environment for creativity. *Academy of Management Journal,* in press.

Amabile, T. M., and N. Gryskiewicz. 1989. The creative environment scales: The work environment inventory. *Creativity Research Journal* 2:231–254.

Amabile, T. M., and S. S. Gryskiewicz. 1987. *Creativity in the R&D laboratory.* Technical report no. 30. Greensboro, N.C.: Center for Creative Leadership.

Amabile, T. M., B. A. Hennessey, and B. S. Grossman. 1986. Social influences on creativity: The effects of contracted-for reward. *Journal of Personality and Social Psychology* 50:14–23.

Amabile, T. M., K. G. Hill, B. A. Hennessey, and E. Tighe. 1994. The work preference inventory: Assessing intrinsic and extrinsic motivational orientations. *Journal of Personality and Social Psychology* 66:950–967.

Amabile, T. M., E. D. Phillips, and M. A. Collins. 1994. *Creativity by contract: Social influences on the creativity of professional artists.* Unpublished manuscript, Brandeis University.

Amabile, T. M., and E. Tighe. 1993. Questions of creativity. In *Creativity: The Reality Club 4,* edited by J. Brockman. New York: Touchstone, 7–27.

Baer, J. 1994. Divergent thinking is not a general trait: A multidomain training experiment. *Creativity Research Journal* 7:35–46.

Bartis, S., K. Szymanski, and S. G. Harkins. 1988. Evaluation and performance: A two-edge knife. *Personality and Social Psychology Bulletin* 14:242–251.

Bartko, J. J. 1966. The intraclass correlation coefficient as a measure of reliability. *Psychological Reports* 19:3–11.

Berretta, S., and G. Privette. 1990. Influence of play on creative thinking. *Perceptual and Motor Skills* 71:659–666.

Besemer, S. P., and K. O'Quin. 1986. Analyzing creative products: Refinement and test of a judging instrument. *Journal of Creative Behavior* 20:115–126.

Brunke, M., and M. Gilbert. 1992. Alcohol and creative writing. *Psychological Reports* 71:651–658.

Burns, M. 1988. Music as a tool for enhancing creativity. *Journal of Creative Behavior* 22:62–69.

Carney, S. 1986. *Intrinsic motivation in successful artists from early adulthood to middle age.* Ph.D. diss., University of Chicago.

Cheek, J. M., and S. Stahl. 1986. Shyness and verbal creativity. *Journal of Research in Personality* 20:51–61.

Collins, M. A. 1992. *Contextual influences on the effect of restricted choice on problem-solving creativity.* Unpublished manuscript, Brandeis University.

Collins, M. A., and T. M. Amabile. 1992. *Intrinsic motivation and artistic creativity: The effects of naturally-occurring interest, affect, and involvement.* Paper presented at the Annual Meeting of the Eastern Psychological Association, Boston, Mass., April.

Comadena, M. 1984. Brainstorming groups: Ambiguity tolerance, communication apprehension, task attraction, and individual productivity. *Small Group Behavior* 15:251–264.

Conti, R. 1992. *A potential danger in the use of productivity goals.* Unpublished manuscript, Brandeis University.

Conti, R., and T. M. Amabile. 1995. *Problem solving among computer science students: The effects of skill, evaluation expectation and personality on solution quality.* Paper presented at the annual meeting of the Eastern Psychological Association, Boston, Mass.

Conti, R., T. M. Amabile, and S. Pollak. 1995. The positive impact of creative activity: Effects of creative task engagement and motivational focus on college students' learning. *Personality and Social Psychology Bulletin* 21:1107–1116.

Conti, R., M. A. Collins, and M. Picariello. 1995. *Differential effects of competition on the artistic creativity of girls and boys.* Unpublished manuscript, Brandeis University.

Conti, R., H. Coon, and T. M. Amabile. In press. Some support for the componential model of creativity: Secondary analyses of three studies. *Creativity Research Journal.*

Cropley, A. 1990. Creativity and mental health in everyday life. *Creativity Research Journal* 3:167–178.

Csikszentmihalyi, M. 1988. Society, culture, and person: a systems view of creativity. Chapter 13 in *The nature of creativity,* edited by R. J. Sternberg. Cambridge. Mass.: Cambridge University Press, 325–339.

Csikszentmihalyi, M., and R. Robinson. 1986. Culture, time, and the development of talent. In *Conceptions of giftedness,* edited by R. J. Sternberg and J. E. Davidson. New York: Cambridge University Press, 264–284.

Dacey, J. S. 1989. Discriminating characteristics of the families of highly creative adolescents. *Journal of Creative Behavior* 23:263–271.

Deci, E. L., and R. M. Ryan. 1985. *Intrinsic motivation and self-determination in human behavior.* New York: Plenum.

Delbecq, A. L., and P. K. Mills. 1985. Managerial practices that enhance innovation. *Organizational Dynamics* 14:24–34.

Eisenberger, R., and M. Selbst. 1994. Does reward increase or decrease creativity? *Journal of Personality and Social Psychology* 66:1116–1127.

Ekvall, G., J. Arvonen, and I. Waldenstrom-Lindblad. 1983. *Creative organizational climate: Construction and validation of a measuring instrument.* Report 2. The Swedish Council for Management and Organizational Behaviour.

Fabes, R. A., J. D. Moran, and J. C. McCullers. 1981. The hidden costs of reward and WAIS subscale performance. *American Journal of Psychology* 94:387–398.

Feldhusen, J., and P. Clinkenbeard. 1986. Creativity instructional materials: A review of research. *Journal of Creative Behavior* 20:153–182.

Feldman, D.H., M. Csikszentmihalyi, and H. Gardner. 1994. *Changing the world: A framework for the study of creativity.* Westford, Conn.: Praeger.

Forgays, D., and D. Forgays. 1992. Creativity enhancement through flotation isolation. *Journal of Environmental Psychology* 12:329–335.

Gardner, H. 1988b. Creativity: An interdisciplinary perspective. *Creativity Research Journal* 1:8–26.

Gardner, K. G., and J. D. Moran. 1990. Family adaptability, cohesion, and creativity. *Creativity Research Journal* 3:281–286.

Gondola, J. 1986. The enhancement of creativity through long and short term exercise programs. *Journal of Social Behavior and Personality* 1:77–82.

Greenberg, E. 1992. Creativity, autonomy, and evaluation of creative work: Artistic workers in organizations. *Journal of Creative Behavior* 26:75–80.

Greer, M., and E. Levine. 1991. Enhancing creative performance in college students. *Journal of Creative Behavior* 25:250–255.

Gruber, H. E. 1988. The evolving systems approach to creative work. *Creativity Research Journal* 1:27–59.

Gruber, H. E., and S. N. Davis. 1988. Inching our way up Mount Olympus: The evolving-systems approach to creative thinking. In *The nature of creativity,* edited by R. J. Sternberg. Cambridge: Cambridge University Press, 386–426.

Gryskiewicz, S. S., and D. A. Hills, eds. 1992. *Readings in innovation.* Greensboro, N.C.: Center for Creative Leadership.

Harackiewicz, J. M., S. Abrahams, and R. Wageman. 1991. Performance evaluation and intrinsic motivation: The effects of evaluative focus, rewards and achievement orientation. *Journal of Personality and Social Psychology* 63:1015–1029.

Harrington, D. M. 1990. The ecology of human creativity: A psychological perspective. In *Theories of creativity,* edited by M. A. Runco and R. S. Albert. Newbury Park, Calif.: Sage Publications, 143–169.

Harrington, D. M., J. H. Block, and J. Block. 1987. Testing aspects of Carl Rogers' theory of creative environments: Child rearing antecedents of creative potential in young adolescents. *Journal of Personality and Social Psychology* 52:851–856.

Heinzen, T. E., C. Mills, and P. Cameron. 1993. Scientific innovation potential. *Creativity Research Journal* 6:261–269.

Hennessey, B. A. 1989. The effect of extrinsic constraints on children's creativity while using a computer. *Creativity Research Journal* 2:151–168.

_____. 1994. The consensual assessment technique: An examination of the relationship between ratings of product and process creativity. *Creativity Research Journal* 7:193–208.

Hennessey, B. A., and T. M. Amabile. 1988. Story-telling: A method for assessing children's creativity. *Journal of Creative Behavior* 22:235–246.

Hennessey, B. A., T. M. Amabile, and M. Martinage. 1989. Immunizing children against the negative effects of reward. *Contemporary Educational Psychology* 14:212–227.

Hennessey, B. A., and S. Zbikowski. 1993. Immunizing children against the negative effects of reward: A further examination of intrinsic motivation training techniques. *Creativity Research Journal* 6:297–308.

Hill, K. 1991. *An ecological approach to creativity and motivation: Trait and environment influences in the college classroom.* Ph.D. diss., Brandeis University.

Hill, K. G., T. M. Amabile, H. M. Coon, and D. Whitney. 1994. *Testing the componential model of creativity.* Unpublished manuscript, Brandeis University.

Hocevar, D., and P. Bachelor. 1989. A taxonomy and critique of measurements used in the study of creativity. In *Handbook of creativity,* edited by J. Glover, R. Ronning, and C. Reynolds. New York: Plenum Press, 53–75.

Isaksen, S. G., and K. B. Dorval. 1993. Toward an improved understanding of creativity within people: The level-style distinction. In *Understanding and recognizing creativity: The emergence of a discipline,* edited by S. G. Isaksen, M. C. Murdock, R. L. Firestien, and D. I. Treffinger. Norwood, N.J.: Ablex Publishing Corporation.

Isaksen, S. G., K. B. Dorval, R. B. Noller, and R. L. Firestien. 1993. The dynamic nature of creative problem solving. In *Discovering creativity,* edited by S. C. Gryskiewicz. Greensboro, N.C.: Center for Creative Leadership, 155–162.

Isaksen, S. G., M. C. Murdock, R. L. Firestien, D. J. Treffinger, eds. 1993. *Understanding and recognizing creativity: The emergence of a discipline.* Norwood, N.J.: Ablex Publishing Corporation.

Isen, A. M. 1987. Positive affect, cognitive processes, and social behavior. Vol. 20 of *Advances in experimental social psychology,* edited by L. Berkowitz. New York: Academic Press, 203–253.

Isen, A. M., and K. A. Daubman. 1984. The influence of affect on categorization. *Journal of Personality and Social Psychology* 47:1206–1217.

Isen, A. M., M. S. Johnson, E. Mertz, and G. F. Robinson. 1985. The influence of positive affect on the unusualness of word associations. *Journal of Personality and Social Psychology* 48:1413–1426.

Jussim, L., S. Soffin, R. Brown, J. Ley, and K. Kohlhepp. 1992. Understanding reactions to feedback by integrating ideas from symbolic interactionism and cognitive evaluation theory. *Journal of Personality and Social Psychology* 62:402–421.

King, S. 1990. Introduction to *Four past midnight.* New York: Viking Penguin.

Kirton, M. J. 1976. Adaptors and innovators: A description and measure. *Journal of Applied Psychology* 61:622–629.

Koestner, R., R. Ryan, F. Bernieri, and K. Holt. 1984. Setting limits on children's behavior: The differential effects of controlling vs. informational styles on intrinsic motivation and creativity. *Journal of Personality* 52:233–248.

Lynn, S. J., and J. W. Rhue. 1986. The fantasy-prone person: Hypnosis, imagination, and creativity. *Journal of Personality and Social Psychology* 51:404–408.

_____. 1988. Fantasy proneness: Hypnosis, developmental antecedents, and psychopathology. *American Psychologist* 43:35–44.

McFadden, M., and E. Demetriou. 1993. The role of immediate work environment factors in the turnover process: A systemic intervention. *Applied Psychology: An International Review* 42:97–115.

McKeachie, W. J. 1983. National symposium on the applications of psychology to the teaching and learning of music. Session 3: Motivation and creativity. *American Psychologist* 38:855–857.

Meador, K. S. 1992. Emerging rainbows: A review of the literature on creativity in preschoolers. *Journal for the Education of the Gifted* 15:163–181.

Michel, M., and S. Z. Dudek. 1991. Mother-child relationships and creativity. *Creativity Research Journal* 4:281–286.

Mooney, R. L. 1963. A conceptual model for integrating four approaches to the identification of creative talent. In *Scientific creativity: Its recognition and development.* Edited by C. W. Taylor and F. Barron. New York: Wiley, 331–340.

Necka, E. 1984. The effectiveness of synectics and brainstorming as conditioned by socioemotional climate and type of task. *Polish Psychological Bulletin* 15:41–50.

O'Quin, K., and S. P. Besemer. 1989. The development, reliability, and validity of the revised creative product semantic scale. *Creativity Research Journal* 2:268–278.

Pellegrini, A. D. 1984–85. The effects of exploration and play on young children's associative fluency. *Imagination, Cognition, and Personality* 4:29–40.

Phillips, E. 1992. *Assessing the creativity of expert artworks: An extension of the Consensual Assessment Technique.* Unpublished manuscript, Brandeis University.

_____. 1993. *An examination of children's motivation to draw: A developmental approach.* Unpublished manuscript, Brandeis University.

Picariello, M. L. 1992. *The effects of motivational orientation on children's creativity.* Paper presented at the Meeting of the Eastern Psychological Association, Boston, Mass., April.

_____. 1994. *Children's perceptions of autonomy in the classroom: Implications for intrinsic motivation, learning, and creativity.* Ph.D. diss., Brandeis University..

Pollak, S. 1992. *The effects of motivational orientation and constraint on the creativity of the artist.* Unpublished manuscript, Brandeis University.

Radio-Gaynor, J. R., and M. A. Runco. 1992. Family size, birth-order, age-interval, and the creativity of children. *Journal of Creative Behavior* 26: 108–118.

Raikov, V. 1992. Hypnosis as an active creative act and post-hypnotic development of enhanced creativity. *Journal of Creative Behavior* 26:148–155.

Robinson, S. E., S. L. Roth, and L. L. Brown. 1993. Morale and job satisfaction among nurses: What can hospitals do? *Journal of Applied Social Psychology* 23:244–251.

Rose, L., and H. Lin. 1984. A meta-analysis of long-term creativity training programs. *Journal of Creative Behavior* 18:11–22.

Runco, M. A., and M. D. Bahleda. 1987. Birth order and divergent thinking. *Journal of Genetic Psychology* 148:119–125.

Runco, M. A., and W. R. Smith. 1992. Interpersonal and intrapersonal evaluations of creative ideas. *Personality and Individual Differences* 13:295–302.

Ruscio, J. 1994. *Exploratory analysis of the creative process in problem-solving.* Unpublished manuscript, Brandeis University.

Ruscio, J., D. Whitney, and T. M. Amabile. 1995. *How do motivation and task behaviors affect creativity? An investigation in three domains.* Unpublished manuscript, Brandeis University.

Russell, R. D., and C. J. Russell. 1992. An examination of the effects of organizational norms, organizational structure, and environmental uncertainty on entrepreneurial strategy. *Journal of Management* 18:839–856.

Ryan, R. M., and W. S. Grolnick. 1986. Origins and pawns in the classroom: Self-report and projective assessments of individual differences in children's perceptions. *Journal of Personality and Social Psychology* 50:550–558.

Salvolaninen, T. 1990. Expanding human-computer interaction by computer aided creativity. *Interacting with Computers* 2:161–174.

Shrout, P. E., and J. L. Fleiss. 1979. Intraclass correlations: Uses in assessing rater reliability. *Psychological Bulletin* 86:420–428.

Siegel, S. M., and W. F. Kaemmerer. 1978. Measuring the perceived support for innovation in organizations. *Journal of Applied Psychology* 63:553–562.

Simonton, D. K. 1984. *Genius, creativity, and leadership.* Cambridge, Mass.: Harvard University Press.

_____. 1988. Age and outstanding achievement: What do we know after a century of research? *Psychological Bulletin* 104:251–267.

_____. 1989a. The chance-configuration theory of scientific creativity. In *The psychology of science: Contributions to metascience,* edited by B. Gholson, A. C. Houts, R. A. Niemeyer, and W. R. Shadish. Cambridge: Cambridge University Press, 170–213.

_____. 1989b. The swan-song phenomenon: Last-works effects for 172 classical composers. *Psychology and Aging* 4:42–47.

_____. 1990. Creativity in the later years: Optimistic prospects for achievement. *Gerontologist* 30:626–631.

_____. 1991. Creative productivity through the adult years. *Generations* 15:13–16.

_____. 1992. The social context of career success and course for 2,026 scientists and inventors. *Personality and Social Psychology Bulletin* 18:452–463.

Stein, M. I. 1953. Creativity and Culture. *Journal of Psychology* 36:311–322.

Sternberg, R. J., ed. 1988. *The nature of creativity: Contemporary psychological perspectives.* Cambridge, Mass.: Cambridge University Press.

Sternberg, R. J., and T. I. Lubart. 1991. An investment theory of creativity and its development. *Human Development* 34:1–31.

_____. Creative giftedness: A multivariate investment approach. *Gifted Child Quarterly* 37:7–15.

Suedfeld, P., J. Metcalfe, and S. Bluck. 1987. Enhancement of scientific creativity by flotation REST (restricted environmental stimulation technique). *Journal of Environmental Psychology* 7:219–231.

Szymanski, K., and S. G. Harkins. 1992. Self-evaluation and creativity. *Personality and Social Psychology Bulletin* 18:259–265.

Thornburg, T. 1991. Group size and member diversity influences on creative performance. *Journal of Creative Behavior* 25:324–333.

Tighe, E. M. 1992. *The motivational influences of mood on creativity.* Ph.D. diss., Brandeis University.

Weber, R. J., and D. N. Perkins. 1989. How to invent artifacts and ideas. *New Ideas in Psychology* 7:49–72.

Whitney, D., J. Ruscio, T. Amabile, and M. Castle. 1995. *Effects of planning on creativity.* Paper presented at the Annual Meeting of the Eastern Psychological Association, Boston, Mass.

Witt, L. A., and M. N. Beorkrem. 1989. Climate for creative productivity as a predictor of research usefulness and organizational effectiveness in an R&D organization. *Creativity Research Journal* 2:30–40.

Woodman, R. W., J. E. Sawyer, and R. W. Griffin. 1993. Toward a theory of organizational creativity. *Academy of Management Review* 18:293–321.

Woodman, R. W., and L. F. Schoenfeldt. 1990. An interactionist model of creative behavior. *Journal of Creative Behavior* 24, 10–20.

Ziv, A. 1988. Using humor to develop creative thinking. *Journal of Children in Contemporary Society* 20:99–116.

About the Book and Author

Creativity in Context is an update of *The Social Psychology of Creativity*, a classic text for researchers, students, and other interested readers. *Creativity in Context* incorporates extensive new material, going far beyond the original to provide a comprehensive picture of how the motivation for creative behavior, and creativity itself, can be influenced by the social environment.

Teresa Amabile describes new findings both from her own research and from the work of many others in the field, detailing not only the ways in which creativity can be killed by social-psychological influences, but also the ways in which it can be maintained and stimulated. The research and the theory have moved beyond a narrow focus on the immediate social environment to a consideration of broad social influences in business organizations, classrooms, and society at large; beyond a documentation of social influences to a consideration of the cognitive mechanisms by which social factors might impact creativity; and beyond subject populations consisting of children and college students to an inclusion of professional artists, research scientists, and other working adults.

Amabile describes a greatly expanded set of methodologies for assessing creativity, and introduces a set of methodologies for assessing the social environment for creativity in nonexperimental studies. Throughout, the book maintains a clear focus on a comprehensive view of creativity—how the social context can influence motivation and how motivation, in conjunction with personal skills and thinking styles, can lead to the expression of creative behavior within that context. The result is a clarified theory of how creativity actually happens, with strong implications for supporting and increasing essential aspects of human performance.

Teresa M. Amabile is professor of business administration at Harvard University.

Credits

Index